NEGROES

AND THE GUN

NEGROES
AND THE GUN

THE BLACK TRADITION OF ARMS

NICHOLAS JOHNSON

Prometheus Books

59 John Glenn Drive
Amherst, New York 14228

Published 2014 by Prometheus Books

Cover image © Media Bakery
Cover design by Grace M. Conti-Zilsberger

Inquiries should be addressed to
Prometheus Books
59 John Glenn Drive
Amherst, New York 14228
VOICE: 716–691–0133
FAX: 716–691–0137
WWW.PROMETHEUSBOOKS.COM

18 17 16 15 14   5 4 3 2 1

Library of Congress Cataloging-in-Publication Data

Johnson, Nicholas, 1959-
    Negroes and the gun : the Black tradition of arms / by Nicholas Johnson.
        pages cm
    Includes bibliographical references and index.
    ISBN 978-1-61614-839-3 (pbk.)
    ISBN 978-1-61614-840-9 (ebook)
    1. African Americans—Civil rights—United States—History. 2. Firearms ownership—United States—History. 3. Firearms—United States—Use in crime prevention—History. 4. Self-defense—United States—History. I. Title.

E185.61.J695 2014
323.1196'073—dc23

2013033057

Printed in the United States of America

To
Jane, Nicky and Ellen
Mom and Dad
Than and Nita
Cleo and Buddy
The Crump Brothers
and the Church Folk

CONTENTS

ACKNOWLEDGMENTS

This book started with an essay I was asked to write for the *Harvard Law and Policy Review*. That work produced a manuscript so long that it was unsuitable for the format. It expanded from there, and I finally whittled it down into an article published as the centerpiece of the *Connecticut Law Review*'s 2013 *Commentary Edition*. Along the way I realized that the essay turned article was really a book.

I have benefited from the insights and comments of people who read versions of this work. Thanks to Bob Kaczorowski, Shelia Foster, Marc Arkin, Russ Pearce, Howie Erickson, Dan Richmond, Kimani Paul-Emile, Jack Krill, Nelson Lund, Jenny Brown, Laura Bair, Dick Lohkamp, Bob Levy, Steve Halbrook, Alice Marie Beard, Joyce Malcolm, Robin Lenhardt, Tanya Hernandez, and to the participants in the 2010 Fordham Law School Faculty Scholarship Retreat where I presented a version of this work. Thanks also to my coauthors on *Firearms Law and the Second Amendment*, Dave Kopel, George Mocsary, and Mike O'Shea, for their insights along the way. I owe a particular debt to Robert Cottrol and Don B. Kates for their friendship and pioneering scholarship.

Thanks to the research assistants who worked on different versions of this project. Tammem Zainulbhai and John Hunt helped at the beginning, before I thought that this was a book. John Paul Sardi, Giancarlo Stanton, Jacob Laksin, and Ellen Johnson saw it through to the end. Thanks to my wife, Jane, who, in typical fashion, was adept at something I was not good at and tracked down many of the images that appear in the book. Thanks to Katherine Epanchin-Butuc, Juan Fernandez, and Larry Abraham at the Fordham Law Library for retrieving a variety of obscure texts. Thanks to Fordham University for the sabbatical grant that gave me the time to distill a mountain of information into 150,000 words. And thanks generally to family and friends for tolerating in good cheer the countless hours that this project drained from other equally worthwhile things.

AUTHOR'S NOTE

This book raised two notable stylistic challenges. The first was whether to capitalize *black* in the frequent references to Black people. Many consider capitalization the new norm. And some have argued that the failure to capitalize *Black* is a slight that sensitive writers will avoid. But people are plainly divided. My daughter observes that her Black professors uniformly capitalize *Black* and her white professors generally use the traditional lowercase form. In many contexts, including my textbook and in the law-review article that is the foundation for this book, I have capitalized references to Black people and Black concerns. The publisher of this book, on the other hand, follows the traditional usage of referencing black people in the lowercase. After extensive conversations, we chose to use the lowercase form here primarily as a matter of aesthetics. This book makes frequent reference to black and white people within the same sentence or paragraph. Capitalizing *Black* but not *white* seemed visually distracting. Capitalizing both *Black* and *White* seemed equally distracting.

The second challenge was in sourcing. This book uses the sourcing style familiar to readers of law reviews and other legal texts. Notes at the end of paragraphs or a sequence of paragraphs will identify the sources for the quotations and the factual claims that appear above them. My goal was to provide sources for every significant factual claim and quotation in the book. That goal was in tension with the practical constraints of book publishing. Sourcing in the precise style of law reviews would have produced well over one hundred pages of endnotes. (The forty-thousand-word law-review article on which this book is based came in at more than six hundred source notes). The endnotes here run roughly thirty-five pages. In some instances, for the sake of efficiency, I have collapsed references for several paragraphs into a single endnote. This may require readers to proceed through several paragraphs to reach the endnote that provides the source. The text of an endnote may contain references to several sets of pages from a single source, and it might also list more than one source. The cited sources here will generally proceed in sequence. So, for example, an endnote following a sequence of three paragraphs indicating pages "3-4, 12, and 23-24" will designate the sources for those paragraphs in sequence.

INTRODUCTION

Gun! Just the word raises the temperature. Add *Negroes* and the mixture is incendiary, evoking images of hopeless young gangsters terrorizing blighted neighborhoods.

This book tells a dramatically different story. It chronicles a tradition of church folk, merchants, and strivers, the very best people in the community, armed and committed to the principle of individual self-defense. This black tradition of arms takes root early and ranges fully into the modern era. It is demonstrated in Frederick Douglass's advice of a good revolver as the best response to slave catchers. It is evident in mature form in 1963, when Hartman Turnbow of Mississippi fought off a Klan attack with rifle fire. Turnbow considered this fully consistent with the principles of the freedom movement, explaining, "I wasn't being *non-nonviolent*, I was just protectin' my family."

The black tradition of arms has been submerged because it seems hard to reconcile with the dominant narrative of nonviolence in the modern civil-rights movement. But that superficial tension is resolved by the long-standing distinction that was vividly evoked by movement stalwart Fannie Lou Hamer. Hamer's approach to segregationists who dominated Mississippi politics was, "Baby you just got to love 'em. Hating just makes you sick and weak." But, asked how she survived the threats from midnight terrorists, Hamer responded, "I'll tell you why. I keep a shotgun in every corner of my bedroom and the first cracker even look like he wants to throw some dynamite on my porch won't write his mama again."[1]

Like Hartman Turnbow, Fannie Lou Hamer embraced private self-defense and political nonviolence without any sense of contradiction. In this she channeled a more-than-century-old practice and philosophy that evolved through every generation, sharpened by icons like Ida B. Wells and W. E. B. Du Bois, pressed by the burgeoning NAACP, and crystalized by Martin Luther King Jr., who articulated it this way:

> Violence exercised merely in self-defense, all societies, from the most primitive to the most cultured and civilized, accept as moral and legal. The principle of self-defense, even involving weapons and bloodshed, has never been condemned, even by Gandhi. . . . When the Negro uses force in self-defense, he does not forfeit

support—he may even win it, by the courage and self-respect it reflects. . . . But violence as a tool of advancement, involving organization as in warfare . . . poses incalculable perils.[2]

In practice and in policy, from the leadership to the grass roots, this view dominated into the 1960s—right up to the point where the civil-rights movement boiled over into violent protests and black radicals openly defied the traditional boundary against political violence. That violent and radical turn was the catalyst for a dramatic transition, as the movement ushered in a new black political class. Rising within a progressive political coalition that included the newly minted national gun-control movement, the bourgeoning black political class embraced gun bans and lesser supply controls as one answer to violent crime in their new domains. By the mid-1970s, these influences had supplanted the generations-old black tradition of arms with a modern orthodoxy of stringent gun control.

The first seven chapters of this book chronicle the rise, evolution, and decline of the black tradition of arms. Chapter 8 details the pivot from that tradition into the modern orthodoxy.

The secondary theme of this book, distilled in the last chapter, addresses an intriguing tension. On one side is the tragic plague of violent young black men with guns and the toll that this violence takes on many black communities. On the other is the fact that recent momentous affirmations of the constitutional right to keep and bear arms were led by black plaintiffs, Shelly Parker and Otis McDonald, who complained that stringent gun laws in Washington, DC, and Chicago left them disarmed against the criminals who plagued their neighborhoods. The modern orthodoxy would cast Parker and McDonald as dupes or fools. But the black tradition of arms places them in a more complex light and raises critical unexamined questions about the modern orthodoxy. Chapter 9 engages those questions, highlights the diversity of interests and views about the gun question, and assesses the current implications of the black tradition of arms.

In the several years that I have been working on this project, people have asked what motivated it. What did I hope to achieve? To the first question, this book, like much of my work, is motivated by a rural sensibility, a familiarity with and affection for people and places that are underacknowledged in both in popular culture and in policy making.

To the second question, my goal here is to answer a longing that I have observed in a variety of contexts. It is evident when people, especially young people of color, probing the narrative of the civil-rights movement, wonder plaintively whether anyone ever fought back. There is a palpable yearning for something more than the images of Negroes in church clothes flattened by baton charges, attacked by dogs, and sometimes hanged from tree limbs. Many of these people were heroes. But they were also victims, and that leaves us unfulfilled, grateful for their sacrifice but still not fully proud. The question lingers, where is our Leonidas? Where is our classic champion who meets force with force even in the face of long odds? Some may find an answer within the black tradition of arms.

Of course, many episodes here end badly for Negroes with guns. And any worry about overglorifying violence is further leavened by accounts of prosaic black-on-black violence and desperate, failed efforts that are more pathetic than heroic. But other episodes, like Hartman Turnbow's defiant stand, leave us wondering how different is this, really, from the tale of gallant young cavalrymen charging artillery placements with sabers?

Black folk still await their Tennyson. But his raw material is in these pages.

CHAPTER ONE

BOUNDARY-LAND

Robert Williams returned home from the army in the spring of 1946 to the same bitter irony that had confronted countless black veterans before him. They shed blood to protect democracy abroad, and bled again under racial apartheid at home.

Monroe, North Carolina, remained much the same as when Williams was a boy and witnessed a scene of petty brutality that confirmed what it meant to be on the wrong side of the color line. Turning the corner toward the courthouse, he stepped into the scene of a burly white cop arresting a woman in a fashion that captured the status of Negroes across the South. The man with a badge was "Big Jesse" Helms Sr., father of the future United States senator. For the rest of his life, Williams carried the image of Big Jesse flattening that woman with a sock to the jaw, and then dragging her off to jail with her dress up over her head and screaming as the concrete singed her back and thighs. As an old man, Williams the revolutionary—leaning on a cane, sporting a big, grey afro—would talk like it was yesterday about the laughter of the white bystanders and how the cluster of black courthouse loiterers hung their heads and scurried away.

The courthouse loiterers represented a particular stripe of man. Some would say that Robert Williams was a different kind of man. Maybe so. But more important is that Robert Williams was not alone. He is an exemplar, but he was not unusual. He was part of a long tradition of black men and women who thought it just and natural to answer aggression with corresponding force. They kept and carried guns and believed in self-defense as a fundamental right. Their story is obscured by the popular narrative of the nonviolent civil-rights movement. But alongside that narrative, deep in the culture, is a rich vein of grit and steel. Robert Williams was heir to that tradition. His bloodline was thick with it.

Williams's early experiences confirmed the privilege of white skin, but that did not cow him. Even though his people were no match for the power of the state and the culture of Jim Crow, when pushed to the wall, they bucked up and fought back. There is a hint of this in the Williams clan back as far as grandfather Sikes. Over the course of his life, Sikes Williams was a slave, a farmer, a reconstruction newspaper editor, a perpetual optimist, and finally, always, a realist. In the middle of a hostile environment, with powerful reasons to despair, Sikes Williams worked hard and hoped for the best for himself and his family. He also understood his responsibility in that moment where his next breath or the safety of those he loved was threatened by imminent violence. One of Robert's prized possessions was a rifle that, according to family lore, had been used by Sikes Williams in matters of life or death.

Grandpa Sikes was a hero of Robert's imagination. But the firsthand confirmation of the Williams family backbone came in another childhood episode, when word spread that a mob was forming to lynch a Negro who had fought with police. Rumor circulated that in addition to dragging the man from his cell for a hanging or burning, the mob also was planning to run some black folk out of town. The old people, and some young ones, who had witnessed the terror of the lynch mob, hid or prepared to flee.

Williams's father, "Daddy John" heard the rumors too. But when it was time to head out for work on the graveyard shift at the mill, he picked up his lunch pail and left the house as usual. The only difference this time was, before stepping out the door, he slipped a pistol into the pocket of his overalls. Fortunately, neither the lynching nor the chasing came that night. But Robert never forgot his father's steel in that environment of fear and carried with him the image of that pistol, slipped quietly into the overalls pocket of a man who was not looking for trouble.

Later, when Robert Williams became an inflammatory figure, white people would say he should be more like his father, someone they considered a good Negro who kept his place. Robert knew the only difference between them was that Daddy John had the luck never to face a threat that would have turned him into a bad Negro with a gun. While the casual observer might take his kindness for weakness, even as an old man, Daddy John thanked his luck and still prepared for the worst. "Always the shotgun was there," Robert remembered, "it was always loaded and it was always at the door. And that was the tradition."[1]

Robert Williams was honorably discharged from the service, but only barely so. He served at least one stint in the brig for insubordination, or, in his words, "refusing to be a nigger." Back home, he faced a similar problem. Monroe in 1946 was Klan territory. And it was not long before the insubordinate soldier was in conflict with the Invisible Empire.

Bennie Montgomery was Williams's childhood friend. Bennie was wounded in the Battle of the Bulge and discharged with a metal plate in his head. He was never really the same after that. Out of the service, Bennie cycled quickly back to his ordained place in the Jim Crow South—into the fields, chopping and shoveling. Home only a few months, he got into a scrap with his white employer. With the pleasures of Saturday night on his mind, Bennie approached the boss around noon and asked for his wages. Workers were always paid at the end of the day, and Bennie knew it. The boss rewarded his impudence with a slap and a kick. They tussled. By the end of it, Bennie had pulled a knife and killed the man. Later, police found Bennie, still in bloody clothes, drinking beer at a local dive, just sitting there like nothing had happened.[2]

The Klan threatened to lynch Bennie. So the authorities moved him from Monroe. He was quickly convicted of murder and executed. But the execution of Bennie Montgomery did not satisfy the Klan. When the state shipped his body back home for burial, the Klan proclaimed that the remains belonged to them. They planned to drag Bennie's body through the streets.

Before that could happen, the black men of the community met at a barber-shop and worked up a plan. By the time the Klan motorcade reached the Harris Funeral Home to seize Bennie's body, forty black men with rifles and shotguns were already in place, hidden where the cover allowed. The motorcade stopped. The black men showed themselves and leveled their guns. Unprepared for a real fight, the Klansmen drove away and Bennie got a civilized burial.[3]

Robert Williams was one of the men who drew down on the Klan that night. That same year across the South, black veterans marched and protested and armed themselves against reprisals in Birmingham, Alabama; Decatur, Mississippi; and Durham, North Carolina. Among these men was a young Medgar Evers, home from the army and pressed to the edge of an armed confrontation at the Decatur court-house, where a mob rose against his attempt to register to vote. Robert Williams was not alone.

Monroe had a slippery hold on Williams. After marrying Mabel and seeing his first son born, he ranged north to Detroit for work on the assembly lines. But almost as soon as he was gone, he talked of returning home. By 1950, he had moved the family back south and enrolled under the GI Bill in the North Carolina College for Negroes in Durham. He wanted to be a writer. A year before finishing, with his government money spent, Williams moved north again for work. He and Mabel sublet a little apartment on Eighty-Eighth Street, in New York City. The building was not generally available to blacks, but the Williamses got in through some radical unionist friends Robert had met at work. The white neighbors were less enlightened than Williams's progressive coworkers. Retreating from the hostility, Mabel stayed in the apartment most of the time. She kept a 9-millimeter pistol close by. It was not a place to make a home, and the Williamses soon left, with Robert chasing work wherever there was promise or rumor of it.

In 1954, induced by promises of training in radio and journalism, Williams enlisted in the Marine Corps. Posted at Camp Pendleton, California, he was promptly installed as a supply sergeant. The promise of training in journalism evaporated with the explanation that blacks did not work in the Information Services. Angry and defiant, Williams fired off missives to Congress complaining about the bait and switch. Then he sent a nasty letter and a telegram to President Eisenhower, threatening to renounce his US citizenship in protest of his mistreatment. This ultimately was enough to earn him a dishonorable discharge from the Marines and a train ticket back to Monroe.

Despite Williams's immediate circumstances, the outlook actually was brightening for blacks in 1954. The United States Supreme Court had ruled in *Brown v. Board of Education* that "separate but equal" was unconstitutional. But it would take far more than a Supreme Court opinion to kill off Jim Crow. White opposition to *Brown* was deep and often vicious. North Carolina governor Luther Hodges, immediately went nuclear, fulminating about black and white amalgamation. State government bureaucrats schemed to maintain de facto segregation. In Monroe, the white reaction against those who aimed to live the message of *Brown* ran from veiled warnings to economic reprisals, to threats and acts of violence.

In 1956, the Klan held a huge rally, led by Reverend James "Catfish" Cole, a tent evangelist and carnival barker from South Carolina. Cole stirred up support through a series of rallies, some drawing more than fifteen thousand people. In the space of a few months, two murders, a cross burning, and dynamite attacks were attributed to the Klan. The combination of economic pressure and violence dampened local enthusiasm for the NAACP's efforts to press enforcement of *Brown*.

When Robert Williams joined the Monroe NAACP, membership was down to six, and the chapter was ready to disband. Fearing economic sanctions as well as Klan violence, the comparatively middle-class folk who had run the branch handed Williams the presidency and soon abandoned the organization. Set adrift by the cautious strivers, Williams recruited new members from people who had been ignored by the clique of black bourgeoisie. He went to the pool halls, the street corners, and the tenant farms, and to the black veterans, some of them comrades in the 1947 defense of Bennie Montgomery's remains. Within two years, Williams would grow the Monroe branch from basically just him, to more than three hundred members.

One of Williams's first controversial acts as chapter president came after a young black boy drowned at a local swimming hole. Monroe had a pool for whites. It was built with public money but excluded blacks, who were relegated to ponds, lakes, or old quarries. Every summer black children drowned in these makeshift swimming holes. The Monroe Parks Commission briefly considered granting black kids one or two days a week to swim. But that was deemed too expensive because of the need to change the pool water after Negroes used it. When Williams and his allies continued to press the issue, including one encounter where he brandished a pistol to escape a threatening crowd of counter-protesters, whites circulated a petition asking that "local Negro integrationists especially Williams and NAACP Vice President, Dr. Albert Perry, be forced to leave Monroe."[4]

The petition was at least nominally democratic compared to the work of Klan potentate Catfish Cole. Cole whipped up sympathetic crowds screeching that "a Nigger who wants to go to a white swimming pool is not looking for a bath. He is looking for a funeral." Cole held five rallies over as many weeks. At the end of each one, the Klan drove through Monroe's black section, blaring horns, throwing debris, and shooting into the air. At the head of these drives was Monroe Police chief, A. A. Mauney, who described them as "motorcades" that he led simply to keep order. On at least one occasion, members of the motorcade fired shots into Dr. Albert Perry's home. Williams complained and requested intervention from the mayor and the governor and with notable persistence sent another letter to President Eisenhower. The only evident response was from local politicians who explained that the Ku Klux Klan had a right to meet and organize, same as the NAACP.[5]

Around the same time, the death threats started. The main targets were Williams and Dr. Perry. Williams began wearing a Colt .45 caliber automatic pistol wherever he went. The gun was familiar, identical to the US Army Model 1911 sidearm. Surplus Colts were widely available in the civilian market and sometimes sold through the US government's Civilian Marksmanship Program, administered by the National Rifle Association, which Williams promptly joined. Williams carried the big gun in a hip holster, "cocked and locked," the hammer clicked back (some would say menacingly), so with a quick swipe of thumb safety, the gun would fire eight fat 230 grain slugs as fast as he could press the trigger.

Williams carried the .45 out of legitimate fear of attack, but it was still an inflammatory act. Up to that point, the Monroe NAACP had enjoyed a smattering of support from progressive whites. That support had faded when Williams pushed the swimming-pool issue. It ended entirely when he began wearing the Colt.[6]

Although Williams was president of the Monroe chapter, many whites felt that the vice president, Dr. Albert Perry, was the greater threat. He was comparatively affluent, and many suspected he was the group's primary financial backer. Unlike many middle-class black folk, Perry was relatively immune from white economic pressure.

One night, Perry's wife interrupted a chapter meeting with a panicked call. They had received another death threat. She knew about the earlier threats, of course. But this was the first time she had answered the phone herself and heard a voice dripping with venom say we are going to kill you.

Dr. Perry rushed home. The rest of the men disbanded the meeting, retrieved their guns, and went to guard Perry's house. They camped that night in his garage, some sitting up in folding chairs with shotguns and rifles across their laps, others standing watch and napping on cots, with rifles and shotguns stacked nearby. They soon determined that the threat was too serious for such ad hoc measures and developed an organized system of rotating guards. Off and on, more than sixty of them guarded the Perrys in shifts.[7]

In October 1957, Catfish Cole held another big Klan rally in Monroe, followed by the traditional motorcade. The destination was Dr. Albert Perry's house. As they approached, some of the hooded revelers fired shots at Perry's neat brick split-level. They were surprised at the response. Anticipating the threat, Williams and the black men of Monroe fired back from behind sandbags and covered positions. One account puts it this way:

> It was just another good time Klan night, the high point of which would come when they dragged Dr. Perry over the state line if they did not hang him or burn him first. But near Dr. Perry's home their revelry was suddenly shattered by the sustained fire of scores of men who had been instructed not to kill anyone if it were not necessary. The firing was blistering, disciplined and frightening. The motorcade of about eighty cars, which had begun in a spirit of good fellowship, disintegrated into chaos, with panicky, robed men fleeing in every direction. Some abandoned their automobiles and had to continue on foot.[8]

Maybe exaggerated in memory, another defender recalled, "When we started firing, they run. We run them out and they started crying and going on. . . . The Klans was low-down people that would do dirty things. But they found out that you would do dirty things too, then they'd let you alone. [They] didn't have the stomach for this type of fight. They stopped raiding our community." In the aftermath, the local press was actually critical of the Klan, attributing the incident significantly to the provocative motorcade. The city council agreed. In an emergency meeting, it passed an ordinance banning KKK motorcades. Outside Monroe, however, the defiance of Williams and his neighbors prompted sympathetic responses like the $260 contribution from a congregation in Harlem to purchase rifles and requests from other communities for help in setting up black rifle clubs.[9]

This was a time of tremendous stress for Williams. His financial situation was precarious. White employers or lenders often tightened the screws on blacks who pressed the civil-rights agenda. At least partly due to his activism, Williams had difficulty finding and keeping work. His frustration is evident in an article he wrote for the newsletter, the *Crusader*. He disdained "Big cars, fine clothes, big houses and college degrees." Manhood, Williams claimed, was more elemental. It meant standing up and taking care of people who depended on you.

But what precisely did that mean? What about the chance that standing up got you knocked down or carried off? Then what good were you to your family and community? Williams's thinking on these questions would soon be sharpened. The lesson came from an unlikely confrontation between the nearby Lumbee Indian tribe and the Klan.

The Lumbee incident was instigated by the now-familiar Catfish Cole, this time exercised by reports of race mixing between whites and Lumbees. Cole laid this sin at the feet of the Lumbee women, disparaging their morals and their "half-breed" children. He announced publicly, "we are going to have a cross burning and scare them up." After several small cross burnings and public fulminations about mongrelization, Cole's Klan planned a widely advertised rally, near Maxton. Before the rally, Cole was warned by the sheriff against further provoking the Lumbees. He had gotten perfunctory warnings like this before. Undeterred, he continued plans for the big event.[10]

On the appointed day, in a roadside field, the Klansmen gathered in the darkness. They set up a portable generator, a PA system, and a kerosene-soaked cross. As the speechmaking started, a Lumbee man swooped in on Catfish Cole. Out of the surrounding darkness, more Lumbees, some would later say several hundred of them, gave a war cry and fired guns into the air. Many of the Klansmen were armed but were unprepared for a gun battle with unknown adversaries hidden in the darkness. Klansmen ran for their cars, abandoning their generator, their little buttons and pamphlets, and their cross. Catfish Cole fled into the swamp, leaving his wife, Carolyn, behind. Four people were injured, reportedly by falling bullets.

The Lumbees' celebration was carried by the national news. After pushing Carolyn Cole's Cadillac out of the ditch and bidding her good-bye, the Indians lit the Klan cross and burned an effigy of her husband. The next day, some of them strutted in Klan robes and hats abandoned by members of the Invisible Empire. *Life* magazine featured a playful photograph, taken several days later, of a beaming Simeon Oxendine, a Lumbee leader, wrapped in a confiscated Ku Klux Klan banner. Even a few local papers seemed to celebrate the Lumbee rout of Cole and his minions, quoting Simeon Oxendine, that "if the Negroes had done something like this a long time ago, we wouldn't be bothered with the KKK."[11]

Oxendine's assessment is intriguing because it raises questions that would plague Robert Williams. Williams was committed to standing like a man and fighting back. But the tougher questions were how much fighting, what type, and within what boundaries? The Lumbees were a tiny slice of the population and insignificant at the ballot box. Their rout of Catfish Cole, the carnival barker, was a sideshow that did not threaten the balance of political power. Responding to Cole's threats to return to Lumbee territory with thousands of armed Klansmen, Governor Hodges pressed the state to indict Cole on charges of inciting a riot. Cole was convicted and served more than a year in prison.

Ultimately, Williams's admiration for the Lumbees was cautious. He was under no illusions that the conviction of Catfish Cole was an endorsement of any broader claims for justice, certainly not black claims. Whites could jokingly salute the Lumbee triumph over the Klan because Cole was a clown and the Indians, long conquered and their population decimated, posed no political threat. Blacks, on the other hand, were far more numerous, an actual majority in many places. This evoked the old demons of Reconstruction and Negro rule. Groups of Negroes with guns, threating political violence either tacitly or overtly, would be provocative on a different order from the almost-quaint Lumbee rout of Catfish Cole.

Negroes with guns had defended Bennie Montgomery's body from desecration and had backed down Klansmen intent on savaging Dr. Albert Perry. But those episodes could still be cast as simple self-defense against Klan provocation. Certainly, Williams saw them that way. They did not clearly cross the line into organized political violence.

This had been a crucial distinction for generations. In different ways over time, blacks recognized the folly of political violence. Ultimately outnumbered and outgunned, Negroes would win nothing as a people through violence. The only plausible tools for group advancement were moral suasion rooted perhaps in religion or American ideals and generally dependent on coalitions with white progressives or enlightened pragmatists. Like generations before him, Williams was acutely conscious of the essential boundary between self-defense and political violence. And, at least in his own mind, he was cautious not to step over it.

Of course, even legitimate private self-defense could be perilous for blacks. Even those who took up arms and protected themselves against imminent threats might still be at the mercy of some sheriff or prosecutor or all-white jury, who would say their violence was not justified. But many times, things did not get that far. Many blacks benefited from the phenomenon, now confirmed by modern researchers, that in most episodes of armed self-defense, no shots are fired and in the remaining fraction, mostly no one is hit. So even in an era where the justice system was overtly biased against blacks, it was plausible to gamble on armed self-defense. And many people would.[12]

Even where shots were fired and someone was injured or killed, the aftermath could vary greatly. In black-on-black confrontations, white authorities might easily dismiss the incident as just a black thing, not worth pursuing. This fueled responses like the 1940s initiative of the Mississippi Delta Committee for Better Citizenship to "ensure greater punishment for Black criminals who committed offenses against Blacks." As circumstances changed, white intervention could also complicate things further, as reflected in one activist's lament that "a Negro who is the favorite of an influential white man can kill another Negro with impunity."[13]

Black-on-white self-defense was another thing altogether. The most cynical assessment is that self-defense simply delayed the violence; that blacks who survived an initial threat would quickly be consumed by the violence of the state or the mob. So it is some proof of the visceral draw of self-defense that this logic did not dissuade Williams or countless others. Sure, it was safer to avoid the threat altogether if you could—better to dissemble, to step back with eyes averted after a slap across the face, or just to flee. But when stripped of those choices and forced to decide about being brutalized today or to gamble on self-defense, countless black people, guns in hand, chose to fight back.

Black protest against injustice was growing across the South. The evolving political strategy—pressed by national civil-rights organizations (some of them capitalizing on interracial coalitions and formally disavowing violence), their local affiliates, and independent grass-roots groups—was mainly passive resistance using the tools of sit-ins, marches, and boycotts. The white reaction was sometimes vicious, and self-defense by blacks under those circumstances risked a spillover into political violence. This was the atmosphere in which Robert Williams sparked an incident that captures the strategic burden, continuous tactical assessment, and boundary drawing that frame the black tradition of arms.

In May 1960, at the Union County Courthouse, Lewis Medlin stood charged with rape. Medlin was white. His accuser, Mary Ruth Reed, was black. At the time of the alleged attack, she also was pregnant. According to the charge, Medlin came to her cabin while her husband was in the fields and tried to rape her as her five children stood by. Mary Ruth broke away and fled into the yard, where Medlin caught her and beat her. A white neighbor intervened and then called the police.

The Reeds resisted both blandishments and threats in pursuit of their full measure of justice in the courts. With Mary Ruth's white neighbor backing up her story, there was reason to be hopeful. But Medlin's lawyer had a good feel for the dynamics of the place and time. He pursued a two-prong defense, arguing first that Medlin was innocent because he was just "drunk and having a little fun." Next, he brought Medlin's wife to the stand, introduced her as "a pure flower of life . . . one of God's greatest gifts." Then he asked the jury of twelve white men whether it was plausible that Medlin would have strayed from his beautiful southern flower—then pointing to Mary Ruth—"for that!" The jury deliberated for about half an hour and then acquitted Medlin.[14]

Blacks in the balcony of courtroom erupted in anger. Medlin was skirted out the side door. Robert Williams, who had urged calm and pressed people to let the system work, was besieged by the angry and the tearful. Some of them, most cuttingly the women, who over time had come to trust Williams as a man in the community they could depend on, actually blamed him for urging restraint. It was a tipping point for Williams. Later, he would recall it in grander themes, invoking the long American tradition of armed resistance to tyranny. But on the day of the acquittal, his reaction was visceral, provoked by raw impulses of sex, race, and a code of honor as old as the South. The case had drawn enough attention that national news organizations were on hand to broadcast Williams saying this.

> We cannot take these people who do us injustice to the court and it becomes necessary to punish them ourselves. In the future we are going to have to try and convict them on the spot. We cannot rely on the law. We can get no justice under the present system. If we feel that injustice is done, we must right then and there, on the spot be prepared to inflict punishment on these people. Since the federal government will not bring a halt to lynching in the South, and since the so-called courts lynch our people legally, *if it's necessary to stop lynching with lynching*, then we must be willing to resort to that method.[15]

Williams's statement triggered the perennial worry. An organized program of violence risked an overwhelming violent response and promised to alienate essential white allies. It also highlighted the paradox that despite the worry about political violence hurting the broader freedom movement, armed self-defense was a crucial private resource for blacks. Through rhetoric, policy, and practice, emerging leaders and ordinary black folk tried to accommodate these two concerns by maintaining a clear boundary between foolish political violence and righteous self-defense. In the view of some people, Robert Williams had crossed over the line.

The headlines blazed, "NAACP Leader Urges Violence." The *Carolina Times* called it the biggest civil-rights story of 1959. Southern editorials attributed Williams's "bloodthirsty remark" directly to the national office. The *Charleston News and Courier* ranted, "Hatred is the stock in trade of the NAACP. High officials of the organization may speak in cultivated accents and dress like Wall Street lawyers, but they are engaged in a revolutionary enterprise."[16]

When word of Williams's statement reached NAACP headquarters in New York, Executive Secretary Roy Wilkins was immediately on the phone to him. The gravity of the situation was plain, and Wilkins recorded the call. Hearing that Williams was planning to make a follow-up statement on national television, Wilkins warned, "You know, of course, that it is not the policy of the NAACP to advocate meeting lynching with lynching. You are going to make it clear that you are not speaking for the NAACP?" After a tense exchange, and realizing that Williams's statement was now firmly linked to the NAACP, Wilkins dispatched a telegram suspending him as branch president.[17]

At a press conference the next day, Williams dialed back his tone, stating that he was not advocating any sort of group political violence by blacks and was not advocating retaliatory lynching. But still he insisted, "Negroes have to defend themselves on the spot when they are attacked." At NAACP headquarters, Roy Wilkins was not convinced by Williams's contrition and worried privately that Williams's rhetorical opposition to political violence was a facade deployed to win sympathy and perhaps gain reinstatement.

With Wilkins unmoved, Williams appealed his dismissal directly to the membership at the 1959 annual convention. The body upheld Wilkin's decision but added an important caveat: "We do not deny but reaffirm the right of an individual and collective self-defense against unlawful assaults." The report of the Resolutions Committee that brought the issue to the floor noted in its preamble, the NAACP's long support of the right of self-defense, "by defending those who have exercised the right of self-defense, particularly in the Arkansas Riot Case, the Sweet case in Detroit, the Columbia, Tennessee Riot cases and the Ingram case in Georgia."[18]

This view was underscored and systematized by Martin Luther King's separate assessment of the Williams controversy. King's treatment is the signal statement of the thrust and boundaries of the black tradition of arms, capturing the organic policy and practice of generations.

In a widely reprinted exchange of essays with Williams, King articulated three distinct categories of response to violent attacks and political oppression. The first, pure nonviolence, is difficult, King said. It "cannot readily or easily attract large masses, for it requires extraordinary discipline and courage." The second response, said King, was implicit in the freedom struggle and should not discourage outsiders from supporting the movement:

> Violence exercised merely in self-defense, all societies, from the most primitive to the most cultured and civilized, accept as moral and legal. The principle of self-defense, even involving weapons and bloodshed, has never been condemned, even by Gandhi. . . . When the Negro uses force in self-defense, he does not forfeit support—he may even win it, by the courage and self-respect it reflects.

This explicit endorsement of armed self-defense, contrasted with King's third assessment, illustrates vividly the core theme of the black tradition of arms. The third approach, Williams's approach, said King, advocated "violence as a tool of advancement, organization as in warfare . . . [and posed] incalculable perils." Political goals, King argued, were best achieved by nonviolent, "socially organized masses on the march."[19]

King's assessment was only one aspect of a robust community engagement of the issue. Louis Lautier of the influential *Baltimore Afro-American* argued that Williams had not advocated political violence, but merely that "colored people should defend themselves if and when violence is directed at them." In the *Arkansas*

State Press, legendary activists Daisy and L. C. Bates, longtime gun owners who soon would fire shots in self-defense, were equivocal on Roy Wilkins's contention that Williams had crossed the line into advocacy of political violence. Wilkins offered the Bateses a series of blandishments to secure their support in the fight against Williams. Wilkins got his vote, but Daisy and L. C. Bates remained firm on the principle of private self-defense, warning that "nonviolence never saved George Lee in Belzoni, Miss., or Emmett Till, nor Mack Parker at Poplarville, Miss." Anne Braden, enduring white activist for racial justice, reprinted the King and Williams essays in the *Southern Patriot*, and her summary succinctly captured the black tradition of arms. No one disputes the right to defend home and family, she explained, "What the nonviolent movement says is that the weapons of social change should be nonviolent."[20]

The NAACP national office received protests from the branches that supported Williams. In Monroe, the branch showed its continuing support for Williams by electing his wife, Mabel, president in his place. The Brooklyn branch wired Roy Wilkins in protest of the "illegal and arbitrary removal from office of Robert F. Williams for expressing sentiments to which we subscribe." This and other support for Williams raised the question of whether some in the community had abandoned the traditional commitment to avoid political violence at all costs. As we will see, this was neither the first nor the last time that this commitment would be challenged.[21]

Fig. 1.1. Robert and Mabel Williams in the 1950s. (From the personal collection of Mabel R. Williams.)

A more moderate tone was exhibited by black journalist John McCray, in a *Baltimore Afro-American* article titled, "There's Nothing New about It." McCray's assessment confirmed the basic boundaries of the black tradition of arms. On issues of social change, he said, "A minority group cannot hope to win in campaigns of violence." On the other hand, McCray acknowledged without criticism that black self-defense had deep roots. "Today, thousands of our people have secured 'protection' in their homes, mostly with the intent to repel night riders who, years ago, were terrors to their forbearers."[22]

With debate raging, Roy Wilkins defended his position in a pamphlet titled *The Single Issue in the Robert Williams Case*, arguing that his approach was consistent with the black tradition of arms. "There is no issue of self-defense. . . . The charges are based on his call for aggressive, premeditated violence. Lynching is never defensive." Here, Wilkins wrapped himself a century-old philosophy. While condemning political violence as a hazard to the movement, he recognized armed self-defense as a crucial private resource. At a June 1959 fundraising dinner in Chicago, Wilkins pressed the point, drawing applause and Amens. "Of course, we must defend ourselves when attacked. This is our right under all known laws."[23]

Wilkins reiterated this position throughout his life. On national television in 1967, Wilkins affirmed his support for private firearms ownership. The nation was wrestling with urban rioting, militant rhetoric, and violence from black radicals, and was weighing proposals for sweeping firearms restrictions. Asked whether he would endorse a "massive effort to disarm the Negroes in the ghettos," Wilkins maintained the legitimacy of armed self-defense. "I wouldn't disarm the Negroes and leave them helpless prey to the people who wanted to go in and shoot them up. Every American wants to own a rifle. Why shouldn't Negroes own rifles?" In his 1982 memoir, Wilkins confirmed, "Like [Robert] Williams, I believe in self-defense. While I admire Reverend King's theories of overwhelming enemies with love, I don't think I could have put those theories into practice myself. But there is a difference between self-defense and murder, and I had no intention of getting the NAACP into the lynching business."[24]

The Williams affair is remarkable for the detail in which it elaborates the black tradition of arms and shows the community openly endorsing armed self-defense. But it is just a single episode in a more-than-century-long tradition of Negroes with guns, one where the legitimacy and utility of firearms was an article of faith and where the best people in the community were armed.

This is the story of those people and that tradition.

CHAPTER TWO

FOUNDATION

*"The True Remedy for the Fugitive Slave Bill is a good revolver,
a steady hand, and a determination to shoot down any man
attempting to kidnap."*

—Frederick Douglass, 1854[1]

T here was no sign of anything special happening when the slave boy Fred
Bailey stood up and fought the rawboned Maryland planter they called
"Covey the Nigger-breaker." Negroes had been striking back against the prosaic violence of slavery since the beginning. The nature of that resistance and its impulses
are contested today, and these cavils may never be settled. But at the core, the deeds
and decisions of earlier generations of slaves, fugitives, and freemen ground Martin
Luther King's twentieth-century debate with Robert Williams and frame the black
tradition of arms.

Violence in the freedom struggle resonates differently over time. Political
nonviolence so dominates the story of the modern civil-rights movement that it
obscures the tradition of individual self-defense. And while the folly of political violence seems plain today, the case against it did not always sway black folk. Indeed,
luminaries of the nineteenth-century leadership class advocated organized violent
resistance against slavery as a matter of considered policy. And before that, cryptic
accounts of early American slavery, evidence abundant individual and organized
resistance.

Martin King and Robert Williams debated the boundaries of an established
tradition. But the roots of that tradition, like births and deaths and black family
trees that fade to dust under slavery, are not fully recorded in the fashion of other
important American developments. So the early story, we piece together—some of
it from rare accounts by black folk and more of it as remnants from the stories of the
conquering class.

Partly this yields unsympathetic renderings of quick, violent outbursts and loosely organized, swiftly quashed revolts—the widely recounted insurrections of Denmark Vesey, Gabriel Prosser, Charles Deslandes, Nat Turner, and an estimated 250 more obscure episodes. In other brief accounts and sterile court records, we see the familiar, unplanned human reflex to meet violence with violence that reflects why philosophers speak of a natural right to self-defense. [2]

Some scholars argue that early arrivals from Africa were culturally inclined against organized violence and favored individual combat charged with African ritual. Others contend that lingering tribal rivalries and language barriers hindered planning for group resistance. Still others say that organized slave revolts had a clear African base and that it was American-born blacks who adopted practical survival strategies that eschewed suicidal rebellions.

Records of early criminal convictions suggest that direct violence against masters or other whites was more likely from "unseasoned" slaves new to the Americas. "Seasoned" slaves, acclimated to the culture, were more likely to resist surreptitiously. Eighteenth-century prosecutions and executions for arson and poisoning suggest that this was not uncommon. [3] Many acts of resistance defy rigid boundaries, demonstrating both a personal fight against the immediate violence of slavery and a political resistance against the slave system. The black tradition of arms grows out of this milieu. [4]

Fred Bailey's situation was common. He had been rented out to Edward Covey by his master, Thomas Auld. Bailey was young, just coming into manhood. Some said that the handsome mulatto had been coddled. And Auld perhaps thought that too. A year away with Covey would train him up right.

Covey wrung a living out of the silty loam of Maryland's eastern shore. He drove Negroes hard. With a nod and a knowing smile, men called him "Nigger-breaker," in earnest respect for his particular talent and general disposition. Like others of his type, Covey was the slavers' medicine for young bucks with too much spirit.

Fred Bailey was not the typical problem, though. Relatively speaking, he was soft, his early life spent in the comparative comfort of the Baltimore home of Hugh Auld, Thomas's brother. It was there, as bonded companion to Hugh and Sophia Auld's young son Tommy, that Bailey learned to read from the Bible at the knee of the kindly Sophia.

Bailey surely was a slave, presented to Tommy as "his Freddy," and formally charged with serving and protecting the younger boy. But the work of servile big brother was not taxing and often left Bailey free to roam the streets and docks of Baltimore. Fieldwork under Covey's lash was a jolting immersion into the more common experience of American Negro slavery.

One steamy afternoon in 1833, the August heat dragged down the tenderfoot. Part of a team of four assigned to threshing, Bailey lagged, stumbled, and then passed out. His job was to carry raw, stalked grain to the thresher. When he stopped working, the threshing stopped. The commotion of threshing was profit. Silence was loss. And Covey was quick to investigate.

Bailey was laid out in a shady spot next to the thresher when Covey approached and demanded explanations. Bailey, in a heat daze, mumbled excuses. Covey figured first to kick him back to work and planted a boot hard in his side. Bailey rose partway, fell back, got another kick, and then another. Crab-walking, attempting to stand, then falling again, Bailey was somewhere between up and down when Covey bashed him in the head with an oak-barrel stave. The blood flowed. And this time Bailey stayed down, resigning himself to dying right there if that was his fate.

The beating was having the opposite effect Covey wanted. He was worn out from giving it, and Bailey was no closer to resuming work. Covey stomped off in disgust. Bailey, splayed out on the ground, bleeding from the head, resolved, if he survived the moment, to flee.

At the first clear chance, Bailey crawled off into the woods, barefoot and bleeding. His destination was St. Michaels, seven miles away. There, he imagined finding relief in the self-interest of Master Thomas. It was fair to think that Auld would object to Covey abusing his valuable property. Bailey might even have thought to prevail on whatever advantage rested in the whispers that Auld was actually his father. It was not an unreasonable hope. Auld had twice rescued Bailey from the fate of a field hand, arranging for soft duty in Baltimore with Hugh, Sophia, and Tommy.

The welcome in St. Michaels was disappointing. Bailey looked how you would expect from a kid who had dropped from heatstroke, taken a beating, and then fled barefoot through seven miles of forest and swamp. But Thomas Auld had little sympathy either for Bailey's appearance or for his story. Auld knew Covey. Covey was a good man. Whatever had happened, Bailey must have deserved it. And, of course, as a matter of law, there was really nothing to be done. Covey had leased Bailey for a full year. It would be legally, nay, morally wrong to welsh on the bargain.

In another era, biographers, speculating about the blood connection and Auld's multiple rescues, would claim that there had been something like love binding Fred Bailey and Thomas Auld. Maybe this exaggerates things. But whatever affection there was, Auld's refusal to intervene with Covey was the end of it for Bailey. Bailey's later depictions of Auld exhibit only disdain.

Early the next morning, ordered to return to Covey or be whipped and returned by force, Fred Bailey reversed course and trudged seven miles back to the scene of his escape. Climbing over the rail fence into the front pasture, he encountered Covey charging toward him, bullwhip in hand. Whatever impulse had moved Bailey to run off, Covey intended to beat out of him. But he had to catch him first.

Bailey fled to the high corn and crawled down low. Covey lost the scent. Exhausted and hungry, Bailey spent the day in the woods, at the edge of the fields, deciding whether to run back to St. Michaels to a whipping, surrender to Covey for a whipping, or stay in the woods and starve.

That night, Bailey roamed the fields and woodlots until he came to the little cabin of Sandy Jenkins, who is recorded either as a free black or a slave who enjoyed a degree of independence, living in his own place with a free black woman. Sandy let Bailey wash up and shared his simple dinner as they talked about what to do.

Sandy was at least a generation older than Bailey. He had longer experience with the violence of slavery. He also was the keeper of secrets. While Sandy's wife cleaned up, man and boy walked out into the darkness. Sandy said Bailey must surrender to Covey. He also promised Bailey something that seems fanciful today, but less so then.

Deep into the woods, where the light from the cabin fire was lost, Sandy worked under the moonglow, scratching and probing. Then, on his knees, clawing into the black loam, he tugged up a root from the breathing forest.

Years later, after he had escaped from slavery, thrown off the name Bailey, and become what the *New York Times* called the "foremost man of his race," *Frederick Douglass* recounted how wise old Sandy had bestowed on him "a certain root, which, if I would take some of it with me, carrying it always on my right side, would render it impossible for Mr. Covey, or any other white man, to whip me."

Looking back, it is pleasing to speculate about the magic of the root and the forces of destiny that were taking hold. What we can say for sure is that the next encounters between the "Nigger-breaker" and the nascent abolitionist, orator, writer, publisher, and freedom-movement pioneer Frederick Douglass were to be profoundly different from what had passed before.

Away for several days now, with only a brief appearance and a retreat into the corn, Douglass returned to the Covey farm early on the Sunday, buoyed gingerly by the promise of Sandy's root magic. Walking toward the main house, he spied Covey, dressed for church. His temperament reflecting his destination, Covey acknowledged Douglass calmly and gave him instructions for a bit of work that would not take long. Douglass finished the work and spent the remainder of the day contemplating the magic of the root, the wonder of the Sabbath, and the other mysteries that had pacified Covey since their last meeting.

Like countless Mondays before and since, the warmth and charity of the Sabbath had faded by the next morning. It was not yet daylight when Douglass was lured into the stable with instructions to tend the horses. He was climbing down from the loft when Covey entered with a rope, lassoed him, and yanked him to the floor. Douglass later recounted it this way:

Covey seemed now to think he had me, and could do what he pleased; but at this moment—from whence came the spirit I don't know—I resolved to fight; and suiting my action to the resolution, I seized Covey hard by the throat; and as I did so, I rose. He held on to me, and I to him. My resistance was so entirely unexpected, that Covey seemed taken all aback. He trembled like a leaf. This gave me assurance, and I held him uneasy, causing the blood to run where I touched him with the ends of my fingers.

Covey called out to his cousin, Hughes, for help. Hughes waded in just long enough to get a strong kick in the ribs from Douglass and was out of the fight. Covey went for a stick, but Douglass intercepted him and flung him by the neck back to the ground. Covey yelled for help to Bill, another rented slave. Bill objected that he was a valuable working man whose master would not want busted up.

From there, it was just Douglass and Covey, fighting like men until they were spent. And like most episodes of violence, the aftermath was crucial. Here, the odds shifted sharply against Douglass. Violence against whites, even in self-defense, was a hazardous bet for slaves. With the legal status of mules, they were treated accordingly by American courts. And it is a compelling intuition that, except for self-defense in the course of a successful escape, violence against whites would more likely just delay injury or death than prevent it.[5]

Douglass himself wondered why Covey did not have him taken to the constable and "whipped for the crime of raising my hand against a white man in defence of myself." The answer, he thought, was that Covey had a reputation as a breaker of Negroes, and his brand would suffer if he were forced to send a defiant sixteen-year-old to the public whipping post.

Whether it was this or something grander and preordained that accounted for Covey's reticence, is impossible to know. What we do know is that Douglass was transformed. Filthy and sweating, Covey dragged himself up out of the mud and admonished that he "would not have whipped him half so much" if Fred had not resisted. Douglass saw it differently. "*He had not whipped me at all.* I considered him as getting entirely the worst end of the bargain; for he had drawn no blood from me, but I had from him."

For Douglass this was the turning point in his life as a slave that kindled his quest for freedom, and marked his passage into manhood. "I was nothing before. I was a man now.... And determined to be a FREEMAN!... I resolved that, however long I might remain a slave in form, the day had passed forever when I could be a slave in fact. I did not hesitate to let it be known of me, that the white man who expected to succeed in whipping, must also succeed in killing me."[6]

Frederick Douglass was far from the first to fight. And given the danger that even vaguely suspected aggression might trigger severe punishment, it is evidence of the power of the self-defense impulse that slaves fought back with some frequency. A study of seventeenth- and eighteenth-century criminal convictions shows that violence against masters lead the next closest category of slave crimes (theft) by a factor of three.[7]

For episodes that made it to the courts, slave self-defenders typically met quick, severe punishment. This is illustrated in early Missouri court records, where the aftermath of slave violence was predictable. Punishment was swift in 1818 for a St. Louis slave who stabbed and killed his owner in order to avoid a whipping. He was tried, in a fashion, and quickly hanged. It happened again in 1828, when John Tanner's slave, Moses, somehow acquired a gun and shot and killed Tanner. Missouri courts were unsympathetic to Moses's claim that Tanner had "acted disgracefully" toward Moses's wife. Denied the prerogatives of honor that might be extended to a white man, Moses was summarily tried and hanged.

The scenario repeats in 1859, in the town of Buchanan, where a young slave who had been sold off to a slave trader managed to conceal a pistol, shoot the trader, and escape. He was apprehended and swiftly hanged. It happened again in 1863, when a slave named Henry shot his master after being threatened with a whipping. The shooting occurred in July. Henry was hanged by the end of August.

In another variation on the theme, a free Negro in St. Louis shot and killed a deputy and wounded another in an attempt to keep one of his neighbors from being carted back to slavery. The effort failed on all counts. The fugitive was hauled off in a yoke, and the free black Samaritan was burned at the stake by a mob.

Negro violence yielded slightly better results in 1843 in Boone County, Missouri. There, a group of five slaves plotted to kill their master, who had threatened to whip the lot of them. With axes and the advantage of numbers, they hacked Hiram Beasley to death and ran off. Two of them were apprehended and hanged, but the others escaped.[8]

In an exceptional North Carolina case, *State v. Negro Will*, a slave sentenced to death for killing his overseer had his conviction reduced to manslaughter by the North Carolina Supreme Court. For the time and place, it was an extraordinary recognition of a Negro's basic self-defense interest. Will killed the overseer in a conflict over a garden tool. His title challenged, Will decided no one would have the thing. He snapped the handle and stomped off. Inflamed by this defiance, the overseer, Baxter, chased Will down and emptied his revolver at him. When Baxter came in close, Will sprang forward and killed him with a knife. Will's owner was convinced it was self-defense and paid two leading North Carolina lawyers $1,000, approximately Will's cash value, to represent him.

Negro Will was an exceptional case. More emblematic of the times is the North Carolina court's far harsher assessment in *State v. John Mann*, which overturned the conviction of a slaver who shot his Negro girl as she attempted to flee. The case underscored the basic principle that masters were not criminally liable for violence against their slaves, bolstering the intuition that slave self-defense was more of a desperate last act than a viable survival strategy.[9]

In this sort of environment, it is hard to say that Douglass's fight with Covey and countless other episodes of slave resistance were fully rational acts. But how then to classify them? It is common across history to celebrate doomed fights against impossible odds as the essence of heroism. But those fighters generally have champions among poets and storytellers in cultures hungry for such heroes. The black tradition of arms will yield many folk who fought desperately against long odds. But query whether there is space in our culture to think about them as anything more than victims.

For Frederick Douglass, looking out from the middle of the nineteenth century, there was slim reason to believe that Negro resistance in the fight for freedom would ever be celebrated within the American story. Even after he had achieved fame, some fortune, and international acclaim, Douglass was still stigmatized by the United States Supreme Court as part of a class who held no rights that the white man was bound to respect.[10]

Despite that blighted logic, or perhaps because of it, Douglass's rise from less than nothing is actually the most American of stories. At age twenty, or nineteen, depending on whether we credit Douglass's guess or biographers' research, he stole away from slavery out of Baltimore, disguised as a sailor. He would become one of America's most formidable abolitionists, so talented as an orator and writer that incredulous racists would charge that his claim of escaping from slavery was a fraud.[11]

Douglass was one of the earliest and most prominent blacks to wrestle publicly with the role of violence in the freedom struggle. Even in his early career, still under the sway of pacifist abolitionists who "discovered" and advanced him, Douglass had difficulty translating pacifist appeals to the conscience of slavers into something that resonated for Negroes.

The terror of slavery and the fugitive slave laws ultimately pushed Douglass to advocate not just armed self-defense but overt political violence and slave insurrection. By the middle of the nineteenth century, having broken away from William Lloyd Garrison's pacifist abolitionists, Douglass offered a bold prescription for the man-hunters who were licensed by the final and most damnable of the fugitive slave laws. Speaking to both fugitives and freemen, Douglass advocated, "A good revolver, a steady hand and a determination to shoot down any man attempting to kidnap.... Every slave hunter who meets a bloody death in his infernal business is an argument in favor of the manhood of our race."[12]

Fig. 2.1. *Fighting the Mob in Indiana*, an artist's rendering of Frederick Douglass fighting a proslavery mob (1843). (Courtesy of Documenting the American South, the University of North Carolina at Chapel Hill Libraries.)

In some sense, it was inevitable that Douglass's advice spilled over from self-defense into political violence. Putting aside debates of higher law, slave hunters were not criminals. Their nefarious craft was explicitly authorized by the Constitution of the United States, enshrined in Article IV, Section 2, and embellished subsequently by statute, in the Fugitive Slave Act of 1793. This was still deficient, said slavers, because it was weak on federal enforcement and permitted free-state laws that interfered with slave recapture and exposed man-hunters to assault and kidnapping charges.

The final and harshest fugitive slave law was rendered by the Compromise of 1850, which aimed to ease the tensions over whether new states would enter the union slave or free. With the nation pulsing under the fever for westward expansion, the Compromise of 1850 brought California into the union as a free state, let voters in other new states decide about slavery for themselves, and put federal law enforcement squarely behind the recapture of slave property.

In later generations, black leaders would assess political violence from inside the fence. Nominally citizens, nominally right-bearers, and ultimately outnumbered, blacks would largely reject violence as a tool for achieving political goals. The better bet was to shame America into fulfilling the promise of its founding ideals.

But under slavery, the calculation was different. Negroes were excluded entirely from the system, branded as an inferior cast with no basic human rights, let alone political ones. So the appeal of political violence, desperate and doomed as it might be, is understandable. There was little reason to worry about maintaining some strategic boundary between political violence and self-defense.

For much of his activism, this was Douglass's calculation. And for many Negroes, it had long been so. Many fugitives were pressed either to fight or to return to bondage. Whether you called it self-defense or political violence mattered little. And starting early on, fugitive and freeman, *these Negroes fought*.

From the beginning, free blacks were a threat to slave culture and an important resource for fugitives. Associations of free blacks date to the beginning of the American state. Some were formal, like the Philadelphia Free African Society, formed in 1787 as white America framed its Constitution. Other groups were less organized and more thinly recorded, often just clusters of caring neighbors, clear-eyed about the utility and morality of violent self-defense. In 1804, one of these groups in Lancaster, Pennsylvania, interdicted a slave catcher, stripped him naked, "and beat him soundly with hickory switches." In most cases, though, folk were more effectively armed.

In 1806, near Dayton, Ohio, a gun was Ned Page's most important possession. Ned and his wife Lucy were technically free people, brought from Kentucky under circumstances that extinguished claims to them as property. So said Ohio.

But words in law books often don't translate into reality. If things happened fast enough, decisive action would trump the parchment barriers of Ohio law.

The Pages were laid over in a makeshift tavern when two armed men entered intent on hauling them back south in chains. Ned Page pulled a pistol from his pack, squared up his sights and threatened to kill rather than be taken. A clutch of friends surrounded him in support. The slave catchers were apprehended and charged with breach of the peace.

In 1810, armed black men rode to the rescue in Jefferson, Ohio, after an informer set slave catchers onto a family of fugitives. The capture was easy. The return was not. The kidnappers had the family yoked and headed south when they were intercepted by a group of fifteen to twenty "colored men armed with guns pistols and other weapons." The two sides maneuvered to a standoff and the Southerners agreed to the offer of a white attorney to present their claim to the authorities. The local magistrate rejected the slavers' claims and released the Negroes. In a final insult, the slave hunters were charged with assault. They posted bail and rode off, forfeiting their bond.

Many early episodes where fugitives got their hands on guns shifted quickly into primitive combat. This accords with the firearms technology of the time. When Frederick Douglass advised blacks to acquire a good revolver, practical applications of that multishot technology were only a few decades old, made viable by Sam Colt's percussion-cap revolver in 1836 and Horace Smith and Daniel Wesson's more efficient cartridge system in 1851. Before that, armed self-defense generally involved single-shot or, more rarely, multi-barrel guns, sparked by flintlocks or percussion caps. Except where people had multiple guns, additional fighting meant contact weapons. John Reid's resistance in 1820 is illustrative.

Reid was a fugitive slave living in Kennett Township, Pennsylvania. He was sitting by the fire in his cabin when armed slave catchers began breaking through his door. Reid grabbed his gun, and shouted, "It is life for life!" The first man through the door was Samuel Griffith, Reid's owner come to claim him. Reid shot Griffith dead. The second man through was Reid's former overseer, Peter Shipley. His firearm spent, Reid killed Shipley with a club strike to the head. Reid was charged with murder. But the antislavery sentiment in the area was such that the jury acquitted him on the murder of Griffith and convicted him of a lesser charge in the death of Shipley.[13]

So where did nineteenth-century Negroes get their guns? The answer varies substantially by place. Free blacks and fugitives who escaped to the North could acquire guns through a variety of legitimate channels, constrained mainly by their resources. But Southern blacks had to navigate the first generation of American arms-control laws, explicitly racist statutes starting as early as Virginia's 1680 law, barring clubs, guns, or swords to both slaves and free blacks.

It is a fair intuition that that slaves obtained guns mainly by theft. But there are indications that some slaves were actually entrusted with guns by their masters. Slave-state gun-control laws actually reflect this. An eighteenth-century Maryland law commanded that "no Negro or other slave, within this province, shall be permitted to carry any gun or any other offensive weapon, from off their Masters land, without license from their said master." A similar Georgia law declared that no slave could possess a firearm except where accompanied by "a white person of at least 16 years old, or while defending crops from birds."[14]

In some cases, slave access to firearms entirely defies modern intuitions. Court records from prewar Vicksburg, Mississippi, show that some slaves had direct access to the market for firearms, alcohol, and other contraband, through trading with white merchants who were periodically arrested and prosecuted for selling to blacks.

One of the exacerbating factors in this illegal trade was the practical limit on the kind of oversight that masters could exercise over their slaves. Some bondsmen found relative freedom in the unavoidable circumstances of their work. Many of the wagon and carriage drivers around Vicksburg enjoyed a great deal of autonomy because it was impractical to supervise them as they chased fares and hauled cargo.

Slave masters often found it simply more profitable to assign Negroes to unsupervised tasks or to allow trusted slaves to hire themselves out or even run their own businesses. One planter in prewar Vicksburg, Mississippi, actually bragged that his boys were so enterprising and such prodigious savers, that he had borrowed money from them himself. One slave couple was reported to have accumulated thousands of dollars' worth of property, including two tracts of land held in trust for them by a white attorney. Another slave named William Hitch, who lived and worked in town away from his master, commented that he had been essentially "free since he was a boy" because his owner allowed him total control in hiring out his time.

Some slaves from this class used their accumulated capital to buy their freedom. Others remained in place, building resources, and in some instances, aided by their owners, passed their assets on to heirs. In some places this dynamic gave rise to the "nominal slave," whose relative freedom was alternately a blessing and a curse for whites.

Many whites considered the freer rein given to nominal slaves a hazard. In 1859, Vicksburg papers editorialized that the "class of Negroes now among us who are pretended to be owned by a white men [are] a pest and annoyance of the town." These "quasi-slaves" were derided as "vicious and insolent . . . keepers of half-wild horses, cattle and dogs."

This often-unsupervised slave culture facilitated trading of both alcohol and guns. Court records in Warren County, Mississippi, reveal more than one hundred cases alleging illegal trading by whites with slaves. Many of these are sales of alcohol. But some cases, like the prosecution of Christian Fleckenstein, provide rich evidence about illicit trading of firearms.

Fleckenstein was a threadbare merchant and widely rumored seller of contraband to slaves. Suggesting the division of interests between slavers and the merchant class, one local slave owner, fed up with Fleckenstein's illicit trade, set a trap to build a case against him. The planter sent one of his slaves into Fleckenstein's store with three dollars and clear instructions. The slave returned with a bundle containing liquor and a gun.

Fleckenstein was arrested and tried. The litigation is an interesting insight into the slave world and the difficulty owners had in simultaneously controlling their slaves and extracting their full economic value. The court charged the jury that Fleckenstein should be found guilty unless he could produce a note giving the slave permission from his master to purchase the gun and the alcohol. The court was willing to acknowledge that a master might plausibly send a slave on an errand to buy either item.

Fleckenstein, of course, had no such proof and was convicted. On appeal, his conviction was reversed on technical deficiencies in the indictment. Fleckenstein continued trading with slaves and evidently was joined by a handful of other "disreputable groceries." Over time, the low trade generated fat profits that allowed the disreputable grocers to build sturdy brick homes.

Another incident in Vicksburg suggests that blacks had access to firearms through theft or through a loose trading culture well before the sting operation on Christian Fleckenstein. In 1835, white Vicksburgers pursued a private remedy against the abundant gambling, drinking, and prostitution in "the Kangaroo," a local haven for slaves, nominal slaves, and free blacks. After heated conversations and the passing of resolutions, a group representing the good people of the town marched in military formation to one of the hangouts in the Kangaroo. The show of force was repelled when the blacks launched a volley of gunfire that killed one man. Whites sent for reinforcements and ultimately prevailed, apprehending and hanging five occupants of the house.

There is no explicit detail on where the Negroes of the Kangaroo got their guns. But the indications that many of them were armed suggests a level of access to firearms beyond the random opportunity to steal one. The "nominal" slave class, with assets and broad trading opportunities, probably had access to guns and would have been a source of guns for Negroes with more limited opportunities.[15]

Another hint about the nature of slaves' access to firearms appears at the end of the Civil War in an 1865 debate of a white vigilance committee about disarming the freedmen in and around Somerton, South Carolina. In what seems to be an unusual objection for the time and place, Lauren Manning, a lowland planter, opposed disarming newly minted freedman, arguing that "some of his slaves carried weapons for the protection of the plantation before the war, and now these men had been made free and therefore had a right to carry arms."[16] Manning's objection was overruled, and the vigilance committee set out with some vigor to disarm local Negroes. But Manning's statement that his slaves had carried firearms confirms that slaves sometimes accessed guns in ways that may seem surprising today.

Still, the intuition that theft accounted for a substantial portion of slave access to firearms remains sound. When the slave couple Loveless and Pink ran off with their three children from Leon County, Florida, in the mid-1830s, they stole master Cornelius DeVane's shotgun and all the provisions they could carry.[17] Fugitive slave Henry Bibb not only stole his master's gun but later wrote a book about his adventures that describes the gun theft this way: "For ill treatment we concluded to take a tramp together. . . . Before we started I managed to get hold of a suit of clothes the Deacon possessed, with his gun, ammunition and bowie knife."[18]

Theft also was the source of the guns used by two young runaways who were pursued by patrollers on horseback. When the horsemen closed on them, the slave boys opened fire with a brace of pistols, ending the pursuit and escaping. And on the Manigault plantation in coastal Georgia, overseers confirmed that slaves were stealing and hoarding ammunition when they discovered a cache of shot and powder hidden by a slave named Ishmael who confessed his plans to run off.[19]

Other episodes leave us wondering more intently about the source of slave armament. Cryptic reports of armed bands of escapees suggest multiple thefts or stockpiling in preparation for escape. A mass slave escape from southern Maryland in 1845 is indicative. The fugitives, numbering between seventy and eighty, were led by a free Negro named Bill Wheeler. On a stifling hot July evening, the unsupervised men snuck off and then assembled as a body, marching in discipline, carrying pistols, blades, and farm tools improvised into weapons. With a semblance of military planning that defies intuitions of spontaneous escapes, the group separated into two companies and proceeded along alternate routes. Eventually, the larger group was corralled outside Rockville, Maryland. The blacks closed ranks and exchanged gunfire with their pursuers. Several Negroes were wounded, two of them stood trial, and one was executed.

A similar incident occurred the same year when ten slaves escaped from Hagerstown, Maryland. On their way to Pennsylvania, they confronted an equal-sized white posse. As the pursers closed in, the slaves "drew themselves up in battle order" and attacked with pistols and tomahawks. Eight of the fugitives managed to escape, leaving behind two of their own dead and several wounded whites.[20]

In 1848, forty-seven blacks armed with guns and knives fled Kentucky bound for Ohio. Before reaching the Ohio River, they were surrounded by three hundred armed whites. The fugitives stood and fought in two separate skirmishes but ultimately surrendered. Many of the escapees were put on trial for sedition and insurrection. Three were convicted and hanged. Several others were saved by their masters, on the argument that the benefit of more hangings was less than the value of the men as property. Armed fugitives had more success in 1855 when a group of six runaways from Virginia deployed pistols and knives to fight off bounty hunters who detained them in Maryland. Here the full group managed to get away.[21]

The escape story of Reverend Elijah P. Marrs is particularly instructive, in that it contains an explicit admission of gun theft. Marrs was born into slavery in Shelby County, Kentucky, in 1840. He rose to become a revered clergyman, educator, and standout in Reconstruction-era politics. During the early stages of the Civil War, Marrs risked retribution at the hands of Shelby County rebels for reading and writing letters for local slaves. As the war progressed, the danger mounted for the "Shelby County Negro clerk," and he soon decided to run off to the Union Army.

In the late summer of 1864, Marrs organized a group of twenty-seven slaves who set out for Union lines. Confirming the surmise that theft was a source of guns for slaves, Marrs reports that his group was "armed with . . . war clubs and one old rusty pistol, the property of the captain."[22]

It is not clear whether Elijah Marrs's group actually fired their solitary gun or whether they gained some advantage by brandishing it. Researchers say that brandishing guns without firing them is the most common form of armed self-defense today.[23] Although it is impossible to know how often slaves benefited from brandishing guns, if the modern trend applied, those episodes would far exceed incidents of actual gunfire, and those nonshooting defensive gun uses would likely go unrecorded.

Some evidence of nonshooting, defensive gun uses under slavery survives because it involved famous Negroes. Consider the long practice of Harriet Tubman, storied conductor of the Underground Railroad, who reportedly guided more than seventy slaves out of bondage. There are no accounts of Tubman exchanging gunfire with slave catchers. But she is widely reported and depicted carrying a rifle, a musket, or a pistol. Some modern researchers, queasy about the notion of a gun-toting Tubman, argue that her guns were unloaded—a theory hard to square with Tubman's scouting for the Union Army.

Tubman was not the only guide on the Underground Railroad to carry a gun. Lesser-known black abolitionist John P. Parker not only carried guns in his forays south, but also claimed to have used them in what he described as "warfare" with slaveholders. By the middle of the nineteenth century, Parker had settled in Ripley, Ohio, where he harbored scores of fugitives, brawled, brandished guns against slave-hunting gangs, and "never thought of going uptown without a pistol in my pocket, a knife in my belt, and a blackjack handy." One account credits Parker with making Ripley "as important an escape route as any in the nation." Parker was clearly not the only armed conductor in the vicinity of Ripley. Fugitive slave Francis Fredric recounted escaping through Ripley, where he was "well-guarded by eight or ten young members with revolvers."[24]

Fig. 2.2. Harriet Tubman, conductor of the Underground Railroad. (Woodcut ca. 1865.)

HARRIET TUBMAN.

In the mid-1850s, Parker aided in a daring raid into Kentucky, under the planning of white abolitionist minister John Rankin. A group of runaways was stranded on the riverbank in slave territory. Parker reports that Rankin asked him to come to their typical meeting place and bring every gun he owned. Parker wrote later,

I had been told to bring all my firearms, which I did, including an old musket. I knew something serious was up, because this was the first time I'd ever been called on to come, armed with anything but small arms. . . . I can still see the pale face of Reverend Rankin as he sat in the center of this council of war, arguing for his plan of rescue. . . . To go heavily armed . . . and take the group forcibly from anyone who got in the way.

That night, a squad of seven men spread across three boats and armed with everything they had, landed in slave territory and retrieved the shivering clutch of runaways.[25] The scene repeats in the story of John Henry Hill, who escaped to and continued to agitate from Canada. Hill reports engaging in a gunfight with his master before fleeing Richmond, Virginia, armed with "a brace of Pistels."[26]

William Still, a freeborn Negro, hailed as the "father of the Underground Railroad," produced a remarkably textured eight-hundred-page account of fugitive slave escapes, including episodes that fulfill the longing for the detail that is missing in so many accounts of fugitive slaves wielding guns. Working through the Philadelphia Anti-Slavery Society, Still aided hundreds of escaping slaves and eventually began interviewing them and recording their stories. One of the most iconic images of Negroes with guns during slavery appears in Still's account of the escape of Barnaby Grigby, Mary Elizabeth Grigby, Frank Wanzer, and Emily Foster. They were fugitives from Virginia who stole their master's "best horses and carriage" and fled north on Christmas Eve 1855. They made it as far as Maryland without incident. Then, as they entered the Cheat River Valley, a group of "six white men and a boy" thought them suspicious, perhaps the subjects of a reward, and aimed to apprehend them. Still records their story this way:

> The fugitives verily believing that the time had arrived for the practical use of their pistols and dirks, pulled them out of their concealment—the young women as well as the young men—and declared they would not be taken! One of the white men raised his gun, pointing the muzzle directly towards one of the young women, with the threat that he would "shoot" etc. "Shoot! Shoot! Shoot!" she exclaimed, with a double barreled pistol in one hand and a long dirk knife in the others, utterly unterrified and fully ready for a death struggle. The male leader of the fugitives by this time had "pulled back the hammers" of his "pistols," and was about to fire! Their adversaries seeing the weapons, and the unflinching determination on their part of the runaways to stand their ground, "spill blood, kill, or die," rather than be "taken" very prudently "sidled over to the other side of the road" leaving at least four of the victims to travel on their way.[27]

The worry about the veracity of such oral accounts is diminished by a corresponding newspaper report that "Six slaves . . . from Virginia came to Hoods Mill . . . and some eight or ten persons gathered round to arrest them; but the Negroes drawing revolvers and bowie knives, kept their assailants at bay, until five of the party succeeded in escaping. . . . The last one . . . was fired at, the load taking effect in the small of the back [and was captured]. He ran away with the others the [next] evening."[28]

A BOLD STROKE FOR FREEDOM.

Fig. 2.3. Fugitives defy slave catchers, from William Still's account of the 1855 Barnaby Grigby escape. (From William Still's *The Underground Railroad* [Philadelphia: Porter & Coats, 1872], p. 125. Courtesy of the House Divided Project at Dickinson College.)

Equally prominent in William Still's account of slave escapes is the *Conflict in the Barn*, an image depicting Robert Jackson and his little band of fugitives with guns fighting for their freedom and their lives against a band of border-country slave catchers. Jackson was a fugitive from Virginia, traveling under the alias of Wesley Harris. He had run off after fighting with his overseer, who attempted to whip him for some trifle. Jackson resisted, grabbed the whip, and gave the white man a taste of his own lash. When Jackson's master heard about it, he decided to sell off Jackson at the next offense.

The mistress of the house had embraced Jackson as a favorite and warned him of her husband's plans. When Jackson learned that another slave—a fellow named Matterson—and his two brothers, were planning to run off, he conspired to go with them. On the next dark moon, they struck out. It took them two days to reach Maryland. A friendly Negro there warned them of slave catchers scouring the border and advised them to hide. They headed to the countryside and took shelter in the barn of an ostensibly friendly white farmer who "talked like a Quaker," and promised to help them travel northward to Gettysburg.

Something about the Good Samaritan did not sit right with Jackson, and that sixth sense was a sound barometer. In the morning, eight armed men including a constable descended on the barn, asking questions, demanding to see travel passes, and determined to take the Negroes to the magistrate. Jackson warned, "if they took me they would have to take me dead or crippled." Then one of Jackson's companions spied the farmer who had betrayed them and "shot him, badly wounding him." The constable seized Jackson by the collar, and Jackson responded with pistol fire. He recounted later:

> I at once shot him with my pistol, but in consequence of his throwing up his arm, which hit mine I fired, the effect of the load of my pistol was much turned aside; his face, however, was badly burned besides his shoulder being wounded. I again fired on the pursuers, but do not know whether I hit anybody or not. I then drew a sword I had brought with me, and was about cutting my way to the door, when I was shot by one of the men, receiving the entire contents of one load of a double barreled gun in my left arm.

With the help of the Philadelphia Anti-Slavery Society, Jackson survived his wounds. William Still reports that the committee "procured good medical attention and offered the fugitive time for recuperation. . . . And sent him on his way [to Canada] greatly improved in health and strong in the faith that *he who would be free, himself must strike the blow*."[29]

Fig. 2.4. An artist's rendering from William Still's account of fugitive slave Robert Jackson's 1853 fight for freedom. (From William Still's *The Underground Railroad* [Philadelphia: Porter & Coats, 1872], p. 50. Courtesy of the House Divided Project at Dickinson College.)

Certainly many acts of resistance did not involve firearms. Sometimes the fugitive himself was the main weapon. In Fairfax, Virginia, for example, two slaves were sentenced to death for a barehanded assault on slave patrollers. The record is richer surrounding the 1844 abduction of "Big Ben" Jones from Bucks County, Pennsylvania. Jones was literally a giant, nearly seven feet tall and correspondingly strong. Jones had escaped from Maryland almost fifteen years earlier. Undeterred by time, his master and four accomplices found Jones in a forest clearing, splitting logs. They approached with pistols and bludgeons and demanded his surrender. Jones feigned submission but then with fists, feet, and his ax, laid into his abductors, taking down two of them before he was overcome. Finally beaten into submission, Jones was hauled into the back of the carriage that could be tracked, said witnesses, by the stream of blood dripping from the floorboards.[30] We are left just to wonder whether a gun would have made a difference.

Many Negroes were better prepared than Big Ben Jones, and their reported acts of armed resistance meant that the exhortations of abolitionists like Frederick Douglass were no empty rhetoric. Douglass was less a policy advocate than a reporter of the facts on the ground. In a published speech in 1857, Douglass celebrated recent acts of armed self-defense:

> The fugitive Horace at Mechanicsburg, Ohio, the other day, who taught the slave catchers from Kentucky that it was safer to arrest white men than to arrest him, did a most excellent service to our cause. Parker and his noble band of fifteen at Christiana, who defended themselves from kidnappers with prayers and pistols, are entitled to the honor of making the first successful resistance to the Fugitive Slave Bill. But for that resistance, and the rescue of Jerry and Shadrack, the man-hunters would have hunted our hills and valleys, here—with the same freedom with which they now hunt their own dismal swamps.[31]

It was not just Douglass who championed violent resistance against the fugitive slave law. In 1846, white abolitionist congressman Joshua Giddings of Ohio gave a speech on the floor of the House of Representatives, advocating distribution of arms to fugitive slaves. Giddings saw resistance to slavery as fully within the boundaries of self-defense, declaring, "If a slave killed his master in a struggle to prevent his arrest in Ohio, he would be justified in the eyes of the law and I would call him a good fellow." Untroubled by the implications, Ohio senator Thomas Morris cast resistance to slave catchers as the ultimate political violence, declaring that the kidnapping of blacks by slave catchers was "an act of war."

The technical legal claims here are intriguing. The Fugitive Slave Clause in the Constitution plainly recognized slave catchers' rights through the euphemism that "person[s] held to service or labor" had to be "delivered up" to their masters. This constitutional provision and its 1793 statutory embellishment had no enforcement mechanism, and many free-state laws defied slave catchers. Pennsylvania, for example, made slave catching a crime and indicted man-hunters who chased quarry into the Keystone State. Under this sort of state law, which underscored the violence inherent in the slave catcher's craft, resistance using deadly force seems fairly within the boundaries of self-defense.

Even with passage of the 1850 Fugitive Slave Act, which put federal authority explicitly behind the claims of slave catchers who ventured into free states, black fugitives and some radical white abolitionists remained untroubled by any theoretical weakness in their stance of righteous violence. This sentiment is evident in an editorial from the *Pittsburgh Gazette*, which responded to the 1850 law advising blacks "to arm themselves and fight for freedom if need be, but not to run away."[32]

Although most slaves did not escape, it is a testament to the spirit and grit of those who did that the storied Henry Clay of Kentucky stomped to the floor of the United States Senate in 1849 to rant that "it posed insecurity to life itself for slave-owners to cross the Ohio River to recover fugitives." That same year, decrying abolitionist agitation and fugitive resistance, John C. Calhoun agonized that "citizens of the South in their attempt to recover their slaves now meet resistance in every form." A constituent complained to Calhoun that Pennsylvania's antikidnapping law made slave property insecure and that rumor of the law had drawn slaves to escape from the upper south in gangs.[33]

During this same period, there was a great deal of abolitionist agitation directly on the question of arms for self-defense. As early as 1838, the abolitionist paper the *Liberator*, decried state laws that deprived free Negroes of the basic rights of citizens like suffrage, assembly, and the "right to bear arms."[34]

After the Compromise of 1850, the pacifist voices that had dominated commentary in the *Liberator* were challenged by more aggressive types who advanced the constitutional right to keep and bear arms not merely as an incident of citizenship, but also in practical terms, as a response to slave catchers. In 1851, abolitionist firebrand Lysander Spooner connected higher constitutional principle to the practical security interests of fugitive slaves, declaring:

> The Constitution contemplates no such submission, on the part of the people, to the usurpations of the government, or to the lawless violence of its officers. On the contrary, it provides that "the right of the people to keep and bear arms shall not be infringed." This constitutional security for the right to keep and bear arms implies the right to use them—as much as a constitutional security for the right to buy and keep food would have implied the right to eat it. The Constitution, therefore, takes it for granted that, as the people have the right, they will also have the sense to use arms, whenever the necessity of the case justifies it.[35]

In 1853, the New England Antislavery Convention pressed the finer technical point of precisely how the Constitution guaranteed fugitive slaves a right to arms. Arguing that the word *persons* in the Representation Clause of the Constitution (where slaves were counted as 3/5 a person for determining seats in Congress) was intended to mean slaves and therefore "all the guarantees of personal liberty given to persons belong to slaves also." From there, the convention reasoned, fugitive slaves were among the "people" who "were guaranteed the right to bear arms and of course by implication to use them."[36]

The rhetorical skirmishes over the idea of armed self-defense carried none of the risks of actually fighting with a gun, and there are many reminders that using a gun in self-defense was no guarantee of a good or just result. Certainly the gods were distracted in 1836 when a fugitive in southern Ohio grabbed a rifle to protect his family against a gang of kidnappers. He used his single shot to no avail, was quickly subdued, and then stomped to death. That same year, two black fugitives managed to acquire rifles and escape from Missouri into Illinois. They poached some livestock and were cooking dinner when pursuers surrounded them and demanded their surrender. The fugitives decided to fight. The decision left one of them dead and the other apprehended on charges of escape and attempted murder for wounding one of the slave catchers.

Successful and not, continuing episodes of resistance show a budding culture of gun ownership and a commitment to self-defense. Civil-rights activist James Forman would comment in the 1960s that blacks in the movement were widely armed and that there was hardly a black home in the South without its shotgun or rifle.[37] Anyone surprised by this should reflect on the early episodes of entire well-armed communities turned out against slave catchers in defense of fugitives.

This is evident in 1836, in Swedesboro, New Jersey, where a black family was captured by a professional bounty hunter and held in the basement of a local tavern. A little before midnight, forty black men—neighbors and friends of the captives—armed with rifles, muskets, and pistols, riddled the building with bullets and grape shot. The tavern owner, now ad hoc warden, got the worst of the deal. His building was ventilated and his return fire hit no one except a white bystander.

The armed community was in evidence again when fugitive Thomas Fox of Red Oak, Ohio, was apprehended by bounty hunters from Kentucky. The commotion brought out his neighbors, who confronted the Southerners and freed Fox. Several weeks later, on a Sunday morning, slave agents returned to the neighborhood with reinforcements and dragged a black man out of church. An armed, interracial group of rescuers assembled on horseback and interdicted the kidnappers, who released their black quarry without a fight.[38]

But this respite was only temporary. The Kentuckians were soon back across the border, this time eighteen strong and well-armed. They quickly encountered an armed group dead set against any neighbors being carted back to slavery. This time, the slave catchers identified a young woman, Sally Hudson, as a runaway and moved to seize her. When Sally tried to flee, one of them shot her in the back. This was deemed so cowardly by both sides that it actually diffused the conflict. To the disgust of local abolitionists, an Ohio grand jury refused to indict the man who killed Sally Hudson.

Fig. 2.5. Farmer with a gun. (Illustration by E. W. Kemble, from Paul Laurence Dunbar, *The Strength of Gideon and Other Stories* [1900].)

When racial violence broke out in Cincinnati in 1841, blacks took up arms and fought the surging mob. Initial press reports claimed multiple white casualties, but final assessment showed that only one man, an instigator from across the river in Kentucky, was killed.[39]

The scene repeats in 1844 in Chester County, Pennsylvania, where slave catchers again encountered an assembly of resisters. The slavers' target was a black man named Tom who lived with his family on the Myers' farmstead. As the man-hunters broke through the door of his cabin, Tom grabbed an ax and gave battle. One of the slave catchers fired his pistol in an attempt to cow Tom and his wife, now wielding an ax of her own. The warning shot went astray and actually hit one of the slave catchers.

The gunshot also alerted Tom's neighbors, who ran to help, carrying guns, axes, and garden tools. Three of the slave catchers ran to seek help for their wounded man. Two of them stayed behind, guarding Tom and nervously threatening death to anyone who interfered. Sensing his advantage, one bold black man, pistol in hand, stepped forward, seized Tom, and freed him. Their bluff called, the slavers now implored some whites in the crowd to protect them from the circling Negroes. The threat was staunched when a constable arrived and arrested the Southerners for kidnapping.[40]

The willingness of neighbors and loosely knit groups to come to the rescue sometimes exceeded their effectiveness. But the fashion in which they appeared shows a more than incidental rate of gun ownership. In 1847, in Dauphin County, Pennsylvania, ten fugitive slaves were captured by slave agents from Maryland. They had been hiding out on the farm of a Pennsylvania abolitionist. After an initial confrontation of bluff, bluster, and retreat, both sides sent for reinforcements. Responding to the call, close to forty armed black men arrived on horseback from nearby Harrisburg. This time the putative rescuers were ineffective. The slavers' rein-forcements had arrived first, taken their human property, and were already away.

Sometimes loose confederations of ordinary folk with guns propped up a failed official response. Beginning in 1847, Kentucky slaver John Norris started a years-long quest in pursuit of a family of slaves who had escaped from his Boone County farm. Eventually, Norris captured several of his runaways, who were living free in Michigan. Traveling with his prize through Indiana, Norris encountered difficulties in South Bend, where more than one hundred residents, armed with guns and clubs, slowed him long enough for local abolitionists to get a sheriff's order for release of the blacks. Norris and his cohorts brandished pistols and denied the sheriff's authority.

Defying the sheriff turned out to be easier than confronting the second wave of black men who arrived in response to some unrecorded call for assistance. Variously reported as seventy-five to four hundred strong, the group, organized in military fashion, entered the village "in companies." Against this show of force, Norris gave up the chase, retreated south, and filed a lawsuit that dragged on for seven years before granting him a small measure of relief.[41]

In the border states of the lower North, slaves often depended on the help of sympathetic whites who typically had better resources and easier access to firearms. A century later, strategists in the modern civil-rights movement would worry about political violence alienating sympathetic whites. There was some risk of that under slavery as well. Abolitionists were a slim minority of the population. Many were avowed pacifists. But some abolitionists actually were friendly to violent slave resistance.

In 1838, for instance, Illinois abolitionist Gamaliel Bailey applauded fugitive slaves who defended themselves with guns. Moving beyond rhetoric, a Pennsylvania abolitionist in Indiana County warned slave catchers to be careful of local Negroes, "as they were armed, had guns and knives and most likely would fight." What he didn't tell the man-hunters was that two of these fugitives worked on his farm and he was certain they were armed because he gave them the guns.[42]

Negroes with guns were a fleeting comfort for abolitionist missionary Jarvis Bacon, who in 1851 attempted to guide a group of fugitives out of Kentucky to a free labor settlement in Ohio. The escape plan was detected by patrollers before it really got started. Obviously thwarted, the "well-armed" fugitives still decided to fight, killing one of the pursuing posse and wounding four others.[43]

In a high-profile incident in 1852, two slaves owned by a Georgia congressman were aided in flight from Washington, DC, by white abolitionist William Chaplin. Hidden in Chaplin's carriage, the fugitives were jolted to a halt when district police jammed a fence rail into the carriage spokes and stormed in.

The episode is notable because of the technology. Many early reports of fugitive resistance describe the discharge of firearms followed by hand-to-hand combat. The implication is that the resisters were armed with common, single-shot firearms. Developing repeating technology was relatively expensive and probably harder for free blacks and fugitives with meager resources to acquire.

Reflecting the status of their patron, Chaplin's charges had state-of-the-art revolvers. As the lawmen pounced, Chaplin and the fugitives fired in anger and got an equal measure in return. They exchanged nearly thirty shots before the slaves and Chaplin were finally subdued. That same week, two captured slaves in transit back to Maryland pulled out hidden pistols and opened fire in a renewed attempt to escape. These men, it seems, were equipped with single-shot technology and with guns empty, were easily subdued.[44]

∞

The 1850 Fugitive Slave Law gave Negroes new things to worry about. It pressed government agents and even civilians into the aid of slave catchers. This amplified threat was both practical and symbolic, and blacks responded with renewed vigilance. When a black man was apprehended in New York and remitted to his owner, the community reacted by "arming to the teeth" and forming mutual-aid committees against further incidents.

The new fugitive law also escalated the war of rhetoric. Hyperbolic abolitionists warned that even white people were at risk. One radical pamphleteer argued, "there are in the South, already, slaves as white as any of us, who have in our veins the purest Saxon blood. . . . The whiter the slave—especially if it is a female—the more extravagant the price. The more desirable the victim."

There was actually a flash of this in New Albany, Indiana, where an apparently white woman, her daughter, and her grandson were handed over to an Arkansas slaver whose claim satisfied the legal formalities. This type of incident seems rare. More common was the objection of Northern whites that the new law dragooned them as "slaves" into the man-hunting business.

The Fugitive Slave Law also chased some blacks farther north into Canada. In 1850, a body of 150 fugitives fled Pennsylvania, determined to fight anyone who stood in their way. According to one sympathetic report, "many are armed and resolve to be free at all hazard, an attempt to arrest them would be no child's play."

The pressure of the 1850 law also pushed more blacks to advocate political violence. In Chicago, a group of three hundred assembled to endorse a pact of mutual self-protection against stalking slavers. Their preamble expressed a preference to avoid violence, but the operative provisions promised that no matter what the law said, "if driven to the extreme," these Negroes would "defend themselves at all hazards."

In Ohio, a similar meeting produced the resolution that "all colored people go continually prepared that they may be ready at any moment to offer defense in behalf of their liberty." This reference to going prepared does not explicitly mention firearms. But in Philadelphia, the articulated resolve of a similar group following an abduction of a well-known member of the community was plain. They advised the "colored race to arm themselves and shoot down officers of the law" complicit in the capture of fugitives.

Some of the most explicit advocacy of political violence came from interracial gatherings of antislavery groups. In December 1850, short months after the new statute was passed, Robert Purvis, a black conductor on the Underground Railroad, spoke candidly to the Pennsylvania Anti-Slavery Society. Black men, said Purvis, had a responsibility to arm themselves. Purvis argued that by standing up with arms and defending themselves, blacks would show the world that they were men and "not worthy of slavery."

Some in the audience were avowed pacifists and urged Purvis to follow the example of Christ. Purvis's answer was earnestly practical. "What can I do when my family are assaulted by kidnappers? I would fly and by every means endeavor to avoid it, but when the extremity comes, I welcome death rather than slavery and by what means God and nature have given me, I will defend myself and my family."

In strongholds of aggressive abolitionism, the press openly urged fugitive slaves: "Arm yourselves at once. If the catcher comes, receive him with powder and ball with dirk or bowie knife or whatever weapon may be most convenient. Do not hesitate to slay the miscreant if he comes to re-enslave you or your wife or child." Radical abolitionist Ohio congressman Joshua Giddings went further, claiming that blacks would not fight alone, that the white people of northern Ohio would engage in warfare to resist slave catchers and their federal-government enforcers.

As the rhetorical war escalated, armed resistance continued apace. In 1850 in Lawrence County, Ohio, six "well-armed" fugitives fired on a group of Kentucky slave catchers. Like many of these incidents, once the single shot firearms were spent, the Negroes descended on their pursuers with clubs, leaving them for dead and then escaping into the forest.

There was continued confirmation during this period that the results of violent resistance could vary dramatically. Pursued by slavers over the border into Indiana in 1853, a group of ten fugitives resisted with gunfire but were overcome by better-armed whites. With two slaves and one slaver wounded, the blacks were apprehended and carted back to an unrecorded fate.

Under the new Fugitive Slave Law, hunters of human property could now demand the assistance of United States Marshals. But this federal "authority" made little difference to blacks fighting for their lives. A willingness to defy the federal government and fight the marshals too was evident in 1850, in Coatesville, Pennsylvania, where a free black couple opened fire on a marshal and posse who were pursuing a fugitive in their care. Their firearms spent, the free man and his wife commenced fighting with axes, giving the fugitive cover to escape. Later, they displayed wounds from the fight as badges of honor.

A similar incident occurred in 1856 when Robert Garner, his wife, their four children, and two other adults fled out of Kentucky to Cincinnati. They were resting at the home of a free black man, Elijah Kite, when their Kentucky masters and a United States Marshal broke through the door. Both Kite and Garner responded with pistol fire, wounding one of the intruders.

The violence then took a horrific turn. Garner's wife was the spark. Seeing that the men might lose the fight, Margaret Garner shouted that she would kill her children before returning them to the yoke. By the time the slavers and their government accomplice gained control, Margaret had strangled the life from her two-year-old daughter. For Northerners, Margaret Garner's infanticide underscored the evils of slavery. Southerners said it was just another example of the baffling Negro and con-firmation of his inferior status in law and in nature. After extended legal squabbling, the Garners were given up to their master, who sold them to slave traders in New Orleans.

Another US Marshal was the target of gunplay when an interracial group in the abolitionist bastion of Oberlin, Ohio, blocked the pursuit of Kentucky fugitive John Price. When the slave catchers and their federal man brought the fight, the resisters brandished guns, to a temporary stalemate. The aftermath reflected the simmering conflict between federal law and technically preempted state statutes that deemed slave catchers kidnappers. State and federal bureaucra-cies initiated disparate proceedings. The federal process charged the resisters with violating the Fugitive Slave Law. Ohio, on the other hand, indicted the marshal and three Southerners for kidnapping. The conflict eventually was settled with reduced sanctions against combatants on both sides.[45]

While Negro life in free states and territories was certainly an improvement over slavery, these places fell far short of the promised land. Opposition to slavery did not necessarily mean full political and social embrace of Negroes. This is evident in various free-state laws restricting Negro rights. Ohio's early constitution denied free blacks the right to vote, and in 1807 the state passed a loosely enforced law requiring Negro immigrants to post a $500 bond and a guarantee of their good behavior signed by two white men. The Indiana Territory prohibited Negroes from testifying in court against whites. In 1857, Wisconsin voters reversed a previous statute granting black suffrage. An 1857 Oregon statute prohibited blacks from set-tling in the state. And Illinois, Indiana, Michigan, and Iowa all prohibited interra-cial marriage.

It was the violation of one of those interracial marriage bans in 1845 that sent Rose Anne McGregor of Marion County, Iowa, running for her gun. Rose Anne had the temerity to fall in love with a white man, Tom McGregor, and he with her. They beat the first prosecution for violating the ban by getting the proceedings moved to a Quaker community where a sympathetic grand jury refused to indict them.

Officials then ordered Rose Anne McGregor either to post manumission papers and a $500 bond or to be sold to the highest bidder. The McGregors were defiant and vowed to do neither. While Tom was away, the sheriff and a deputy came out to arrest Rose Anne. She saw them approaching and warned that she was armed and was a crack shot. It was one of those instances where just the threat of gunfire seemed to be enough, at least until nightfall. Under the cover of darkness, the sheriff sneaked to the door, kicked it down, and seized Rose Anne McGregor before she could get a shot off.

Rose Anne was captured, but not for long. As they trotted back to town with

Rose Anne bound up on horseback, she kicked her mount hard in the ribs and held on as the animal bolted off into the night. She soon met up with Tom, and they abandoned their Iowa home in search of a more welcoming environment.[46]

❧

The black tradition of arms ultimately elevates and enshrines the distinction between self-defense against imminent threats and organized political violence seeking group advancement. But in the fight against slavery, there was little concern for that distinction. In a practical sense, slavery was a state of war, and some in the burgeoning black leadership put it basically that way.

At the 1854 National Emigration Convention of Colored People in Cleveland, Ohio, black abolitionist Martin Delaney cast resistance to slavery as straightforward warfare, declaring, "Should we encounter an enemy with artillery, a prayer will not stay the cannon shot, neither will the kind words or smiles of philanthropy shield his spear from piercing us through the heart. We must meet mankind, then as they meet us—prepared for the worst."

With an appreciation of the young nation's revolutionary struggle, escaped slave Andrew Jackson defended his own and the broader use of violence in the pursuit of liberty, proclaiming, "If it was right for the revolutionary patriots to fight for liberty, it was right for me, and is right for any other slave to do the same. And were I now a slave, I would risk my life for freedom. Give me liberty or give me death would be my deliberate conclusion." In Ohio around the same time, John Isome Gaines advocated a slave revolution to overthrow the slaveocracy and install a "government of God that would secure universal liberty and equality."

Commenting on John Brown's failed 1859 raid at Harpers Ferry, black abolitionist Charles Langston invoked America's revolutionary principles, and with a plain note of sarcasm, declared that the "renowned fathers of our celebrated revolution taught the world that 'resistance to tyrants is obedience to God,' that all men are created equal and have the inalienable right to life and liberty. These men proclaimed death, but not slavery, or rather give me liberty or give me death." On these principles, Langston argued, Brown's raid and similar acts of resistance were entirely justified.

One of the most famous calls for violent resistance was David Walker's "Appeal to the Colored Citizens of the World." Walker urged his brothers in bondage to rise up and "kill or be killed." He declared that "the man who would not fight . . . in the glorious and heavenly cause of freedom . . . ought to be kept with all his children or family in slavery, or in chains to be butchered by his cruel enemies."

Similar sentiments were expressed by fugitives who escaped to freedom and became spokesmen for the race. Fugitive activist H. Ford Douglas, publisher of the *Provincial Freeman*, advocated the violent overthrow of slavery in unequivocal terms. Similarly, David Ruggles, founder of the New York Vigilance Committee, urged that blacks "must look to our own safety and protection from kidnappers, remembering that self-defense is the first law of nature."[47]

In 1843, the Michigan Negro Convention repeated this theme, calling on blacks to wage "unceasing war" against the tyranny of slavery. Soon after that, in 1844, Moses Dickson formed a shadowy organization called the International Order of Twelve of the Knights and Daughters of Tabor, with the agenda of over-throwing slavery by any means. Pressing an agenda beyond abolition, Reverend Henry Johnson gave a militant speech at the 1845 Colored Suffrage Convention in New York, proclaiming that "the colored population were ready to take the musket, if necessary, to defend our churches, our family associations, and the rights of our neighbors." The details and activities of many of these individuals and organizations are thinly researched, but a few episodes are more richly recorded.[48]

In 1848, Henry Highland Garnet advanced David Walker's earlier appeal and indulged no fine distinctions between self-defense and political violence. Garnet characterized slaves as "prisoners of war in an enemy's country" and urged, "by all the rules of war, you have the fullest liberty to plunder, burn and kill." Garnet con-sidered slavery a broad and continuing license for violent resistance. "If hereditary bondsmen would be free, they must strike the first blow. . . . It is your solemn and imperative duty to use every means intellectual and physical that promise success. . . . You had better all die—die immediately, than live as slaves and entail your wretchedness upon your posterity. . . . Let your motto be resistance! Resistance! Resistance!"

Garnet presented his address for inclusion in the platform of the National Negro Convention. The body rejected it, with the opposition led by Frederick Douglass and Charles Remond, at that stage still under the sway of the pacifist Garrisonians.[49]

But both Douglass and Remond eventually advocated violence as a tool for ending slavery. In June 1849, Douglass gave a speech in Boston that fairly shocked his audience of pacifist abolitionists. In language reflecting his emerging militancy, Douglass said that he would welcome slave rebellion in the South and would cel-ebrate any news that "the Sable arms which had been engaged in beautifying and adorning the South, were engaged in spreading death and devastation." Although the precise curve of Charles Remond's transformation is unclear, his view had changed by 1851 when he celebrated the violence of three fugitive slaves who shot and killed their pursuing master.[50]

Militant rhetoric raised objections from pacifist abolitionist and sparked con-flicts that illustrated the difference between black and white stakes in ending slavery.

Henry Highland Garnet was a particular target of pacifist William Lloyd Garrison's paper, the *Liberator*. White abolitionist Maria Weston Chapman denounced Garnet in a lengthy *Liberator* article, suggesting that he had fallen under the influence of "bad counsel."[51]

The implication was that Garnet had not developed his own views but had been lured and manipulated into militancy by some shadowy white Svengali. Garnet bristled at the suggestion that "his humble productions have been produced by the Council of some Anglo-Saxon." In a letter to the *Liberator* that models the objections of modern black contrarians to presumptuous white paternalism, Garnet chided, "I have expected no more from ignorant slaveholders and their apologists, but I really look for better things from Mrs. Maria W. Chapman . . . , editor *pro tem* of the Boston *Liberator*. I can think on the subject of human rights without 'counsel' either from men of the West or women of the East."[52]

Despite pacifist discomfort, militant abolitionists continued to advance black resistance in heroic terms. The *New York Independent* observed,

> The framers of this new [fugitive slave] law counted upon the utter degradation of the Negro race—their want of manliness and heroism—to render feasible its execution but it was the cowardly Negro, the worm and not the serpent upon whom they set their foot. They anticipated no resistance from a race cowed down by centuries of oppression and trained to servility. In this however they were mistaken. They're beginning to discover that men, however abject, who have tasted liberty, soon learn to prize it and are ready to defend it.[53]

In some of the most widely reported revolts against the fugitive slave law, blacks, sometimes accompanied by radical white abolitionist allies, defied the authority of the state and attempted to snatch fugitives from the process of the law. In Syracuse, New York, in 1851, black and white abolitionists stormed the courtroom and rescued William McHenry of Missouri, who was offered up to his master under the 1850 law. Federal marshals beat back the crowd and retrieved McHenry, only to lose him again in the tumult.

McHenry was hustled off to Canada. But two dozen people, half of them Negroes, were indicted for violating federal law by aiding in the escape. Suggesting the sentiments of the community, three of the indicted whites were acquitted. Six blacks who were primary instigators, fled to Canada. One of that group, Reverend Jermaine Loguen, had already articulated his contempt for the 1850 law in print: "I don't respect this law. I don't. I won't obey it! It outlaws me, and I outlaw it and the man who attempts to enforce it on me. I place governmental officials on the ground that they placed me. I will not live a slave, and if force is employed to re-enslave me, I shall make preparations to meet the crisis as becomes a man."[54]

A similar incident occurred in 1851 in Boston, where fugitive Frederick Wilkins was apprehended and taken into custody on the strength of the 1850 law. In a tactic that was repeated in Ohio, Pennsylvania, New York, and elsewhere, and in overt defiance of any government authority over Wilkins, Negroes burst into the courtroom, stole Wilkins away, and skirted him off to Canada. When two blacks and two whites involved in the rescue were acquitted on state charges, President Millard Fillmore threatened federal prosecution against the "lawless mob."[55]

Commentary from fugitive activists captures the sentiment that under the circumstances, blacks had little to lose from political violence. One commentator, exiled in Canada, rebuked President Fillmore, arguing that because blacks were not protected by the law of the United States, they could not be "censured for opposing its execution." In Pennsylvania, William Parker, soon to be famous for leading the Resistance at Christiana, expressed it this way: "The laws for personal protection are not made for us and we are not bound to obey them. Whites have a country and may obey the laws. But we have no country." As for the federal protection and assistance granted to slave catchers, Parker retorted, whether the kidnappers were clothed with legal authority or not, "I do not care to inquire, as I never had faith in nor respect for the Fugitive Slave Law."

Religious scruples were no clear bar on such sentiments. In New York City, a mass church gathering resolved that fugitives from slavery should resist "with the surest and most deadly weapons."[56] The militancy of the group was underscored by the thunderous response to William Powell's question, "Shall the bloodthirsty slaver be permitted by this unrighteous law to come into our domiciles, or workshops, or the places where we labor, and carry off our wives and children, our fathers and mothers, and ourselves, without a struggle—without resisting, even if need be onto death?"

Surviving accounts distill what probably was a diverse range of views among black congregations. One longs for a transcript of the 1850 meeting at the Colored Congregational Church in Portland, Maine, resolving "that recognizing no authority higher than the law of God, . . . We pledge to resist unto death any and every effort to take from the city for the purpose of enslaving him any person to whom we are united by the ties of brotherhood." One member of the group invoked the theme of the American Revolution, declaring that "not a man is to be taken from Portland. Our motto is liberty or death."[57]

In 1851, the black state convention of Ohio officially endorsed physical resistance to slave catchers. The sentiment was captured by activist Sam Ward, who concluded that the 1850 law "throws us back upon the natural and inalienable right of self-defense" and warned, "Let the men who would execute this bill beware."

The impulse toward resistance trumped the worry of alienating white allies. In Pittsburgh in 1851, black activist Martin Delaney gave a fiery speech in front of the white political establishment. His declaration dripping with irony, Delaney exhorted,

> Honorable Mayor, whatever ideas of liberty I may have, had been received from reading the lives of your revolutionary fathers. I have therein learned that a man has a right to defend his castle with his life, even unto the taking of life. Surely, my house is my castle; in that castle are none but my wife and my children, as free as the angels of heaven, and whose liberty is as sacred as the pillars of God. If any man approaches that house in search of a slave—I care not who he may be, whether constable or sheriff, magistrate or even judge of the Supreme Court—nay, let it be he who sanctioned this Act to become law, surrounded by his cabinet as his body-guard, with the Declaration of Independence waving above his head as his banner, and the Constitution of his country upon his breast as his shield—if he crosses the threshold of my door, and I do not lay him a lifeless corpse at my feet, I hope the grave may refuse my body a resting place and righteous Heaven my spirit a home. No! He cannot enter that house and we both live.[58]

There is more than enough hyperbole in Delaney's speech. But the content and the venue show how he was moved by desperation to an overt policy of political violence. The statements of Robert Williams, little more than a century later, are tame by comparison.

The harshness of the 1850 Fugitive Slave Law pressed dedicated black acolytes of William Lloyd Garrison to a more militant stance. Robert Purvis of Westchester was both a Garrisonian and a Quaker. The 1850 law pushed him to this: "Should any wretch enter my dwelling, any pale-faced specter among them, to execute this law on me or mine, I'll seek his life and I'll shed his blood."[59]

Although Frederick Douglass would recoil from John Brown's folly at Harpers Ferry, advising Brown that he was going into "a perfect steel trap," he condemned the 1850 fugitive slave law with a militancy that reflected his now open estrangement from Garrison.[60] Writing in the *Frederick Douglass Paper* in August 1852, Douglass declared that "the only way to make the Fugitive Slave Law a dead letter is to make half a dozen or more dead kidnappers."[61] He pressed the theme in a widely reprinted speech exhorting black solidarity against slavery.

> When the insurrection of the southern slaves shall take place, as take place it will unless speedily prevented by voluntary emancipation, the great mass of the colored men of the North, however much to the grief of any of us, will be found by your side, with deep-stored and long-accumulated revenge in their hearts and with death-dealing weapons in their hands.
>
> The colored American, for the sake of relieving his colored brethren, would no more hesitate to shoot an American slaveholder, than would a white American,

for the sake of delivering his white brother, hesitate to shoot an Algerine slave-holder. The state motto of Virginia, "Death to Tyrants," is as well the black man's, as the white man's motto. . . . If American revolutionists had excuse for shedding but one drop of blood, then have the American slaves excuse for making blood flow even unto the horse bridles.

If your oppressors have rights of property, you, at least, are exempt from all obligations to respect them. For you are prisoners of war, in an enemy's country—of a war, too, that is unrivalled for its injustice, cruelty, and meanness—and therefore by all the rules of war, you have the fullest liberty to plunder, burn, kill as you may have occasion to do to promote your escape.[62]

Much of the scattered evidence of the emerging tradition of arms during this era reflects the marginal status of slaves, fugitives, and freemen. It appears briefly and unsympathetically in the records and writings of the dominant class. But sometimes we find something richer. A fully textured account of black resistance emerges from in the widely chronicled violence at Christiana, Pennsylvania. Variously dubbed the Christiana Resistance, Riot, Uprising, or Tragedy, depending on who was talking, the event is significant because one of the surviving accounts comes from the central black figure in the conflict.[63]

The driving force in the Christiana Resistance was a physically imposing escaped slave named William Parker. Parker was a contemporary of Frederick Douglass and knew him as Fred Bailey when they were slaves in Maryland. Parker settled in central Pennsylvania, bordering the slave fields of Maryland, and was an active conductor on the Underground Railroad.

Parker was harboring several Maryland runaways in his home outside Christiana when their master, Edward Gorsuch, accompanied by several relatives and three government marshals, rode in to retrieve his property. Parker's account is filled with bravado that demands cautious evaluation. But independent reports confirm an episode of fierce resistance.

By the time the slavers approached Parker's modest, two-story farmhouse, the community already had experienced several abductions and was primed for conflict. Parker himself had fought with slave catchers hunting in the area. In one incident, Parker and a loosely organized vigilance group intercepted a band of Maryland kidnappers, rescued a neighborhood girl, and left two of the abductors badly wounded. In another, Parker and a band of seven exchanged gunfire with slave catchers who were retreating with their prize back to Maryland. This time, the slavers prevailed and Parker suffered a gunshot wound. Shortly after that, still nursing his injury, Parker went out alone in pursuit of hunters from Maryland who had abducted his neighbor, Henry Williams. Again he was thwarted and worried aloud, "Whose turn will come next?"

Parker was forewarned when slave hunters advanced on his home in early September 1851. An agent of the Philadelphia Anti-Slavery Society's Vigilance Committee, was stationed on the steps of the magistrate's office where fugitive slave warrants were issued. He transmitted the news that Gorsuch had procured papers authorizing the capture of his Negroes from Christiana.

The man-hunters had their papers and their law. But that meant nothing to the armed blacks who answered the alarm and came running with guns and cutlery. Exactly how many folk came is contested. Some estimates say fifty to eighty. Some surely exaggerated accounts of two hundred seem intended to elevate the danger facing the slave hunters and tacitly excuse the fact that several of them fled the scene.[64]

The detailed account of the combat is disputed. But most agree that Gorsuch was insistent on recovering his slaves even though some of his party advised retreat. Gorsuch rejected this counsel, declaring that he would "have his slaves or perish" in the attempt.

We do not know exactly what sorts of guns the combatants used, whether they were older single shots or state-of-the-art repeaters. But it is certain that all of the firearms that day were charged with black powder, a propellant that renders thick clouds of white smoke. So even assuming the low estimates about the number of combatants, the pasture and woodlot of Parker's homestead would have been thick with gun smoke.

Soon after the shooting started, the discipline of the slave catchers evaporated. A few fled, or as they later put it, went for help. The others took cover and attempted to nurse their wounded. By the end of it, Gorsuch was obliged his arrogant demand: He was denied his slaves. But he did perish.

With Gorsuch crumpled dead in the mud and two of his party badly wounded, the aftermath was both predictable and surprising. In the midst of frenzied reporting and swirling accusations, Parker, several of his compatriots, and two of Gorsuch's slaves fled north, chased by federal and state lawmen. Under political pressure from the slave states, indictments for treason were issued against forty-five members of the group who came to Parker's aid. In federal court in Philadelphia, before Circuit Judge Robert Grier, United States prosecutors charged the first defendant, white collaborator Casner Hanway, with "treasonous levying of war, a conspiracy of a public nature, aimed to nullify a law of the United States."[65]

The charge basically captures the idea of resistance as political violence that ran through much of the rhetoric of the burgeoning black leadership class. So it is ironic that Judge Grier instructed the jury in a fashion that disputed this characterization and laid the foundation for Hanway's acquittal. Treason, Grier explained,

involved a conspiracy of a public nature, aimed to overthrow the government or
hinder the execution of the law. He cast the efforts of the Christiana resisters in
far more personal terms. "A number of fugitive slaves may infest a neighborhood,
and may be encouraged by the neighbors in combining to resist the capture of any
of their number; they may resist with force and arms. . . . Their insurrection is for a
private object and connected with no public purpose."

Fig. 2.6. An artist's rendering of the Resistance at Christiana. (From William
Still's *The Underground Railroad* [Philadelphia: Porter & Coats, 1872], p.
351. Courtesy of the House Divided Project at Dickinson College.)

This instruction was pivotal in the acquittal of Hanway. And that acquittal was
sufficient to discourage further treason prosecutions. Without appreciating the full
implications over coming generations, Grier distilled the essential question that
would frame assessments of legitimate and illegitimate violence within the black
tradition of arms.

After Hanway's acquittal, it seemed better to abandon the treason prosecutions
and to charge the remaining black defendants with riot and murder. But federal
prosecutors worried that remanding them for trial on these state offenses would
result in lenient treatment by the county court. And that is precisely what happened. Ultimately, no one who aided William Parker was convicted of a crime. And
the implication that the resistance was moral and righteous resonated widely.

The Christiana Resistance became a focus of black attention around the
country. Contributions to the legal fight and statements of support came from black
communities in San Francisco, Chicago, Columbus, and New York, and from fugi-

tives living in Canada and England.[66] In churches and lodge halls, blacks passed resolutions of support. A group in Seneca County, New York, resolved "that the recent shooting of the kidnapper in Pennsylvania kindles the hope that the day may yet dawn when the colored man, both North and South, will offer a proper and manly resistance to their mean and murderous oppressors." Evidencing some concern that this stance would offend white abolitionist allies, the resolution acknowledged that "while there may exist a difference of opinion among the friends of liberty in relation to the mode of resistance, yet all must firmly believe that unflinching resistance, at whatever cost, is what is imperatively called for to confound and conquer these tyrants and win the sympathy of the world."[67]

The black newspaper the *Impartial Citizen* compared Christiana to recent acts of European resistance that had been applauded by white America:

> Had a band of Austrian mercenaries attacked Kossuth in Turkey with the avowed purpose of delivering him into the hands of their government, and had his companions met them with the same sort of resistance which was offered at Christiana, the act would have been trumpeted to every wind as an instance of noble and self-sacrificing heroism for which no wreath of glory was too bright, no words of panegyric too warm. But the black men of Christiana, whose feelings prompted them to a similar act in the service of their friends—what of them? They must be tried for treason against a government based upon the principle that all men are created equal and endowed by nature with certain inalienable rights, among which are life, liberty, and pursuit of happiness.[68]

The *National Antislavery Standard* was more graphic, stating, "It need surprise nobody that in the game of slave hunting it should sometimes happen that the hunted become the mark for bullets, [and] the law of self-preservation, and not the Fugitive Slave Law, be obeyed and triumph." The *Standard* showed the same sympathy for the dead slaver Gorsuch that he and his class showed for their quarry. "That Gorsuch should have been shot down like a dog seems to us the most natural thing in the world." This result, said the *Standard*, should be duplicated at every opportunity. "The example . . . set at Christiana we have no doubt will be followed and perhaps improved upon hereafter, for colored flesh and blood . . . is very like that of a lighter shade, and shrinks from stripes and chains, and will be prompt to try a measure which even in its worst result is better than slavery."[69]

Black abolitionist Charles Remond, originally an acolyte of the pacifist Garrisonians, cast the violence at Christiana grandly as the opening of a new American Revolution. "It is ours to point to Attucks, of bygone days; and we could, if we would, to Freeman, and Parker, and Jackson of Christiana celebrity; for if Washington and Attucks opened the revolution of the past, Parker, and Jackson, and Freeman, open the revolution of the present, when they shot down Gorsuch and his son at Christiana."[70]

With the aid of various sympathizers, Parker's band of fugitives, hounded by an escalating reward for their capture, fled on foot, on horseback, by stagecoach, and by steam train to Rochester, New York. Parker's account says only that he was sheltered there at the home of a friend. This friend we know for certain to be Frederick Douglass, who years later described Parker in heroic terms and acknowledged his own role in Parker's escape.

> I could not look upon them as murderers. To me, they were heroic defenders of the just rights of man against man stealers and murderers. So I fed them, and sheltered them in my house. Had they been pursued then and there, my home would've been stained with blood, for these men who had already tasted blood were well armed and prepared to sell their lives at any expense to the lives and limbs of their probable assailants. What they had already done in Christiana, and the determination which showed very plainly especially in Parker, left no doubt on my mind that their courage was genuine and their deeds would equal their words.

It is fitting that Parker's last act on US soil was to embrace Frederick Douglass. The two of them had come of age as slaves in Maryland. One of the first abolitionist meetings Parker attended featured Douglass, then a rising star of the Garrisonians. They both had fought slavery in their own ways, Parker mainly with physical strength and courage, Douglass with an increasingly polished and cutting intellect.

Douglass probably handed Parker a wad of money and gave some instructions about his contact across the water. And we know for sure what Parker handed to Douglass, who wrote about it this way:

> The work of getting these into Canada was a delicate one. . . . The hours they spent at my house were therefore hours of anxiety as well as activity. . . . There was danger that between my house and the landing or at the landing itself we might meet with trouble. As patiently as I could, I waited for the shades of night to come on, and then put the men in my "Democrat carriage" and started for the landing on the Genesee. . . . We reached the boat . . . without remark or molestation. I remained on board till the order to haul the gangplank was given; *I shook hands with my friends, and received from Parker the revolver that fell from the hand of Gorsuch when he died, presented now as a token of gratitude and a memento of the battle for liberty at Christiana.*[71]

For the rest of his life, Douglass counted the revolver, pried from the dead hand of the slaver Gorsuch, as one of his prized possessions.

CHAPTER THREE

━━━━━━━━━━━━━ ∽ ━━━━━━━━━━━━━

PROMISE AND BREACH

"**R**ise Now and Fly to Arms!" That was Henry Highland Garnet's exhortation to young black men when Abraham Lincoln finally opened the Union Army to Negro soldiers. Garnet devoted his life to the freedom struggle, and for a time during the mid-nineteenth century, was a better bet than Frederick Douglass to become titular leader of the race. A militant Presbyterian minister, Garnet had implored Negroes to fight slavery to the death. And when the opportunity came, he urged young black men to fight for the Union, despite the slights of unequal pay and a long delay before they were deemed worthy to serve.[1]

As a war hawk, Garnet advocated the ultimate form of political violence. But he also had a keen appreciation for the utility of private violence. A gun likely saved his life as a young man when he was beset by mobbers. It was 1835, and Garnet was student at the Noyes Academy in Canaan, New Hampshire. Noyes was established the previous year by New England abolitionists on the principle of admitting "colored youth of good character" on equal terms with whites. But Canaan was not universally welcoming.[2]

A group of local men, agitated by talk of amalgamation, and spurred on by visiting Southern slave owners, vowed to stamp out the hazard in their midst. They did, however, go through the form of democracy, holding two town meetings and voting to remove the Noyes Academy from Canaan. They took the removal mandate literally, and in August 1835, hitched up "ninety yoke of oxen" and pulled the school building off its foundation, into a swamp half a mile away. They warned the Negroes to be gone within the month or die. Some thought the one-month deadline too lenient, and a contingent of them descended late that night on the house where the black boys were boarding. Garnet's housemate Alexander Crummell describes the scene.

> Under Garnet as our leader, the boys in our boardinghouse were moulding bullets, expecting an attack upon our dwelling. About eleven o'clock at night the tramp of horses was heard approaching, and as one rapid rider passed the house and fired

at it, Garnet quickly replied by a discharge from a double barreled shotgun which blazed away through the window. . . . That musket shot by Garnet doubtless saved our lives. Notice, however, was sent to us to quit the State within a fortnight.[3]

Garnet was a fugitive from Southern justice. Born into slavery in Kent County, Maryland, in 1815, he escaped north with his family around age nine. Passing into free territory, they sheltered in Wilmington, Delaware, with a Quaker abolitionist named Thomas Garrett. It is likely that the family, in the fashion of many escaped slaves, adopted the name Garnet (sometimes Garnett) as a loose tribute to Thomas Garrett, who aided their escape.[4]

Garnet was a dark black man with deep-set eyes and a strong jaw. Racists of the day said he was a "pure negro" and thus doubly suspect on all the prevailing stereotypes. But Garnet wore the label proudly, tracing his lineage to the warrior class of the Mandingo tribe. And his militancy reflected that temperament. He calculated that once black soldiers were armed and trained, America would be unable to deny their freedom, at least "not without a good fight."[5]

Roughly two hundred thousand Negroes served in the Union Army. Many said that Negroes did not have the temperament for soldiering. But after black men fought and died bravely at Port Hudson and Milliken's Bend, Louisiana, and Fort Wagner in South Carolina, the assessment changed dramatically. After the battle of Port Hudson, the *New York Times* said, "they were comparatively raw troops and were yet subjected to the most awful ordeal. . . . They charged upon fortifications through the crash of belching batteries. The man, white or black, who will not flinch from that will flinch from nothing. It is no longer possible to doubt the bravery and steadiness of the colored race." A reporter on the ground wrote, "it is useless to talk anymore about Negro courage. The men fought like tigers." Charles Dana, reporting to Secretary of War Stanton, affirmed the assessment, writing, "The sentiment in regard to the employment of Negro troops has been revolutionized by the bravery of the blacks in the recent battle of Milliken's Bend. Prominent officers, who used to in private sneer at the idea, are now heartily in favor of it."[6]

Commentators looking back argue that some black soldiers were so intent on proving themselves that they exhibited courage bordering on recklessness. This was evident not just in the fighting but also in their reactions to battlefield wounds. One black soldier with his leg blown off below the knee dismissed efforts to take him to the rear for attention. Instead, he perched against a log "sat with his leg a swaying and bleeding" and continued fire on the enemy. Two days later, he was dead. Another resilient soul from the 30th US Colored Infantry was shot in the head, leg, shoulder, and wrist in four separate battles. He declared confidently to his commander, "I don't reckon I'se gwine to get killed in dis wah." And he didn't.[7]

Fig. 3.1. Depiction of black Union troops in combat. ("A Negro Regiment in Action," wood engraving by Thomas Nast, *Harper's Weekly* magazine, New York, March 14, 1863.)

Negro soldiers would distinguish themselves in uniform. But the Civil War started and progressed without expectation of black military service or commitment to emancipation. Early in the war, General George McClellan, projecting the stance of his commander and the calculations of strategists both north and south, promised Unionist slaveholders in Virginia that he would not confiscate their human property. As answer to the hopes of Negroes that the war meant greater opportunity for escape or resistance, McClellan committed "with an iron hand, [to] crush any attempt at insurrection."

Not all Union officers agreed with McClellan. General Benjamin Butler of Massachusetts, commander of the Union stronghold at Fortress Munroe in Hampton, Virginia, treated fleeing slaves as contraband of war rather than returning them to their masters. Butler's aggressiveness on this point extended to recruiting blacks as spies and scouts.

The man reputed to be the first black armed for service in the war, a fugitive slave named George Scott, was deployed under General Butler. Although Scott was a new and novel addition to the Union force, he was thoroughly familiar with firearms. He had been on the run and hiding in the South for more than a year, carrying a pistol and a bowie knife taken in a fight with his master on the eve of his escape.[8]

Knowledge of the local terrain made Scott a valuable scout in hostile territory. More than a year before President Abraham Lincoln decided to deploy black troops, Scott was assigned to accompany a Union force into the Battle of Big Bethel in York County, Virginia. In violation of policy and defying the bias of many white soldiers, General Butler commanded the squad, "George Scott is to have a revolver."

George Scott's unsanctioned service was not unique. The war emboldened a whole class of daring and defiant Negroes. Some of them fled bondage on the news or rumor of the Union advance. Many left their plantations but stayed local, subsisting off of the land, stealing and poaching food. Some of them organized into bands of maroons forging, stealing, and fighting where they must.

The knowledge and skills these men brought to the fight were acknowledged in the compliment of a Union officer that, "Nowhere in the swamps of North Carolina, can you find a path where a dog can go that a Negro does not understand." One observer in New Bern, North Carolina, commented in 1862 that more than fifty volunteers from this class of men were serving as spies, scouts, and guides, even though they were denied the status of soldiers. These black men ventured into hostile territory without the protection of the laws of war and spent weeks in the swamps and marshes with only meager provisions "and a good revolver."[9]

When war policy changed and escaping Negroes were officially accepted, if not welcomed, behind Union lines, many of them settled in contraband camps that posed their own hazards. Recent escapees and their free black brethren built communities with all of the undertakings one would expect, including provisions for their personal security. Along with schools and burial societies, the shanty communities that grew up around Union strongholds also established private militias and vigilance squads. There was no formal program for arming these groups, and we can only speculate about the ease or difficulty with which they obtained firearms.

These communities could quickly turn hazardous with the shifting tides of battle. The possibility of Confederates retaking the field and raids by Confederate guerrillas posed deadly threats. This hazard to civilians was acute in Holly Springs, Mississippi. Union and Confederate forces fighting along the Tennessee border captured and recaptured Holly Springs fifty-nine times. Confederate forces showed little sympathy for Negro noncombatants. In December 1862, Confederates raided Holly Springs, carrying off and burning Union supplies stored there under a light guard. In the midst of flames and gunfire, were "negroes and abolitionists begging for mercy."[10] In Plymouth, North Carolina, fighting again degraded into the killing of black civilians settled behind shifting Union lines. In the aftermath of battle, Confederate troops, led by Colonel James Deering, executed twenty-five black prisoners in uniform and killed at least eighty more blacks, including women and children who were fleeing into a nearby swamp.[11]

But Negroes were not always victims in these contests. When Confederate defenders lost Vicksburg in July 1863, blacks celebrated by raiding the homes of their former masters. In one case, a white planter shot at a group of black women who were rummaging through what was left of his property. A week earlier, this would have been an unremarkable response to black criminality. This time, however, the planter faced the wrath of armed black men who whipped him and then put a gun to his head and demanded that he call *them* master. These men are not recorded as soldiers, and we can only guess the sources of their guns.[12]

Even after they were given a uniform and a government rifle, Negroes were still dogged by the racial attitudes of the day. Rank was no shield from this blight. Witness the trials of Lieutenant John V. DeGrasse, a black doctor from Boston who traveled to North Carolina to enlist black recruits. He was accosted by white Union sailors who demanded to know on what authority he was there "recruiting niggers." When they moved in close, DeGrasse drew his revolver and faced them down. As friends ran to his aid, the situation defused without gunfire. Some said that DeGrasse's armed stand helped establish the credibility of Negro recruiters and black officers generally.

A unique hazard to black Union soldiers was the refusal of Confederates to recognize them as legitimate combatants. Confederate murders and abuse of captured Negroes was a terror that continued throughout the war. There were reports of Confederate massacres of black soldiers in Tennessee, South Carolina, Louisiana, Arkansas, Virginia, and Florida.

A report from the *Charlotte Observer* reflects the attitude that fueled these massacres. "Ransom's brigade," said an enlisted man, "never takes any Negro prisoners." Major John Graham of Ransom's outfit wrote to his father about passing through Suffolk, Virginia, where the ladies of the town implored them to "kill the Negroes." This plea was unnecessary, he said, because "it is understood amongst us that we take no Negro prisoners."

One of the few white officers to effectively combat atrocities against black prisoners, General Edward Wild, was court-martialed for the attempt to protect his black troops. His sin was taking hostages from the families of Confederate guerrillas and publicizing that his captives would get the same treatment as his black soldiers in Confederate hands.[13]

As word spread about Confederate abuse of black prisoners, Negro soldiers themselves resolved to retaliate. Following the murder of black troops captured at the Battle at Fort Pillow, Tennessee, Negro soldiers adopted the battle cry "Remember Fort Pillow," and retaliated by executing Confederate prisoners in Louisiana and South Carolina. One eyewitness, a cavalryman from Maine, wrote home, "we had 200 niggers soldiers with us it did not make eny difference to them about the Rebs surrendering. They would shoot them down. the officers had hard work to stop them from killing All the prisoners. when one of them would beg for his life the niggers would say rember Fort Pillow."[14]

Fig. 3.2. Coverage of the New York draft riots. ("The Riots at New York— the rioters burning and sacking the colored orphan asylum," wood engraving, *Harper's Weekly* magazine, August 1, 1863, p. 493.)

As the war chewed up resources and Union fortunes flagged, Congress enacted conscription that sparked draft riots in the North, and this riot rage was naturally channeled at blacks. In the summer of 1863, draft riots in New York City left 120 Negroes dead, thousands more injured, and a black orphanage in ashes.[15]

The gruesome details of these riots are well chronicled. Accounts like that of the hapless man hoisted up a tree while chunks of his flesh were carved out and thrown to the quivering mob fuel the intuition that blacks fled and cowered under a wave of unhinged violence. But some of them plainly fought back. Although the end result was tragic, Augustus Stuart was one who fought.

Stuart was armed with a pistol when he was set upon by a roving gang. He managed to escape the immediate attack, but in the fading light, he mistakenly perceived a company of soldiers as the mob back in pursuit. Stuart fired at them, and one of the mounted soldiers, appreciating only that he had been shot at, charged Stuart with his sword and ran him through.

Guns rendered a better result for a group of black laborers who were attacked by a mob of "two or three hundred vagabond Irishmen." They fought off the attack with revolver fire until police arrived. The mob actually attacked the police in an attempt to get at the blacks but was repelled.[16]

We do not know whether or how often other versions of these scenarios repeated during the draft riots. Nor do we know how many blacks retreated to some dark, quiet place and rode out the riots, quietly clutching guns. But in a related context, the calculations of Northern blacks illustrate a discernible culture of armed self-defense.

In 1864, 144 delegates met at the National Convention of Colored Men, in Syracuse, New York. This meeting was the genesis of the National Equal Rights League, one of the earliest national civil-rights organizations. Notable in attendance were Frederick Douglass and Henry Highland Garnet.[17]

Not everyone in Syracuse was friendly to the Convention of Colored Men. Before the proceedings even began, a group of Irish immigrants accosted Garnet, one of them kicking him from the behind and another sending him to the dirt with blow to the head. When Garnet's friends learned of the assault, they grabbed their revolvers and went searching for the attackers, who now had scattered into the night. While it is unclear whether Garnet was armed at the time of the attack, the report of his friends' armed response suggests the habits of the group.

One of the other men at the meeting, Abraham Galloway of North Carolina, was widely known to travel armed, and researchers report that this was typical of convention delegates, several of whom were fugitives from slavery. These men were painfully aware of the draft riots in New York City only a year earlier. Plus they had lived and fought through the full range of hazards that plagued Negroes through the middle of the nineteenth century. It would be surprising if they were not armed.[18]

The end of the Civil War left an army of occupation in the South. The natural tensions of military occupation were exacerbated by black troops. When the 46th US Colored Infantry entered Union-occupied territory in Mississippi, white planter John Bobb could not abide the insult of black soldiers on his property, picking his flowers. He attacked one of them with a brick. The soldier, Sergeant William Anderson, responded with superior force, shooting Bobb dead.[19]

These sorts of conflicts became more common with the changing complexion of the federal army. Only a fraction of Union troops occupied the South after the war, and the balance mustered out according to length of service. Because blacks were not admitted into ranks until the middle of the war, they were retained at a higher rate, making the occupying force "blacker" than the one that won the war. Estimates put black soldiers at about 10 percent of fighting forces. But by the last quarter of 1865, blacks made up about one third of the occupation army. Many Southerners took this as a deliberate Union insult.[20]

The recorded violence is surely only a fraction of the total, but it confirms that Negroes with guns and the authority of uniforms grated hard on defeated Confederates. One cryptic report of the killing of a black soldier explains the outcome as a predictable result of the soldier taking "rather more liberty than an Anglo-Saxon likes to submit to." Considering that prewar legal standards had justified white-on-black violence for offenses like "insolence," it is easy to understand how Negroes in uniform, behaving like soldiers, inflamed many whites.[21]

Fig. 3.3. Henry Hyland Garnet. (Albumen silver print by James U. Stead, ca. 1881.)

The spectacle of Negroes with guns actually sent one old man into hysterics. As a column of Negro soldiers passed by to the cheers of a boisterous entourage of freedmen, the old Southern gentleman threw up his hands in horror and pleaded, "Blow Gabriel blow, for God's sake blow"—an evident plea for the world to end.[22]

The racial tensions within ranks that afflicted black troops during the war extended into the period of uneasy peace. In Wilmington, North Carolina, Sargent John Benson of the 6th United States Colored Troops came to an armed standoff with white Union officers after attempting to arrest a white woman who had pointed a pistol at one of his soldiers. Although they wore the same uniform, Benson's superiors had less allegiance to him than to the Southern belle. After being driven off at gunpoint, Benson published a letter in the *Wilmington Herald*, protesting the episode. This got him arrested, stripped of his sergeant's stripes, and imprisoned on the charge of insolence to commissioned officers.[23]

Black civilians experienced similar treatment as Union soldiers found race a more compelling bond than politics. Union commander Quincy Gilmore noted numerous clashes between white Union soldiers and black civilians in Charleston, South Carolina. Gilmore records that "street quarrels have taken place, in some instances, arising from insolence and brutality of soldiers toward the Negroes" and sometimes where blacks were reported as the aggressors.

The interracial tinderbox progressed into shots fired when a fight between white soldiers and black civilians was joined by black soldiers who waded in to aid the freedmen. Union soldiers traded gunfire along racial lines for more than twenty minutes, and brief firefights broke out around Charleston over the next several days, with disputed reports of casualties.

There is good evidence that black soldiers did not treat the returning Confederates delicately. Members of the 35th US Colored Troops were disciplined for entering the homes of white Charlestonians and confiscating guns. In other cases, black soldiers duplicated the looting and ravaging of their white counterparts.[24]

In North Carolina, black soldiers exploited the threat value of their firearms to seek vengeance on a white ferry captain who could not abide the change wrought by Northern victory. Whites and blacks had always ridden the New Bern–Roanoke ferry. But blacks were barred from the upper deck. When black troops ventured into that prohibited space, the captain responded with a barrage of racial insults.

The soldiers did not leave the upper deck, and they did not forget the insults. A few days later, in the fog of dawn, they rowed out to the ferry with guns drawn. They captured the captain and his clerk and, back ashore, tied them to a sticky yellow pine and beat them bare-assed with government-issue belts.[25]

In April 1865, soldiers from the 52nd US Colored Infantry descended on the Vicksburg, Mississippi, plantation of Jared and Minerva Cook. Some of them evidently had been slaves of Cook before the war. Brandishing revolvers, they demanded that Cook turn over his guns and ransacked the house. Then they demanded the silver. Before it was over, they had shot and killed Minerva Cook and wounded Jared. When their crimes were detected, the men were court-martialed, and several of them were hanged.[26]

In Victoria, Texas, black troops did their own hanging, dragging a white man accused of murdering a freedman from his jail cell and stringing him up. And again in South Carolina, black troops formed a lynch party to avenge the fatal stabbing of a black sergeant who had fought with a Confederate veteran after refusing to leave a white railway car. The black troopers tried the rebel by "drum-head court-martial" and then shot him down.[27]

❧

Almost as soon as the shooting war stopped, the Southern governments moved to reinstitute slavery through a variety of state and local laws, restricting every aspect of Negro life, from work to travel, to property rights. Gun prohibition was a common theme of these "Black Codes."

White anxiety about free Negroes with guns was fueled by episodes like the scene Thomas Pickney encountered when he returned to his plantation on the Santee River in South Carolina. Already warned that his Negroes had looted the place, Pickney called them around to explain that he wanted to pay them wages and restore the plantation to profitability.

Pickney chose his words carefully because most of the newly minted freemen had come to the assembly armed. Their reaction to his proposal was chastening. Now unafraid to look him in the eye, Pickney's boys said they planned to work for themselves and refused to work for any white man. If they refused to work for a white man, Pickney asked, where did they propose to go? The answer brought him up short. "We ain gwine nowhar." Their plan was to stay where they were and work the land "whar we wuz bo'n an'whar belongs tuh us."

Although these men were surely unfamiliar with the legal principle of restitution, where without any formal agreement, assets are reallocated to prevent unjust enrichment, their instincts were consistent with that theme. And in the spirit of the common law, they were intent on enforcing their claim through self-help if necessary. One black man wearing a Union Army coat made the point dramatically. Standing in the doorway of his cabin, his hand clutched around a rifle, he slammed the butt of the gun to the floor and declared that he would work the land under his feet. And he challenged any man to "put me outer dis house!"[28]

Other armed Negroes were similarly provocative. One clear-eyed veteran from Louisiana embraced the war's lessons about force, incentives, and cooperation and advised "every colored soldier, bring your gun home." Another Negro veteran showed clear appreciation for these themes, recounting in 1865 how, "When de war ended, I goes back to my mastah and he treated me like his brother." He was under no illusions about this evident change of heart, concluding, "Guess he was scared of me 'cause I had so much ammunition on me."

Mississippi minister Samuel Agnew exhibited the worry of many Southerners, writing in late 1865 that "our Negroes certainly have guns and are frequently shooting about." It signaled conflicts to come that local freedmen were in "high dudgeon" over recent efforts by roving gangs of "regulators" to disarm them. The blacks, according to Agnew, were now demanding that they had "equal rights with a white man to bear arms."

A Freedman's Bureau agent from Florida lamented the wide practice among freedmen of traveling armed. And a Bureau agent operating in the Sea Islands of Georgia and South Carolina reported that the Negroes under his charge were widely armed and "these guns they prize as their most valued possessions next to their land."

In North Carolina, appeals to the governor's office displayed a simmering fear among defeated rebels about Negroes with guns. One correspondent wrote candidly of his worry that "the design is to organize for a general massacre of the white population. Nearly every Negro is armed not only with a gun [long gun], but a revolver. . . . The meeting of a thousand or two of Negroes every other Sunday, with Officers and Drilling, I think a serious matter." In October 1865, Mississippi planter E. G. Baker similarly complained in a letter to the state legislature, "it is well known here that our Negroes through the country are well equipped with firearms, muskets, double barrel shotguns and pistols."[29]

These sorts of fears fueled overtly racist gun laws like Mississippi's Act to Regulate the Relation of Master and Apprentice Relative to Freedmen, which prohibited blacks from owning firearms, ammunition, dirks, or bowie knives.[30] Alabama prohibited "any freedman, mulatto or free person of color in this state, to own fire-arms, or carry about this person a pistol or other deadly weapon."[31] An 1865 Florida law similarly prohibited "Negroes mulattos or other persons of color from possessing guns, ammunition or blade weapons" without obtaining a license issued by a judge on the recommendation of two respectable citizens, presumably white. Violators were punished by public whipping up to "39 stripes."

The federal government, with an occupying army still in place, countermanded much of the discriminatory arms legislation. In January 1866, General Daniel Sickles, commander of federal occupation troops, issued a general order that "the constitutional rights of all loyal and well disposed inhabitants to bear arms will not be infringed."[32]

Black Code drafters also faced the problem that has always afflicted weapons embargoes. Even for ruthless postwar lawmakers, *saying* that guns were banned to blacks was different from actually prying them away. The assessment of a black trooper assigned to the Freedman's Bureau in Mississippi is instructive here. In a letter to a Bureau commissioner, Private Calvin Holly described an incident in Vicksburg involving armed black men. He noted, "they was forbidden [by the Black Code] not to have any [guns] *but did not heed.*"

Attempts to disarm the freedmen appeared not only in state statutes, but also in local ordinances and private contracts. In a report to President Andrew Johnson, General Charles Schurz described a series of local ordinances in Louisiana that prohibited blacks from owning any type of weapon without permission from their employer and separate approval by the mayor. In other cases, petty plantation tyrants put conditions in long-term labor contracts prohibiting blacks from possessing firearms.[33]

The Black Code and labor contract restrictions were a piece with violent attempts to disarm blacks perpetrated by local police, white state militias, and Klan-type organizations that rose during Reconstruction to wage a war of Southern redemption. The formal Ku Klux Klan emerged out of Tennessee in 1866. But across the South, similar organizations cropped up under names like the White Brotherhood, the Knights of the White Camellia, the Innocents, and the Knights of the Black Cross. Black disarmament was part of their common agenda.[34]

∞

Many black veterans left military service with their issue weapons or war prizes and probably were better armed than the general black population. But the public conversation shows that arms for self-defense were a particular concern of the broad swath of black civilians. This is evident in the reaction to occupation-army commands affirming freedmen's right to keep and bear arms. These orders were widely reprinted in black newspapers along with commentary that spoke to the community's concerns. A good example appears in the *Christian Recorder* published by the African Methodist Episcopal Church, which editorialized:

> We have several times alluded to the fact that the Constitution of the United States guarantees to every citizen the right to keep and bear arms. Gen. Tilson, assistant Commissioner, for Georgia, has issued a circular in which he clearly defines the right as follows: . . . "The Constitution of the United States gives the people the right to bear arms and states that this right shall not be infringed. Any person, white or black, may be disarmed, if convicted of making an improper and dangerous use of weapons; but no military or civil officer has the right or authority to disarm any class of people, thereby placing them at the mercy of others. All men, without the distinction of color, have the right to keep arms to defend their homes, families or themselves." We are glad to learn that Gen. Scott, Commissioner for this state, has given freedmen to understand that they have as good a right to keep firearms as any other citizens. The Constitution of the United States is the . . . law of the land, and we will be governed by that at present.[35]

The black newspaper the *Loyal Georgian* reprinted General Sickles's Order No. 1, followed by an editorial explaining that that blacks were now citizens who had a right to have guns for self-protection.

> Have colored citizens a right to own and carry firearms? . . . Almost every day we are asked questions similar to the above. We answer certainly you have the same right to own and carry arms that other citizens have. You are not only free but citizens of the United States and, as such, entitled to the same privileges granted to other citizens by the Constitution of the United States. . . .
>
> Article II of the Amendments to the Constitution of the United States gives the people the right to bear arms and states that this right shall not be infringed. Any person, white or black may be disarmed if convicted of making an improper or dangerous use of weapons, but no military or civil officer has the right or authority to disarm any class of people, thereby placing them at the mercy of others. All men, without distinction of color have the right to keep and bear arms to defend their homes, families or themselves.[36]

Negroes claiming their constitutional right to arms also sent petitions to Congress, protesting racist state gun-control laws. One typical petition implored Congress, "We ask that, inasmuch as the Constitution of the United States explicitly declares that the right to keep and bear arms shall not be infringed and the Constitution is the supreme law of the land—that the late efforts of the legislature of the state to pass an act to deprive us or [*sic*] arms be forbidden, as a plain violation of the Constitution." The Joint House and Senate Committee of Fifteen of the 39th Congress, which eventually drafted the Fourteenth Amendment, heard many such complaints about Black Code and private terrorist attacks on freedmen's right to arms.[37]

Congress received many other reports and complaints about schemes to disarm blacks. A report of the commissioner of the Kentucky Freedman's Bureau confirms black complaints that "the civil law prohibits the colored man from bearing arms. Their arms are taken from them by the civil authorities. . . . Thus the right of the people to keep and bear arms as provided in the Constitution is infringed." The congressional testimony of General Rufus Saxon, formerly a commissioner of the Freedman's Bureau in South Carolina, adds texture. In February 1866, Saxon described to a congressional committee how white planters tried to use peonage contracts backed with threats of violence to deprive freedmen of their firearms. "They desired me to sanction a form of contract which would deprive the colored men of their arms, which I refused to do. The subject was so important, as I thought, to the welfare of the freedmen that I issued a circular on this subject."[38]

Saxon also reported the attempt by private terrorists to disarm Negroes, recounting how "in some parts of the state, armed parties are, without proper authority, engaging in seizing all firearms found in the hands of the freedmen. Such conduct is plain and direct violation of their personal rights as guaranteed by the Constitution of the United States." Another Freedman's Bureau commissioner, General Wager Sayne, reported to Congress how militias in Alabama attempted to disarm freedmen and that his force blocked those attempts.[39]

Reports to the Reconstruction Congress verify the importance of defensive firearms to freedmen. A Freedman's Bureau report from Tennessee describes an incident where a band of Klansman attacked a group of eight freedmen. Several of the black men were armed with pistols and drove off their attackers. Freedman's Bureau commissioner Howard confirmed the widespread possession of arms by the rising black political class, noting, "no Union man or Negro who attempts to take any active part in politics, or the improvement of his race is safe a single day; and nearly all sleep upon their arms at night, and carry concealed weapons during the day."[40]

By the end of February 1866, the House of Representatives began debating what became the Fourteenth Amendment to the Bill of Rights—which would declare that blacks were full citizens entitled to equal protection and due process under the law.[41] This debate is some of our best evidence about the scope of the constitutional right to arms. In a revealing discussion of the Civil Rights Act, whose language prefigured the citizenship clause of the Fourteenth Amendment, a representative from New York explained the aim to "make the colored man a citizen of the United States and he has every right which you and I have. . . . He has a defined status; he has a country and a home; a right to defend himself and his wife and children; a right to bear arms."

The passage of the Civil Rights Act of 1866, the Second Freedman's Bureau Act, and ultimately the Fourteenth Amendment, is a rich and complex story that implicates far more than the freedmen's right to arms. But that right was integral to the debate, and was discussed widely outside the halls of Congress. When Congress voted to override President Andrew Johnson's veto of the Civil Rights Bill, the *New York Evening Post* editorialized about the evils that the bill sought to remedy. Prominent here was the attempt across the South to deprive freedmen from "keeping firearms."

By the end of April 1866, the full Congress began debate on the proposed Fourteenth Amendment. Senator Howard introduced the proposal, explaining that the "great object" of the amendment is to "restrain the power of the states and compel them in all times to respect these great fundamental guarantees. . . . Secured by the first eight amendments of the Constitution [including] the right to keep and bear arms." Concurrent with this debate, Congress also passed legislation abolishing the Southern state militias. This was necessary, explained one of the sponsors, because the state militias had been used to disarm the freedmen.[42]

Initially the rebel states unanimously rejected the Fourteenth Amendment.

But, chafing under federal military rule and the stipulation that they could not reenter the Union unless they approved the amendment, they eventually capitulated. (This coercion would fuel twentieth-century segregationists' claims that the Fourteenth Amendment was illegitimate and that the Constitution still sanctioned racial apartheid.) By 1868, the Fourteenth Amendment was the law of the land and laid a broad foundation for the protection of a range of liberties essential to the rise of the freedmen, including the right to keep and bear arms.

The grand constitutional efforts to affirm the freedmen's right to arms carried an important *symbolism*—free men had a right to arms, slaves did not. But for Negroes navigating a multitude of threats after the war, it is hard to overestimate the *practical* importance of firearms. This is demonstrated dramatically in episodes of gunfire but more prosaically in the accounts of freedmen who never fired their guns—men like Cato Carter, who spent most his life in slavery and then endured what passed for freedom in postwar Texas. So far as we know, Carter never fired a gun in self-defense. And it is just by happenstance, in a set of regional slave narratives, that we learn about his practice of arms.

Carter confirmed that in some ways freedom was more hazardous than slavery. As a valuable piece of white man's property, he actually enjoyed a measure of legal protection that disappeared after emancipation. So when white terrorists launched into high gear, Carter was happy to have an effective self-defense tool. Bands of whites, said Carter, "was allus skullduggering 'round at night." He does not tell where he got it, but Carter calculated that the wise response was to keep and carry a gun to protect his home and family.[43]

Cato Carter was no aberration. A report from the Texas legislature describes a series of conflicts in the postwar period where freedmen were "generally as well armed as the whites," and this sort of small-scale parity fueled intermittent black victories. In Washington County, Texas, white men rode out to break up a black political meeting. The whites were armed, but not really prepared for a shootout. When they fired into the crowd of Negroes, the freedmen shot back, scattering their attackers. Later, a white man broke into the home of one of the black organizers and threatened her with a gun. Armed black men tracked him down, arrested him, and turned him over to military authorities.[44]

The ability and decision to acquire a gun for self-defense surely varied according to individual circumstances, disposition, and calculations about surrounding hazards. Some hazards were public, some were private, and some were hybrids—private threats backed by a badge of office and flavored by the racism of the day.

The case of Al McRoberts is one of the latter. McRoberts started carrying a gun after W. A. Harris, a Danville, Kentucky, police officer, threatened to kill him. A Christmas Eve street encounter culminated with McRoberts firing three shots from his revolver at Harris. McRoberts was arrested, but later that evening, a mob seized him, took him to the edge of town, and hanged him from a sturdy oak. The inquest report concluded that "McRoberts came to his death by hanging by some parties unknown."[45]

Many of the reports of Negroes with guns during this period lack texture. One longs for detail on the specific worries and fears that caused these folk to acquire and carry guns. What comfort did they draw, amidst news of the latest terrorist attack, from a revolver, rifle, or shotgun close to hand? And what about the harms avoided, incidents where Negroes brandished guns and chased off some threat? Modern surveys tell us that this type of scenario, vastly underacknowledged even now, is by far the most common category of armed self-defense.

Narratives from the increasingly literate class of freedmen are suggestive here. The little-noticed autobiography of Reverend Elijah Marrs is one of these. Born into slavery in Shelby County, Kentucky, in 1840, Marrs ran off to join the Union Army in September 1864. Entering service toward the end of the war, he was among the latecomers who made the Union Army a proportionally "blacker" force than before.

In early 1866, Elijah Marrs was on furlough, visiting his family in Shelbyville, Kentucky. He was welcomed by black folk as a returning hero. But many whites took the opposite view of his service. Marrs had just arrived at his parents' home when a fire broke out on Main Street. Instinctively, he dropped his gun belt and ran to help. But his good deed drew unwanted attention. With the fire still smoldering, three white men wielding knives charged Marrs, one of them fulminating about "niggers in uniforms."

Marrs picked up a stick and fought his way home. Then he "wheeled and ran into the gate, around the house, and into the back door . . . seized pistols, threw open the front door, and opened fire on them." Under a hail of lead, Marrs's attackers ran for cover and then escaped. Accommodating his family's fears that the men might return during the night with reinforcements, Marrs sat up until dawn, with revolvers ready. The night passed without violence, and Marrs managed to survive his three-week furlough with only one further incident that he defused by drawing his revolver and taking steady aim at a menacing young man who scurried off in search of a softer target.[46]

When Elijah Marrs finally mustered out of the army in late 1866, he returned to Shelby County. With an established reputation as a literate black man, he was persuaded to start a school in nearby Simpsonville. Black schools and teachers were targets of terrorist violence, and Marrs's school was no exception. One night, hooded men rode into his yard and threatened to flog everyone in the house. Marrs reports, "I stole downstairs, and, armed with my old pistol, stationed myself in a chimney corner, prepared to fight my way through should occasion demand it." The terrorists ultimately did not break in and Marrs did not venture out. But that did not stop the other occupants of the house celebrating him as their savior.

By 1869, Marrs had become politically active and was elected president of the county Republican Club. He was visiting with a group of political friends at the home of Elder Lewis in Lagrange, Kentucky, when breaking glass signaled the arrival of local terrorists. One of Marrs's cohorts, a man named Roberts, grabbed a pistol and brandished it to full effect, staunching the attack.

But the evening was young and with the lessons of similar attacks behind them, Marrs, Roberts, and Lewis sat up, clutching guns, anticipating a renewed assault. "About midnight," Marrs reports, "they came again, and as they got near me I called to them to halt and then fired." The gunfire was effective in dissuading at least this band of Klansmen from Lagrange.

By 1870, Marrs had moved to Henry County, Kentucky, to run a school in New Castle. Henry County was thick with KKK, and "a colored man in public business dared not go five miles outside of the city for fear of assassination." After a close call with belligerent Klansmen, Marrs organized the black men of the town into "a society for self protection, [called] the Loyal League."

Marrs then describes something that leaves us wondering what similar episodes have gone unrecorded. While there are no surviving minutes of his Loyal League, Marrs details his own preparation as part of the group and opens the speculation that he was not unique. "For three years," says Marrs, "I slept with a pistol under my head, an Enfield rifle at my side, and a corn knife at the door, but I never had occasion to use them."[47]

We can only guess how many other members of Marrs's Loyal League made similar preparations. And what about their friends and neighbors? Given the times, what was the reasoning of Negroes who decided against owning a gun? Were they convinced that some government agent would protect them, or did they just pray and hope for the best?

Some of the inputs on decisions to keep and bear arms are demonstrated in the records of the United States Senate Committee on Southern Reconstruction. A letter from a teacher at a freedmen's school in Maryland demonstrates one set of concerns. The letter contains the standard complaints about racist attacks on the school and then describes one strand of the local response. "Both the Mayor and the sheriff have warned the colored people to go armed to school, (which they do) [and] the superintendent of schools came down and brought me a revolver."

In other testimony, a music teacher from Virginia described attacks on Union men who "drew their revolvers and held their assailants at bay." This affiant then volunteered that he also was constantly armed.[48] A Freedman's Bureau commissioner from Richmond, Virginia, described how common folk were widely armed and resisted the various efforts to take their guns. To the committee's question, "Are there many arms among the blacks," he responded "Yes sir; attempts have been made in many instances to disarm them; it has not been allowed; they [citizens patrols] would disarm the Negroes at once if they could."

Fig. 3.4. Depiction of Negro Soldiers and the Klan. (Still taken from *The Birth of a Nation*, directed by D. W. Griffith, 1915.)

A reporter from Texas noted that communities of freedmen had successfully resisted attempts to take their guns and celebrated their victories with ostentatious displays. "Negroes are seldom molested now in carrying the firearms of which they make such a vain display. In one way or another, they have procured great numbers of old army muskets and revolvers, particularly in Texas, and I have in a few instances, been amused at the vigor and audacity with which they have employed them to protect themselves against the robbers and murderers that infest that state."[49]

Although we cannot track it through the kind of empirical assessments that are common today, black firearms ownership also generated plenty of intragroup violence in the postwar era. This included a component of domestic violence of the type illustrated in the 1866 prosecution in Mississippi of W. D. Chase. Chase lived in the Negro quarters of Vicksburg, with his wife, Phyllis. Neighbors reported that they quarreled about money, about his drinking, and about apparent visits of a white soldier to the home when Chase was gone. Witnesses heard the couple fighting about a pistol, and one neighbor reports Chase yelling, "I will shoot any woman who will take a white man and leave me." That oath was followed by a gunshot, and neighbors gathered to find a despondent Chase crying, "Oh ma if you die I want to die too."

Even during the war, there were indications that the contraband camps that grew up behind Union lines suffered from prosaic black criminality involving firearms. Reporting on the camp towns around Vicksburg, Mississippi, describes frequent gunfire, theft, and other crime. One editorial, from an admittedly unsympathetic white newspaper, chided that there was money to be made by anyone who could fashion a bulletproof covering for the meager structures of the Vicksburg camp.[50]

For the immediate postwar period, we are left to surmise from surrogate evidence that a significant part of the violence that affected blacks was intraracial. An unusual postslavery experiment is instructive. The venue was the imagined slave utopia of Mississippi planter Joseph Davis, brother of Confederate president Jefferson Davis. Spurred by the theories of English social reformers, Joseph Davis sought to establish a model slave community. He built sturdy cottages with plaster walls and fireplaces to quarter his 350 slaves and established a court where slave juries decided complaints about misbehavior and whether a slave should be punished. Before whipping a slave, overseers were required to get a conviction against the culprit by a jury of his peers. In April 1862, Joseph Davis fled his plantation, leaving his slaves behind as Union forces advanced.[51]

Sometime around the end of the war, Davis transferred ownership of the plantation to one of his favored slaves, Benjamin Montgomery, who appropriated Davis's vision and reconfigured the place as the town of Davis Bend. Montgomery sat as judge in a variety of disputes between the free blacks of Davis Bend. Perhaps reflecting the broader trend, roughly one third of the cases involved crimes of violence.

A broader assessment in Warren County, Mississippi, between 1865 and 1867 confirms the hazards that blacks faced during that period from both whites and other blacks, and it helps us understand why they might seek out guns for self-defense. While court records do not always specify race, one observer claimed that not a day passed without news of some robbery or murder of a black victim.[52]

The program of congressional Reconstruction initiated by radical Republicans, over the objections and vetoes of President Andrew Johnson, exacerbated simmering fears about rising black political power and looming retribution. Rumors spread of armed blacks drilling in nightly conclaves, waiting for some signal to unleash a massacre. Those fears often centered on black rifle companies that were common in the postwar era.[53]

The fears and rumors provoked by the black rifle companies are easy to understand. And it is also worth pausing to consider just the existence of these groups. One longs for some detailed record of the membership, activities, sources of guns, and agenda of such groups. But, like many chapters in the black experience, the details here are thin. Still, there is enough evidence to demonstrate that many blacks during this period owned guns, knew how to use them, and saw firearms as important personal-security tools.

Black veterans played a significant role in rifle companies like David Cooper's group in Cape Fear, North Carolina, and John Eagles's Wilmington Rifle Guard. The Wilmington Rifle Guard drilled every week and was a central feature in the annual Emancipation Day parade. This and other celebrations by black Wilmington were often followed by Creedmoor-style target-shooting competitions that drew hundreds of participants and spectators.[54]

In the fall of 1867, two independent black militias drilled publicly in Washington, DC, displaying arms that they had purchased from the federal government. President Andrew Johnson's order to disband sparked controversy, and the military commander of the district responded that absent a declaration of martial law, he had no authority to enforce the president's order. The mayor of the district confirmed that the black militia had not broken any local laws. The Negroes finally did stop parading, but they kept their arms and did not disband.[55]

The activities of the rifle clubs and militias were not the exclusive province of veterans. Organized practice and competition with firearms drew participation from the broader community at open public events. In 1866, for example, roughly four hundred blacks gathered at a Pitt County, North Carolina, plantation for a Fourth of July celebration that included "target practice with Springfield rifles."[56]

George Washington Albright of Mississippi further demonstrates that black rifle companies were not dependent on leadership from veterans. Albright was a carpenter and a teacher, who organized a black volunteer militia aimed "to keep the common people on top and fight off the attacks of the landlords and former slave owners."[57]

Much of the public practice of arms by Negroes in the postwar era was connected to the burgeoning political development of the freedmen. Channeling this political ambition, black chapters of the Union League formed throughout the South. Their secrecy, ritual, late-night meetings, and posting of armed sentinels fueled rumors of armed black men intent on mayhem. Despite the often-innocuous content and consequence of Union League meetings, they were, in fact, a venue where Negroes with guns assembled. And sometimes this was more than just for show.

Fig. 3.5. "The Colored Creedmoor," a comic depiction of postwar black gun culture. ("The Colored Creedmoor," wood engraving by Thomas Nast, *Harper's Weekly* magazine, New York, August 28, 1875.)

In Harnett County, North Carolina, a league chapter threatened violence to secure release of colored orphans bound out to white planters. A league chapter in Brazos, Texas, under the leadership of Reverend George Brooks, battled a party of the hooded night riders in 1868, and the episode spurred blacks to acquire more guns and step up public military-style drills. Demonstrating again that arms are no guarantee of safety, league leader George Brooks was subsequently murdered.

In Morgan County, Georgia, George Flemister reorganized a league chapter that had dissolved under Klan pressure. The reconstituted Morgan County League was instrumental in Republican electoral gains and then attempted to expand its influence to community protection. When a black man named Charles Clark was arrested on a specious rape charge, a squad of armed Union League members rallied to guard him from lynching. Believing the threat had passed, they dispersed. Later, a group of white men in "long gowns . . . and some great sharp things upon their heads" broke into the jail and killed Clark. They then ransacked Flemister's little shoe-repair business and ran him out of town.

In Grant, North Carolina, Union League leader Wyatt Outlaw, son of a slave mother and a white Unionist, organized league members to establish a school, a church, and a vigilance committee that patrolled the community. He actually urged blacks to rely on his patrols and avoid individual violence. Ultimately,

Outlaw was unable to keep a lid on the violence. Incensed by his political activism, members of the White Brotherhood seized Wyatt Outlaw and hanged him in the town square.

In Maury County, Tennessee, league members stood by their promise of mutual defense when night riders threatened their leader, Pleasant Hill. They rushed to the scene with "muskets and revolvers [and] in this way kept them off and defended ourselves . . . until daylight." In Darlington County, South Carolina, a league chapter redoubled its preparations on the rumor of an impending Klan attack, and with weapons displayed, they took control of the town.

Similar episodes were recorded in Macon, Mississippi, and Granville County, North Carolina. The show of force by the Granville County League was enough to prompt a democratic leader to offer terms. He proposed that if the blacks would stand down, "he would stop the Ku Klux." In Oktibbeha County, Mississippi, an entire league chapter marched with arms to the county seat, spurred by lynch rumors following the arrest of one of their members.[58]

In South Carolina and Alabama, league chapters rejected the authority of the state and county courts, setting up their own judicial system and selecting a community sheriff. This led to charges of insurrection, and the Alabama movement leader was arrested.

An 1867 conflict involving Union League activists in Hale County, Alabama, triggered an escalating cycle of violence. It started with a fight in the town of Greensboro, between a white merchant and Alex Webb, a black Union League activist who served as registrar of voters. The merchant ended up shooting Webb, who died a short while later. Suspecting some larger plot, and fearing that the murderer had been aided by townsfolk, armed Negroes flooded into town. Then they scoured the countryside in search of suspected conspirators and dragged one half-naked man back into town as evidence of their effort.

The familiar worry about escalation was soon fulfilled. The black show of force spurred the formation of a new Klan organization in Hale County. Over the next several years, Hale County Negroes would battle the Klan in repeating cycles of violence. In one episode, Klansmen rode into Greensboro to depose a partisan Republican judge. Unable to locate him, they attacked the jail and freed one of their cohorts. Blacks responded by torching the livery stable of an apparent Klan sympathizer. Later, Klansmen fired into a Negro prayer meeting. Blacks responded with a failed retaliatory attack, resulting in another Negro dead.[59]

In August 1868, in Camilla, Georgia, the threat of black electoral success triggered a violent scene reported as the "Camilla Riot." At the heart of the controversy was the contest over who would represent the state's Second Congressional District, where blacks outnumbered whites by almost two to one. Under Reconstruction policies, Republicans controlled the governor's office and the legislature. Whites had already demonstrated their opposition to the Republican candidate, William Pierce, at a rally in nearby Americus, where Pierce was lucky to make it out alive.

When Pierce scheduled a rally in Camilla, where whites were a slim majority, he was warned, "this is our Country and we intend to protect it or die." Local blacks, still agitated about a racially motivated shooting in Camilla four months earlier, had already resolved that they would never go to Camilla unarmed.

The political rally for Pierce started in the countryside and gathered momentum and participants as it moved toward town. By the time they reached the village of China Grove, just outside Camilla, the noisy parade, led by a wagonload of musicians, numbered perhaps three hundred. About half of the men were carrying some sort of firearm. The procession was fully in the style of the Union League and Republican clubs of the period, who often paraded this way to draw out community support on election days. But many whites viewed these processions as threatening mobs. In Camilla, the news quickly spread that an armed body of Negroes was approaching.

Before the group reached town, the sheriff, backed by a freshly appointed citizens committee, rode out and warned them not to enter town carrying guns. The Negroes said they intended to have a peaceful rally at the courthouse. After some debate and a failed attempt to secure an alternative site, they marched into Camilla. By this time, the sheriff had deputized most of the white men in town, and they were girded for conflict.

The Negroes marched toward the courthouse to music of drums and fifes. The sheriff later reported that they marched in military fashion, four deep, surrounded by outriders on horseback. Squads of armed whites assembled adjacent to the courthouse square. The shooting started when a drunk white man wielding a shotgun ran out and demanded that the drummers cease their racket. They refused, he fired, and the battle was on.

As is common in these encounters, the blacks were armed with the guns of poor folk, often single-shot shotguns loaded with cheap birdshot. They were also at a tactical disadvantage, assembled in the middle of the street, while their opponents stalked the perimeter. The blacks fired and fled for cover. The whites fired with effect and pursued fleeing Negroes into the swamps. Nine blacks were killed and many others were wounded. Whites proceeded through the countryside over the next two weeks, beating and warning Negroes that they would be killed if they tried to vote in the coming election.

Back in Albany, Negroes agitated for retaliation. Reverend Robert Crumley, pastor of the African Methodist Church, complained that the Camilla group failed to heed his advice. He had warned that them not go to Camilla with less than 150 armed men. Then he urged Albany blacks to ride to Camilla the next day and "burn the earth about the place."

The Albany Freedman's Bureau agent managed to dampen the rage with the promise to send for federal troops. By Election Day, tempers had cooled, but the climate of violence had cowed many weaker souls. Low black turnout resulted in a Democratic victory in the majority black Republican congressional district.[60]

Fig. 3.6. A Freedman's Bureau agent stands between rebels and freedmen. ("The Freedmen's Bureau," drawn by A. R. Waud, *Harper's Weekly* magazine, New York, July 25, 1868, p. 473.)

Other political violence of the Reconstruction era centered on official Negro state militias operating under radical Republican administrations. State militias were distinct from the private militias and rifle companies, and they posed a different set of concerns. Immediately after the war, Southern state militias were an enforcement arm of the Black Codes, the muscle behind the attempt to reinstitute slavery in a different form. Membership in these militias often overlapped with budding private terrorist groups like the Klan. Congress attacked the problem by disbanding the state militias of the former Confederacy through a rider to the 1867 Reconstruction Act.[61]

As Reconstruction progressed and radical Republicans took control of Southern state governments, they asked Congress to reauthorize the state militias. In 1869, Congress reauthorized state militias for North Carolina, South Carolina, Florida, Alabama, Louisiana, and Arkansas. Virginia, Texas, Mississippi, and

Georgia were excluded on worries that Republicans were not sufficiently established there. As Republican tools, the reauthorized militias were disdained by most whites. Blacks, on the other hand, were more than willing to serve.

The work of the Negro militias varied substantially, oscillating with Republican fortunes. In several states, they were barely worth mentioning. Alabama never deployed its Negro militia, even at the height of Klan violence in the state. In Florida, Republican governor Harrison Reed went through the motions of organizing a Negro militia but avoided using them for fear of white backlash. In other states, Negro militias marched mainly as a political show.[62] But in some places, Negro militias fought in significant episodes of political violence, supporting the programs of Republican governors to ends that were sometimes detached from the immediate interests of black folk.

In Texas, Governor Edmund Davis deployed Negro militia in an attempt to retain his office after being defeated by rival Richard Coke. In Louisiana, Negro militias were deployed for threat value by competing Republican factions. And in Arkansas, Negro militias fought in a full-scale military conflict, dubbed the Brooks-Baxter War.

The Brooks-Baxter War grew out of a schism between regular Republicans (the Minstrels) and a liberal Republican faction (known as Brindle-Tails). This split fueled a contest for the governorship in 1872. Elisha Baxter was the nominal winner, but Joseph Brooks contested the results. Fifteen months after Baxter took office, a county judge ruled that Brooks actually won the election. Both sides appealed to President Ulysses S. Grant, who cautiously refused to weigh in.

Insistent that he was the rightful governor, Brooks gathered three hundred Negro militia and set up a parallel administration. Baxter, who had nominally prevailed in the election, declared martial law also enforced by Negro militia. In the ensuing weeks, both sides vied for reinforcements and built up stores of arms. With all the trappings of war, they fought three separate engagements. About twenty men were killed and scores were wounded. President Grant finally ended the conflict with a proclamation that Baxter was the rightful governor and with a grant of immunity to all combatants. The broader consequences for Negroes were more worrisome. The conflict weakened the Republican Party in Arkansas and contributed to the ascension of Democrats.

White backlash against rising black political power and the specter of armed Negroes was multilayered. Confederates had lost the war of secession but now were battling for the soul of the South. Fear of Negro rule unified whites and fueled political violence in ways that nothing else could. Occupation by black troops, black suffrage, and the rise of Negroes to office generated resentment and resistance. Through rough politics, trickery, and violence, the white South would soon "redeem" its institutions and culture from the revolutionary social inversion of Reconstruction. This Southern "Redemption," solidified by federal abdication on Reconstruction, resubordinated blacks and carried deadly lessons about the risks of political violence and the importance of private self-defense.

Whether as police forces, private militias, or terrorist night riders, ex-Confederates pursued a ruthless campaign of political violence to disarm and dis-enfranchise blacks. Even in places where blacks might make a rational postwar decision to disdain political violence, in many cases, violence was unavoidable.

Operating under the loose imprimatur of law, bands of white militia raided Negro homes, searching and seizing firearms. For blacks, the distinction between these official militias and terrorist organizations like the KKK was often thin. Sometimes there was not even a pretense of distinction. Witness Colonel Roger Moore, commander of the New Hanover County, North Carolina, militia, who also headed the Wilmington KKK.[63]

Conflicts between Negroes and ex-Confederates holding badges as police or claiming membership in some militia were predictable. One conflict between a black veteran and a white policeman left one of the combatants cut and the other nursing a bullet wound. Another fight between a black soldier of the occupying force and a Confederate veteran repurposed as a Wilmington, North Carolina, policeman lead to protests, gunfire and death. The black soldier was reprimanded for his part in the initial fight. Angered by the perceived mistreatment of the black trooper, his friends in uniform and a crowd of black civilians surrounded city hall in protest. They were attacked by a group of whites and quickly dispersed. But during the night, they reconstituted into small, armed bands and attacked Confederate veterans on the police force, killing at least one man.

The reaction here exemplifies the worry about escalating cycles of violence. After the black show of force, the city administration recruited more policemen and requested guns from the governor, "with which to arm the police and other [white] citizens." Confederate General Robert Ransom, with a cadre of handpicked Confederate veterans, was installed as the new police chief, and he moved aggressively to disarm Wilmington's Negroes. He was aided by the policy of Union Army officers who gave him "carte blanche" in dealing with black soldiers.

Ransom's new police force was a continuing terror for blacks. One officer of the Freedman's Bureau reported they "are the hardest and most brutal looking and acting set of civil or municipal officers I ever saw." A Freedman's Bureau agent reported how two of these stout men apprehended a scrawny black woman for public intoxication. They laughed and goaded her for nearly half an hour, and when they tired of her antics, one of them knocked her cold with his baton.

Election season in Wilmington brought fiery spectacles and thundering midnight Klan rides that tested the black resolve to vote. The black response was defiance. Demonstrating that earlier disarmament attempts had failed, Wilmington blacks divided themselves into armed patrols. They rode throughout the night, firing randomly in their own show of force and confirmation that the Klan did not rule.[64]

In the run-up to the fall elections of 1868, the *Wilmington Daily Journal* decried that "there are many Negroes in this city who . . . almost constantly go armed." Black state senator Abraham Galloway, now standing for the office of presidential elector, wore a pistol, conspicuously displayed, wherever he went. He traveled with a squad of armed black men who later formed a dedicated black militia for community defense. The well-armed community again rebuffed the attempts at intimidation. On Election Day, Galloway became North Carolina's first black elector and delivered the district's votes to the Republican, Ulysses Grant.[65]

Fig. 3.7. Abraham Galloway. (Courtesy of the House Divided Project at Dickinson College.)

The 1868 elections in Tennessee were also shadowed by threats and intimidation. As Election Day approached, Klansmen made countless attempts to disarm blacks, resulting in shootouts with Negroes who resisted. One man recounted how a Klansmen attempted to drag him from his home, but, "I prevented him by my pistol, which I cocked, and he jumped back. I told them I would hurt them before they got away. They did not burn nor steal anything, nor hurt me." Another Tennessee freedman faced down terrorists who apparently believed his warning that "the first man who broke my door open I would shoot."[66]

The hazard of Klan violence was exacerbated by the sometimes-close connection and shared personnel between the terrorist organizations and the agents of government. At many points during the black freedom struggle, folk would claim that law enforcement and other officials were sympathetic to the Klan. But several incidents during the Reconstruction era provide vivid confirmation.

A report to Congress in 1871 tells of an elderly freedman in rural Tennessee who shot his way out of a Klan attack on his home. After he killed one of the group, the others fled. When he unmasked the dead man, it turned out to be the local constable. Subsequent investigation revealed that the county sheriff was also among the attackers. A jury deemed the shooting to be legitimate self-defense.

In another Tennessee incident, a gang of Klansmen fired into the home of a black family, wounding a female occupant. Black men in the house responded with gunfire, hitting the leader of the gang, who fell dead on their porch and was abandoned by his friends. At sunrise, the Negroes ventured out to find that the dead man on their steps was a deputy sheriff.

To Republican congressmen aimed at curbing the wave of Klan violence, this Tennessee shooting was an entirely salutary result. Representative Benjamin Butler of Massachusetts, proclaimed from the House floor, "I thank God for the courage of that Negro, who, in defending his own roof-tree and hearthstone, shot down the Sheriff and Constable who, as leader of the Ku Klux Klan invaded both!" Butler's Republican colleague Job Stevenson of Ohio lamented the violence and threats that kept Republican voters from the polls but celebrated the cases of armed self-defense reported during congressional investigations. Stevenson applauded the fact that many freedmen were armed and had defended themselves. It was evident, in his view, that Negroes with guns were an important deterrent to racist violence as, "seldom do they attack a man until they have him disarmed."

An episode from Georgia reported to a congressional committee in 1871 supports Stevenson's assessment. There a freedman was shot three times by Klansmen but managed to return fire. When he hit one of them, the entire group retreated, dragging away the wounded man.[67]

In 1875, in Independence, Texas, armed white men interrupted an interracial group of Republican political activists. Two black men in the group, one of them reportedly a Baptist preacher, fought off the intruders with shotguns. Later, in the little town of Graball, Texas, black men, fearing that Democrats would steal or stuff ballot boxes, posted armed guards around the tally houses and voting sites. In one predominantly black precinct, a Negro named Polk Hill shot it out with a band of hooded men who broke into the polling place to steal ballots. He killed one of them, who turned out to be the son of the Democratic candidate for county commissioner.[68]

In Charleston, South Carolina, where white rifle clubs attempted to intimidate blacks from voting in the 1876 election, clashes with armed blacks ended in standoffs. And in one case, a few weeks before Election Day, blacks sent white Democrats fleeing, with a show of force that left five whites and one black dead. At a rally of at least one thousand blacks, following the killing of a black rifleman, the community adopted a resolution calling for retaliation against the terror, declaring, "We tell you that it will not do to go too far in this thing. Remember that there are 80,000 black men in this state who can bear Winchester rifles and know how to use them."[69]

The political violence of the era was not just a Southern phenomenon. In Philadelphia, in 1871, Republicans wielding the black voting bloc challenged the Democratic political machine and swept to power on Negro support. But four blacks died in a spate of election eve violence. The Philadelphia police, controlled by the Democrats, let the violence proceed unchecked. Details of the black resistance are thinly recorded, but one observer described the conflict as an "eye for an eye and a tooth for tooth in every instance."

A conflict commensurate with modern intuitions occurred in Mississippi in 1875, where a Negro militia confronted a white volunteer force organized by Democrats in anticipation of the 1876 election. For weeks before the voting, both groups paraded with arms and executed jarring artillery salutes demonstrating their preparedness.[70]

At the center of the conflict, and a particular target, was black sheriff Peter Crosby. Faced down by a group of several hundred armed white men who challenged his claim to office, Crosby fled to the state capital. His plea for help was rebuffed by the governor, who told him to stand up and fight. White men had faced bullets to free blacks, said the governor, and blacks must fight to maintain that freedom.

Crosby returned to Vicksburg and organized a body of men to retake the sheriff's office by force. The white opposition was dug in on high ground. Accounts conflict about who fired first, but scores of men, the majority of them Negroes, died in the shooting. In the days following, whites ransacked black homes, searching out and confiscating firearms. Peter Crosby would survive the violence, and, with the aid of federal troops, was reinstated to his office. But he would soon resign under a wave of continuing threats and declining political fortunes.[71]

The places where blacks were a clear majority of the population raise pointed questions about the risks and opportunities of armed resistance against the forces of Southern Redemption. In Mississippi, for example, violence and the threat of it suppressed the black vote in 1875 and gave Democrats control in counties where blacks constituted two thirds (Oktibbeha and Amite Counties) to three fourths (Lowndes County) of the population.

From what we can tell today, whites were better organized, better armed, and potentially more desperate in the fight against Negro rule, which to them represented a world gone mad. A crucial aspect of the Democrat's victory was disarmament of black Republicans. The full details of how a white minority managed to disarm and overcome the black majority in these counties are lost. But the assessment of Albert

Morgan, formerly Republican sheriff of Yazoo County and ally of carpetbag governor A'Delbert Ames, is instructive. Both Morgan and Ames fled Mississippi in the wake of the Democratic ascent. Morgan lamented his potential role in that rise, explaining, "when the general arming of the whites first became known to me . . . I counseled the colored man against irregular arming, advising all to rely upon the law and its officers. I hoped by steadfastly pursuing this course, by offering no pretext for violence, we might pass the ordeal I saw approaching." Acknowledging the tactical error, Morgan conceded, "I was unused to guerrilla warfare."

Blacks were also a majority in regions of South Carolina. Riding the wave of Reconstruction, these black majorities gained powerful Republican friends in the legislature and the governor's office. In the shadow of Negro rule, white Democrats formed private rifle clubs and looked for opportunities to provoke conflict with the black majority. With the advantage of numbers, and at least nominal official support, blacks in this region sometimes prevailed against white political violence. A conflict in 1876 known as the Ned Tennent Riot is instructive.

Ned Tennent was the flamboyant commander of a black militia company in Meriwether Township, Edgefield County. Tennent relished the pomp of military drill and inflamed whites with his arrogant demeanor and commander's hat adorned with an ostrich plume. After members of a white rifle club fired shots into his home, Tennent summoned two hundred black militiamen and fueled rumors of a coming wave of black vengeance. The white rifle clubs girded for battle.

The next incident was in the predominantly black town of Hamburg in July 1876. The avowed strategy of the rifle clubs was to suppress black voting by killing "a certain number of niggers' leading men." The plan was "if they could be successful in killing those they wanted to kill in Hamburg, they [Democrats] would carry the county."[72]

The black community of Hamburg was relatively well organized under the leadership of a man named Prince Rivers, who had served in the Union Army and as a South Carolina legislator. Hamburg had also just revitalized its militia, which was led by black veteran Dock Adams. Adams was less flamboyant than Ned Tennent, but he was a meticulous and demanding commander.

As part of Independence Day celebrations, Adams was parading his militia on Main Street when he encountered two young white men in a buggy who demanded that he yield the street. The young men were from the planter class and expected a deference that Adams refused. They subsequently filed a complaint with Prince Rivers, who was also the trial justice in Hamburg. Dock Adams filed a counterclaim, and Rivers set a hearing date to resolve the matter.

News of the case spread widely, and on the day of the hearing, the white plaintiffs arrived accompanied by armed men from various white rifle clubs, including the unit led by future United States senator Ben "Pitchfork" Tillman. Tillman flatly rejected Rivers's authority and demanded that Adams's militiamen turn over their weapons and apologize to the white plaintiffs. Adams refused and deployed to a building that he had appropriated as an armory.[73]

Throughout the afternoon, more white rifle companies trickled into Hamburg, and the lawyer for the white plaintiffs went to secure reinforcements and artillery. By nightfall, the gunfire started, and it continued for nearly five hours. Facing continuing white reinforcements, Dock Adams's militia was outnumbered, outgunned, and by daybreak was clearly defeated. A black marshal and a militia lieutenant were killed, many were wounded, and thirty of Adams's militia were captured. Some captives were executed with bullets to the head, and others were fired upon after the order to run. Dock Adams somehow managed to escape.

While blacks lost this conflict in South Carolina, they did not lose every battle. In the village of Cainhoy, just outside Charleston, black militia with superior numbers and firepower confronted whites who attempted to break up a Republican political meeting. When the shooting stopped, five whites lay dead and fifty more were wounded.

While large black populations were a political threat, that did not always lead directly to interracial violence. Sometimes black voting power could be co-opted. And that generated interesting secondary turns of political violence. In 1875, before the effort to suppress black voting fully took hold, Democrats tried the carrot in addition to the stick, enticing selected Negroes into the party with various blandishments. One of these men, disgruntled Republican Martin Delaney, a former Union Army officer, campaigned in earnest for South Carolina Democrats in the fall of 1876. Democratic governor Wade Hampton also made overtures to Negroes. He was even accompanied by a mounted armed guard of five hundred men led by ex-slave Richard Mack during the 1876 campaign. On Election Day, Hampton managed to garner roughly five thousand black votes. For their part, black Republicans played very rough with fellow Negroes who were rumored to support the Democrats. These early contrarians were threatened, beaten, and even shot at for their apostasy.

In heavily black districts of South Carolina, the "shotgun politics" of the rifle clubs alone was insufficient to secure victory for the Democrats. Ultimately, it took massive ballot fraud to wrest control from the Republicans. In many places, blacks still managed to vote in large numbers, and the ballot fraud was evidenced by returns in some white precincts that exceeded the voting population.[74] Perched in the United States Senate, commenting on the violence, Ben "Pitchfork" Tillman reflected, "We have done our level best. We have scratched our head to figure out how we can eliminate the last one of them. We stuffed ballot boxes. We shot them [Negroes]. We are not ashamed."[75]

For a brief period during the Reconstruction era, the federal government attempted to quell the Klan-style terrorism. In 1871, for example, federal prosecutors indicted Klansmen from York County, South Carolina, for violating the rights of blacks to assemble, vote, keep and bear arms, and be free from unreasonable searches and seizures. This prosecution was rooted in a spree of Klan violence including assaults and disarmament of blacks and threats that they would be killed if they tried to vote. It culminated in the murder of black militia captain Jim Williams.

Williams had been a particular worry for South Carolina Democrats, who depicted him essentially as an outlaw who had to be dealt with. Williams's militia company was armed with efficient Enfield breach-loading rifles and flaunted the weapons in armed pre-election parades.[76]

After breaking into various black homes and disarming occupants, Klansmen confirmed Williams's location from a black neighbor who reported that Williams had at least twelve guns hidden in his home. The Klan descended on Williams's cabin, seized his guns, and then dragged him away over the screaming tempest of his wife, Ruby. At daybreak, two of Williams's neighbors went searching for him and found his corpse hanging from a tree. Federal prosecution of the men who killed Jim Williams and terrorized his neighbors ended with a single Klansman convicted and sentenced to eighteen months in prison.[77]

Of all the violence in the campaign to redeem the South from Reconstruction, the bloodiest episode occurred in Grant Parish, Louisiana, in a town called Colfax. Fueling the conflict was a cynical Republican governor who courted black Republicans and attempted to placate unreconstructed white Democrats, all while snookering his more radical Republican rivals. Political scheming resulted in competing claims for county offices. And that sparked a wave of political violence that the region and the country would not soon forget.

Colfax was the brainchild of Willie Calhoun, heir to a fourteen-thousand-acre plantation in the Red River Valley. Willie's father had ruled over more than seven hundred slaves before the war. Raised half his life in Europe and laboring under a physical handicap, Willie fell, philosophically, quite far from the tree. He responded to emancipation and Reconstruction far differently from his neighboring planters. Just the name of the place suggests Willie Calhoun's unusual view of things. On Willie's initiative, the thousands of acres handed down by his father were established as a new parish, named for President Grant. The county seat, previously Calhoun's Landing, was renamed after Grant's vice president, Schuyler Colfax.

When the war was over, Willie handed out plantation livestock to former

Calhoun slaves, helped start a black school, and rented acreage at fair prices to blacks. When agents of the Freedman's Bureau arrived to aid the transition from slavery to freedom and mediate conflicts with ex-Confederates, Willie Calhoun welcomed them and their mission.

Like many places, Grant Parish had seen its share of terrorist violence. That prompted Grant Parish blacks, with at least the initial backing of the governor, to form a militia for the security of the population. It was commanded by William Ward, a former slave from South Carolina who had escaped into Union lines, enlisted in the army, and risen to the rank of sergeant. Seventy-five black men filled the ranks of Ward's militia company.

Election season yielded the discord sowed by Governor Henry Warmoth's machinations. The seat of power in Colfax was the courthouse, formally one of Willie Calhoun's stables. Black Republicans secured it first and staked their claims to the offices that it represented. When local whites bragged within earshot of their Negro help about the plans to take the courthouse and oust the Republican team, word soon reached William Ward. Ward raised the alarm with Republicans, who armed for defense of the courthouse. Soon, two dozen black men with guns arrived to guard the courthouse and the Republican administration.[78]

The first shooting occurred when a scout posse of blacks encountered a force of mounted whites and exchanged shotgun fire. Again, the technology is significant. The shotgun is a devastating weapon at close range. But the forces here were at least two hundred yards apart. At that range, the shotgun load has spent most of its energy. So it is no surprise that no one was hurt in this first exchange.

Other skirmishes followed. On April 5, one of William Ward's men, Benjamin Allen, led a patrol into the countryside to search for a black man who was rumored to have been abducted. They encountered a group of twenty armed whites and exchanged gunfire. With the horses spooked, the two sides dispersed, again with no casualties.

Cooler heads from both sides attempted a parlay, each offering to cease hostilities if the other would surrender its claims to government office. The negotiations broke down when one of Ward's men burst into the meeting, shouting that a band of whites had just killed Jesse McKinney, a freedman who worked a small patch of land at the edge of Colfax. This was the tipping point.

Blacks from around the countryside poured into Colfax, and William Ward's men dug in. On April 6, skirmish squads clashed again. Both sides were mounted, and the blacks had the advantage of surprise. They laid in ambush, sending out a white ally as a decoy. The plan worked, and the blacks fired with effect from cover. The whites fled across a muddy stream, firing back over their shoulders. The worst casualty was one white man getting his thumb shot off. The black patrol returned to Colfax triumphant.[79]

Black victories and stalemates in sporadic small conflicts led white Democrats to call for reinforcements. By April 13, more than 150 white men had assembled on the outskirts of town. They were led by a man who claimed the office of sheriff under the order of a county judge, whose own authority was rooted in the contested election results. Men answered the call from several adjoining counties, including a contingent from the Knights of the White Camellia and the Old Time Ku Klux Klan. The recruiting effort also yielded a four-pound cannon from a sympathetic riverboat owner.

The blacks at Colfax were superior in number but not in fighting quality. The group of 150 included women and children from the countryside who had set up a little camp around the courthouse. Many of the black men reportedly were not armed, and the guns that they did have were largely shotguns and hunting pieces. About a dozen black men had Union-issue, breach-loading Enfield military rifles. The bigger problem was that they had only enough ammunition for each man to fire a few shots. They also attempted to construct a jerry-rigged cannon from pieces of steam pipe, but the thing blew up when they tried to test-fire it.

On Sunday, April 9, a preconflict parlay began with demands of surrender and refusal. Finally, the white force warned the courthouse defenders that they had thirty minutes to remove the women and children. This was the point where the two white men in the courthouse—an ambivalent Republican and a Northern traveling salesman—decided to flee. Except for the hapless Negro the Democrats would force at gunpoint to throw a firebomb onto the courthouse roof, the coming conflict would be purely black against white.

The white force advanced in a skirmish line to clear out preliminary guards and traps. At three hundred yards, they set up the canon and began firing. The Negroes fired their remaining improvised cannon. It blew up just like the first one.[80]

The groups traded small-arms fire for about two hours. Blacks' hopes rose and then fell on the empty speculation that the whistle of a passing steamboat signaled Republican reinforcements. They were heartened again by a lucky shot that took out one of the white cannon crew. But he was quickly replaced.

Finally, with most of their ammunition spent, the black courthouse force succumbed, and then it was pure slaughter. The whites gave no quarter. Bill Cruickshank, later infamous as a defendant in a historic Supreme Court case stemming from the conflict, made a game of lining up Negroes close together so that he could kill two of them with a single shot. When some objected to the shooting of prisoners, others responded, "we are only shooting the wounded." In later testimony, one of the surviving blacks summarized the scene this way:

> They told us to stack our arms and they wouldn't hurt us and for us to march out; then they set the courthouse on fire; . . . They made me go among the prisoners;

. . . They kept me prisoner until midnight; they took me and another man out to shoot us; one bullet struck me in my neck, stunning and dropping me; the other man was killed; they did not shoot me again; I laid on the ground until morning; fearing to move.

When a riverboat stopped at Colfax toward sundown, travelers witnessed the carnage of a battlefield. Most of the dead were black. The armed white men who still roamed the area explained that blacks had been riled up by radical Republicans to seize the courthouse and provoked a fight. Estimates of the death toll range from 80 to 150 blacks and a handful of whites.[81]

The alleged leaders of the prevailing whites were prosecuted in litigation that went all the way to the United States Supreme Court. The prosecutions held powerful lessons for black folk. Ninety-five whites were indicted on various charges. But only a handful of men were ultimately tried, and even they were acquitted on most charges. An editorial in the *New Orleans Republican* cast the lesson this way:

> The colored folks will hereafter depend to some extent upon the same weapons for defense that their enemies use for attack. A jury is really no match for a firearm. If it be generally known that in each Negro cabin in the County there is a lively weapon of defense, there will not be such a constant recurrence of homicides as have disgraced the annals of this state for many years. We expect these shotguns to prove famous peacemakers.[82]

Looking back, this assessment seems unsatisfactory. Armed Negroes at Colfax had been annihilated. Urging blacks to get guns, or more guns, seems like a fruitless recipe for escalating violence. The prescription seems desperate, reflexive, not fully rational. But viewed against the unfolding pattern of state malevolence and diminishing options, it is easier to understand how a fight doomed to failure might actually have been the best among the dreary options.

Political violence aimed at suppressing black advancement was a fact of life almost from the moment the Confederacy lost the war. It was an integral part of a strategy that paid off in 1877 when Democrats resolidified white rule through a political deal that ended the brief experiment of Reconstruction and ceded the Negro issue to Southern home rule.

That deal was born out of the viciously contested presidential election of 1876, between the Republican, Rutherford B. Hayes, and the Democrat, Samuel Tilden. Violent intimidation and cheating were rife in 1876, and by some accounts Tilden won the election. A more realistic account is that Democrats stole the election through violence, intimidation, and fraud, and Republicans stole it back through a politically tilted election review commission that overturned the ostensible Tilden victory in three Southern states and handed it to Hayes.

The election commission's decision fueled competing claims to the presidency that some feared might lead again to war. The Democratic slogan of the time was "Tilden or Fight." Conflict was averted through negotiations in a literally smoke-filled room at the Wormser Hotel, in Washington, DC, where Southern Democrats ceded the presidency to the Republicans in exchange for economic stimulus, the removal of federal troops from the South, and home rule over Negroes. The country was weary of the Negro issue and anxious for reconciliation and a new prosperity. Reconstruction was dead.

The end of Reconstruction opened the period some would call the nadir of the black experience in America. The political outlook was dim. Black political aspirations had been quashed by a program of violence and fraud, and now by federal abdication. Many have chronicled this story, but one of the best summaries comes from a black man of the times. In 1884, black publisher T. Thomas Fortune said this.

> It is sufficient to know that anarchy prevailed in every southern state; that a black man's life was not worth the having; that armed bodies of men openly defied the Constitution of the United States and nullified each and every one of its guarantees of citizenship to the colored man. Thousands of black men were shot down like sheep and not one of the assassins was ever hung by the neck until he was dead.[83]

With the diminishing promises of citizenship came greater personal exposure to violence. This posed a profound dilemma. State and local governments would grow increasingly hostile to Negroes. The notion of relying on the state for personal security or anything else would seem increasingly absurd against the rise of convict labor schemes, state-sponsored Jim Crow rules, and lynch law.

It was an important moment in the black tradition of arms. There were growing reasons to believe that whatever blacks now had in the political arena was all they would get. Black political violence would steadily decline. Individual self-defense would become the predominate theme of the tradition as Negroes came to grips with the fact that the brand of citizenship they enjoyed carried shrinking benefits and increasing risks that the state would care little for their physical security or general welfare. In the dangerous times to come, Negroes pushed to the wall by violent threats would be very much on their own and would have to decide whether to just crumple or to stand and fight.

CHAPTER FOUR

NADIR

"The Winchester rifle deserves a place of honor in every Black home." So said Ida B. Wells.

What would drive a four-and-a-half-foot tall colored schoolteacher to say such a thing? What did she witness? What did she fear? What were the rumors and threats that shrouded her rise from slavery to the vanguard of the black freedom struggle? And what was the culture that allowed this eminent leader of the race to exalt a gun that was the assault rifle of her day, without censure and, indeed, to wide affirmation?

Wells came of age during the period many consider the nadir of the black experience in America. She witnessed the violent defeat of Reconstruction and chafed under the menace of John Lynch and the indignities of Jim Crow. It was a period filled with hazards where the government was not just neglectful of Negro security but was often an overt menace. Wells's praise of the Winchester reflected hard lessons and worries about the next dark night, passed along on the whispers of black folk.

By age twenty, Wells had been orphaned by a yellow-fever epidemic; had become caretaker of her siblings; and had moved from her childhood home of Holly Springs, Mississippi, to Memphis, where a coveted teaching contract introduced her to the city's black elite. It was the start of her journey into journalism, publishing, and her destiny as America's foremost antilynching crusader.

Memphis in 1881, was a relative haven of opportunity for Negroes, whose performance on criteria like employment and arrest rates would be the envy of modern policy makers. But other aspects of the climate in Memphis were not so salutary. Blacks and Irish immigrants competed for much of the same low-cost housing and unskilled work. Black war veterans were natural combatants with the Memphis police force, which was 90 percent Irish and was described by a white army officer as "far from the best class of residents."

Political leaders of the period were candidly unsympathetic to Negro interests. Tennessee governor William Brownlow hopefully predicted that, with no masters to care for them, most Negroes would perish from starvation and disease within a generation. It turned out that these folk were of heartier stock.[1]

Ida Wells's fighting instinct first erupted on board a Chesapeake and Ohio passenger train. The traveling strategy for colored ladies of the day was meticulous grooming and impeccable manners, with the hope of avoiding the demeaning, random ejections from the first-class car. Wells pursued this strategy in the fall of 1883, but would only play the game so far.

When she handed her first-class ticket to the conductor, he ordered her to move to second class. Wells ignored him and turned to her novel. Provoked by her impudence, the conductor grabbed her luggage and hissed that he was attempting to treat her like a lady. Wells answered that he should leave the lady alone. Now fed up, the conductor grabbed at Wells, intent on dragging her out like cattle.

Wells set her feet wide against the seat-front and clutched hard into the headrest. When the conductor tried to pry her away, she sank her teeth into his hand. She was defeated only after several passengers helped the bleeding conductor lift away the entire seat section where Wells was anchored and throw it and her into the smoky second-class car.

Bruised, her dress torn, and her ego battered, Wells left the train at the next stop, to the jeers of the first-class passengers. The episode triggered the first stage of her activism. She sued the C&O Railroad and followed with a series of lawsuits against other rail lines. Some companies responded with separate cars for black first-class passengers. Although the accommodations were rarely first-class in fact, the United States Supreme Court soon affirmed the constitutionality of these so-called separate but equal accommodations.

Wells began her activism suing railroads, but she built her legend fighting lynching. Early on, like many respectable black folk, she tried to distance herself from the terror of lynching by thinking about it as only a sort of disproportionate justice inflicted on black criminals. That changed in 1892 with the triple lynching of Tom Moss, Calvin McDowell, and Will Stewart.

Moss was a good friend of Wells's. He was president of People's Cooperative Grocery, which served the predominantly black Memphis community along Walker Avenue, known as "the Curve." People's Grocery was new competition to a store run by W. H. Barrett. Barrett was white, but he relished the profits from selling to blacks in the racially mixed neighborhood around the Curve.

The violence that ended in the lynching of Tom Moss started with a fight between black boys and white boys over a game of marbles. Angry that his son had come out badly, Cornelius Hearst took a horsewhip to one of the black kids. A group of angry black fathers then gathered outside Hearst's home and incidentally next to People's Grocery.

As tension built, W. H. Barrett exploited rumors of impending black violence to convince a local judge to issue arrest warrants for "agitators" who gathered around People's Grocery. Armed with the knowledge that the warrants would be served, Barrett then spread the rumor that a white mob was intending to raid the store.

The managers of People's Grocery got their guns and prepared for the attack. When they saw a group of armed men approaching the back of the store at around ten o'clock that night, their fears seemed confirmed. The advancing group, none of them in uniform, actually was deputized and charged with serving the warrant insti-gated by W. H. Barrett. There is dispute about who fired the first shot. But it is clear that three deputies were wounded in the exchange of gunfire.

While bystanders fled, the remaining deputies sent for reinforcements, and the occupants of People's Grocery were arrested. Tom Moss was not among them but was later described as the ringleader and the person who shot at least one of the deputies. Moss claimed to be at home with his wife during the gunfight, and another man was initially charged with firing the shot later blamed on Moss. The white press depicted the event as a bloody riot and ambush by a murderous band of Negroes. Scores of white men were deputized. They arrested at least thirty alleged conspirators.

Fearing mob action, a black militia guarded the jail for two nights. But on the third night, the black guard dissolved. With the jail unguarded, a crowd seized Tom Moss, Calvin McDowell, and Will Stewart, dragged them to a spot north of town, beat them, gouged their eyes, and finally—mercifully—shot them.

Lynching was nothing new in in this era. But the killing of Moss, McDowell and Stewart was different. It was the first time in Wells's experience that "respect-able" black folk had been lynched. None of the men had any sort of criminal record and all of them worked in jobs that were essentially middle-class. The killing of Tom Moss also was intensely personal for Wells. She was godmother to his daughter and she wrote later that Moss and his family were her best friends in Memphis.

Black reaction to the lynching ranged from outrage to fearful talk of leaving the city for destinations as varied as Liberia and newly opening territory in Oklahoma. Wells was not in Memphis the night of the lynching, but when she returned, she wrote an angry editorial charging that Memphis had "demonstrated that neither character nor standing avails the Negro if he desires to protect himself against the white man or become his rival." Wells condemned the city's attempt to disarm black citizens and ban gun sales to blacks while deputizing white men and boys to enter black homes, seize firearms, and help themselves "to ammunition without payment."[2]

The lynching provoked wide outrage in the black press, with angry calls for justice and even vengeance. The *Kansas City American Citizen* editorialized that the lynching "called for something more than patient endurance—it calls for dynamite and bloodshed." The *Langston City Herald* asked, "what race or class of people on God's footstool would tolerate the continual slaughter of its own without a revolt?"

Wells joined the charge, expanding her criticism to the federal government and black federal officeholders, asking, "where are our leaders when the race is being burnt, shot, and hanged?" This was partly a condemnation of vanishing federal support for blacks under the collapse of Reconstruction, but it also targeted the handful of Negroes on the public payroll who feared that agitation would jeopardize their positions.

At a practical level, Wells responded in familiar fashion. Prompted by the inability of even well-intentioned public officials to stop eminent violent threats, she explained later, "I had bought a pistol first thing after Tom Moss was lynched." She was in some sense tardy in this precaution. Over in Nashville, eighteen-year-old W. E. B. Du Bois, a freshman at Fisk University, observed in 1886 that his classmates, shaken by the rising tide of lynchings, were habitually armed whenever they ventured into the city.[3]

Wells now developed a sharper critique of the nature and impulse for lynching. She had seen black criminals lynched. But this was different.

> I had accepted the idea meant to be conveyed—that although lynching was irregular and contrary to law and order, unreasoning anger over the terrible crime of rape led to lynching; that perhaps the brute deserved to die anyhow and the mob was justified in taking his life.
>
> But Tom Moss, Calvin McDowell, and [Will] Lee Stewart had been lynched . . . with just as much brutality as other victims of the mob; and they had committed no crime against white women. This is what opened my eyes to what lynching really was. An excuse to get rid of Negroes who were acquiring wealth and property and thus keep the race terrorized and keep the "nigger down."

During the period that white America dubbed the Gay Nineties, lynchings of blacks in the South averaged about two per week. Wells's increasingly cutting assessment of the terror launched her into dangerous territory. She started suggesting that frequent claims of rape by white women proved too much. "Eight Negroes lynched since last issue of the *Free Speech* . . . on the same old racket, the alarm about raping white women. If southern white men are not careful, they will overreach themselves and public sentiment will have a reaction; a conclusion will then be reached which will be very damaging to the moral reputation of their women."[4] The implication here was incendiary. The *Memphis Commercial* fulminated that southern white men would not long tolerate "the obscene intimations" of Wells's editorial. It was an accurate assessment.

Wells was in New York when white men went on the warpath. Before it was over, Wells's coeditor at the *Memphis Free Speech* was run out of town, and the paper's offices were destroyed. Wells was warned that it would hazard her life to return. She decided to stay in New York after learning that some of the black men of Memphis were risking their lives by organizing an armed squad to protect her.

Ironically, being exiled from Memphis launched Wells onto the broader stage of New York City and dramatically widened the audience for her work. With her investment in the *Memphis Free Speech* consumed by the mob, Wells joined T. Thomas Fortune's *New York Age*, where her reporting would garner national and international recognition.[5]

From New York, Wells's attack was unrelenting. She struck hard at the myth that lynching was the product of the lawless element. She hammered the shibboleth of black rapists, arguing that the facts clearly viewed would "serve . . . as a defense for the Afro-American Samsons who suffer themselves to be betrayed by white Delilahs." Then, without the cover of euphemisms, she stated boldly that "there are many white women in the South who would marry colored men if such an act would not place them at once beyond the pale of society and within the clutches of the law."

Her most blistering tactic was to use white sources and reporting to make her case. She reveled in the report of Mrs. J. C. Underwood, an Ohio minister's wife who claimed she had been raped by a black man, then recanted, acknowledging the "strange fascination" the Negro had for her. She admitted to lying about the rape on the worry that she might have contracted venereal disease or become pregnant with a black child.

Wells found plenty of other fodder in the southern papers. In one short spate, the white Memphis press covered six cases of white women taking black lovers. From all across the South, Wells gathered stories showing poor, middle-class, and affluent white women, the prostitute and the physician's wife, as willing sexual partners with black men. She reprinted news of white women who had given birth to black children and refused to name the father. She gloried in a *Memphis Ledger* report in June 1892 decrying the circumstances of Lillie Bailey, "a rather pretty white girl, seventeen years of age, who . . . is the mother of a little coon" and refused to identify "the Negro who had disgraced her." For Wells this demonstrated that the pretty white girl had some affection for the father of the "little coon."[6]

Along with her ever more incisive critique of lynch terror, Wells developed a keener sense of the necessity and value of defensive firearms. Celebrating the recent evidence of blacks defending themselves and preventing lynchings through armed self-defense in Jacksonville, Florida, and Paducah, Kentucky, she advanced her classic prescription for armed self-defense. "*The lesson this teaches and which every*

Afro-American should ponder well, is that the Winchester rifle should have a place of honor in every black home. The more the Afro-American yields and cringes and begs, the more he is insulted, outraged and lynched."[7]

It was a bold prescription, perhaps even foolhardy. But Wells was keenly aware of the hazards. She understood firsthand from the lynching of Tom Moss the danger of drawing guns, only to be outnumbered and finally outgunned. But she also saw clearly the potential utility of firearms and the moral case for fighting back against violent aggressors. The implications of this simple insight, ancient in its roots, would resonate throughout her life's work.

Like Frederick Douglass, who advised Negroes to acquire a good revolver against the threat of slave catchers, Wells seems to have avoided getting into any gunfights. Indeed, while we know that Wells purchased a pistol after Tom Moss was lynched, it is not clear whether she actually owned a Winchester rifle. But the circumstances of Wells's purchase of part interest in the *Memphis Free Speech* newspaper are suggestive.

Wells shared ownership in the paper with Reverend Taylor Nightingale. Pushed by the mounting anger over a *Free Speech* editorial applauding Negroes' violent response to a lynching in Georgetown, Kentucky, Nightingale would flee Memphis for the Oklahoma Territory. The style of the editorial suggests that Wells actually wrote it:

> Those Georgetown Kentucky Negroes who set fire to the town last week because a Negro named Dudley had been lynched, show some of the true spark of manhood by their resentment. We had begun to think the Negroes—where lynching of Negroes has become the sport and pastime of unknown (?) White citizens— hadn't manhood enough in them, to wriggle and crawl out of the way, much less protect and defend themselves. Of one thing we may be assured, so long as we permit ourselves to be trampled upon, so long we will have to endure it.[8]

Although this was likely Wells's work, the editorial was unsigned and the immediate blame was laid on Nightingale, whose known militancy included urging everyone in his congregation to buy Winchester rifles. Wells and Nightingale were sympathetic friends, and perhaps both of them found the idea of the Winchester simply a potent rhetorical tool. But at least one researcher concludes that Nightingale did in fact own a Winchester rifle. And given the times, it would be no surprise if both he and Wells counted Winchesters among their important possessions.

The Winchester reference appears again in the public bickering between Wells and black leaders in Memphis. Writing from New York, Wells poked again at the rape theme, asking facetiously why white women of the South were so often in the position to cry rape so long after the supposed fact. Attempting to keep the city from exploding over the insult, black minister B. A. Imes published a letter criticizing Wells, including a gratuitous attack hinting at promiscuity. Wells answered with her own personal attack, demonstrating to all that Reverend Imes was overmatched. This actually built sympathy for Imes and raised the objection that it was unfair for Wells, sitting in New York, to criticize people like Imes, who remained "in a bloody city while looking along the barrel of a ready Winchester."[9]

The repeated references to the Winchester seem purposeful. It was the state-of-the-art repeating rifle of the day. One formal review of the Henry Model Winchester reported "187 shots were fired in three minutes and thirty seconds and one full fifteen shot magazine was fired in only 10.8 seconds. A total of 1,040 shots were fired and hits were made from as far away as 348 feet at an 18 inch square target with a .44 caliber 216 grain bullet." This gun was the assault rifle of its day. With its medium-range ballistic superiority (compare the Winchester's .44 caliber, 216 grain projectile to the .22 caliber, 55 grain AR-15 round), it still surrenders little to its twenty-first-century progeny.[10]

When Ida Wells advised black folk on the virtues of the Winchester rifle, one of her practical examples was the averted lynching in Paducah, Kentucky. She was referencing the episode in July 1892 where, following another lynching just a month earlier, a Negro was arrested for peeking into windows at white women. Primed for the threat, community men gathered to guard the jailhouse. As expected, a group of white toughs eventually showed up.

With no attempt to parlay, the Negroes fired on them, fatally wounding one. For whites, this confirmed rumors that blacks had been stockpiling weapons and planning retaliation for the earlier lynching. Local papers warned of the race war to come.

The governor sent in the state militia, and police seized guns from the hardware stores and distributed them among the white men of Paducah. For blacks, they took the opposite approach, searching black homes and confiscating firearms. In a natural survey of the scale of Negro gun ownership, they seized more than 200 guns from black homes. Eventually tensions subsided to an uneasy peace.[11]

The second averted lynching occurred on July 4, in Jacksonville, Florida. In the early afternoon, a Negro teamster named Ben Reed and a white shipping clerk at the Anheuser-Busch brewery got into a row over Reed's tardiness in making a delivery. The shipping clerk was a young man, excited to close down early and join the Independence Day festivities. Reed was pushing forty and resented the harsh talk from a white kid. They exchanged insults, then blows. The combat escalated as they attacked each other with the tools and hardware of the loading dock. By the end of it, Ben Reed was in police custody, charged with the murder of the young white man.

As the news spread, so did the lynch rumors. Considering the times, the response of the black community was no overreaction. The *Florida Times-Union* provided the account that would soon make its way to Ida Wells.

> Every approach to the jail was guarded by crowds of negroes armed to the very teeth. The city was virtually under their control. . . . Sentinels stood on every street corner, and when a white man would pass they would question him about where he was going, etc. A whistle signal would then be passed on to the next corner and the pedestrian would be surrounded and followed. If he went in the direction of the jail, the Negroes would close in upon him and he would soon find himself covered by fifty or more cocked revolvers. He would be interrogated again and after being treated to abusive language would then be ordered to go back.

Over the next three days, the crowd of armed Negroes surrounding the jail grew to nearly one thousand, and a counterforce of whites began pouring in from as far away as north Georgia. Finally, on July 7, a show of force by the governor's militia, brandishing a Gatling gun, and a spate of torrential rains dispersed the crowds without bloodshed. Except for the cocksure young man who goaded Ben Reed, no one died in those tense moments at Jacksonville. Reed was convicted of murder and sentenced to life imprisonment at hard labor.[12]

Other, similar episodes confirmed the potential for Negroes with guns to thwart lynch violence. In 1888, in the village of Wahalak, Kemper County, Mississippi, armed black men exchanged gunfire with an impromptu posse that pursued a black kid into the Negro quarters. The black boy had fought a local white kid to a draw. This prompted a band of Kemper County men to ride to the defense of white superiority. Two whites and several blacks were killed in gunfire. But the Negro boy who dared to come out even in a fair fight was not lynched.[13]

In 1899, in the town of Darien, Georgia, a prominent black man was jailed on the familiar charge of rape. The rumor spread that the sheriff planned to turn him over to the mob. The blacks of Darien were numerous and organized enough to thwart the mob with armed sentinels posted at the jailhouse and an understanding that folk should rush to the jail if they heard the bell of the nearby Baptist church. These defensive efforts were a troublesome show of defiance to whites who dubbed it the "Darien Insurrection."[14]

Of course, these arguably salutary results are not the full story. Legitimate or not, violence can unleash a whirlwind. The background worry of armed blacks provoking white backlash is illustrated by a lynching in Mayfield, Kentucky, just thirty miles from Paducah. The spark was the fear of black retribution for earlier lynchings nearby.

Jim Stone, one of the Negroes who would die in Mayfield, was rumored to be the leader of the conspiracy. The evidence of an impending Negro attack was the unusual insolence of Mayfield's blacks and the fact that they were increasingly going about armed. That was enough to send the mob after Jim Stone, who was lynched in December 1896.

There was no community intervention against the lynching of Jim Stone. But there was suspected retaliation in the form of mysterious fires and the shooting of a white man who boldly ventured into a black saloon. The violence culminated with the deputizing of one hundred white men who attempted to fully disarm the blacks of Mayfield. These deputies tore through the community, burned four homes, and shot up others. By the end of it, now mostly disarmed and cowed, the blacks who had not fled delivered a hundred-signature petition to the municipal government, praying to end hostilities and promising no more revenge for the recent lynchings. Their terms of surrender were accepted, and a peace of sorts was restored to Mayfield.[15]

The ending was similar in Danville, Virginia, where a gunfight precipitated a cycle of violence. It was 1883, and tensions were already high in anticipation of upcoming elections when black and white men passed too close on the sidewalk. Arms touched. The white man took offense. They argued, and the black man's insolence sent the white man for his revolver. They scuffled and that drew a crowd, and then there was gunfire. By the end of it, three black men and one white were killed, and six blacks and four whites were wounded. Armed whites then locked down the town, warning Negroes to stay off the streets. This climate suppressed the black vote on Election Day and helped Democrats to prevail.[16]

Although diminished compared to the Civil War period, black political violence continued into the late nineteenth century. The populist movement of the era offers good examples. Ideally, populism subordinated racial distinctions to shared values and political concerns of the working class. In practice, race still trumped. But despite the failed ideals of racial harmony, the impulse toward collective action by working people still generated episodes of armed resistance that contribute to our thinking about the black tradition of arms.[17]

In Jefferson County, Georgia, populist leader Thomas Watson made direct appeals to black voters and exhorted mixed-race audiences of populists. Although Watson rejected black and white social equality, he pressed the common political concerns of working men. Campaigning in 1892, Watson appeared on the stage with Negro populist Reverend H. S. Doyle. Doyle's life was threatened several times during the campaign, and a shot fired at him during a Jefferson County meeting actually killed a white man in the crowd. When Doyle was subsequently targeted for lynching, he retreated to Watson's farm, where two thousand armed populists, black and white, rallied to guard him.[18]

In 1886, in Lasky County, Arkansas, about forty Negro workers affiliated with the populist Knights of Labor, struck the Tate plantation, seeking a wage increase. The Knights had enjoyed some recent organizing success, and that spurred the black men to further militancy. They boldly warned the local sheriff not to interfere with their strike. He dismissed the warning and rode with help to break them up. When one of the workers confronted him, the sheriff shot the man, wounding him. The gunshot drew attention, and soon the sheriff and his little squad were surrounded by 250 armed Negroes. The sheriff retreated but later returned with reinforcements. By then, many of the black men had dispersed. The remaining strikers briefly resisted, but after a few volleys of gunfire, they scattered.[19]

In Leflore County, Mississippi, Negro farmworkers of the Colored Alliance overplayed the power of bluff after one of their leaders was threatened. They drafted an angry letter, promising to defend their leader by force, and signed it "3000 armed men." Then 75 of them assembled in military order and marched to town to deliver it. While many of them were armed, they were not three-thousand-strong. Their letter fueled rumors that blacks were massing for an attack. Soon, the call was out to the governor, who sent in three companies of Mississippi National Guard. This force, accompanied by a large group of armed civilians, plus the sheriff with his own force, rode out after the supposed conspirators. Before it was over, scores of Negroes were shot down.[20]

In the modern debate, many approach armed self-defense empirically, extrapolating from general trends whether or not it is a good bet. Some object that this strips out variables that make every case unique and demand private choice. Others invoke higher principles and exalt even failed self-defense as heroism.

Ida B. Wells fit into this last group. Where some saw foolish, fruitless acts of armed resistance, Wells saw the stuff of legend. This is nowhere more evident than in her 1900 paean to Robert Charles of New Orleans. The white press called Charles a lawless desperado. But Wells projected the evident black consensus that Charles was the "hero of New Orleans."[21]

Robert Charles was conceived in slavery but born into freedom in the vicinity of Vicksburg, Mississippi. He was a decently hard worker, with a man's fondness for liquor and women. Like many men of the time, he habitually carried a pistol.

The extent of this practice is suggested by studies of southern convict labor schemes, which used the charge of carrying a concealed weapon and other minor offenses like vagrancy, using obscene language, and selling cotton after sunset, to funnel cash-poor black men into a system that leased them out to whoever paid their fines. The crime of carrying a concealed weapon, enforced primarily against Negroes, was, by the turn of the century, one of the most consistent methods of dragooning blacks into the system.[22]

So it was not unusual that Robert Charles and his friend Leonard Pierce tucked .38 caliber Colt revolvers into their belts and headed out into the sticky July evening. At around 11:00 p.m., Charles and Pierce were sitting on the stoop of a row house, awaiting the return of Charles's sister and her roommate, when two white New Orleans policemen approached. The progression from "What's your business here?" to violence was quick.

As Charles attempted to stand, one of the cops grabbed him. Charles pulled back, and the cop drew his club and then his revolver. Charles drew his own gun and they both fired, each taking nonfatal bullet wounds. Charles took off, leaving Leonard Pierce behind. Pierce identified Charles and told police where to find him.

Slowed by his wound, Charles eventually made it back to his rented room, where he retrieved his Winchester rifle. The New Orleans police were not far behind. A squad of them approached and yelled for him surrender. Charles flung open the door and killed the captain with a bullet to the heart. Then he fired on two others, killing one of them with a shot through the eye. Two more in the rear retreated to an adjacent apartment. Charles stalked them briefly and then fled.[23]

The flight of Robert Charles precipitated more than a police manhunt. It provoked a mob that ranged through the city, attacking targets of opportunity. It then descended on the parish prison, aiming to lynch Leonard Pierce. The prison was well defended, and there were no jailers willing to hand over Pierce, so the mob went back to random attacks. By morning, mobbers had killed three blacks and beaten approximately fifty others.

The next day, police investigated a tip that Charles was hiding out in the home of friends on Saratoga Street. Charles had been there for hours, casting bullets and loading cartridges. As two officers entered the building, Charles shot them both with a barrage from his Winchester.[24]

In the street, the crowd that had followed the cops was growing by the minute. By the early evening, one thousand armed men surrounded the building. Soon there would be more than ten thousand. People ducked for cover when Charles popped up from a second-story window and opened fire, killing one man in the crowd. Thoroughly surrounded, Charles surely appreciated that this was where he would die.

The details of the gun battle seem embellished over time, with reports of five thousand shots fired into the second story where Charles huddled. If the reports are to be believed, Charles's marksmanship and his capacity to avoid return fire were uncanny. Under a deluge of gunfire, Charles got off another fifty shots, killing two men in the crowd before finally succumbing to multiple wounds. Charles was dead, but the unsated mob spread through the city, killing three more Negroes and burning a black school.

The incident is partly an affirmation of the danger of spillover and escalation from one incident into a cycle of violence and retribution. But it also raises the question, what motivated Robert Charles? Some contend that Charles was smoldering over the grotesque lynching of Sam Hose in Newman, Georgia, and focused his ire on the state government, which had recently stripped the vote from blacks. When his first victim, the New Orleans flatfoot, drew his club and pistol, Charles was already primed for war. Other reports said that Robert Charles was driven mad by cocaine. Republicans and Democrats said the episode demonstrated the worst ramifications of the opposing party's policies. The Democratic press painted Charles as a prime example of a dangerous breed, the "bad nigger."[25]

For all the carnage he wrought, Robert Charles received remarkably sympathetic treatment from Ida B. Wells. But her assessment ranged far beyond the immediate conflict. For Wells, the incident was part of a broader current that included the lynching of Sam Hose, who had killed his employer in self-defense, and a dozen other lynchings that she had covered in the previous few months. The root problem, Wells said, was the cops' "assurance born of long experience in the New Orleans service . . . that they could do anything to a Negro that they wished," even though Charles and Pierce "had not broken the peace in any way whatever, no warrant was in the policeman's hands to justify arresting them and no crime had been committed of which they were suspects."

Just as she did in the attacks on lynching, Wells turned white press reports to her advantage. The *Times Democrat* revealed the reason Charles and Pierce were confronted in the first place. The neighborhood had been "troubled with bad Negroes" and the neighbors were complaining to the Sixth Precinct police about them. Charles and Pierce had been sitting on a doorstep long enough that someone considered them suspicious, and police came to run them off.

Some would say that the greatest hazard was the black men carrying guns in the first place, that Charles was no hero but was simply foolish. But Wells's depiction of Charles's last stand sounds like a Texan describing the heroes of the Alamo:

> Betrayed into the hands of the police, Charles, who had already sent two of his would-be murderers to their death, made a last stand in a small building, 1210 Saratoga St., and still defying his pursuers, fought a mob of 20,000 people single-handed and alone, killing three more men, mortally wounding two more and seri-

ously wounding nine others. Unable to get him in his stronghold, the besiegers set fire to his house of refuge. While the building was burning Charles was shooting, and every crack of his death-dealing rifle added another victim to the price which he had placed upon his own life. Finally when fire and smoke became too much for flesh and blood to stand, the long sought for fugitive appeared in the door, rifle in hand, to charge the countless guns that were drawn upon him. With a courage which was indescribable, he raised his gun to fire again, but this time it failed, for 100 shots riddled his body, and he fell dead face front to the mob.[26]

The Robert Charles shooting is a dramatic episode within a broad practice of arms that included plenty of prosaic beneficial gun use as well as ordinary crime and stupidity. Textured renditions of those more pedestrian episodes are rare. But there is a good example in the account of young Louis Armstrong, who reveals a pivotal episode of stupidity with a gun within a subculture that seemed to have plenty of it.

Armstrong's autobiography suggests that firearms were common among the denizens of black New Orleans at the turn of the century. Before he became the world-renowned horn player, Armstrong waded through the streets and dives of New Orleans and actually was set on his way to fame and fortune by a foolish act with a gun.

As a teenager, Armstrong, armed with a pistol, dived into a stupid contest of bravado that leaves one thinking sympathetically about modern stop-and frisk programs. Armstrong and his fledging musical troupe were roaming the streets, singing for money. According to Armstrong, it was common to celebrate the holidays by "shooting off guns and pistols or anything loud so as to make as much noise as possible." So when he ventured out New Year's Day, he took the .38 caliber revolver that his mother kept in a cedar chest. It was a common gun, the same type that Robert Charles had carried.

On Rampart Street, Armstrong's little group passed by a kid who had made similar preparations. Armstrong was laughing and singing when "all of a sudden a guy on the opposite side of the street pulled out a little old six-shooter pistol and fired it off." Armstrong's friends goaded him, "Go get him, Dipper." Armstrong pulled his gun "and let her go." Armstrong's gun was evidently a larger caliber. The noise and smoke frightened the other kid away, and Armstrong proceeded down Rampart Street, triumphant. He reloaded and started to shoot into the air again, when "a couple of strong arms came from behind" and dragged him off to jail.[27]

Armstrong's recklessness earned him a stay in the Colored Waifs Home, where he picked up a cornet from a little shelf of cast-off instruments. Armstrong's story ended well. Many Negroes who reached for a gun were not nearly so lucky. And it demonstrates the power of the self-defense impulse that a robust black tradition of arms developed in spite of the unpredictable and often-tragic results of owning and using guns.

Ida Wells surely wrestled with the worry that violence is an unpredictable catalyst.[28] Although we have sparse good data on black gun crime at the turn of the century, we know that by 1920 the black homicide rate in many southern cities exceeded the exceptional murder rates of today's black underclass. Anecdotal evidence suggests that this tracks earlier trends. Wells surely was aware of the ordinary interracial violence and common stupidity with guns illustrated by Louis Armstrong's boyhood recklessness. Still, she erred toward folk having the option of armed self-defense, and that judgment was shared by prominent blacks of the day.

Having already lost so much politically, and pushed further by the horror of lynch law, blacks at the end of the nineteenth century were operating in perhaps the most desperate time of their American experience. And lest anyone think that things could get no worse, the United States Supreme Court would soon invite further indignities in *The Civil Rights Cases*, concluding that neither the Thirteenth nor the Fourteenth Amendment were sufficient authority to sustain the public accommodations sections of the Civil Rights Act. This gave a green light to the full array of Jim Crow Laws and demonstrated for many the need for a national civil-rights organization to defend black interests. It also underscored the importance of self-help on a number of measures, including personal security.[29]

No one was more animated on this point than the man who sheltered Ida Wells after she burned her bridges in Memphis, fiery editor of the *New York Age*, T. Thomas Fortune. Fortune was born a slave in Florida, in 1856. He came of age during Reconstruction and witnessed its promise and disappointment as his father Emanuel rose and fell in the tide of postwar politics. Like many blacks who staked their hopes on Reconstruction, Emanuel Fortune confronted white opposition united in its disdain for black rule—Whigs, Democrats, the landed rich, the rural poor, and the merchant class put aside their differences and coalesced around their common whiteness. Their opposition to Reconstruction was not just political but violent.[30]

A delegate to the 1868 Florida constitutional convention, Emanuel Fortune was a rising star among black Republicans. And that made him and his political friends targets of violence. Just after nightfall in 1869, one of Fortune's cohorts, Freedman's Bureau agent W. J. Purman, was shot from the shadows while walking across the town square. Purman limped to safety and managed to survive. In the days that followed, a group of armed black men paid him a discreet visit and pledged to sack the village if Purman gave the word. It is not clear if Emanuel Fortune was part of this group. But it is clear that Fortune was armed and prepared to fight.

Even before the shooting of W. J. Purman, Emanuel Fortune was wary of the mounting threats. Fearing ambush, he stopped traveling after nightfall, developed an enviable skill with a rifle, and made detailed preparations for any attack on his home.

At the first hint of trouble, the children were to run upstairs. His wife, Sarah Jane, would then open the door and shield herself behind it. Emanuel, from the cover of a barricade he built in the center of the room, would open fire with his rifle.[31]

One longs for more on the effect that this planning had on young Timothy as he passed by the barricade every day, and played on and around the bulking reminder that any random night might bring a gunfight. So far as we can tell, Emanuel Fortune's defensive plan was uncashed insurance, but the fighting spirit it reflected burned hot in his son Timothy.

Soon after the election of 1876 closed the door on Reconstruction, Timothy Thomas Fortune moved to New York, where he would eventually establish a newspaper that became the *New York Age* and later simply *The Age*. Fortune proved to be a kindred spirit for Ida Wells, at least for a time. He surrendered nothing to her in his militancy, and he endorsed armed self-defense just as fervently, although perhaps less colorfully.

T. Thomas Fortune and Ida Wells were part of a new generation of activists in the freedom struggle. Some of them started newspapers—men like Harry C. Smith, who established the *Cleveland Gazette*, and W. Calvin Chase, who started the *Washington Bee*. Others, like New York lawyer T. McCants Stewart, made their mark in the professions or in business. Richard T. Greener, the first black graduate of Harvard, characterized this new generation as "Young Africa, stronger in the pocket and mildly contemptuous of the lofty airs of the old decayed colored aristocracy." These men and women channeled the voice of the "New Negro," a rising class of black agitators who, Fortune asserted, were "the death knell of the shuffling, cringing creature in black who for two centuries and a half had given the right-of-way to white men."[32]

Fortune was an articulate but volatile affiant of the black tradition of arms. Although he proposed to respect the line between political violence and self-defense, his passion fueled a rhetorical style that sometimes treaded close to the boundary. Describing the agenda and strategy of his proposed national civil-rights organization, the Afro-American League, Fortune exhorted, "we propose to accomplish our purposes by the peaceful methods and agitation through the ballot and the courts. But if others use the weapons of violence to combat our peaceful arguments, it is not for us to run away from violence. . . . Attucks, the black patriot—he was no coward! . . . Nat Turner—he was no coward! . . . If we have work to do, let us do it. And if there comes violence, let those who oppose our just cause 'throw the first stone.'"[33] Looking out desperately toward the new century, Fortune declared, "to be murdered by mobs is not to be endured without protest, and if violence must be met with violence, let it be met. If the white scamps lynch and shoot you, you have the right to do the same."[34]

Some criticized him for agitating from the relative comfort and safety of New York City, but Fortune had endured his share of racism and did not shy from a fight. In fact, he seems consciously to have picked one in 1890 when he entered the bar at the Trainor Hotel on Thirty-Third Street and demanded a glass of beer. He was refused service, as he apparently expected. In the record from a subsequent trial, the bar owner claimed that Fortune threatened to "mop up the floor with anyone who laid hands on him."

Fortune gave a different account of the conflict. He sued the bar owner for assault, solicited donations for a litigation fund, and ultimately won a thousand-dollar jury verdict. The black press celebrated Fortune's victory. He was the model of the New Negro, said the *Indianapolis Freeman*, adding that in the past "the Negro's greatest fault was being a magnificent sufferer."[35]

The allegation that Fortune had threatened to mop up the floor with anyone who laid hands on him is consistent with his editorial stance. Denouncing a Georgia court decision allowing railroad conductors to send black first-class passengers back to the smoking car, Fortune advised Negroes to "knock down any fellow who attempts to enforce such a robbery."

Cognizant that he was advising Negroes to strike the first blow, Fortune equivocated, "we do not counsel violence; we counsel manly retaliation." Then, capturing the dilemma that state failure and malevolence posed for blacks, he reasoned, "in the absence of law . . . we maintain that the individual has every right in law and equity to use every means in his power to protect himself."

Fortune's militant stance extended explicitly to the use of firearms. Commenting on an interracial gunfight in Virginia, Fortune wrote, "if white men are determined upon shooting whenever they have a difference with a colored man, let the colored man be prepared to shoot also. . . . If it is necessary for colored men to arm themselves and become outlaws to assert their manhood and their citizenship, let them do it."[36]

This editorial drew a harsh response from the white press. One paper argued that Fortune's advice would provoke a race war that blacks could not win. Fortune responded with an essay titled "The Stand and Be Shot or Shoot and Stand Policy": "We have no disposition to fan the coals of race discord," Thomas explained, "but when colored men are assailed they have a perfect right to stand their ground. If they run away like cowards they will be regarded as inferior and worthy to be shot; but if they stand their ground manfully, and do their own a share of the shooting they will be respected and by doing so they will lessen the propensity of white roughs to incite to riot." On the last passionate turn, Fortune argued that a man who would not defend himself was properly deemed "a coward worthy only of the contempt of brave men."

Fortune's prescription here teases back and forth into the boundary-land between political violence and individual self-defense. The editor of the *Cincinnati Afro-American* saw Fortune's approach as utter folly and welcomed inclusion on "the list of cowards," arguing that it was indeed "better for the colored man to stand and be shot than to shoot and stand." This dissent provokes the question whether Fortune was on the edge of community sentiment or in the middle of it.

One signal of how Fortune's views resonated in the community is the long-standing but largely secretive connection between him and the conservative Booker T. Washington. In a decades-long relationship, Fortune was sometimes a daily correspondent with Washington and often served as ghostwriter for Washington's books, speeches, and editorials. Washington secretly financed Fortune's journalistic efforts, and when the *New York Age* was incorporated, Washington took a block of stock in exchange for his past and future support of the paper.

Fortune was a passionate race man and sometimes, especially in extemporaneous speeches, he projected a militant tone that the Wizard of Tuskegee surely deemed unwise. This was certainly the case in 1898 when an irate Fortune unleashed a tirade against President William McKinley's tour of reconciliation through the South. Incensed that McKinley was honoring Confederate dead while blacks were being lynched in the name of white supremacy, Fortune ranted, "I want the man whom I fought for to fight for me, and if he don't I feel like stabbing him."[37]

Later Fortune said that he had not advocated "physical assassination" but rather meant to stab McKinley at the ballot box. Still, his comments were widely criticized, and Booker T. Washington surely was not happy with the attack on the Republican president, who still held more promise for blacks than the Democrat alternative.[38]

We are left just to wonder about the conversations Washington and Fortune had on questions of defensive violence. When Washington died, his people scurried to retrieve their correspondence. But we know for sure that Washington was a gun owner. In 1915, the Tuskegee faculty presented the aging headmaster with a shotgun as a token of their affection. One of his biographers says that the gift reflected the faculty's desire that the aging and overworked Washington get some rest and recreation. But it also suggests Washington was familiar with firearms and reflects the prosaic nature of gun ownership in the culture of Tuskegee.[39]

Booker T. Washington's support of T. Thomas Fortune overlapped with a variety of controversial statements. At a speech at the African Methodist Episcopal Zion Church in Washington, DC, Fortune boiled over at reports from a recent conference, where prominent white university professors, ex-governors, and presidential cabinet members opined on the state of the Negro postemancipation. Several of them had seriously proposed repealing the Fifteenth Amendment, which guaranteed black male suffrage. Here Fortune saw no need to dance around the edges of political violence. He threatened that the same amount of blood that had secured the Fifteenth Amendment would be required to revoke it. He advised black folk, "if the law can afford no protection, then we should protect ourselves, and if need be, die in defense of our rights as citizens. The Negro can't win through cowardice."

The white press criticized that Fortune's prescription was folly "verge[ing] on crime." But Fortune put the question in terms of essential manhood and whether some versions of life are worse than death.

> The black man's right of self-defense is identically the same as the white man's right of self-defense. Tell me that I shall be exterminated, as you do, if I exercise that right and I will tell you to go ahead and exterminate—if you can. That is a game that two can always play at. And suppose you do exterminate me, what of it? Am I not nobler and happier exterminated while contending for my honest rights than living a low cur that any poor white sneak would feel free to kick?[40]

Fortune's passion spilled over again at a Philadelphia meeting of the Afro-American Press Association. Motivated by a new spate of lynchings, Fortune raged, "we have cringed and crawled long enough. I don't want anymore 'good niggers.' I want 'bad niggers.' It's the bad 'nigger' with the Winchester who can defend his home and children and wife." Fortune was followed by W. A. Pledger, editor of the *Atlanta Age*, who invoked the Winchester as the optimal tool against the mob.[41]

Fortune's response to turn-of-the-century rioting in Atlanta that destroyed neighborhoods and killed scores of blacks was unsurprising. "The trouble will go on in Atlanta," he said, "until the Negro retaliates—until driven to bay, the Negro slays his assailant." In correspondence with Emmett Scott, chief aid to Booker T. Washington, Fortune seethed, "What an awful condition we have in Atlanta. It makes my blood boil. I would like to be there with a good force of our men to help make Rome howl." Fortune dismissed "nonresistance," arguing to Scott that incidents like the Atlanta riot invited "contempt and massacre of the race."[42]

Fortune offered a series of episodes as models for black self-defense, including, prominently, an 1888 incident in Mississippi. It started with a black man's refusal to step aside for white people on the sidewalk and escalated into a nasty scrap. When the talk turned to lynching, the black men of the community grabbed their guns, laid an ambush, and, on Fortune's telling, fired on the "lynching party of white rascals, killing a few of them." Fortune excoriated the northern white press for casting the blame on the black men.

Fortune saw this incident as a model of black resistance, arguing that if whites "resort to the gun and the torch . . . let the colored men do the same, and if blood must flow like water and bonfires be made of valuable property, so be it all around, for what is fair for the white man to do to teach the Negro his place is fair for the Negro to do to teach the white man his place."[43]

There is some instinct to dismiss Fortune's rhetoric as a fringe voice in a sea of more levelheaded, nonviolent folk. But that dissolves under the assessment of Kelly Miller, dean of Howard University, who wrote in the *Amsterdam News* that Fortune "represented the best developed journalist that the Negro race has produced in the Western world. His editorials were accepted throughout the journalistic world as the voice of the Negro. Between the decline of Frederick Douglass and the rise of Booker T. Washington, Fortune was the most influential Negro in the country."[44]

There are many confirmations that Fortune was channeling community attitudes about armed self-defense. It is evident in the black reaction to the 1898 coup that extinguished Negro influence in Wilmington, North Carolina. Wilmington had a black voting majority and numerous black officeholders supported by a fusion ticket of populists and Republicans. Republicans controlled the board of aldermen, where three black members served. Blacks served prominently in the local judiciary, and black postmasters numbered more than twenty. All of this rested on a thriving black middle class of hoteliers, merchants, druggists, bakers, and grocers.

This success bred tensions, and things boiled over when Alex Manly, editor of the black newspaper the *Daily Record*, launched his own attack against the rape justification for lynching, arguing, "every Negro lynched is called a big burly black brute, when in fact, many of those who have thus been dealt with had white men for their fathers, and were not only not black and burly, but were sufficiently attractive for white girls of culture and refinement to fall in love with, as is very well known to all." Manly was doubly offensive as the embodiment of his own critique. He was the acknowledged mulatto son of former North Carolina governor Charles Manly.

These accumulated affronts drove Democrats over the edge. Backed by Klan-type organizations dubbed "Red Shirts" and "Rough Riders," Democrats summoned thirty-two of the city's prominent blacks and laid out their demands: All black officeholders in Wilmington must resign and Alex Manly must leave Wilmington.

Then, while the black elite were formulating a response, the Democrats launched a wave of violence that steamrolled the scattered Negro opposition. The Republican-Populist administration was ousted and replaced with Democrats. More than 1,400 blacks abandoned their property and fled the city. One commentator called it "the nation's first full-fledged coup d'état."[45]

Across the country, black reaction to the coup was visceral. A protest rally at the Fifth Avenue Baptist Church in Washington, DC, is emblematic. To a chorus of sympathetic cheers and angry tears, Colonel Perry Carson raged against the coup in Wilmington and lamented the lack of preparedness. Wilmington, he said, was an object lesson that blacks must, "prepare to protect yourselves; the virtues of your women and your property. Get your powder and your shot and your pistol." The

Washington Post was apoplectic, not so much about the Wilmington coup, but that a previously sensible colored man like Carson was urging Negroes to arms.[46]

Fig. 4.1. Newspaper coverage of the Wilmington race riots. (*New York Herald*, Friday, November 10, 1898.)

Lesser incidents provoked similar responses in the black press and even among the clergy, who extolled the self-defense impulse even where there was little hope of prevailing. In the *Cleveland Gazette*, Reverend C. O. Benjamin celebrated the heroism of a black man in Mississippi who resisted his white assailants, urging that "Negroes should stand like men."[47] Speaking before the Afro-American Press Association in 1901, W. A. Pledger of the *Atlanta Age* similarly advised that terrorists "are afraid to lynch us where they know the black man is standing behind the door with a Winchester."[48]

Pressing against the boundary of political violence, Bishop Alexander Walters of the AME Zion Church urged development of a national black organization with an explicit focus on community self-defense. In a March 10, 1898, letter in the *New York Age*, Walters exhorted, "after the late outrages perpetrated against postmasters Loften of Hogansville, Georgia, and Lake of Lake City, South Carolina, for no other reason than their race and color . . . it becomes absolutely necessary that we organize for self-protection."[49]

After the torture and burning at the stake of Sam Hose in 1899, with its incomprehensible carnival atmosphere, Walters was moved beyond restraint and openly advocated political violence. In an address to the New Jersey Methodist Conference,

Walters juxtaposed the recent American bloodshed to "free" Cubans and Filipinos from Spanish domination, with the barbarism of the southern lynch mob. "The greatest problem of America today," said Walters, "is not the currency question nor the colonial processions, but how to avoid the racial war at home. You cannot forever keep the Negro out of his rights. Slavery made a coward of him for 250 years, he was taught to fear the white man. He is rapidly emerging from such slavish fear and ere long will contend for his rights as bravely as any other man. In the name of the Almighty God, what are we to do but fight and die?"

When Bishop Walters's first concrete action after the Sam Hose lynching was to call for a day of prayer and fasting, W. Calvin Chase saw it as a retreat and criticized that it would have no impact on "cutthroats, lynchers and murderers." Chase said that blacks were "praying when they needed to strike." Julius F. Taylor, editor of the *Salt Lake Broad Axe*, affirmed this sentiment, urging that "the Negro must not expect to have his wrongs righted by praying, fasting and singing, but he must rely on his own strong arm to accomplish that objective."[50]

Although he may have been short on follow-through, Bishop Walters's statements are significant as a suggestion of how self-defense resonated within the community. And it speaks to the power of the self-defense impulse that, even within the black clergy, he was not alone. In 1897, following the lynching of two men in Louisiana, AME bishop Henry McNeal Turner wrote in the *Voice of the Missions* newspaper that Negroes should defend themselves with guns against the lynch mob. He urged blacks to acquire guns and "keep them loaded and ready for immediate use." Turner admitted that his views might be considered an unseemly departure for a man of God and that he had held his tongue for many years, out of concern for the religious organization he represented. But after the latest lynchings, he was now urging, "Get guns Negroes, get guns, and may God give you good aim when you shoot."[51]

This sentiment was shared by emerging black intellectual John Edward Bruce, lecturer, editor, self-taught historian, and founder of the Negro Society for Historical Research. Bruce reserved nothing in his condemnation of lynch violence. His October 5, 1889, speech in Washington, DC, urging violence in kind against the mob, is representative. "The man who will not fight for the protection of his wife and children," said Bruce, "is a coward and deserves to be so treated. The man who takes his life in his hand and stands up for what he knows to be right will always command the respect of his enemy." Bruce seemed unconcerned about treading over into advocacy of political violence:

> Let the Negro require at the hands of every white murder in the South or else-where a life for a life. If they burn your houses, burn theirs. If they kill your wives and children, kill theirs. Pursue them relentlessly. Meet force with force, every-where it is offered. If they demand blood, exchange with them until they are

Fig. 4.2. Negro leaders of the late nineteenth century, Frederick Douglass *(center)*, T. Thomas Fortune *(upper left)*, Booker T. Washington *(upper right)*, Garland Penn *(lower left)*, and Ida B. Wells *(lower right)*, circa 1900. (Courtesy of the New York Public Library; Schomburg Center for Research in Black Culture; Manuscripts, Archives, and Rare Books Division.)

satiated. By vigorous adherence to this course, the shedding of human blood by white men will soon become a thing of the past. Wherever and whenever the Negro shows himself to be a man he can always command the respect even of a cutthroat. Organized resistance to organized resistance is the best remedy for the solution of the vexed problem of the century which to me seems practical and feasible.[52]

Publisher and philanthropist Mrs. C. C. Steward urged that black folk take a lesson from their white neighbors, "The white man knows how to shoot and keeps his Winchesters. He teaches his wife and his baby boy to shoot." This was a lesson, said Steward, that "the Negro needs to learn. . . . A good double barrel rifle and plenty of ammunition will go a great deal further in protecting our families from being mobbed and lynched than all the prayers which can be sent up to heaven."

Considered against the sentiments of his peers, T. Thomas Fortune's views about armed self-defense were not at all unusual. And he did not build one of the highest-circulating Negro papers in the country by being out of step with the mood of black folk. On the theme of self-defense, Fortune's exhortations were not some tough medicine he was pushing onto the masses. He was channeling the sentiment of the community.

This sentiment was fueled in part by the failure of government at all levels to protect and serve black folk, a failure that drove calls for an array of black self-help strategies and spurred the development of national civil-rights organizations that Fortune and Ida B. Wells would help start. Fortune despaired at the lack of grassroots financial support for the Afro-American League, the organization he conceived in 1886. It would never really thrive, but the pulse of the league fueled development of the Afro American Council, the Committee of Twelve, the Niagara Movement, and ultimately the National Association for the Advancement of Colored People.[53]

∞

With federal abandonment of Reconstruction, rising lynch violence, and disenfranchisement of black voters, the outlook for blacks in the late nineteenth century seemed so dim that many Negroes thought the best thing to do was to leave. The grand schemes to settle in Liberia or the Caribbean are familiar. But there were also small-scale movements within regions.

In some cases, Negroes fled to urban centers, spurred by violence in the countryside. But there was also an impulse in the other direction. Following race riots in the urban North, Henry Highland Garnet advised flight to the countryside, complaining that "prejudice is so strong in cities, and custom is so set and determined, that it is impossible for us to emerge from the most laborious and the least profitable occupations. . . . For instance in the city of New York, a colored citizen cannot obtain a license to drive a cart! Many such inconveniences beset them on every hand."

Garnet surely idealized the countryside. But he was driven by an impulse familiar to many Negroes that there must be someplace better than where they were. And that impulse drove many black folk to strike out for the American West.[54]

The story of Negroes in the West is obscured by the dominant narrative of the white cowboy. Some research traces this tilt to the class and racial bias of Owen Wister, whose classic novel *The Virginian* in many ways frames the canon that feeds the popular narrative and drives much of the American mythology of the gun. But the reality was far richer than the myth. The real American West was not the lily-white scene portrayed in film but a far more racially mixed affair that contributes abundantly to the black tradition of arms.[55]

By 1870, roughly 284,000 blacks accounted for 12 percent of the population of sixteen Western states and territories. But Negroes actually show up as early as 1790, in a Spanish census, where roughly 20 percent of the populations of San Francisco, San Jose, Santa Barbara, and Monterey acknowledged African ancestry. Until the United States' conquest of the Mexican territory, about 15 percent of Californians continued to acknowledge African heritage. But with the coming of US rule, the incentive to deny Negro blood resulted in the large-scale "disappearance" of that population. These largely mixed-race people were still there, of course. But now they had stronger reasons to disclaim their African roots.[56]

The most obvious prewar path west for blacks was slavery. One underacknowledged aspect of this movement is the population that went west as slaves of Indians who were displaced from the southeast under the Indian Removal Act of 1830. Among the Five Civilized Tribes forced from the East, only the Seminoles of Florida abjured slavery and actually developed alliances and friendships with blacks in two separate waves of interaction.

As early as the 1690s, Spain tempted slaves from the English colonies into Florida with the promise of freedom under Spanish rule. In 1739, an African named Francisco Menendez actually commanded the stronghold at Fort Mose, with the assignment of protecting St. Augustine from attack. In 1740, his forces helped repel an English attack led by Georgia governor James Oglethorpe.

By the 1780s, Florida was home to Spanish-speaking Africans, fugitive slaves from the colonies, and indigenous and migrated Indian tribes, including the Seminoles. Fugitive slaves established maroon settlements in Spanish Florida with names like "Disturb Me If You Dare" and "Try Me If You Be Men." By 1819, when the United States purchased Florida from Spain, General Andrew Jackson commented that the transaction had finally closed "this perpetual harbor for our slaves."

Equally instructive is the 1837 assessment of the Second Seminole War by Major General Thomas Sidney Jessup: "This you may be assured, is a Negro, not an Indian war; and if it be not speedily put down, the South will feel the effects of it on their slave population before the end of the next season." Modern research echoes this view, concluding that the Second Seminole War is better described "as a Negro insurrection with Indian support."[57]

Fig. 4.3. Escape into the Swamps. (Drawing by B. West Clinedinst, from Harriet Beecher Stowe, *The Writings of Harriet Beecher Stowe* [Houghton, Mifflin/ Riverside Press, 1896].)

When the Five Nations were driven west under the 1830 Indian Removal Act, the four slave-owning tribes (Choctaw, Chickasaw, Cherokee, and Creek) took their Negro slaves with them. Wealthier members owned enough Negroes to constitute up to 15 percent of the tribal populations. Settling in newly designated Indian Territory (much of modern-day Oklahoma), they continued to hold and acquire slaves with the encouragement of Indian agents in the employ of the United States government.[58]

Negroes enslaved by Indians were generally better treated than the slaves of whites, a trend that caused one Indian agent to recommend bringing in white men to show how American slavery was supposed to be done. Still, the impulse to resist slavery generated breaks for freedom, and slaves sometimes deployed firearms in the attempt.

In November 1842, a group of Negroes in Weber Falls, Indian Territory, seized guns, horses, and supplies and fled to Mexico. Some suspected that Seminoles had incited the revolt. The fugitives were pursued by their Cherokee masters and fought them off in a two-day gun battle. Finally, Cherokee reinforcements subdued the runaways and returned them to punishments of whipping and hanging.[59] In other parts of Indian Territory, the population of runaway slaves was substantial enough to produce robust fugitive communities. One group of about two hundred built a fort on the Washita River and was blamed for raids and killings in the area for more than a decade.

Indian Territory would be surrounded by the Confederacy, and the Five Civilized Tribes aligned with the South during the Civil War. Tribal slaves freed after the Civil War accounted for one strand of the black population in the west, although, in a curious detail, slavery in Indian Territory was not dissolved by the Thirteenth Amendment in 1865 but by treaty in 1866.

Within the Indian nations, blacks fought for equal rights in a fashion that resembled the broader national struggle. But black Indians also acknowledged an advantage to living under the jurisdiction of the Indian Nations versus the United States. Black Indian leader O. S. Fox reminded his friends that "the opportunities for our people in that country far surpassed any of the kind possessed by our people in the U.S."

When the federal government divided tribal lands among individuals in the 1880s, freedmen of Indian masters were treated like members of the tribe and received homesteads of eighty-eight acres. While in the rest of United States, the final decades of the nineteenth century was one of the lowest points of the black American experience, in 1884, the Indian Nations were arguing the question of full equality for black members.[60]

The appetite for western expansion eventually consumed large parts of Indian Territory. In 1889, the federal government forced Indian tribes to surrender their land in exchange for cash and sparked the rush of homesteaders into Oklahoma Territory. Among those who lined up to claim their portion, approximately ten thousand were Negroes. The black Indians already in the territory dubbed these newcomers "State Negroes."

For blacks from the east, the promise of free land was an opportunity to build an independent black society. One of the most ambitious promoters of this movement was Edwin P. McCabe. McCabe had the grand vision of transforming the Oklahoma Territory into a black state where he would serve as governor. Toward that dream, McCabe founded the town of Langston, which seeded twenty-seven other black towns in the territory.

McCabe's ambitions were ill received by whites. An 1890 article from the *Kansas City News* reports that whites "almost foam at the mouth whenever McCabe's name is suggested for Governor [and] also at the idea of Negroes getting control." A concurrent *New York Times* report speculated that McCabe might soon be assassinated.

McCabe and his community appreciated the hazards. The threat was palpable in September 1891, as the Sac and Fox Indian reservations were scheduled to open for settlement. McCabe had been coaxing blacks for more than a year to come and claim their share of the bounty. He also was candid about the challenges.

Blacks had been run out of several other staging towns. But in Langston City, more than two thousand armed Negroes assembled in preparation for the land rush. After sporadic bouts of gunfire, McCabe himself was accosted and fired on by three white men. He was rescued by a group of friends wielding Winchester rifles. It was exactly the kind of scenario that prompted Ida B. Wells to advocate a Winchester in every Negro home. And within seven months of Negroes wielding Winchesters in defense of Edwin McCabe, Wells would walk among them in Oklahoma.[61]

Fig. 4.4. Portrait of Edwin McCabe.

After the Tom Moss lynching, the *Langston City Herald* solicited blacks in Memphis, urging that it "would be a good place for the colored people to leave." Some claimed that Tom Moss spent his last breath urging Negroes to abandon Memphis and head west. Exiled in New York, Ida B. Wells put a sharp point on the assessment of those in the Memphis emigration movement. "Many of our exchanges have been calling Memphis hell, without stopping to think they were doing the real hell an injustice. Hell . . . is a place of punishment for the wicked—Memphis is a place of punishment for the good, brave and enterprising."

Wells was serious about the prospect of western migration, but she was also cautious about endorsing a place she had never seen. In 1882, she undertook a fact-finding mission, traveling as a guest of her cousin's husband, I. F. Norris. Norris was an emigration agent paid to promote black settlement in Oklahoma. He arranged for Wells to see for herself whether Oklahoma was a promising destination for Negroes. Wells arrived in Oklahoma in April and spent three weeks there. She had meetings with the *Langston City Herald*, and it would be surprising if she did not discuss the recent attack on Edwin McCabe and his rescue by black men with Winchesters.[62]

Wells took the dignitary's tour, traveling from Langston City to the territorial capital of Guthrie, to Oklahoma City, and to the town of King Fisher. Along the way, she was encouraged to see black councilmen, constables, and school committees. But Wells also detected a clear sentiment of opposition to the "Africanizing" of Oklahoma manifested by multilayered threats.

Simmering hostilities in the town of King Fisher confirmed the wisdom of Wells's views about armed self-defense, and the black men of King Fisher were precisely in accord with Wells. They formed a squad of men armed with Winchester rifles and threatened to sack the town if anyone in their community was harmed. A traveling journalist observed, "the colored men in Oklahoma mean business. . . . They have an exalted idea of their own rights and liberties and they dare to maintain them. . . . I found in nearly every cabin visited a modern Winchester oiled and ready for use."[63]

Wells's final assessment of the Oklahoma Territory was skeptical. She might have been encouraged by the fact that a justifiable shooting of a white man by a Negro, like the incident in the black town of Boley, could conclude without a lynching. But she saw insufficient employment opportunities to support "an indiscriminate exodus of our people." And she probably was right about the inability of the territory to absorb a mass of blacks looking for jobs and neighborhoods like they would leave in Memphis. Still, *folk came.*[64]

The black towns in Indian Territory are only one aspect of the rich black presence in the west. Even among the solitary mountain men and trappers who operated on the edge of the frontier, Negroes carved their place. Notable among them was Jim Beckwith, son of a white man and a slave woman. Beckwith trapped beaver, survived gunfights, and lived and finally died among the Crow Indians. But for the happenstance of telling his story to a traveling reporter, Beckwith and his exploits would be lost to us. And while the number of these black mountain men cannot be determined for certain, it is clear that Beckwith was not unique. Witness Edward Rose, who appears in a broader treatment of the western mountain men of the 1830s. His reported exploits with the gun satisfy every western stereotype.[65]

Frontier-era conflicts along the color line become blurred and complicated as red, black, and white men mixed together in various contexts. A typical pathway for blacks into Texas was as slaves to migrating whites. These Negroes sometimes found themselves fighting Indian raiding parties that had attacked their white masters. In other situations, blacks actually joined with Indians in renegade raiding parties like the ones that attacked the Hoover family in 1861 and Texas rancher George Hazlewood in 1868. In some cases, Negroes were actually on both sides of the conflict, as in 1869 when a group of Indian fighters led by a black man attacked a dozen cowboys, killing three of them and wounding five others. They were finally run off by gunfire from a rescue party headed by a Negro cowboy.

In 1845, when Texas entered the union, it had about 100,000 white settlers and 35,000 slaves. By 1861, the slave population had grown to about 182,000. The promise of freedom in Mexico was a particular draw for slaves along the southern border. An 1845 report from Houston illustrates the character of that resistance. According to the *Houston Telegraph*, a group of twenty-five Negroes escaped from Bastrop, "mounted on some of the best horses that could be found, and several of them were well armed. It is supposed that some Mexican . . . enticed them to flee to the Mexican settlements West of the Rio Grande."[66]

The draw to Mexico was strong enough that in 1854, the *Austin State Times* reported that more than 200,000 slaves had escaped to Mexico. This estimate is fantastically exaggerated (the 1860 census reported 182,556 slaves in Texas). But it does show that slave escapes into Mexico were a pressing concern. A more realistic estimate of Texas fugitives appears in the complaint of southwest Texas slave owners that more than four thousand fugitive Negroes were living across the border.[67]

The worry about Mexico as a growing haven for fugitives boiled over in 1855. A border settlement of Indians and fugitive Negroes led by a chief named Wildcat had been a particular lure for Texas slaves. The settlement was such a draw for runaways that south Texas slaveholders raised $20,000 for a punitive expedition against it. In 1855, one hundred thirty Texans led by a captain of the Texas Rangers rode across the border to break up the settlement and retrieve fugitive slaves. They were repelled by a superior force of Negroes, Indians, and Mexicans who were waiting in ambush. Roundly whipped, they fled back across the border carrying their wounded and some baubles from the little town of Piedras Negras that they looted on the way out.[68]

Presidents James Polk and Zachary Taylor both pressed Mexico to return fugitive slaves to their owners. The precise Mexican reply, that "no foreign government would be allowed to touch a slave who had sought refuge in Mexico," probably never filtered down to the average Texas slave. But there was plainly an appreciation among Negroes that freedom lay south. This was the draw for a slave girl named Rachel who, along with two others, stole guns and fled across the border. A slave named Bill followed the same script. The "bright mulatto . . . knocked down his overseer and ran off with a double barrel shotgun."[69]

Although dwarfed by the population of slaves, free blacks pursued their own opportunities in the prewar west. A rare and striking case is the Ashworth family, which in 1850 owned two thousand acres of land, more than five thousand head of cattle, and at least a dozen slaves. In a swirl of jealousy, ambition, and tribalism, they tumbled to the center of what came to be known as the Orange County War.

Originally from Louisiana, the Ashworths settled around the east Texas town of Madison (now Orange) in the early 1830s. Census records show four brothers and their families. There is some dispute about whether they fought for the Republic of Texas in its war of independence from Mexico. At least two of them sent substitutes.[70]

Technically the Ashworths were mixed-race people. At least one of the brothers was reportedly married to a white woman, although the distinction between them would have been difficult to discern just by looking. But the Ashworth's African lineage was sufficiently recorded that it took an act of the Texas Congress in 1840 to exempt them from legislation requiring free blacks to leave the republic.

This was quite a political feat for any Negro in the nineteenth century, and it reflected the bonds of business, family, and friendship that the Ashworths had built among the whites of east Texas. This included the county sheriff who, through business interests or some vague family connection, was a staunch ally of the Ashworths'.[71]

The Orange County War started over a hog. Clark Ashworth was charged with stealing it. And the proud Ashworth clan took offense at the accusation. The deputy who arrested Clark Ashworth for hog theft was from a different local faction than the sheriff. When Sam Ashworth confronted him, the deputy arrested Sam too, citing a law that punished "abusive language by Negroes."

After a trial where Sam Ashworth's African lineage was established by witnesses who said they considered him mulatto, the judge sentenced him to "thirty lashes on the bareback." The sentence was never executed because Sam's ally, the sheriff, allowed him to escape. But now Sam Ashworth had been provoked beyond consoling and plotted revenge. Aided by one of his younger cousins, Sam Ashworth laid an ambush for the deputy. They killed him with a barrage of shotgun and pistol fire. The sheriff went through the motions of investigating the shooting. But his allegiance was to the Ashworths.

Disgusted by the sheriff's perfunctory investigation, a faction of men who had long despised the Ashworths organized a gang of "Moderators" who rode down on the Negro community, burning houses and barns and warning them to leave the county. The sheriff organized a competing interracial force of "Regulators." After a series of gun battles with casualties on both sides, the Moderators prevailed, killing the sheriff and chasing Negro families across the border into Louisiana.

Sam Ashworth fled into Indian Territory, where he lived with the Choctaws until the beginning of the Civil War. And in demonstration of his odd status as a slave-owning Negro with few discernible African characteristics, he joined the Army of the Confederacy and was killed in 1862 at the Battle of Shiloh.[72]

The experience of Greenburry Logan was less dramatic and maybe more typical of free Negroes in prewar Texas. Logan arrived in 1831, answering Stephen Austin's call for settlers. He was wounded fighting in the war for independence from Mexico and was granted Texas citizenship. His hapless appeal for exemptions from the race-coded disabilities that had taken hold in Texas by 1841 suggests that he had fewer or less powerful friends in the establishment than did Aaron Ashworth.

> I cam here in 1831 invited by Col. Austin. I got letters of sittizeship . . . and one quarter league of land insted of a third. But I love the country and did stay because I felt myself mower of a free man then in the states. It is also known that Logan was in every fite with the Maxacans during the camppain of 35 until Bexhar was taken in which event I was the 3rd man that fell. Every previleg dear to a free man is taken away and Logan libel to be imposed upon by eny that choose to doo it. No chance to collect the debt without witness, no vote or say in eny way yet liable for Taxes.[73]

Greenburry Logan's appeal to the Texas Congress fell on deaf ears, his fighting sacrifices for the republic dismissed as an inconvenient footnote to the bourgeoning slaveocracy.

The black experience in the west was plainly impacted by the secession of Texas from the union. Fifty Thousand Texans fought for the Confederacy, and that allegiance resonated in the postwar period. Just as in the southeast, the Ku Klux Klan was active in the west, and former Confederates focused their ire on "lawless" freedmen, complaining about free Negroes "getting drunk, flourishing weapons, stealing horses and insulting whites." While there was no doubting an element of criminality among the freedmen, there also were abundant legitimate reasons for them to own and carry firearms.[74]

Negroes were an integral part of the culture of the open range, where the boon of free grazing fueled the famous cattle drives and legends of longhorn steers and salty men on horseback. Of the estimated thirty-five thousand men who worked the western trail drives, roughly one third were Negroes and Mexican, and the majority of that fraction were black. One detailed study estimates that of the typical eight-man trail crew, two or three men would have been Negroes.[75]

The vastness of the American west created demands and opportunities that add a peculiar layer to the black tradition of arms. Something about the space or the culture, particularly the life of the black cowboy, sometimes lent a more benign character to the prevailing racism. Against intuition, we find numerous reports of armed black heroes risking their lives for friends across racial lines.

We learn by happenstance of the Negro cowboy named Lige, who repelled a ruffian named Sam Grant with gunfire after Grant ambushed Charlie Siringo. Siringo produced one of the first factual memoirs published by a cowboy and provided sufficient accounts of Negroes to support the conclusion that blacks were a good fraction of the population.

The presence of blacks in the west is also memorialized in the landscape, in places like Nigger Hill, Nigger Creek, and Nigger Gulch, named for the black prospectors who worked mining claims in those areas. Often the evidence of individual Negroes appears in the invective or perhaps just the descriptor *nigger* before their given name—men paid wages under the names "Nigger Jeff," "Nigger Newt," and "Nigger Bob."[76]

The possibility that *nigger* was more descriptor than an insult is evident in attempts to compliment the talents or toughness of men called "Nigger Add" and "Nigger Jim." Nigger Add was revered as a horse breaker, gave orders to white men, and, after he had topped out in the ranch hierarchy, commented that he would "run this outfit if not for this old black skin."

"Nigger Jim" Kelly commanded similar respect as the top hand of Texas rancher Print Olive. When Olive was ambushed in a Kansas saloon in 1872, Kelly flew to the rescue with gunfire and saved Olive's life. Print Olive's respect for Kelly and Kelly's reputation for toughness sometimes smoothed the sharp edges of cow-town racism. When an Irish saloonkeeper refused to serve him, Kelly moved his hand to the hilt of his six-gun. White cowboys intervened, advising the barkeep, "That's Nigger Jim, Print Olive's bad nigger. Pay you treat him right."

A similar scene played out in Abilene in 1870 when a saddle-weary trail crew camped on the outskirts of town and then rode in seeking entertainment. Their black cook consumed more than his share of cheap whiskey and started firing his revolver into the air. The booming cow town had just built a new jail, and the black cook was its first occupant. His stay was cut short when his hungry trail mates broke him out at gunpoint, making him both the first prisoner and the first escapee from the new jail.

No doubt there was plenty of discrimination and racial harassment in the cow towns that led to gunfire. And sometimes, as in the case of John Hayes, Negroes did all of the shooting. John Hayes was refused service in a saloon that was attempting a "whites only" policy. Hayes, with a budding reputation as the "Texas Kid," drew his revolver and shot up the saloon.

John Hayes's violence was gratuitous. But Henry Hilton was literally pulled into a fight that ended in deadly gunfire. Hilton owned a small ranch near Dodge City, Kansas. He was in town for provisions when a group of white cowboys aimed to make sport of him. They exchanged tough talk, and Hilton warned them that he would not stand for any "hazing, even if he was a nigger." Then one of the men lassoed him and tried to pull him off his horse. Hilton drew his revolver and killed the man. Before he could appear on the shooting charge, Hilton got into a late-night saloon brawl with a black cowboy named Bill Smith over some unrecorded slight. The two men emptied their revolvers and died from their wounds.

This was not the only time black cowboys shot one another. In the winter of 1870, the *Laramie Weekly Sentinel* reported that a man named Pressley Wall was shot and killed at the Bullard Saloon by Littleton Lawrence, "both colored." In Cheyenne, an argument at a black prostitute's crib left a Negro known only as Dozier limping to the train station, bleeding from three bullet wounds presumably from a black assailant.[77]

Although film depictions suggest otherwise, blacks participated on both sides of the infamous Lincoln County War that propelled Billy the Kid into legend. At least three black men rode with Billy the Kid. Riding with the opposing forces were "Negro" (probably "Nigger") John Clark, as well as a detachment of black cavalry. At least one of these black men, George Washington, survived the conflict to join territorial governor Lew Wallace's Lincoln County Riflemen in 1879. For a short, violent period, the Lincoln County Riflemen were the dominant force for order in the tumultuous environment.[78]

Black men figure prominently in other, less famous conflicts. In 1883, a black cowboy who answered to "Nigger Jeff" went with his employer, rancher Dick Grier, into Mexico on an invitation to buy cattle. It turned out to be an ambush, and only three of Grier's group made it out alive. One of them was "Nigger Jeff," who covered the retreat of his trail mates with gunfire and then escaped to nurse his own wounds. Other Negroes of the west pursued less honorable paths—men like the nameless gunfighter who was contracted to kill another bad man named Mexican Joe. Mexican Joe was quicker on the trigger.

The recorded story of the black west often focuses on the sensational—the bloody, boozy conflicts that rose to the level of news. The countless less colorful folk who populated the west and made decisions to acquire and carry arms can only be guessed at. We are left mainly to speculate about the practice of arms among the field hands, stockyard workers, miners, saloon entertainers, prostitutes, hoteliers, and ordinary black settlers who populated the American west.[79]

But even within this category of more pedestrian firearms use, colorful tales of men like Willis Peoples survive. Peoples owned a small ranch near Mead, Kansas. The community was agitated about a large wolf that had been killing cattle, and raised a reward for the wolf's hide. Peoples said that if they would leave the wolf alone and give him a few weeks, he would bring it in. Peoples trailed the animal, stalked within fifty feet of it, and killed it with a rifle shot to the head. Riding into town with a nearly seven-foot-long wolf carcass, Peoples became a minor celebrity.

We are also generally left guessing about episodes where men simply brandished guns to staunch some threat or drew guns on one another, then backed down. An 1881 report from Raton, New Mexico, confirms the second category. A Negro and a white cowboy pulled their six-guns over some slight and then backed away without firing. We learn about this averted violence incidentally within the story of the white cowboy dying later that evening in a shootout with another man.[80]

The power of bluster and bluff is underscored in the autobiographical account of Nat Love, also known as Deadwood Dick. At least by his own telling, Nat Love had a talent for otherworldly marksmanship. His stories and self-proclaimed reputation hit all of the stereotypes of western exploits with the gun. Love was a self-promoter whose grand depictions of his multilayered prowess invite worries that some of his claims are exaggerated or fictitious.[81] But the dubious exploits of men like Nat Love gain a degree of credence in light of similar, more readily verifiable adventures of other improbable Negro cowboys.

Some of the best records of blacks in the frontier west come out of the effort to bring a measure of law to Indian Territory. It is not only lawbreakers but also black lawmen who frame the scene. What passed for law in the territory was mainly federal, and starting in 1875, was famously administered out of Fort Smith, Arkansas, by hanging Judge Charles Parker. Parker's records chronicle a significant black presence in the violent territory. Among the criminals who came before him, Parker hanged thirty whites, twenty-six Indians, and twenty-three blacks.

The black population in Indian Territory also produced abundant lesser criminal activity and armed conflicts fulfilling the stereotypes of western violence. It hosted notorious black outlaws like Dick Glass and Crawford Goldsby. Glass led a life of violence and crime that ended in 1885 in a shootout with Indian policeman Sam Sixkiller.[82] Crawford Goldsby survived long enough to build a bigger legend. He was the son of a black woman with Indian and European linage and a light-skinned Buffalo Soldier named George Goldsby, who sometimes passed for Mexican. George disappeared when Crawford was only two years old, under circumstances that are interesting in their own right.

In 1878, Sergeant George Goldsby commanded a squad of black soldiers at Fort Concho, Texas. The relationship between white Texans and the Buffalo Soldiers was often tense. There were the typical racial taunts. And sometimes whites took potshots at the black troopers who traveled around Texas towns and homesteads. After one of these episodes, George Goldsby allowed his soldiers to take their rifles to settle a dispute with some local whites. With the shooting done, unwilling to trust the army's judgment of his decision, Goldsby fled and never saw his wife or son again.

With his father on the run, young Crawford Goldsby was shipped east to the Indian school in Carlisle, Pennsylvania. When he returned west as a teenager, he was physically a man and soon found a man's trouble. A saloon quarrel with an older Negro cowboy led to drawn guns and Crawford fleeing the scene as a killer. Sometime during this period, Goldsby picked up the name Cherokee Bill. He answered to it when he joined the Cook Gang, a mostly black outlaw band, some of them ex-slaves of Cherokee Indians.

Fig. 4.5. Shoot-out at Fort Concho. (Frederic Remington's *How the Worm Turned*, oil on canvas, April 1901. St. Lawrence University, Canton, NY.)

Cherokee Bill did everything one expects from a western outlaw—thieving, eluding posses, gun fighting, and murder. Bill's most notorious act of violence was shooting his brother-in-law in an argument over some pigs. Bill also killed a barber, a train-station agent, and a train conductor. After a robbery where he killed a bystander, Bill was arrested and convicted of murder. His saga continued with appeals of his conviction to the United States Supreme Court and an escape attempt with smuggled guns. He finally was hanged in the summer of 1895.[83]

The black outlaws in Indian Territory highlight the blunt errors of formal racial categories. Cherokee Bill's lineage included many strands of the American melting pot. So too, the Rufus Buck Gang, which plundered the territory for a short, violent spurt. They are reported alternately as Indian, black, and mulatto. An arresting officer described the leader, Rufus Buck, as part black. Photographs suggest that the gang members were a blend of Negro, Native, and white. After a short, violent career of robbery and murder, the gang was run to ground by black Creek Indian police. They surrendered after seven-hour gunfight and died under Judge Parker's hanging justice in July 1896.

Other interracial gangs operated along a similar trajectory. Men like Tom Root, Buss Luckey, and Will Smith rode with a gang of train robbers who fought gun battles against pursuing posses and ultimately were executed under sentence from hanging Judge Parker.[84]

Some gun criminals in Indian Territory disappoint the stereotype. Della Humby was a simple bully who killed his wife and ambushed an Indian policeman who tried to arrest him. Other lawmen fell to gunfire from men like "Captain"

Wiley, a Negro living among the Seminoles. Wiley killed a federal marshal in what he called a fair fight. He was arrested and died in custody at Fort Smith. This was not the only episode where white lawmen fell to Negro gunfire. In 1892, on a train between Santa Fe and Gainesville, Texas, a black man and a white marshal shot it out after harsh words that started when the marshal sat in the Negro smoking car. It is disputed who drew first. But the marshal and one Negro died from gunfire, and two other black men were arrested.[85]

Fig. 4.6. Rufus-Buck gang. (Photograph from 1895.)

Black lawmen in Indian Territory demonstrate the diversity of the place. The deputy marshals who extended Judge Charlie Parker's authority into the territory included at least twenty blacks whom we can verify by name and probably others who remain unknown because race was recorded only by happenstance.

Bass Reeves is among the most storied of Parker's black marshals. He is draped in tales of bravery, marksmanship, strength, and stamina that sometimes seem too fantastic to credit. But official reports level out the legend. Reeves is recorded killing fourteen men in the line of duty. He prevailed in numerous nonfatal showdowns and gunfights and rendered hundreds of whites, Indians, and Negroes to Charlie Parker's justice.

The instinct that Parker's black marshals were somehow unique is refuted by men like Willie Kennard, a former Buffalo Soldier, who rode into the town of Yankee Hill,

Colorado, and applied for the marshal's job. A skeptical mayor tested his resolve by sending him to arrest one of the town's notorious villains, a rapist who was drinking in a saloon down the street. In classic western progression, Kennard entered the saloon and the bad man drew his gun. But Kennard was faster. With gun smoke hanging in the air, he dragged the wounded rapist to jail and picked up the marshal's star. He served the town of Yankee Hill for three years before moving on.

Fig. 4.7.
Bass Reeves,
United States
Marshal.

Brit Johnson was not a lawman, but his bravery and exploits fill the expectations about the western hero and form the basis for a tale by a western novelist titled *The Black Fox*. Brit Johnson was probably born a slave, but by 1871, he was living near Fort Griffin, Texas, with his family. He was already renowned for his 1864 rescue of a group of women and children who were abducted from a settlement in Young County, Texas, by Comanche raiders.

In January 1871, Johnson and three other black cowboys were hauling supplies to Johnson's home when a Comanche band attacked. The details of Johnson's last stand were reconstructed at the scene. All of Johnson's trail mates were quickly killed. Johnson finally succumbed after inflicting multiple casualties. The Comanche corpses and nearly two hundred empty shell cases littered around the spot where Johnson lay dead were evidence of his fight to the death and his skill with the gun.[86]

∞

As we already have seen, the Buffalo Soldiers are a familiar landing in the story of the black west. These troops are steeped in irony, famously named by the plains Indians whose plight they might easily have sympathized with and whose final defeat they aided. Compounding this irony was the overhang of race in the interactions between the Buffalo Soldiers and many of the constituency they were assigned to protect. Their job as frontier security force was often complicated by the divide of race. The community feeling was evident in east Texas when two Buffalo Soldiers attempted to arrest a white man for murder. The murderer was a better shot and from a privileged class. He killed both soldiers and was acquitted by a jury of his peers.

For Confederates moving west after the Civil War, black men in uniform were hard to abide. In Lincoln County, New Mexico, in two separate episodes, Confederate veterans shot black soldiers for entering diners and bars where whites were eating and drinking. One of these inveterate rebels, Frank Freeman, recently of Alabama, was captured by a squad of black soldiers and then escaped to tell that the soldiers planned to lynch him.[87]

The fact that they were well-armed and trained to fighting discipline allowed the Buffalo Soldiers to strike back hard either in self-defense or in vengeance. In Kansas in 1867, a mob killing of three black soldiers triggered a gunfight in the streets as their squad mates rode into town seeking retribution. In El Paso, Texas, local police arrested two Buffalo Soldiers, prompting their platoon mates to storm in with government-issue carbines to break them out. Each side lost a man in the gunfire. In Wyoming, Buffalo Soldiers stationed at Camp Bettens endured taunts, threats, and then an attack by townsfolk on two of their platoon mates. They marched into town and retaliated with gunfire. The shootout ended with one casualty, a Buffalo Soldier lying dead in the street. The other soldiers received minor punishments by a military tribunal.[88]

Even with the hardships they endured, the Buffalo Soldiers fared better than many Negroes of the era. The relative appeal of their lifestyle was evident in the decision former slave girl Cathy Williams to impersonate a man, hone her gun skills, and ride with US Colored Troops serving in New Mexico. She concealed her gender and did the work of a soldier until injuries sent her to the post surgeon, who reported that she was a woman and had her discharged.

Fig. 4.8. Buffalo Soldier. (*Dismounted Negro, Tenth Cavalry*, Frederic Remington, 1886. From *The Century Magazine* 1889, vol. 15. General Photograph Collection, MS 362: 068-1095, University of Texas at San Antonio Libraries Special Collections.)

When Ida B. Wells and folk from the east were dreaming of a western promised land at the end of the nineteenth century, being black in America was a challenge no matter where you were. Modern commentators describe this period as the nadir of the black experience in America. Although they might not have used exactly that word, the 1899 assessment of the Douglass Memorial Literary Society of Buffalo Soldiers was basically the same: "Resolved, that there is no future for the Negro in the United States."[89]

That sort of grim assessment, coupled with the focus here on deadly encounters and gunplay, demands a point of caution about the unfolding tradition of arms and the daily lives of Negroes. Even during the bleakest times, other things were going on. Black folk still laughed and loved and relished the comforts of family. So, in tracking the black tradition of arms, we must remember that it grew up from countless individual souls who, even under the common burden of racism, still had richly different experiences. They operated under a multitude of different impulses. They had different capabilities, dispositions, and internal lives. And these things magnified the variations rendered by differences like wealth, occupation, domestic situation, and complexion.

Ida Wells developed an early appreciation for these sorts of differences as she moved gingerly into the circles of Memphis's black elite. As she matured, the interaction of Wells's inner life and her experience in the world produced what some said was a stern and sometimes difficult personality. And it is tempting to conclude that this was predictable. How indeed could someone whose best friend was lynched, someone who advised every Negro household to acquire the assault rifle of the day, have anything but a gloomy countenance?

This sort of pop-psychological assessment often appears in the modern gun debate and likely will extend to assessments of the black tradition of arms. So it is useful to appreciate how the tradition of arms flourished among all kinds of different folk operating under different circumstances—how even during the worst of times, Negroes with guns cannot be fixed into any particular "type." Although we do not always have fully developed pictures of the countless folk who owned, carried, and defended themselves with guns, it is evident that they were a diverse lot.

Ida Wells exalted the Winchester rifle and owned and probably carried a pistol. But she did more talking about guns than actual shooting. Mary Fields, whose late-nineteenth-century exploits in Montana earned her the sobriquet "Stagecoach" Mary, was exactly the opposite. Six feet tall and 200 pounds, Mary Fields worked, joked, drank, fought, cursed, and shot her way into the annals of legend in and around Cascade, Montana.

She was born around 1832, probably in Tennessee. The details of her life in slavery are contested. Her own version was different from the familiar story of victimization. Still tough, vibrant, and feared at age sixty, Mary described it this way. "I learned . . . as a slave to say yes'em, and then do as I damn well pleased." The specifics are difficult to verify, and Mary may have embellished the story of her early life to match her growing legend.[90]

There is, however, agreement that she worked at the Ursuline Convent of the Sacred Heart in Toledo, Ohio, and then traveled west with some of the sisters who were taking Christianity to the Indians of Montana. Mary was the most valuable single resource at the mission, contributing skills as a carpenter, gardener, cook, and even healer, using herb and root knowledge gathered during slavery.

Montana was surely no idyll. And intuitions about the petty indignities that a dark black woman would face there at the end of the nineteenth century are confirmed by reports that for most of her time in Montana, Mary Fields was not called "Stagecoach Mary" but "Black Mary," and she actually signed her name that way.

Mary's black skin was an undeniable fact, but it was not a handicap. One of the first episodes in the legend of Black Mary Fields was a predictable clash along the color line. In the fall of 1892, the sisters at the mission hired John and George Mosney as laborers. The sisters paid the wages, but the daily assignments came from Mary.

The white men objected to "taking orders from a nigger." Then George fetched a bullwhip and threatened to show Mary her place. Mary ignored his taunts, walked to her cabin, and returned shouldering a shotgun. George went from taunting to yelling for help. John answered, running up beside him, rifle in hand. Before John could test Mary's resolve, the mission foreman and Mary's growing friend, Joseph Gump, ran in and diffused the scene. He dismissed the Mosney brothers and warned them against tangling with Mary, whose gun skills he appreciated from their many practice sessions out on the prairie.

Two years later, another arrogant man who could not abide taking orders from Black Mary was not so lucky. This time, Joseph Gump was away fetching supplies and had left Mary in charge of a work group. As Mary was handing out tasks, one of the workers objected that "no white man should take orders from a nigger slave." Mary made a brief attempt at diplomacy, telling a fellow that there were no slaves at the mission. This just provoked him, and he lunged in with a looping punch that sent her to the dirt.

The other men laughed and hooted the way that men will when they see someone get knocked off their feet. And this was the high point for the man who sucker punched Black Mary. She told him to get his gun and meet her behind the barn.

The nuns looked on in disbelief. The workmen took bets. Black Mary gave her tormentor the first move. Then she shot him twice in the chest. Those who bet the odds won money. And both winners and losers spread the legend of Black Mary Fields, who was fast, accurate, and fearless with a gun.[91]

In many circles, her firearms prowess gained Mary the kind of respect that was rarely accorded to women in the Montana Territory. She bragged at the end of her life that she was the only woman, not counting prostitutes, who could drink in the territory's typically all-male saloons. Of course the people at the mission were another matter, and soon after the shooting, Mary was ordered to leave.

This actually launched her into the more storied phase of her life. Needing some way to support herself, Mary secured a job driving stages for the Wells Fargo company. She closed the job interview with a warning to the young fellow who was openly hostile to hiring a black woman driver. "I'm Mary Fields," she said—"*Black Mary*, I can outshoot, outride any man trying for this job. You don't want to try me." It was an unlikely strategy for securing employment, and it is likely that the Wells Fargo agent only hired Mary as a favor to some of the sisters at the mission.

The Wells Fargo job fueled the legend of "Stagecoach Mary," shotgun at her side, revolver in her belt, wearing buckskins that she tanned herself. There was nothing else like her in the territory. Her legend grew when, one winter on haul from Helena to Cascade, she was attacked by wolves. She fought off the pack with shotgun and revolver fire and delivered her load intact and on time.

Mary engaged life richly. She was generally armed while she drank, joked, gambled, and fought in the saloons of Cascade. But she did not always resort to the gun. She probably endured many insults. And legend says that she answered with fists and head butts, and once with a perfect-sized rock that turned her fist into a hammer. An admiring report in the *Great Falls Montana Examiner* said that Mary had "broken more noses" than anyone in Montana."[92]

Although we are always slightly skeptical of western tales of colorful characters (Mary reportedly kept a pet eagle) and prodigious marksmanship, there comes out of the saloons, where Mary drank shots and smoked foul cigars, another seemingly reliable report of her facing down a white cowpoke with her pistol. After some sort of insult led to drawn guns, Mary taught the fellow a lesson with a shot to the earlobe. Only Mary knew for sure whether that was the target.[93]

Age was no obvious regulator on Mary Fields. In 1901, at age seventy-two, now making a living doing laundry, Mary was passing the afternoon in a local saloon. She looked up from her whiskey to spy a fellow whose payment for laundry services was long overdue. She pursued the deadbeat down the street, spun him around, and knocked him flat on his back. Then, figuring the punch was worth two dollars, she leaned in and told the man to forget about the bill.

Some men were rightly afraid of Mary Fields, and some surely despised the powerful black woman in their midst. But many people in Cascade, Montana, apparently loved her. She was caretaker for many kids around Cascade and was an ardent fan of the local baseball team. When her house burned down in 1912, townsfolk got together and built her a new one. One of the people who knew and admired her at the end of her life was Hollywood legend Gary Cooper, who quipped that Mary Fields was "one of the freest souls to ever draw breath . . . or a .38."[94]

So what to make of this black woman who, at the low point of Negro life in America, strapped on a gun and rose to legend, fighting and beating white men in raw contests of violence. It is intriguing that her gunplay never provoked mobbing or backlash. Maybe she was so unusual that she is only some kind of exception that proves some general rule. Perhaps it is some version of the respect paid to those isolated souls who stand up under circumstances where there is no broader political threat. Maybe Mary Fields is like the Lumbee Indians, who routed Catfish Cole's Klan rally in 1958, to the chuckles of the white establishment—no threat to the existing order so no need for the lynch mob.

Fig. 4.9. Mary Fields in Cascade, Montana.

Consider, too, how within our broader matrix, the story of Black Mary fits against Martin Luther King's assessment of individual self-defense. King said that standing up in self-defense might actually gain Negroes some level of respect and admiration for the courage it shows. And that is one way to understand the legend of Black Mary, who stood up alone against angry, violent men and bested them in fair fights. In that sense, it suggests something uplifting about America and signals some truth in the ideal of the American west, where personal courage and character mattered above all else.

All of this is contestable. But at the very least, Mary Fields demonstrates the complexity and diversity of the black experience and adds texture to our understanding of the black tradition of arms. Despite the overhanging threats of the era, black folk did not just wallow in despair, clutching guns. Within diverse constraints, they managed to live their lives. They raised and loved their children, worshiped God, feasted on Sunday; and many of them, on Saturday night, celebrated their pleasures with an intensity that rivaled the privileged classes.

For some Negroes more than others it was possible to coexist peacefully, building friendships and allies at the edges of white society. For the right kind of Negro, under the right circumstances, white folk might even take their part against a white man. Even where that white man ended up dead. Shadrack "Buddie" Shang and Moses Fleetwood Walker were such men.

Moses Fleetwood Walker of the Syracuse Stars can be explained by the appeal of celebrity. He was a baseball player, a catcher, good enough to play in the early professional leagues. So when he killed a white man in 1891, fighting back against a violent attack, it was not startling when he was acquitted by a jury of white men who admired his prowess on the diamond.[95] But how to explain Buddie Shang, fully named Shadrach Meshach Abed-Neo White? Born into slavery in Virginia around 1815, it is unclear how and when he picked up all the pieces of his prodigious appellation or when he began answering to the more easily navigated "Buddie Shang."

Even before a Shelby County, Ohio, jury exonerated him in the shotgun killing of a white man, Buddie Shang had already completed a remarkable journey. Shang and his people walked free out of Virginia, well ahead of the Emancipation Proclamation, released from bondage in the will of their master, John Randolph. Legal squabbling cost them an extra thirteen years in slavery, as Randolph's heirs contested the will. It occurred to no one that they might deserve compensation for those additional years under the yoke. When the courts finally upheld Randolph's wishes, a bedraggled band of them struck out for Ohio, and the black settlement of Rumley.

Buddie eventually gravitated to nearby Sidney, where he took up residence in the black shantytown of Lacyburg. By the 1880s, he was a fixture in Sidney, operating a shoe-shine stand outside one of the local taverns. Within the boundaries of the time, he was more than tolerated. The tavern owner was generous with daily bonuses of spirits that Buddie carried home in an ever-present metal bucket.

In the fall of 1889, Buddie was traveling along a canal bank with his bucket, fishing pole, and shotgun, when a local delinquent started to harass him. Buddie fired a warning shot that scared him off. But as the shot pattern spread in the distance, some of the pellets hit the house of Lewis "Soapstick" Nichols, one of the few downtrodden whites who lived in Lacyburg.

Nichols stormed from his house, picked up a stack of bricks, and charged. Buddie ducked the first assault, and backed away with a contrite, "I was just foolin.'" Nichols was undeterred and launched another brick that barely missed. Figuring that his luck was about to run out, Buddie Shang fired another round from his shotgun, knocking Soapstick Nichols to the ground.

In January 1890, the seventy-four-year-old bootblack stood on trial for his life, charged with the murder of Lewis Nichols. He was represented by a young court-appointed lawyer and judged by a jury of twelve white men. With the evidence in, the jury deliberated for just three minutes. Quick deliberations were familiar in these sorts of cases, often signaling results that reflect the worst tribal impulses. But for Buddie Shang, it took only three minutes for twelve white men to vote not guilty.

Buddy Shang lived on in Lacyburg until 1917, when he died at age ninety-seven. He was revered to the point that his image survives on a period postcard over his stock phrase "Dry as a Hoss," an evident reference to his pail being empty.[96]

Fig. 4.10. Buddie Shang.

We can fight about what lesson, if any, to draw from the story of Buddie Shang. He seems, by comparison to Black Mary Fields, a less threatening, more compliant character. The obvious critique here is that the Negro who knew his place, the kindly uncle, might get a measure of justice—although acquittal of the murder of a white man is extraordinary even within that framework.

Perhaps Buddie Shang is more useful for thinking about the bigger, continuing question of whether guns are worth the trouble. A man died and Shang stood trial for murder because he was "just foolin'" with a shotgun. Wouldn't Buddie Shang have been better off without the gun?

If the answer is yes, then what? Should we jump from there to say that everyone would be better off without the damn things, and enforce that resolve with legal rules? But if Buddie Shang is the proof case for that approach, how do we square that lesson with all that came before him, with what was all around him, and with what was to come?

CHAPTER FIVE

CRISIS

"I bought a Winchester double-barreled shotgun and two dozen rounds of shells filled with buckshot. If a white mob had stepped on the campus where I lived I would without hesitation have sprayed their guts over the grass."[1]

Guts sprayed over the grass? Who would think such a thing, let alone say it? When we learn that it was the stiff-collared, Harvard PhD W. E. B. Du Bois, perhaps still the preeminent intellectual of the race, the black tradition of arms gains new resonance.

William Edward Burghardt Du Bois was born into the relatively benign environment of Berkshire County, Massachusetts. His people had lived free there since the eighteenth century. An acknowledged prodigy, Du Bois demonstrated his gifts early in competitions with white classmates and eased gently into the cauldron of American racism when a little white girl nastily refused his offering in the school's visiting-card exchange.

Du Bois would become the leading voice for the higher aspirations of black folk, famously warring with Booker T. Washington's strategy of uplift through industrial education. His energy and vision were a crucial force in the early development of the NAACP. Through the association's flagship magazine, *The Crisis*, Du Bois spoke to and for the American Negro like no one else on the scene. A Pulitzer Prize–winning treatment of his life is aptly subtitled *Biography of a Race*.[2]

By 1906 Du Bois was ensconced as professor of economics and history at Atlanta University, one of the top Negro schools in the country. His shotgun threat was a response to the carnage of the 1906 Atlanta race riot. The riot was a piece with the times. The immediate catalyst was the claim of assaults by black men on white women. The local press fanned the flames with special editions carrying at least two specious reports of such attacks. These allegations caught hold in the context of widespread white angst about the real and imagined debaucheries of Atlanta's "Decatur Street Dives" and the black criminality that their patrons represented.[3]

This was a period in America where Negroes were regularly lynched. The Fulton County, Georgia sheriff's spitting public assessment reflected the times:

"Gentlemen we will suppress these great indignities upon our fair wives and daughters if we have to kill every Negro in a thousand miles of this place."[4]

By arming himself in Atlanta, Du Bois was something of an aberration, but only in the sense that he was late to the game. Many in his circle owned and carried guns, but he never had. As a freshman at Fisk University in 1886, Du Bois recorded that his classmates commonly carried guns whenever they ventured into Nashville.[5] He was lucky that he was able to find a shotgun for sale and had the money to buy it when the Atlanta rioting broke out.[6]

While no one of note appreciated it at the time, the Atlanta riot also was a formative experience for a young man who would become Du Bois's comrade in arms, young Walter White, later the famous spokesman for the NAACP. With a mob advancing, thirteen-year-old Walter waited with his father, gun in hand, at the front windows of their Huston Street home. Shooting from a nearby building repelled the mob before he was forced to fire. But the episode seared in White's memory and cemented his Negro identity.[7]

Walter White's time would come. But Du Bois was already in the thick of the dilemma that burdened blacks trying to navigate the political disenfranchisement and the private violence of early twentieth-century America. With the lessons of Confederate redemption still vivid, the folly of political violence was evident. But the draw of self-defense against personal threats remained powerful.

The circumstances that sent Du Bois running for a gun held lessons about the danger of armed self-defense spiraling into political violence. Reaction to the riot from outside Atlanta made the boundary against political violence seem quite tenuous. Although Booker T. Washington, ever cautious in his public statements, vaguely urged "the best people" white and black to come together to prevent such episodes of disorder, many folk embraced the more militant thinking that fueled Du Bois's armed stand.[8] Among the rising national organizations, the Afro American Council, the Niagara Movement, and the Constitution League, the reaction was openly militant. At a meeting of the Afro American Council in New York, Dr. William Hunter raised the roof with a speech urging blacks to prepare for self-defense on a national scale, "not with brickbats and fire sticks but with hot lead." To the issue of Negroes chafing under the malevolent authority of officials like the Fulton County sheriff, he advised, "Die outside of jail and do not go by yourself."

Reverend George Lee of the Vermont Avenue Baptist Church in Washington, DC, cast off the restraints of his guild, declaring that the attacks in Atlanta dissolved any obligation of turning the other cheek. "I preached peace after the Atlanta riots," said Lee, "But don't misunderstand me, it was prudence, not my religion. If I had the power to stop that kind of thing, even by force, I'd use it. The trouble is all one-sided now, [but] trouble never stays one-sided for long. There's going to be trouble on the other side soon." The *New York Times* caricatured this militant chorus, but still captured the general sentiment with the headline "Talk of War on Whites at Negro Conference."[9]

Fig. 5.1. The front cover of *Le Petit Journal*, covering the 1906 Atlanta riot. (*Le Petit Journal*, October 7, 1906, "The Lynchings in the United States: The Massacre of Negroes in Atlanta.")

The ostensible militancy of the emerging leadership class was rooted in candid acknowledgement of daily threats and hazards. Most would reject political violence as strategically foolish. But it was hard to deny that arms for self-defense were a crucial private resource for blacks.

Du Bois projected this dichotomy in various ways. In his classic work, *The Souls of Black Folk*, Du Bois argued that organized violence was folly, noting that "the death of Denmark Vesey and Nat Turner proved long since to the Negro the present hopelessness of physical defense." At the same time, in the chapter titled "Of the Coming of John," a tale of violence and private honor, Du Bois championed self-defense as a core private interest.[10]

Responding to real-world threats, Du Bois was adamant about the legitimacy and perhaps the duty of self-defense, even where there was danger of spillover into political violence. Consider his 1916 editorial in the *Crisis* excoriating Negroes in Florida who submitted without resistance to the depredations of a lynch mob.

No colored man can read an account of the recent lynching at Gainesville, Fla., without being ashamed of his people. . . . Without resistance they let a white mob whom they outnumbered two to one, torture, harry and murder their women, shoot down innocent men entirely unconnected with the alleged crime, and finally to cap the climax, they caught and surrendered the wretched man whose attempted arrest caused the difficulty.

No people who behave with the absolute cowardice shown by these colored people can hope to have the sympathy or help of civilized folk. . . . In the last analysis lynching of Negroes is going to stop in the South when the cowardly mob is faced by effective guns in the hands of people determined to sell their souls dearly.[11]

In another *Crisis* editorial, following the 1919 Chicago race riot, Du Bois sharpened the point, pushing the boundaries of legitimate self-defense but still warning against violence as a political strategy.

Today we raise the terrible weapon of Self-Defense. When the murderer comes, he shall no longer strike us in the back. When the armed lynchers gather, we too must gather armed. When the mob moves, we propose to meet it with bricks and clubs and guns. But we must tread here with solemn caution. We must never let justifiable self-defense against individuals become blind and lawless offense against all white folk. We must not seek reform by violence.[12]

Du Bois nurtured the *Crisis* from its inaugural issue into the conscience, ambition, and voice of black America. It circulated far beyond its subscription base, passed from hand to hand and left in barbershops, in beauty salons, and on church pews. The *Crisis* offered a deeply textured critique of Negro life, carrying news ignored by the white press. It was superior to most of the black dailies partly because it was a periodical, which allowed more time to perfect the product. But the bigger difference was Du Bois.

The *Crisis* recorded the common news, culture, and hazards that fueled Du Bois's stance on armed self-defense. There were many contributions by talented guests, but it is doubtful that anything appeared in the *Crisis* that Du Bois did not scrutinize. There were uplifting segments titled *Industry*, *Education*, and *Social Progress*. Other more somber sections like *Crime*, *The Ghetto*, and *Lynching* chronicled the indignities and threats that drove countless decisions by black folk to keep and carry firearms and the many episodes where Negroes fired guns in self-defense. Many of these probably were written by Du Bois, and a sampling of them helps us understand his stance on personal and political violence and the line between them.

- In 1911 at a hotel in Indian Springs, Georgia, a tussle between a white clerk and a black bellboy led to a shootout between blacks and whites where two white men were killed. Four black men were snatched up by a mob but retrieved by authorities and sent to the relative safety of Atlanta. Assaults in retribution continued throughout the countryside around Indian Springs.[13]

- In the summer of 1912, white neighbors attempted to block Negroes from moving into the Cook Avenue section of St. Louis. A house purchased by Negroes was pelted with stones and its windows were broken out. Police were called and managed only to arrest a Negro man, Robert Watson, who was patrolling the street in front of the house. He was charged with carrying a concealed weapon.[14]

- On June 18, 1912, in Mangham, Louisiana, George Clayton was lynched for the murder of his employer, Ben Brooks. Before dying, Clayton gamely fought off the mob with a hail of gunfire that wounded six men in the mob.[15]

- In Pineville, Louisiana, a private conflict boiled over into public violence after a Negro shot a white man in an argument. This sparked a wave of retribution along with warnings that blacks should leave Pineville. When blacks resisted, rioting ensued. Six blacks were shot. Two died.[16]

- In Durant and Caddo, Oklahoma, lynch talk was precipitated by the shooting of a white man by a black man. The shooting victim's companions claimed that they were simply passing by a house in the Negro section and were randomly fired upon. The blacks claimed that the white men were trying to blow up their house and they fired in self-defense.

- In Rocky Comfort, Arkansas, a "plantation Negro" shot a white man in self-defense. Incensed by the Negro having sassed him, the white man was in chase, screaming threats to kill, when the Negro ran to the cabin of a friend, retrieved a gun, and shot his pursuer dead. He was almost immediately laid upon by a mob and lynched. The next night, the mob returned to lynch the owner of the cabin where the black killer had borrowed the gun.[17]

- The *Crisis* applauded Hugh M. Burkett, a successful real-estate broker credited with placing black families on some of the better streets in Baltimore. Burkett was celebrated for furnishing bail to a colored man who fired in self-defense against a mob and had been released with the aid of lawyers hired by the NAACP.[18]

- The praise for Hugh Burkett refers to the case of George Howe, "A colored resident of 95 Hartford Ave., Baltimore [who] in an attempt to protect his home, fired into the mob attacking the house and injured four men." He was arrested as the mob threatened to lynch him. "When tried, he was given a sentence of two months each for the first three offenses, but through the efforts of the National Association for the Advancement of Colored People these decisions were appealed and he is now under $500 bail awaiting a jury trial for the fourth case. None of his white assailants in the mob were arrested."[19]

- Mrs. Lily Hill of Washington County, Tennessee, was pardoned by the governor after being convicted of assault with a deadly weapon. "The pardon record says it appears from the statement of the Attorney General that this colored woman is a respectable and well behaved married woman and had been previously molested by the prosecuting witness in the case, and that she was assaulted . . . in a public street because she resented his attentions a second time and when she was pressed by him, drew a pistol from her handbag and shot him in the arm."[20]

- In 1912 in Hamilton, Georgia, three men were lynched after being arrested on suspicion of murder. They were taken from the custody of the local sheriff, who was the uncle of the murder victim. The dead white man, a planter named Hadley, apparently expressed affection for a black woman named Bertha Hathaway. He was killed by gunshot inside Bertha's home, allegedly by Henry Anderson, who counted Bertha as his future bride. Anderson and two Negroes accused of aiding him were lynched.[21]

- In Hickman, Kentucky, competition for work prompted two white laborers to assault a black man. He defended himself with a gun, killing both of them. In retaliation, a group of white men then shot two Negro boys. No arrests were made.[22]

- Ordinary negligence precipitated the lynching of a black farmer named Ralston in Wichita, Kansas, in 1913. Ralston fired his shotgun to scare away a group of white boys who were raiding his watermelon patch. His warning shot killed one of the boys, and a lynch mob soon formed. Ralston initially eluded the mob and turned himself in to authorities who "lost custody" of him to the mob and watched him die.[23]

- Three incidents from November 1917 show the daily risks of interracial encounters. Rueben Mason, a Negro truck driver in Atlanta, was shot and killed by J. B. McElroy because he was slow in moving his vehicle out of the way. In Moultrie, Georgia, Will McRae, a Negro farmhand, was shot and killed by a white overseer because of insolence. In England, Arkansas, that same week, Sam Cates was shot and killed by a group of white men for "annoying white girls."[24]

- A colored woman in Augusta, Georgia, "shot and killed Earl Harmon, a white private, for robbery."[25]

These examples demonstrate the stream of incidents that Du Bois distilled for reporting to the national community. They put his thinking and writing about armed self-defense in context. And they demonstrate how odd it would have been if he had taken a more pacifist view.

Du Bois was not alone. The *Crisis* included contributions from many other talented folk. Writing in 1921, Mordecia Johnson was unapologetic about black resistance against the backdrop of abandoned Reconstruction and the violent triumph of Confederate redemption. "The swift succession and frank brutality of all this was more than the Negro people could bear. Their simple faith and hope broke down. Multitudes took weapons in their hands and fought back violence with bloody resistance. If we must die, they said, it is well that we die fighting. And the American Negro world looking on their deed with no light of hope to see by, said it is self-defense; it is the law of nature, of man, of God, and it is well." [26]

In 1918, Walter White, future executive secretary of the NAACP, reported on a series of lynchings in Georgia precipitated by the revenge shooting of a white planter, Hampton Smith. Smith was notorious for mistreating blacks, and most would not freely work for him. This sent him dredging the convict labor system for men who could not pay their fines, and thus could be "bought" for however long it took to work off the debt. Hampton Smith used this system to "buy" a Negro named Sydney Johnson. After Johnson had worked off his debt with some excess, he demanded payment for the additional time and then refused to work further. Smith responded by coming to Johnson's home and beating him. As they parted, Johnson reportedly threatened Smith. Within a few days, Smith was dead, shot twice as he was sitting near the window in his parlor.

The reflex was vicious. Over a period of seven days, white mobs lynched at least four men and one woman (the eight-months-pregnant wife of one of the initial victims who dared to complain about the injustice and whose killing was so gruesome that one cannot bear to repeat the details). Johnson was finally cornered in Valdosta, armed with a shotgun and a revolver. He wounded two of his pursuers before dying in a hail of rifle fire.[27]

A 1921 editorial reporting on the NAACP's twelfth annual conference exhibits familiar reverence for self-defense along with a caution against political violence: "Lynching and mob violence against Negroes still loom as our most indefensible national crime. Increasingly the Negro . . . has been forced to give his life in self-defense. No man can do less for his family and people and it is a cruel campaign of lying that represents this fight for life as organized aggression. Negroes are not fools. Eleven million poor laborers do not seek war on 100 million powerful neighbors. But they cannot and will not die without raising a hand when the nation lets its offscourings and bandits insult, harry, loot and kill them."[28] In the same volume, under his own byline, Du Bois asked facetiously, "Why is it that only Negroes must be meek and wait and wait! Why is it that only Negroes should not organize for self-defense against mobs?"[29]

Reports and editorials from the *Crisis* show that armed self-defense, though no guarantee of success, was considered a vital resource for blacks. It was an important component of the broader program for Negro advancement that Du Bois expressed this way in 1921:

> The migration of Negroes from South to North continues and ought to continue. The North is no paradise. . . . But the South is at best a system of caste and insult and at worst a hell. With ghastly and persistent regularity, the lynching of Negroes in the South continues—every year, every month, every day; . . . the outbreaks occurring daily . . . reveal the . . . determination to keep Negroes as near slavery as possible. . . . Can we hesitate? COME North! . . . Troubles will ensue with white unions and householders, but remember that the chief source of these troubles is rooted in the South; 1 million Southerners live in the North. . . . This is a danger, but we have learned how to meet it *by un-wavering self-defense and by the ballot.*[30]

Fig. 5.2. W. E. B. Du Bois at work, early in the 1900s. (Atlanta University, 1909.)

The *Crisis* is only one source of the sentiment of the times. Some things surely escaped Du Bois's attention but fueled the self-defense assessments of the people who witnessed them. These incidents elicited a range of reactions and critiques that expand our understanding of the black tradition of arms.

One reaction to racist terrorism was to move away from areas of risk. In Kentucky, for example, documented movements show that lynch violence pushed many rural blacks toward the protection of burgeoning black communities in Louisville and Lexington. Capitalizing on this trend, some rural towns installed neatly painted signs warning, "Niggers don't be here when the sun goes down." A sign with that warning stood in Corbin, Kentucky, until the 1960s.[31]

While flight was one reaction to the threat of violence and racism, another was to take up arms, pray for the best, and know that someday a fight might come. The precise calculations, the guns acquired, and the way they were kept or carried, cannot be fully retrieved. Still, there is abundant evidence of Negroes with guns fighting back against Judge Lynch and lesser threats.

Some of this evidence raises worries about accuracy that afflicts oral histories. The account by former slave Richard Miller is one of these. But it is independently useful for what he presumes people would credit about the black culture of arms. Miller proudly recounted to an interviewer the heroics of George Bland, a former slave living in Danville, Kentucky. Some offense led to the lynching of Bland's wife by Klansmen, who forced him to watch. Bland asked the terrorists if he could retrieve a blanket to wrap her body. Then, according to Miller, Bland walked into his cabin, "got his Winchester rifle, shot and killed 14 of the Kluxers."[32]

Researchers worry that the tale seems too fantastic to credit, especially the killing of fourteen Klansmen. This is a fair skepticism. On the other hand, the feat was certainly within the capabilities of available technology. Fourteen Klan casualties comports with the capacity of the Winchester Henry rifle, an early test of which records fifteen shots fired in roughly ten seconds.

The era of lynching and nightriders is filled with gruesome tales of hapless victims, running, hiding, and cowering under waves of violence. But there are also plenty of verifiable episodes that track Richard Miller's tale of George Bland. Sometimes, as in the case of George Dinning, these self-defense efforts were even deemed legitimate by the ruling bureaucracy. George Dinning was born a slave, was illiterate, and had at least twelve children. But he also was industrious and frugal. He worked and saved to buy a small farm, and by 1897 he had added more acreage and built up a heard of livestock.

Some of his white neighbors were irritated by Dinning's growing prosperity. In the winter of the new year, twenty-five of them marched to his homestead and demanded that Dinning leave the county within ten days. Their pretext was that Dinning was a thief of chickens and hogs. Dinning protested that he had sponsors, white men of status who would vouch for his honesty. This was taken as impudence that led to harsher words and then shots fired at a backpedaling Dinning. Bullets riddled his house. Dinning was hit twice.

But Dinning was not helpless. He had guns and knew how to use them. Bleeding from his wounds, Dinning scrambled to his rifle and opened fire, hitting and killing one man. With one of their company wounded, the mob scattered off. Expecting them to regroup and return, Dinning fled his home and turned himself in to authorities at the county seat. Learning that Dinning was in custody, the mob went back to his farm, drove off his wife and children, ransacked his house, and then burned it to the ground.

Dinning was tried for murder after two changes of venue and the deployment of state troopers to avert a rumored lynching. On the testimony of the mobbers, Dinning was found guilty of manslaughter by a white jury and sentenced to seven years of hard labor.

It was some flicker of progress that Dinning's story did not end here. Black support for Dinning was overwhelming. Black churches and political clubs bombarded the governor with letters urging him to pardon Dinning. Governor William Bradley, a rare surviving southern Republican, reviewed the trial transcript and published his findings: Twenty-five armed men had attacked George Dinning as he was working peacefully on his own property. They had fired first. Bradley concluded that Dinning, "in protecting himself . . . did no more than any other man would or should have done under the same circumstance and instead of being forced to wear convict's garb he's entitled not only to acquittal but to the admiration of every citizen who loves good government and desires the perpetration of free institutions."

Upon release, Dinning was under no illusion that the Republican governor reflected the sentiments of the broader community. His Kentucky homestead destroyed, Dinning moved his family west to Indiana. Once settled, he hired a lawyer to bring a civil suit in federal court against his attackers. He won a $50,000 verdict against six of them, including a lien on the estate of the mobber he killed.[33]

George Dinning's luck, perseverance, and the measure of justice he scratched from the legal system are remarkable. On the other hand, Dinning's basic fighting instinct, his resolve to arm himself, and his willingness to use his gun in righteous self-defense are far from unique.

Moving into the new century under the shadow of lynch law, Negroes were wary of the sounds and signs of mob violence. The signals were glaring in 1902, when a black man named Charles Gaskins sat in jail, awaiting trial for the murder of a Flemingsburg, Kentucky, police officer. On a raw winter evening, roughly sixty white men rushed the jail and attempted to batter down the cell door with a sledgehammer.

They were quickly distracted from their quarry by shotgun blasts from across the street. Local papers reported, "this had the effect of scattering the mob which left as quickly as it came." The gunfire was rumored to have come from a clutch of black men who were loosely related to the prisoner. But no one was ever definitively named as the savior of Charles Gaskins. And the assumption that Gaskins would eventually be executed anyway turns out to be wrong. He is not in the generally reliable records of executed criminals.[34]

While the armed defenders of Charles Gaskins remain unknown, the case of Jacob McDowell confirms the intuition that relatives of lynch targets would be among the first wave of resistance to mobbers. Jacob McDowell was a "hard-working colored man of mature years" who eked out a living within the boundaries of the opportunities allowed to blacks in western Kentucky in 1908.

We know of him because of a conflict that started over a black girl. McDowell confronted Smith Childress, a deputy marshal, objecting to Childress's relationship with the girl. It is unclear exactly what they said, but the tone was surely hostile. On one account, after McDowell had his say and started to walk away, Childress took a shot at him. McDowell fled into one of the stores on Main Street with Childress in pursuit. They scuffled, and McDowell ended up shooting Childress with his own gun. With Childress lying wounded, McDowell ran to the jailhouse to explain what happened. Familiar with the local history of mob violence, the police judge removed McDowell to the next county, where he could be better protected.

Kentucky officials were not the only ones wary of the mob. McDowell's son, Harve, had seen this scenario unfold before and was skeptical about how much risk jailers would take to protect his father. So he gathered eleven trusted men to help stand guard. They were on foot, traveling toward town, when angry men on horseback approached from behind. Accounts differ about what happened next. Whites said that Harve had hidden on the side of the road with a plan to ambush them. Harve McDowell and his cohorts said they moved off the road to hide so that the whites would pass without confrontation.[35]

According to McDowell, the shooting started as his group was climbing over a fence into the cover of an adjoining field. One of the black men got snagged on the fence and his gun went off, shooting McDowell in the leg. This revealed their position and drew fire from the whites. McDowell and some of his men fired back. Others ran away.

When the smoke cleared, one white man was dead and another one seriously wounded. Both of these men, it turns out, were simply traveling through the area and had come along for the adventure of seeing a lynching. The aftermath was familiar. For the next two days, a mob roamed the countryside, threatening and interrogating Negroes until they learned the identities of the men who had gathered to protect Jacob McDowell.

Meanwhile, Jacob McDowell was returned back to the venue of his original confrontation with Smith Childress. It was a curious decision, because the danger that caused authorities to move him the first place seemed clearer than ever. This was confirmed when a group of masked gunmen entered the jail, dragged Jacob McDowell to the outskirts of town, and riddled his body with gunfire. In a subsequent assessment of the McDowell lynching, a pamphleteer claimed that Smith

Childress, the deputy marshal who fired the first shot in the saga, actually led the lynch mob. The suspicion was that Childress feared that a trial of Jacob McDowell would publicize his tryst with a black girl.[36]

The McDowell case confirms that state agents were sometimes complicit in mob violence. But as we saw in the case of George Dinning, state agents were not always villains. This was decidedly the case in Stanford, Kentucky, where a white jailer acted boldly against type.

The conflict started when an argument between two black boys and three white farmers left a white man down from gunfire, and the two young Negroes behind bars. Word of the shooting, the arrest, and the impending mob traveled quickly. Within hours, armed Negroes from Macksville, a neighboring all-black settlement, arrived in Stanford to guard the jail. They planned for gunplay in dim light by wearing white ribbons on their left sleeves to avoid casualties from friendly fire.

Unlike Charles Gaskins's unknown defenders who fired from the shadows, the Macksville men stayed boldly in the open, building a bonfire in the street behind the courthouse and shooting out at bumps in the night. The effect of this show of force on the white jailer was remarkable. He took uniquely aggressive action, placing his son in the cell with the black prisoners and handing guns to all three of them. This was enough to dissuade the mob.

It is unclear whether Negroes who ran to defend their neighbors in this fashion were calculating the odds of success in any serious way. The Macksville defenders could not have known that a show of force would diffuse the mob without a fight. Neither could the defenders of Dollar Bill Smith, in Wiggins, Mississippi, have predicted trading five hundred shots with a looming mob. Smith was a known "bad nigger," at least according to the mobbers. So they were inflamed by the idea that local Negroes would stand up to save him from the noose. With blacks massed in the Negro section, the mob rolled in to teach them a lesson. The Negroes gave as good as they got. There were multiple casualties on both sides, but evidently no one died.[37]

Of course, there is plenty of evidence from the early twentieth century that armed self-defense could end badly for Negroes. Witness the episode in Sunflower County, Mississippi, home to infamous segregationist Senator James O. Eastland. The senator's uncle James owned a 2,300-acre plantation near Doddsville. In the winter of 1904, he rode to the cabin of one of his sharecroppers, Luther Holbert. He aimed to mediate a conflict between Holbert and one of Eastland's favored workers. The trouble stemmed from a love triangle involving Holbert's woman. Eastland was armed with a revolver. Holbert had a gun in his cabin.

We don't know the words they exchanged, but it is clear that Holbert shot James Eastland, who died on the cabin floor, with two shots fired from his revolver.

A posse combed the countryside for Holbert, and in the process killed two Negroes who ran at the sight of furious, armed men on horseback. Holbert was tracked down and lynched, along with his woman, who fled with him.[38]

The progression of gunplay surrounding Charles Gaskins, Jacob McDowell, Dollar Bill Smith, and Luther Holbert leaves us wondering what sorts of calculations people who witnessed these events made about the risks of owning, carrying, or using guns. Did news of the bloodless Negro triumph in defense of Charles Gaskins embolden Negroes and prompt folk to acquire guns? What about the lynching of Luther Holbert? Did it convince Negroes that armed self-defense was just folly? Or did that also counsel keeping and carrying firearms?

Answers are suggested in the tilt of local lore surrounding the 1901 "Balltown Riot" in Washington Parish, Louisiana. The violence sparked on rumors that blacks were stockpiling weapons in preparation for an attack on local whites. Whether this was a real fear or just an excuse is unknown. But we know for sure that a white mob surrounded and then shot into a black church whose members were at the root of the rumors. The Negroes were prepared for conflict. They returned fire, killing three white attackers. Fifteen blacks died.

The Balltown Riot is ostensibly a story of black defeat, perhaps confirming for modern skeptics the folly of armed self-defense. But the fifteen-to-three body count is the "white" record of the violence. Among the local black folk, the accounting was different. Years later, those who lived through it said that the body count was closer to even, but that white officials had doctored the story. As the details grew into legend, witnesses recounted that three white casualties was a vast undercount. One man, recalled proudly how "old man Creole [himself] killed about six."[39]

This sort of account demonstrates a kind of tribal pride that appears frequently in stories of armed self-defense against terrorists. As we will see in the next chapter, America's preeminent black historian, John Hope Franklin, offers a similar critique of the 1921 race riot in Tulsa, Oklahoma. These kinds of assessments suggest the cast of the black tradition of arms. Armed self-defense was often embraced as a matter practical philosophy, undiminished by utilitarian balancing.

There were many incidents where black defenders, armed with the guns of poor folk, were outclassed by better technology. Economics was one driver of these results. But we already saw under the Black Codes, and will see again in the Jim Crow era, how gun laws administered by an overtly hostile state also impaired Negro self-defense. A lynch episode from 1916 demonstrates a small scale, ad hoc version of this.

The first lesson is in the lynching itself. The location was Paducah, Kentucky, where, in 1892, armed Negroes fought off a lynch mob and earned the praise of Ida

B. Wells. Perhaps it was memory or legend of that fight that moved Luther Durrett to a desperate act in aid of his cousin Brack Henley.[40]

Henley was arrested on the charge of assaulting a white farm girl. A mob stormed the jail and dragged him to the victim's house, where she nodded that yes, he was the one. As they were about to yank Henley up by the neck, Luther Durrett stormed from the brush, waving a pistol and threatening to fire into the crowd. He was vastly outnumbered, quickly overpowered, and strung up on a limb next to his cousin.

The lynchings of Henley and Durrett left blacks seething and fueled white rumors that they were planning a retaliatory attack. Those rumors seemed confirmed when scores of Negroes attempted to buy guns from local hardware stores. They were thwarted by Paducah police, who ordered local merchants not sell guns to blacks.[41] At least fifty Negroes were turned away on these orders.

This ad hoc gun prohibition and the fact that black rage here never resulted in gunfire allows several speculations. One is that blacks were unable to get guns, and that diffused what might have become a swirling cycle of violence. But that assumes that blacks were not already widely armed. And given the other signals of black gun ownership, that would be surprising. The alternate speculation is that the lynch violence in Paducah spurred unfilled black demand for additional firearms consistent with the modern "fear and loathing" hypothesis, which says that incidents of violence spur acquisition of firearms for self-protection.[42]

It turns out in any case that the community was not entirely pacifist in its response to the Henley and Durrett lynchings. One of the lynch instigators, George Ross, fled Paducah after multiple threats to his life. The anger of the community seeped out again against a white police officer who was beaten after responding roughly to complaints about a loud Halloween celebration.[43]

While hostile state actors loom large in the lynch era, that story is complicated by men like Augustus E. Willson, Republican governor of Kentucky, who administered the state in the early twentieth century. Elected in 1907, Willson was, for the time, remarkably aggressive in his criticisms of lynch law and his willingness to combat midnight terrorists. His reaction to the mob murder of David Walker and his family in Hickman, Kentucky, matches our modern outrage.

The Walkers were attacked because they were "uppity" Negroes who did not know their place. One account described David Walker as a "surly Negro" who had cursed a white woman in some commercial transaction and threatened a white man who came to her defense. Later, masked by darkness, midnight terrorists rode to Walker's cabin, crept in close, and yelled for Walker to come out. When Walker refused, they doused the structure with kerosene and set it afire. With his house in flames, Walker fired on the mob and then wilted under a barrage of return fire. His wife ran from the house with a baby in her arms. She and the child were shot down. Three of Walker's other children tried to flee but were also killed. Walker's oldest son refused to leave the burning structure or perhaps was already dead by gunshot.

Governor Willson's response distills the scene. "If two or three men had gone to this poor man's cabin and murdered his family, the crime would've shocked humanity with its revelation of incredible weakness, brutality and dastardly cowardice. That a larger number—some fifty men—joined in such a crime, multiplies its cowardliness and wickedness fiftyfold, and makes every member of the band guilty of murder in the first-degree."[44] Willson rejected the argument that nightriders were just good people frustrated by black criminality, and he castigated public officials who countenanced terrorism on that excuse. The epidemic of lynchings in Kentucky, he said, was "the logical [result] of the toleration of nightrider crimes in the state."

Willson's policy response to terrorist violence had wide appeal among blacks and fits comfortably within the black tradition of arms. In addition to offering a $500 reward for the arrest and conviction of anyone complicit in lynch violence, Willson urged Negroes to defend themselves and promised to pardon anyone who shot a nightrider in self-defense. In a speech to the American Bar Association, Willson declared that "every man who is a member of a lawless band that goes with the double cowardice of those who enter upon lawlessness with the protection of the night and of overwhelming numbers against one poor and helpless man . . . takes his life in his hands and if the victim in despair kills him, no one has any right to complain."

The *Kentucky Courier-Journal* subsequently reported various accounts of nightriders killed by blacks in Birmingham, Golden Pond, and other western Kentucky towns. A judge in Lyon County wrote to Willson that many blacks eventually were driven from the area, but not without taking their share in blood and flesh. "I have learned that a man in this county saw the gang on its march to Birmingham counted them, saw them as they returned . . . and one man was lying on his horse, head hanging to one side feet on the other, another was held in the saddle by a man riding behind . . . four others are visited by a doctor from Kuttawa. . . . There were three secret burials [of nightriders] in this County and one in Marshall."

Willson sent troops to western Kentucky and kept them there for more than a year. He used state funds to provide guns and ammunition to people who were under threat of attack. His pressure on local leaders led to the arrest and trial of several lynch-mob instigators. Finally, though, Willson confronted the boundaries of his power. He could press for arrests and trials, but he could not convict terrorists and murderers. Ultimately, all of the men arrested under pressure from Willson were acquitted by juries of their peers.

The Walker lynchings that so animated Governor Willson demonstrate the uncertain curve of armed self-defense, its potential for making things worse, and the difficulty of making sound after-the-fact-judgments about it. Some reports say that the mob descended on David Walker intending *just* to horse-whip him. But "when he fired into their midst he so aroused their indignation that their thirst for blood was not sated until the last member of the Walker family had been shot."[45]

So did Walker's gun just make things worse? Was he a fool who provoked the deaths of his entire family when he could have avoided it all by taking a whipping? Or was Walker a hero who deserves admiration for his defiant last stand? And is there some inherent value to desperate but failed defiance? Or is it better to sur-render and live another day under the yoke? One would pay to hear David Walker's answers to these questions.

The black tradition of arms grew out of countless decisions by men like David Walker to own and carry guns. These decisions were necessarily calculated. Acquiring guns required balancing of scarce resources. Carrying guns from one situation to the next demanded estimates of oscillating risks and rewards. On the other hand, the decision to actually use the gun in self-defense often seems like just a spontaneous reflex. That probably explains the episode in 1908, in Logan County, Kentucky, where Rufus Browder, a black sharecropper, fought with and ultimately killed his landlord.

They argued over some trifle. Then Browder turned his back to James Cunningham and walked away. This affront, a clear violation of racial etiquette, provoked Cunningham to violence. Cunningham cursed Browder for his insolence and slashed him with a whip.

Browder's immediate response is unrecorded. But he probably struck back, because Cunningham went from the whip to a pistol and shot Browder in the chest. Wounded, but ambulatory, Browder pulled his own pistol and killed Cunningham. Browder was arrested for murder and moved to a jail in Louisville, Kentucky.

Browder escaped lynching, but four of his lodge brothers did not. Browder was a member of one of the many fraternal organizations that blacks developed as sur-rogates for absent social-services networks. These groups administered burial funds, pooled emergency assets, and were sometimes the organizational base for vigilance and self-defense groups. Rumor spread among whites that Rufus Browder's lodge brothers were plotting a preemptive attack on whites who had threatened to mob Browder.

Four lodge brothers were meeting in a private home when police entered and arrested them for disturbing the peace. While they were sitting in the jail in Russellville, Kentucky, a mob of nearly one hundred men descended and demanded that the jailer give them up. He handed over the keys, and the four men were summarily hanged. The mob pinned the message on one of the corpses,

"Let this be a warning to you niggers to let white people alone or you will go the same way."[46]

Negro men were the primary victims of lynch law. But black women were also targets of mobs and sometimes beneficiaries of the armed community. Marie Thompson was both. Around 1904, in Lebanon Junction, Kentucky, Marie Thompson was arrested for murder of a white farmer. The humanized picture of Marie is lost. White press reports caricature her as a "Negro Amazon," an evident attempt to explain how she had managed to kill a stout white farmer who chastised her son over some missing tools. Thompson claimed that she had acted in self-defense.

Anticipating the mob, black men from the community assembled with guns to guard the jail. They repulsed a late-evening attack, and apparently concluded that the danger had abated. But deep into the night, Marie Thompson was snatched from her cell by men who seem to have gotten access without resistance from the jailer.

Bolstering the Amazon legend, Thompson was dangling from a rope, seemingly dead, when one of the mob ventured too close. Thompson sprang to life, grabbed the man by his shirt, snatched a knife from his hand and cut herself free. Now wielding the blade, she waded into the mob. Unwilling to engage her hand-to-hand, the mobbers killed Marie Thompson with a volley of gunshots.[47]

The self-defense impulse played out badly for Marie Thompson. It is hard to avoid the conclusion that everyone would have been better off if she had just stayed out of the conflict between the white man and her son, which might have ended with just harsh words and her boy submitting to a light beating. But the difficulty of translating that insight into general policy is illustrated by the murder of Kentucky farmer Jim Hill.

Jim Hill got into a scrape with a white man named L. J. Swift that left Hill missing three front teeth. Hill sought redress through the legal system, asking the county prosecutor to issue a warrant for Swift. County bureaucrats went through the motions. But Hill's complaint ultimately was dismissed on Swift's testimony that Hill had talked back and made threats.

Unsatisfied with the victory in court, Swift lead a group of men to Hill's farm about a week later. With guns drawn, they forced a sack over Hill's head and dragged him from his home. They did not announce their intentions. Perhaps they planned a beating, perhaps a whipping. Perhaps they only intended to frighten Jim Hill enough that he would never again invoke the law against a white man.

Jim Hill's wife had only seconds to make a decision. And if she had drawn a lesson from Marie Thompson, she might have decided just to let them drag her husband off into the night. She hesitated, and then, fighting off a kind of fear that is difficult for us to imagine today, she pursued the mob with a rifle in one hand

and a lantern in the other. She was willing, but the results leave one wishing she had been more effective. The lantern turned out to be a tactical mistake that made her a target. Ducking under gunfire, she lost her lantern and her gun. With Jim Hill's only defender subdued, the mob dragged him into a field and beat him to a gel.[48]

Individual calculations about the wisdom of owning or carrying guns surely varied. Even today gun ownership rates and the data about how many people carry concealed firearms are only estimates from surrogate information. The early twentieth century offers its own sinister surrogate for estimating the frequency with which Negroes carried guns. A study of the southern convict labor system shows that it was quite common for black men of the era to travel armed. It is contestable whether the convict labor system was more about crime control or more about dragooning cheap labor. There is a strong argument for the latter, given the frequency with which black men were roped into the system on charges like "idleness," "using obscene language," "selling cotton after dark," and "violating contract" with white employers in places where true crime was almost trivial.

    Men arrested on these specious charges were jailed and fined. If they could not pay, and many couldn't, their term was extended and their fines and fees compounded. Now even further in debt, they were essentially sold to anyone who paid their fines and were required to work off the debt. The case of Green Cottenham is emblematic. He was arrested for vagrancy in March 1908, spent three days in jail awaiting trial, then was found guilty and sentenced to a fine or thirty days hard labor. Green Cottenham had no money, so he did the thirty days. But this meant he racked up an array of fees for his keep. Soon his debt equaled one year of hard labor, and the obligation was purchased by a railroad subsidiary of the northern industrial giant US Steel.

    Perhaps as many as two hundred thousand black men were snared into the convict labor system on a variety of pretexts. One of the most common charges was carrying a concealed firearm. This was era when many southern men carried side arms. But the crime of carrying a concealed weapon was enforced mainly against Negroes. By the turn of the century it had become one of the most consistent instruments of black incarceration. The indications that arrests for carrying a concealed gun were more frequent than arrests for things like idleness and using obscene language suggests a robust culture of keeping and bearing firearms that thrived despite the risk that it was a pathway into the convict labor system.[49]

Labor supply was the seed of racial violence in East St. Louis, Illinois. And the aftermath brings another appearance from the storied advocate of the Winchester rifle, Ida B. Wells, now married to Chicago striver Ferdinand Barnett. Negroes had been migrating to East St. Louis for at least a decade. This rising population was either a threat or an opportunity, depending on whom you asked. Democrats saw the influx of likely Republican voters as a threat. Woodrow Wilson worried aloud that the rising black population of East St. Louis was a Republican plot.[50]

On the other hand, Negro labor was an important strategic asset for industrialists in contests with the bourgeoning local labor movement. The country had just entered World War I when white unionists struck local meatpacking and metal-refining companies. Management responded by hiring black replacements who crossed picket lines.

In the spring of 1917, more than three thousand union men marched to City Hall to protest the unfair labor competition. Riled by angry speeches and fearing permanent displacement by cut-rate black labor, the crowd raged through the streets, destroying property and assaulting any Negroes they could lay their hands on. The governor sent troops to quell the rioting, at least for the moment.

But the underlying source of the conflict, Negroes who would work cheaper than whites, remained. And the black folk of East St. Louis knew to prepare for more violence. Black defense preparations also raised the perennial dilemma about whether arming in anticipation of conflict actually elevates the risk. Is it better to avoid such preparations on the worry that they escalate the risk and spur cycle of violence? Or do violent aggressors prey on weakness?

The rioting in East St. Louis ultimately prompted a congressional investigation. The conclusions were contested, but the formal findings laid much of the blame on black defense preparations. The precise focus was community leader Leroy Bundy, a relatively affluent black dentist. After the initial attacks in May, Bundy urged Negroes to keep their guns in good order and to acquire more where they could. According to the congressional report, this set East St. Louis on edge and sparked the conflagration.[51]

Fig. 5.3. Reporting on the East St. Louis riot. (*Springfield Republican*, Springfield, Massachusetts, July 3, 1917.)

The community was armed and primed for conflict when a car full of men drove through, shooting at shop windows and bystanders. When the car returned a short time later, Negroes with guns were prepared and fired preemptively, killing two men inside. But there was a mistake. This was not the same car. This was a car full of plainclothes policemen. And now Negroes had shot and killed two of them.[52]

Whites responded in a rampage that killed at least forty Negroes and destroyed multiple blocks of East St. Louis's black enclave. The NAACP pleaded with President Wilson to condemn the mobbing. Wilson said nothing. Investigators called the black defense preparations a conspiracy to riot instigated by Leroy Bundy. Bundy was charged with the murder of the two slain officers.[53]

Through the intervention of Ida B. Wells and her husband, Ferdinand Barnett, Leroy Bundy ultimately was cleared of the murder charges. In the aftermath, Ferdinand Barnett's advice reflected a common assessment of whether preparing for armed self-defense was a worse option than disarming and hoping for protection from the government. At a mass meeting of Negroes following the riot, Ferdinand Barnett advised his roaringly sympathetic audience, "Get guns and put them in your homes. Protect yourselves. Let no black man permit a policeman to come in and get those guns." Perfectly in sync with her husband's advice, Ida Wells urged that "Negroes everywhere stand their ground and sell their lives as dearly as possible when attacked."[54]

Fig. 5.4. A family portrait of Ferdinand Barnett and Ida B. Wells Barnett. (Photograph from 1917.)

Looking back, we know that things would improve for blacks over the twentieth century. But one wonders how W. E. B. Du Bois thought about the prospects for American Negroes in private moments of candor. Did he question the wisdom of staking his future here? Unlike many black folk, he had options and made a conscious bet on the United States of America.

Du Bois had lived and studied abroad. He had fallen for a German girl, or at least she had fallen for him. He could have stayed in Europe. But he returned, resolved to fight both politically and, if we credit his rhetoric, physically. His writing in the *Crisis* demonstrates that resolve.

But Du Bois was no isolated, intellectual radical. While he extolled self-defense rhetorically in the *Crisis*, the NAACP as an organization expended time, talent, and treasure to uphold the principle on behalf of black folk who defended themselves with guns. That fight consumed much of the young organization's resources.

From our vantage point today, the NAACP's work in support of armed self-defense seems remarkable. What, indeed, to make of the fact that armed self-defense was at the core of the first major case the organization supported? The year was 1910, and Pink Franklin, a South Carolina sharecropper, was accused of murder.

Considering the times, it was fortunate that Pink Franklin was not summarily lynched. His initial offense, the "crime" that started it all, was a basic breach of contract. Today this sends people to court in civil actions, seeking a stingy measure of damages to compensate for their disappointed expectations. Even in 1910, for white folk complaining about breach of contract, that was the remedy. But for a black sharecropper, the stakes were far higher.

Pink Franklin violated a special category of agricultural contract that was regulated under the South Carolina Criminal Code. It was a species of the peonage contracts that defeated Confederates attempted to enforce immediately after the Civil War under the Black Codes. The law said that sharecroppers who breached these agreements with planters could be punished by fines and imprisonment. The injured planter could secure his remedy through an arrest warrant enforced by the local magistrate. Negro contract breakers who could not pay their fines and mounting fees from incarceration might then be sold off under the convict labor system into a life that was just a step away from slavery.

Pink Franklin had indeed breached his contract. He signed on as a tenant farmer with one planter and then left for a better deal at another farm. The first planter claimed that Franklin still owed him money. That was enough to secure a warrant for Franklin's arrest. Lawyers would quibble later over whether the law authorizing the warrant was unconstitutional. But that grand illegal question would not be settled in time to shield Pink Franklin from the wrath and caprice of a jilted employer and a malevolent government agent.

In the dark of the early morning, around 3:00 a.m., armed men descended on Franklin's shanty, dubious warrant in hand. Stories conflict about the details. Franklin said that he was surprised in the middle of the night by strange men in his bedroom. When one of them shot him in the shoulder, Franklin dived to the floor, rolled to the gun he kept in the corner, and came up shooting.[55]

A surviving constable claimed that both the front door to Franklin's home and Franklin's bedroom door were ajar; that they knocked, entered, and then were surprised by gunfire from Franklin, an ax attack by Franklin's woman, and a flying tackle by Franklin's young son. There is no record of exactly what type of gun Franklin used. But it certainly was something more advanced than the single-shot technology often employed by poor folk, because two constables fell to Franklin's gunfire. One of them, Henry Valentine, eventually died from his wounds.

Franklin was convicted of murder and sentenced to death. The NAACP supported the case through an appeal to the United States Supreme Court and then, with the aid of Booker T. Washington, lobbied the governor of South Carolina to commute Franklin's death sentence to life imprisonment. In 1915, Franklin's case was reopened, and he was paroled in 1919.[56]

Shortly after taking on the Pink Franklin case, the NAACP assisted another tenant farmer charged with murder under similar circumstances. Steve Green of Arkansas walked off from his peonage contract after his landlord doubled his rent. On no legitimate authority, the planter forbade Green from ever working in the county again. It was the kind of arrogant demand that only makes sense in that time and place.

Bristling with racial entitlement, Green's jilted landlord came gunning for him after learning that Green was working for a neighbor. He did not come to negotiate. He just rode over to Green's new job and opened fire. The attack left Green bleeding but alive. Green retreated home, briefly tended his wounds, then grabbed his Winchester and went after his attacker.

Green turned out to be a better shot than his former boss, killing him efficiently and then fleeing. With the aid of friends and neighbors who hid him and then pooled money for a train ticket, Green made it to Chicago. Fresh in the big city, he managed to get arrested on a specious charge of petty larceny. From there, police connected him to the incident in Arkansas. Through the NAACP and with the assistance of Ida B. Wells, Green contested extradition to Arkansas. With extradition proceedings pending, Green fled to Canada.[57]

In 1919, a cash-strapped NAACP took on another armed self-defense case, coming to the aid of Sergeant Edgar Caldwell, an active-duty soldier stationed at Fort McClellan, Alabama. In December 1918, Caldwell was traveling into Anniston by streetcar when he provoked the wrath of a white conductor, Cecil Linton. Caldwell had dared to sit in the white section of the car. Linton figured to drag Caldwell from the forbidden zone. But Caldwell had a different idea. With the advantage of either strength or technique, Caldwell launched Linton through a glass divider between the cars. Linton called for help to the motorman, Kelsie Morrison, and they managed to throw Caldwell off the car. As Caldwell lay in the street, the two trolley-men advanced to give him a beating for good measure. Morrison, in his motorman's boots, stomped Caldwell, landing solid blows to the ribs.

Criminologists tracking mid-twentieth-century homicides would document that beating equaled and sometimes surpassed shooting and stabbing as a mode of criminal homicide.[58] Edgar Caldwell had no PhD in criminology, but he was a decorated veteran of World War I. He understood that death could come from hands and feet as well as knives and guns. Trapped on his back, writhing under the boot heels of Linton and Morrison, Caldwell drew his service revolver and shot twice, killing Linton and wounding Morrison.[59] It is encouraging that Caldwell was not immediately lynched. But that is offset by the fact that, during the same period, the NAACP protested a spate of mob killings of returning black veterans who were hanged or burned while still wearing their uniforms.[60]

Due largely to the legal assistance and political maneuvering of the local and national NAACP, including a failed appeal to the United States Supreme Court, Sergeant Caldwell survived for almost two years on death row before being executed. Over this period, Caldwell became a household name among Negroes. Writing in the *Crisis*, W. E. B. Du Bois detailed the efforts to save Caldwell and framed the issue as whether blacks would be afforded the basic prerogatives of manhood. The legendary NAACP Legal Defense Fund had yet to be formed, so the cash-strapped organization made direct appeals in the *Crisis* for donations to fund Caldwell's defense.

In the March 1920 edition, the *Crisis* published a full-length photograph of Caldwell with the appeal, "We want 500 Negroes who believe in Negro manhood to send immediately one dollar . . . for Caldwell's defense." The plea resonated with donors who responded not only with dollar bills mailed to NAACP headquarters in New York, but also notes and cards supporting the ideal of "Negro Manhood" exemplified by Caldwell's armed stand.[61]

After Caldwell's execution, Du Bois eulogized him as a martyr for black manhood and described the execution as, "one more addition to the long list of crimes which have been done in the manner of color prejudice." Du Bois's reaction was actually quite reserved by comparison to at least one other black intellectual of the day.[62]

Commenting on the class of hazards that snared Edgar Caldwell, Hubert H. Harrison wrote in 1921, "I advise you to be ready to defend yourselves. I notice that the State Government has removed some of its restrictions upon owning firearms, and one form of live [*sic*] insurance for wives and children might be the possession of some of these handy implements." Harrison, described by A. Philip Randolph as "the father of Harlem radicalism," was at the time, more militant than Du Bois. Although he is largely unknown today, one source calls Harrison "the foremost Afro-American intellect of his time" and "one of America's greatest minds."[63]

In 1923, the NAACP took another armed self-defense case to the Supreme Court. In *Moore v. Dempsey*, the association came to the aid of a group of black World War I veterans who returned to Elaine, Arkansas, intent on building something better than what they left. Many of the men returned to sharecropping but now demanded fair treatment, fair wages, and accurate accounting.[64]

Organized under the banner of the Progressive Farmers and Householders Union, they had hired lawyers and were gathered outside the town of Elaine to plot strategy. The union threatened many entrenched interests. So it was no surprise when a Phillips County deputy sheriff and agents of the Missouri Pacific Railroad arrived to break up the meeting and discourage any more of them, with a little rough treatment.

Standing on the privilege of race and office, the head lawman fired preemptively on the Negroes. Perhaps he worried that he would kill or injure someone, perhaps not. Maybe he was surprised when the simple black farmers, now steeled by combat, fired back. Whether surprise or anger, it would be the deputy's last emotion before he fell dead from Negro gunfire.

The white response was immediate and overwhelming. The sheriff deputized several hundred men and the governor mobilized troops. This force scoured the countryside ostensibly to find the shooters but ultimately in a campaign of retribution. But the going was harder than they expected, with black resistance yielding five more white casualties. The black casualty count, on the other hand, was at least twenty-five.[65]

Scores of Negroes were indicted for murder by an all-white grand jury. A few perfunctory trials produced verdicts of first-degree murder, which carried the death penalty. After that, most of the defendants pleaded guilty to second-degree murder, with its lesser penalty of life in prison. One of these sham trials lasted less than an hour, with the defendant first meeting his lawyer in the courtroom.

The NAACP pursued the cases to the Supreme Court, buoyed by tens of thousands of dollars of donations from around the country. Writing for a divided court, Oliver Wendell Holmes reasoned that the convictions must be reversed because the so-called trials were essentially an extension of the mob, and a sentence of death or imprisonment driven by mob passions was a violation of due process. The case was a grand victory for the NAACP. The optimistic observer might have taken it as affirmation that at the rudiments of a fair trial would extend even to Negroes who took up guns against capricious state authorities.[66]

In the very early stages of NAACP activism, substantial work occurred in the branches. The Detroit branch was particularly active and pressed several pieces of litigation challenging discriminatory commercial practices. Most of those efforts focused on local problems. But in one case the Detroit branch stretched its reach and captured national attention. Like important cases that followed, it was rooted in an act of armed self-defense.

The violence started in Georgia, where tenant farmer Thomas Ray repelled the threats and assault by his landlord with deadly gunfire. It was 1920, and Ray had a sufficient sense of southern justice to know that he should flee. He almost made it into Canada when he was apprehended by Detroit police.

As word of Ray's plight spread, the Detroit branch flew into action. The branch funded lawyers who blocked Ray's extradition, arguing that he would be lynched if returned to Georgia. And although NAACP branches were often the bastions of the Talented Tenth, the Ray case captured the passions of the entire community.

When rumors spread that whites had threatened to seize Ray from the jail, working-class men from the Negro enclave of "Black Bottom" ran to stand guard around the courthouse. The combination of formal legal proceedings and the community's resolve to protect Ray from the mob ultimately succeeded. In June 1921, more than a year after Thomas Ray had fled Georgia, the governor of Michigan freed him on the determination that he had shot in self-defense.[67]

At the close of World War I, W. E. B. Du Bois proclaimed in the *Crisis* that "we are cowards and jackasses if now that the war is over, we do not marshal every ounce of our brain and brawn to fight a sterner, longer, more unbending battle against the forces of hell in our own land." This militant call was not shared by everyone at the NAACP. And it certainly did not reflect the views of John Shillady, the organization's white executive secretary, a pacifist who abjured violence even at a personal level. After a mob attacked Negroes in Longview, Texas, in 1919, Shillady traveled to investigate. He was there only two days before he was assaulted by a white gang. He applied pacifist tactics and curled up into a little ball while they beat him senseless. Within a year, he had resigned from the NAACP.[68]

Shillady's replacement, James Weldon Johnson, the association's first black executive secretary, took a different stance. Following the July 1919 race riot in Washington, DC, Johnson investigated and offered this assessment of how and why peace was restored. "The Negroes saved themselves and saved Washington by their determination not to run but to fight, fight in the defense of their lives and their homes. If the white mob had gone unchecked—and it was only the determined effort of black men that checked it—Washington would have been another and worse East St. Louis."

The violence in DC was sparked by a rumor that a white soldier's wife had been raped by a Negro. The city was filled with military men back from World War I. It also had been filling for some time with blacks migrating out of the South in search of something better. On a hot Saturday in mid-July, hundreds of white veterans rampaged through DC's black neighborhoods. The violence continued two more days, peaking on Monday after an editorial from the *Washington Post* urged "every available serviceman to gather at Pennsylvania and Seventh Avenue at 9:00 p.m. for a cleanup that will cause the events of the last two evenings to pale into insignificance."

White servicemen answered the call and stormed through black neighborhoods in the southwest and Foggy Bottom. But the going was tougher in northwest Washington, DC, where the forewarned community was barricaded in and well-armed. As the mob approached, Negroes answered with a barrage of gunfire. The mob scattered. In the aftermath, cars were found riddled with bullet holes. Dozens of people were seriously wounded and one black man died by gunshot.

Black gunfire certainly helped staunch the mob. But it also helped that Washington was drenched by torrential rains and that President Wilson deployed two thousand troops to secure the streets. James Weldon Johnson certainly knew this. So his celebration of the black resistance seems like more than just an objective description of the events. It actually reads like a general prescription for black resistance against mobbing.[69]

Fig. 5.5. Portrait of James Weldon Johnson. (Black-and-white photoprints [Series 1], Scurlock Studio Records, ca. 1905–1994, Archives Center, National Museum of American History, Smithsonian Institution.)

In subsequent commentary, the *Crisis* extolled the enduring value of the black resistance in Washington, DC, in reporting about a black professor from Howard University who managed to find someone to sell him a house in a "restricted" area of the district. He was told to get out. When he refused, "his new home was given a battering."

Horrified, his intellectual friends at the college "recommended to him some interesting court procedures." But the militant professor and at least one of his colleagues pursued an alternate strategy. They "took the pains to build a barricade. One of them got his guns together and installed himself in the barricade. The two, fortified further by sandwiches and milk, quietly sat, watched and waited."

Local veterans who had been active in defending the community during the 1919 riots got wind of these rough tactics and sent word that they would keep watch over the militant professor's new home. Cause and effect are murky, but the reporting suggests that from this point, no further attacks occurred. The *Crisis* saw this as vindication. "The professor, using a rowdy principle, had opened up a new and decent area for Negro habitation. Thousands of fine Negroes live there now."[70]

The disappointments and hazards of the early century fueled radical approaches to addressing the plight of black folk. Socialist A. Philip Randolph and Black Nationalist Marcus Garvey rejected any possibility of just treatment for Negroes in America. Disparate philosophies led to bitter personal attacks between Randolph, Garvey, and W. E. B Du Bois.

Randolph, a driving force in the rise of the Brotherhood of Sleeping Car Porters, criticized that the NAACP was a tool of middle-class blacks. Randolph also split with Du Bois on the question of black service in World War I. Du Bois urged blacks to serve, arguing that by fighting they would earn their freedom. Randolph quipped that he would not fight to make the world safe for democracy but was more than willing to die at home to "make Georgia safe for the Negro." Philosophical disagreement led to personal attack, with Randolph calling Du Bois a "handkerchief head . . . hat-in-hand Negro."[71]

Marcus Garvey, who founded the Universal Negro Improvement Association in 1914 with the ambition of massive Negro migration to Africa, advanced a homegrown nationalist philosophy. Garvey castigated the NAACP as an organ of light-skinned, upper-class Negroes and leveled his own personal attack at Du Bois, charging that the rising intellectual leader of the race actually preferred the company of whites to blacks.

Returning the favor, Du Bois and Randolph expressed their disdain for Garvey's gaudy showmanship openly and in print. Both the *Crisis* and Randolph's signature publication, the *Messenger*, condemned Garvey and were sympathetic to established Negro leaders who reported mismanagement of Garvey's Black Star shipping line to the federal government.[72]

But despite their deep philosophical differences and personal animus, these stalwarts of competing factions in the early freedom movement found agreement on the point of individual self-defense.[73] There was, of course, disagreement about root causes of the perils to black folk. Randolph thought the plight of Negroes in America was rooted in capitalism, declaring that "lynching will not stop until Socialism comes."[74] Randolph saw no promise in legislation around the edges, warning, "Don't be deceived by any capitalist bill to abolish lynching; if it becomes a law it would never be enforced. Have you not the Fourteenth Amendment which is supposed to protect your life, property and guarantee you the vote?"[75] Randolph had a much broader assessment and a much grander plan:

> No, lynching is not a domestic question, except in the rather domestic minds of Negro leaders, whose information is highly localized and domestic. The problems of the Negroes should be presented to every nation in the world and this sham democracy, about which American's prate, should be exposed for what it is—a sham, a mockery, a rape on decency and a travesty on common sense. When lynching gets to be an international question, it will be the beginning of the end. On with the dance![76]

Fig. 5.6. Political cartoons from A. Phillip Randolph's *Messenger*, proclaiming the militancy of the "New Crowd Negro" and criticizing W. E. B. Du Bois and the "Old Crowd." (*Left:* "The 'New Crowd Negro' Making America Safe for Himself," *Messenger*, 1919. *Right:* "Following the Advice of the 'Old Crowd' Negro," *Messenger*, 1919.)

Acknowledging that his grand political agenda would take time, Randolph's short-term remedy was reciprocal violence in self-defense. He reconciled this with a broader pacifism, explaining that pacifism controlled "only on matters that can be settled peacefully." He did not equivocate about the legitimacy or utility of violence for people pressed to the wall, advising, "Always regard your own life as more important than the life of the person about to take yours, and if a choice has to be made between the sacrifice of your life and the loss of the lyncher's life, choose to preserve your own and to destroy that of the lynching mob."[77] Randolph's call resonated in the black press, even where people disagreed with his socialist agenda. The *Kansas City Call* celebrated Randolph's appeal to self-defense as the battle cry of the "New Negro," who was done "cringing" and was prepared to fight back.[78]

Marcus Garvey offered his own variation on the theme with a peculiar version of the traditional dichotomy between self-defense and political violence. Garvey openly advocated large-scale political violence, arguing that "all peoples have gained their freedom through organized force. . . . These are the means by which we as a race will climb to greatness."[79] Garvey's hedge was that this violence would occur not in America or Europe but in Africa, where organized blacks would retake what was theirs.[80]

Fig. 5.7. Marcus Garvey *(center)* in full regalia. (Photograph by James VanDerZee, © Donna Mussenden VanDerZee, all rights reserved, Photographs and Prints Division, Schomburg Center for Research in Black Culture, the New York Public Library.)

Domestically, Garvey embraced the traditional boundary against political violence, which he seemed to admit could not succeed in the United States. But on the point of private self-defense against imminent threats, Garvey was a traditionalist.

Although he was roundly criticized for acknowledging common ground with the racially separatist KKK, Garvey also challenged the Klan, writing, "They can pull off their hot stuff in the south, but let them come north and touch Philadelphia, New York or Chicago and there will be little left of the Ku Klux Klan. . . . Let them try and come to Harlem and they will really have some fun."[81]

Du Bois, Randolph, and Garvey embodied the early twentieth-century factions of the rising freedom movement. They were divided by profound philosophical differences. But on the basic point of personal security and response to the hazards that plagued Negroes, they found common ground. Harlem poet and Jamaican immigrant Claude McKay captured the general sentiment in a poem that circulated broadly in Randolph's *Messenger* and was widely reprinted. It was a paean to Negro manhood that closes with this: *"If we must die, let it not be like hogs, hunted and penned in an inglorious spot. . . . Like men we'll face the murderous, cowardly pack, pressed to the wall, dying but fighting back."*

McKay was extolling and encouraging the fighting spirit of the New Negro. He might well have been celebrating the last violent stand of the Three Hundred at Thermopolis.[82]

CHAPTER SIX

LEONIDAS

"**S**on, don't shoot until the first man puts a foot on the lawn and then—don't you miss."

That was the somber instruction from Walter White's father in 1906 as race rioting rocked Atlanta. Walter was only thirteen and entirely unknown to W. E. B. Du Bois, who, not too far away, paced with a shotgun, ready to defend his own family against the mob.

Years later, when they both were pulling heavy oars for the bourgeoning NAACP, Du Bois signaled the growing personal rift between them. Criticizing the ease with which White moved between two worlds, Du Bois complained, "He has more white companions and friends than colored. He goes where he will. . . . And naturally meets no color line, for the simple and sufficient reason he isn't colored."[1]

Du Bois was right that the blond-haired, blue-eyed Walter White lacked the physical characteristics of the typical colored man. But the ability to pass for white was no shield for Walter and his family in Atlanta in 1906. While Du Bois was patrolling with his shotgun, Walter White crouched with a rifle, behind lace curtains in the parlor of his family's neat bungalow.

Walter White came closer to shooting a man that night than most people ever will. The mob approached near enough for him to hear the venomous threat, "That's where that nigger mail carrier lives! Let's burn it down! It's too nice for a nigger to live in!" The only thing that prevented White from shooting that night was that his neighbors fired first. Like Walter and his father, they were armed and barricaded in. They also were quicker on the trigger, with some reports saying that their gunfire drove the mob away and others saying that it just drew them in a different direction.

This early incident with a gun had a profound effect on Walter White and might be the best explanation for why he did not take the smoother path through America as a white man. The Atlanta riot was a hinge point where White was "gripped by the knowledge of [his] identity."[2]

Decades later, a biographer would doubt the veracity of White's story about the gun. White was there, of course, so he should know. But it is still useful to consider that White might have made up the story. That sort of fabrication would suggest that he considered the account compelling, if not heroic, and expected it would resonate with his audience. Since he was writing at least in part to black folk, this would have been a fair surmise, especially considering that across town, Du Bois was doing basically the same thing. And it turns out that White and Du Bois were not the only future NAACP vanguards wielding guns in Atlanta that night.[3]

Walter White rose to power and influence within the NAACP and ultimately butted heads with Du Bois, who resigned his post at the *Crisis* in 1934, having lost the battle of egos and vision. A year after Du Bois's departure, the NAACP elected Dr. Louis T. Wright as chairman of the board. Wright was the first Negro ever to serve in the post. He was a graduate of Harvard Medical School and a Georgia native. Just like Walter White and W. E. B. Du Bois, Louis Wright survived the 1906 Atlanta riot. And just like White and Du Bois, his reaction demonstrated the core self-defense concern that fueled the black tradition of arms. Roy Wilkins, future steward of the NAACP, who observed Walter White, Louis Wright, and W. E. B. Du Bois during the association's early development, reveals, "Louis came from Atlanta. Like Walter he had been through the Atlanta race riot of 1906, and like Walter he had watched through the darkened windows of his home, gun in hand."[4] Louis Wright, W. E. B. Du Bois, and Walter White were among the cream of the Talented Tenth. They reflected a culture where the best people in the community unapologetically owned and carried firearms. They were part of a broader tradition in which the importance of armed self-defense seemed plain.

Like James Weldon Johnson, who recruited him to the NAACP, Walter White was abundantly gifted. He sacrificed greater financial success to pursue the work of a race man. Still, his prodigious talents spilled over into efforts that gained him a measure of fame as a literary figure. His popular novel *The Fire in the Flint* depicted of a black doctor and war veteran who returned to Georgia, aiming to do good work. In the novel's closing scene, the hero succumbs in a fashion that captures the theme of the New Negro, fighting desperately against long odds, outnumbered, plainly destined to die but committed to die fighting."[5]

Walter White's more remarkable achievement in print was the book *Rope and Faggot*, which distilled his firsthand accounts of more than forty lynchings. Passing for white, he witnessed the murderous rage, carnival atmosphere, and unfathomable barbarism of the mob. With few discernible Negro characteristics, Walter White stood in the crowds and reported back on the very worst mob violence of the early twentieth century. Some of the details are so gruesome, they read like slasher fiction, doubly horrifying against the new prosperity of the Industrial Revolution and happy images of flappers dancing the Charleston.

But *Rope and Faggot* is not just a chronicle of the macabre. White offers cutting social, psychological, and political critiques of lynching. He also demonstrates the visceral draw of the self-defense impulse. From Nodena, Arkansas, White reported the case of Henry Lowery, who worked under a contract that made him a virtual slave. Lowery's landlord treated him accordingly. On Christmas Day, 1920, Lowery boldly demand his overdue wages. His landlord responded with curses and kicking. As the two men scuffled, the landlord's son drew a gun and shot Lowery. Wounded, Lowery pulled his own gun. In the exchange of shots, Lowery killed the landlord and the man's daughter (hit by a stray bullet). Lowery ran as far as Texas, where he was captured. On his return, he was seized by a mob, chained to a log, doused with gasoline, and roasted alive.

White's account of the Lowman family in Aiken, South Carolina, demonstrates the typical self-defense scenario where folk were desperate and had no clearly better choices. It was 1925 and Prohibition was in full swing. Sam's whiskey making drew the sheriff and four deputies out to his rural cabin. Sam was gone when they arrived, which left them to concentrate on his wife, Bertha. Bertha must have sassed them because the sheriff punched her square in the mouth. Bertha's mother ran to intervene, and one of the deputies shot her through the heart. Hearing the gunshots, Bertha's brother and cousin came running from the field. They evidently had guns on them or laid nearby, because the next thing was a gunfight that left the sheriff dead and the two black men wounded.

Like all of the episodes in *Rope and Faggot*, this one ended in Negroes killed by a mob. This time it was a crowd of two thousand, and they made a game of it. Jailers helped the mob remove the Lowmans to a tourist camp on the outskirts of Aiken. They set them free and told them to run. Then they shot them down like feral dogs. Prominent in the crowd were local lawyers, businessmen, and several members of the South Carolina legislature.[6]

James Weldon Johnson said that the federal government bore part responsibility for the mobbing in Aiken. The Senate's refusal to act on the Dyer Anti-Lynching Bill, he argued, "was equivalent to serving notice on the lynchers that they could pursue their pastime virtually unmolested."[7] Johnson's mentor, Charles W. Anderson, leveled a similar criticism at Woodrow Wilson's policy of segregating the federal workforce, arguing that Wilson's policy had "the reflex influence of giving anti-Negro elements across the country the feeling that they would not be punished by federal authorities."[8]

Walter White reported another episode in *Rope and Faggot* that prompts us to think again about people who pick up a guns in defense of others. White did not witness this incident, but he drew the details from a report by Georgia governor Hugh Dorsey. The case demonstrates a category of violence where black men tried to protect wives, daughters, and girlfriends from carousing white men. It ended in a fashion that White claimed was typical.

Two drunk white men were roaming the Negro section, trolling for sport. An elderly Negro grabbed his gun and ran to the defense of black womanhood. Before it was over, one of the white men lay dead in the street. The Negro was arrested, broken out of jail, and lynched before he got a decent meal. It is an open question whether this fellow was a selfless hero or just a meddler who transformed a sex prowl into a cycle of death.[9] And we might even ask why violence in defense of others fits under self-defense at all.

The questions that plague violent defense of others are even more poignant where people deploy guns in defense of an idea. One is tempted to say that this kind of violence is inherently political, exactly the kind of thing that the black tradition of arms disdained. Walter White's account of Robert Moton complicates that assessment. Moton succeeded Booker T. Washington as president of Tuskegee Institute and was an unlikely advocate of the gun. Tuskegee was a conservative, some said accommodationist, force in the freedom movement. Robert Moton exhibited that approach. But even an innately conservative and gentle man like Moton could retreat only so far. We learn from Walter White about Moton's preparations in 1923 when the local Klan threatened to destroy Tuskegee.

The conflict sparked over Veterans Administration plans to build a Negro hospital on the grounds of Tuskegee. The NAACP had protested construction of any new segregated hospitals. But Moton welcomed the project because he would have influence over the jobs it brought. Local whites also wanted control over the hospital jobs and deployed the Klan to help them take it. In a show of force designed to quell Negro opposition, the Klan paraded and assembled on the grounds of Tuskegee. Walter White's brother, George, was in Alabama at the time. Passing for white, he gained entry to the Klan assembly, where men talked of torching Tuskegee and killing Moton if necessary.

With the plot brewing, Walter White rushed to Washington to seek intervention by the Veterans Administration, and then to Alabama to strategize with Moton. There he found a changed man. "I sat with him in his home in Tuskegee during the height of the trouble," White recalled. "He pointed to a rifle and a shotgun well-oiled and grimly businesslike, that stood in the corner of the room. Although his words in cold print sound overheroic, they did not sound so to me as he said quietly, 'I've got only one time to die. If I must die now to save Tuskegee Institute, I'm ready. I've been running long enough.'"

The conflict at Tuskegee was defused without gunfire by an army general who commandeered the hospital staffing decisions. But we are left to ponder Robert

Moton's movement to the gun. He had plenty of warning that danger was lurking. He could have guaranteed his personal safety by running away. But Moton took up the gun and stood his ground in defense of place and principle. And it is illuminating to imagine the fallout if he had fired his guns and killed someone under the umbrella of self-defense. A narrow conception of self-defense might say that Moton's failure to retreat on fair warning should block any subsequent self-defense claims; that by laying in wait with guns, Moton was courting violence that was easily avoided. The alternative instinct would affirm Moton's resolve to run no more and leads to a broader conception of legitimate self-defense. These competing impulses illuminate disparate philosophies and the divergent American rules about retreat and the boundaries of self-defense.[10]

The black tradition of arms evolved through a long period where, at least for interracial conflicts, the law was overwhelmingly hostile to Negro self-defense claims. But on this score the odds for black self-defenders actually improved during the lynch era. The Mississippi Supreme Court's intervention in 1919 to save Anthony Williams from the gallows demonstrates the trend. Williams is a proof case because he was not some harmless uncle or a community favorite. Anthony Williams was a common Negro who shot and killed a Mississippi deputy sheriff.

It started with dice. There was a big gathering in the town of Arcola, with attendant drinking and gambling. Williams was shooting dice behind a boarding house when someone was called a cheat, and someone pulled a knife. Then one of the men ran to the sheriff, claiming that Anthony Williams drew a pistol on him.

In the habit of the times, the arrest of Anthony Williams was just the beginning. Intent on confiscating the pistol, sheriff's deputies decided to beat Williams until he coughed up the gun. They dragooned several men to hold him down. They kicked him with heavy boots. Then they stripped him and beat him with the buckle end of a belt until the brass lock broke off.

The beating worked, in a fashion. Williams pleaded for them to stop and promised to show where he hid the gun. They went back to the scene of the gambling and searched all around but did not find the pistol. Now frustrated by the impudent Negro and his elusive gun, the deputies decided to stake him out and give him a full and proper whipping.

As they were dragging him off to be hided, Williams jerked out of the way of a passing horse, prompting one of the deputies to take a shot at him. Williams then ran for his gun, which was hidden all along on his horse, saddled nearby. In the prosecution that followed, the court, quoting his trial testimony, projected Williams's dilemma. "I said Lordy if I don't get it I am killed, and if I do get it I am killed. One mind said get your gun and that time I eased up to my horse and got my gun from under the pommel of the saddle."

The deputies had better guns and more shooters. But Anthony Williams was more efficient, or at least more resilient. He was shot twice but managed to fire back, killing a deputy. He was convicted of murder and sentenced to death. After two trips to the Mississippi Supreme Court, Williams's conviction was overturned on the grounds that he shot the deputy in self-defense against an unlawful beating and whipping.[11]

The case is remarkable first because Williams was not simply lynched. The prosecutor's cynical praise of the nascent lynch mob for their restraint shows that this was a real possibility. Of greater long-term importance was the court's finding that the post-arrest brutality was illegal and sufficient to justify Williams's violent response. This sort of official affirmation is the essential final component of any fully successful act of self-defense and something that Negroes had seldom been able to count on.[12]

Before the decade ended, the Mississippi Supreme Court issued another decision that similarly defies the intuitions fueled by the horrors chronicled in *Rope and Faggot*. In *Byrd v. State*, the court reversed the conviction and dismissed the prosecution of Jack Byrd, who was tried, convicted, and sentenced to life in prison for the Christmas Eve murder of Bilbo Cox in the town of D'Lo.

The first notable thing is that the prosecution miscalculated the influence of white privilege. Race still played significantly in the court's assessment. But here it tilted in favor of the accused Negro who was vouched for by numerous prominent white men. These same sponsors also commented on the low reputation of the dead man and his surviving companion, Burkett Neely.

The credible testimony depicted Cox and Neely as carousing drunks who descended on the "Negro Quarters" around midnight in search of whiskey and sport. They started a row in a colored café, assaulting Wes Byrd, while claiming that they were "the law." The café operator fled to seek intervention from his white landlord, who demurred. Then someone ran to tell Jack Byrd that his brother was in trouble.

Jack Byrd grabbed his shotgun and headed to the café, where Cox and Neely turned to him as new and more interesting entertainment. In a stream of profanity and racial invective, they threatened to kill Byrd if he did not surrender his gun. When Byrd refused, they opened fire with revolvers, wounding but not disabling him. Byrd shot back, killing Cox.

Finding that the two white men "were aggressors from start to finish," the Mississippi Supreme Court acknowledged and criticized the impact that race played at the trial, and articulated the racial baseline against which adjudications of black self-defense were evolving. "We cannot escape the conclusion that if this had been a case where the white man had killed a white man, or a Negro had killed a Negro, or a white man had killed a Negro, there would never have been a conviction. We therefore reverse the verdict and judgment; and . . . we order the defendant discharged."[13]

These types of cases show that things were changing. The viability of armed self-defense seemed greater now than a generation before. One is even tempted to consider that the residual terror of the lynch mob, its influence on the black psyche, perhaps exceeded the actual threat to any particular Negro. Of course, backwater lynch mobs were not the only worry.

Walter White's surreptitious reporting of hangings and burnings from river banks and oak groves demanded the nerve and courage of an undercover agent. But in other work, like his reporting on the Tulsa, Oklahoma race riot, White operated openly as an investigative journalist and social analyst.[14]

The Tulsa riot started with the arrest of a black man for allegedly assaulting a white woman in a downtown building. Dick Rowland was taking an elevator to one of the few places in that part of town where he could use the toilet. The alleged victim, Sara Page, first said that the nineteen-year-old bootblack grabbed her arm. Later she said that Rowland had stepped on her foot. Some surmised that Rowland stepped on her foot and reflexively grabbed her arm to stop her from falling back. Page refused to press charges and the case was dropped. But the mob would not wait for all of that.[15]

Tulsa was an unlikely venue for one of the worst race riots of the era. Walter White noted that "one could . . . find few cities where the likelihood of trouble between the races was as little thought of as in Tulsa." Still, there were discernible seeds of conflict. The oil boom had dropped riches on enterprising blacks as well as whites. A formidable accumulation of wealth was displayed along Greenwood Avenue, known proudly as "Black Wall Street." This was a source of jealousy from less enterprising whites.

Tulsa's Jim Crow practices also fueled tension. The black frontier types who settled the area were prickly in their opposition to Jim Crow and less obsequious than many folk in their dealings with whites. This sort of spirit fueled the rapid response to the rumor that a lynch mob had targeted Dick Rowland.

The rumor was perpetrated in part by the local white press. The *Tulsa Daily Tribune* ran a generally inaccurate story about the elevator incident and a forming mob, under the headline "To Lynch Negro Tonight."[16] The black men of Tulsa were having none of it. On the rumor that a mob was headed for the jail, armed Negroes ran to protect Dick Rowland. They arrived to find the rumor exaggerated. After an exchange with the sheriff, who promised that Rowland was safe, they dispersed.[17] Later that evening, new rumors spread that a mob was staging to assault the jail. Black men assembled again, seventy-five strong, and headed to the courthouse.

The spark of the violence was a testosterone-fueled showdown between one of the black men, an army veteran, and a white man who could not abide the sight of Negroes with guns. The black veteran was carrying his GI Model 1911 .45 caliber, semiautomatic pistol. Eyewitnesses report the white man approaching and demanding, "Nigger where you going with that pistol?"

The black veteran replied, "I'm going to use it if I need to."

"No, you give it to me," said the white man.

"Like hell I will," replied the veteran.

With the confident arrogance of a superior race, the white man strode forward to disarm the Negro. Then he confronted the force of a 230-grain, .45 caliber slug traveling at almost one thousand feet per second. It knocked him down flat even though fired from the hand of a lowly Negro. From there, the sheriff recorded, "the race war was on and I was powerless to stop it."[18]

Like any such conflict, countless individual episodes and calculations go unrecorded. The stories of many of the people who perished will never be told. But from the survivors there is vivid detail of the fighting and dying.

Bill Williams was only sixteen when the rioting broke out. His parents had prospered during the oil boom, extracting from Jim Crow an opportunity to build a garage, a soda fountain, and a theater catering to blacks. Bill's father, John, was among the armed men who assembled to protect Dick Rowland.

Some reports say that the initial violence at the courthouse killed ten whites and a lesser number of blacks. This, of course, was not the end of things. John Williams returned home after midnight, expecting that things would get worse. When Bill awoke at 5 a.m., he found his father, having sat up all night, cradling his .30-30 lever-action rifle. A pump-action shotgun was propped against the wall. As the day progressed, the gunfire intensified and the mob advanced on Greenwood Avenue. For a while, the Williams family held up in the apartment over their business. John Williams fired on the mob from cover until they discerned his position and riddled the building with gunfire.

The Williams family ran out the back, then northward up Greenwood. John Williams left his wife and son with people who were sheltered at a funeral parlor. Then he ran next door to a pool hall, where he could get "a right-hand shot" at the advancing mob. With his rifle, John Williams shot men from the pool hall, aided by another black man who worked the shotgun.

The mob advanced again in another wave, sending John Williams, his wife, and their son, Bill, scattering in different directions. Unlike many families in Tulsa, they reunited the next day with everyone uninjured. But many blacks had not survived the night. Over one thousand black homes were destroyed, and black Wall Street was ashes.[19]

Fig. 6.1. Coverage of the violence from *Tulsa World Daily*, June 2, 1921.

The death toll is contested. Various casualty estimates attempted to shape the story. And there are many possibilities. But one of particular note comes from America's preeminent black historian, John Hope Franklin. Franklin moved to Tulsa in 1925 at age ten. He observed that the black community viewed the 1921 riot as a manifestation of their courage, and as a lesson about the proper response to racist aggression. Franklin recounted the conventional wisdom within the black community that "many more whites were killed during the riot than many whites were willing to admit." He also speculates about the details from his own experience. In the late twenties, Franklin was regularly at the courthouse, observing his father's law practice. He was especially attentive to cases involving the estate of "some white person who died on or about June 1, 1921. One was always tempted to conclude that the deceased lost his life in the riot."

With the historian's careful eye, Franklin acknowledged that community assessments of white casualties were likely exaggerated. But he found that the embellished local lore still had "the desired effect." The fighters at Tulsa were cast in the mold of heroes across the ages who had fought bravely against long odds—the immortalized light brigade charging artillery positions with swords, the Three Hundred Spartans dead to the last man at Thermopolis, and, dare one say, the countless Confederate boys who fell in service of the Lost Cause. Black folk, said Franklin, did not see the death and destruction at Tulsa as an episode of black victimization. According to Franklin, they cast it as a story of classic heroism and marshaled it to profound practical effect.

The self-confidence of Tulsa's Negroes soared, their businesses prospered, their institutions flourished, and they simply had no fear of whites. After 1921, an altercation in Tulsa between a white person and a black person was not a racial incident, even if there was a loss of life. It was just an incident. Such an attitude had a great deal to do with eradicating the fear that a Negro boy growing up in Tulsa might have felt in the years following the riot.[20]

Fig. 6.2. Photograph depicting the burning of black residences and businesses in Tulsa during the race riots. ("Running the Negro out of Tulsa," June 1, 1921.)

The fighting at Tulsa is a piece with the storied 1923 conflict in Rosewood, Florida, an episode so dramatic it would provoke the attention of commercial film-makers, who presented a story of heroes far more militant than the familiar brave folk who endured attack dogs, fire hoses, and baton charges with stoic nonviolence.

The violence at Rosewood had a familiar start. A white woman, named Fanny Taylor, had been assaulted. The suspect was a black escapee from a chain gang. Bloodhounds took a scent from Fanny Taylor's torn clothes and raced away, followed by a crowd of armed men that swelled as word spread. Soon the dogs were on him, or at least onto something, and they were headed straight to the black town of Rosewood.

The dogs chased the scent to the cabin of Aaron Carrier and stopped cold at fresh wagon tracks leading away from Carrier's back door. With the hounds stymied, the posse headed for Carrier's mother's house, where they found Aaron hiding upstairs. With his mother screaming on the porch, they dragged Aaron Carrier out of the house. Then they tied him to the back of a Model T Ford, and dragged him until he admitted that another man, Sam Carter, had helped the rape suspect escape.

The posse fanned out over Rosewood, warning curious Negroes to get out of sight. They broke into Sam Carter's house, put a noose around his neck, and pulled him outside to an old oak tree. They would torture the truth out of him. And after intermittent strangling and mutilation, Carter said that he had driven the suspect to a spot on the edge of the swamp.

They yanked Carter down and made him show them the spot. When the hounds failed to pick up a scent and it seemed that Carter had just said what they wanted after torture, one of the frustrated men, stinking of moonshine, shot Carter point blank in the head. Then they hoisted his body up into a tree and riddled it with bullets.

The violence cycled from there. Rumor spread that blacks were planning to retaliate for the attacks on Sam Carter and Aaron Carrier. At the center of those rumors was a tall, dark-skinned Negro folk in Rosewood called simply, "Man." His Christian name was Sylvester Carrier.

Sylvester Carrier was a quick and accurate rifle shot who lived on what he could harvest from the swamps, along with the occasional stolen head of livestock. He actually had served time for cattle rustling, the whole time arguing that he was set up by whites. And he carried an anger fueled by the claimed injustice of it. Black folk who saw him at church playing the organ and singing had a richer sense of Man. But they also did not doubt his disposition to fight, even against long odds.

Rumor said that blacks were massing at the home of Sarah Carrier, Man's mother. And that was enough to draw a band of armed men, about a dozen of them, to a railroad siding within hollering distance of Sarah's home. It was a cold night for Florida. They built a fire and planned their attack.

Sarah Carrier knew these white men. She actually had nursed two of them. As the men approached, she went out onto the porch and scolded them like she would her grandchildren. "Y'all go on home, get yourselves on home." Someone in the group, no one would say who, didn't like Sarah's tone and shot her through the head. Then they descended on the house, where Sylvester Carrier was waiting with a Winchester lever-action rifle and a pump shotgun.

As the first man stepped foot on the porch, Man shot him through the face. An instant later, a second man up fell to a slug from Man's Winchester. Others retreated as Sylvester Carrier shot rapid-fire through the front and side windows, wounding another man who tried to climb to a second-floor window. After regrouping they attempted one more assault on the house that left two more of them wounded by Man's blistering gunfire.

The word spread like jungle drumming. White men came from across the region, one contingent from Gainesville, others from Jacksonville, and scores more from no-name places in between. Soon there were hundreds of them, aiming to wreak vengeance on the community that had spawned this Negro who raised his gun to such deadly effect against white men. In full froth, the mob raged through Rosewood, killing two blacks who had lingered—one old widow, and an old swamp man who called himself "Lord God."

Finally, the mob descended on James Carrier, the old man of the clan. After a perfunctory interrogation, they dragged him to two fresh graves. There lay Man and his mother and Sarah. They forced James at gunpoint to dig his own grave. It wasn't much of a hole, and the dirt he managed to move with his one good arm before they killed him was washed away by the first rain.

The law, such as it was, arrived belatedly, to a scene of utter destruction. As far as structures, Rosewood was not much of a town in the first place—thirty homes, a few no more than shacks, but three churches, a general store, and a masonic lodge. Now it was just death and ashes.[21]

The white press depicted Rosewood as a riot stemming from the familiar poisonous root of sexual assault, exacerbated by Negroes with guns. But the black press cast the fighters of Rosewood as heroes. The *New York Age* compared the incident to recent acts of self-defense in Chicago where "the Negro was not afraid to fight back and when the fight was over he felt that he had something pretty near a fair chance before the law. Those are two conditions which the suffocating, damning atmosphere of the South does not permit."

Sylvester Carrier was elevated as an exemplar of black manhood by the *Pittsburgh American*, which declared that Rosewood should "make Negroes everywhere feel proud and take renewed hope. For our people have fought back again! They have met the mob with its own deadly weapons, they've acquitted themselves like freemen and were not content to be burned like bales of hay."

This was not just a general endorsement of self-defense, of the type that virtually anyone might make when pressed. The *Pittsburgh American* was talking pointedly about self-defense with guns. "Things have come to the place in this country that the only course for the Negro is armed resistance. Lynchers are free to prowl the earth and butcher any Negro who gets in their path. The only way for the black man then is to keep his powder dry and shoot back."[22]

The *Kansas City Call* was equally resolute that "no man in his right senses expects to run, and run, and run forever. . . . Man created in God's image will always choose to die face to the fore—whenever it is sufficiently clear that he may not live in peace." Leavening this militant stance was at least a rhetorical admonition against political violence. "We cannot establish rights by fighting," said the *Call*, "But how under heaven can we urge our people to die like sheep. . . . How can we ask them to be cowards?"[23]

Walter White was among the many commentators on Rosewood, and he openly despaired that the American conscience was not shocked by the terror. But White was not crippled by despair. Indeed, by some measure, the brutality energized him to fight. Many fought back physically, and White had shown as a boy his courage for the physical fight. But his talents drew him to a subtler form of combat. He would soon become instrumental in building one of the vital institutions of the modern freedom movement. And that work was solidly rooted in the black tradition of arms.

Walter White confronted a multitude of challenges over his long career at the NAACP. But one of the most remarkable episodes began shortly after he was recruited to the association by James Weldon Johnson.[24] Johnson was a polymath— lawyer, educator, newspaper editor, novelist, classically trained musician, and composer whose "Lift Every Voice and Sing" is embraced today as the "Black National Anthem." As a child growing up in the Williamsburg section of New York, Johnson and his friends played at the feet of militant journalist T. Thomas Fortune.[25]

As a young man studying at Atlanta University, Johnson gave a prize-winning speech that captured the early philosophy of the organization he would come to lead. Blacks should seek to rise through industry, education, and the accumulation of wealth, he said. But Johnson also cautioned strongly against submission to oppression, arguing that "half of the suffering of the race would be eradicated" if Negroes fought back against the terror of the lynch mob.[26]

Johnson was counsel to Nicaragua and Venezuela under Republican administrations and had deep personal and political animus for the southern-born Democrat Woodrow Wilson. It was Wilson's reelection in a close contest with Republican Charles Evans Hughes that spurred Johnson to go work for the NAACP. Although blacks had many fair complaints about Republicans by 1916, Johnson was optimistic about the prospects under Hughes, who, as a Supreme Court Justice, had recently written an opinion overturning a discriminatory Oklahoma voting law. Against the backdrop of Democrats' dominance in the South, and Woodrow Wilson's recent praise of the newly released Klan paean, *Birth of a Nation*, Johnson cast his lot with the party of Lincoln. So when Wilson was returned to the White House, Johnson girded for battle.[27]

Johnson aimed to staff the NAACP with people like himself, men from the Talented Tenth. Walter White was firmly in that mold. Indeed, by almost any measure, White was in the top fraction of the Talented Tenth. And whatever resentments his talents and privilege might stir, he answered with a tireless commitment to justice for black folk.

Ossian Sweet was also a man of the Talented Tenth, though some would say just barely so. Sweet was born poor in the little town of East Bartow in rural Florida. His one advantage was hard-working, God-fearing parents who loved him. That turned out to be plenty.

It was a long road for Ossian Sweet from East Bartow into the ranks of the Talented Tenth. Some mixture of courage, prescience, and a lucky affiliation with Florida's African Methodist Church landed Ossian a spot at Wilberforce College in Ohio. Wilberforce had educated Negroes since before the Civil War, operating on the site of the old Tawawa Springs resort. Southern slavers had entertained their black concubines there and then helped repurpose the place as a school for their mulatto children.[28]

Sweet was a good but not exceptional student. So his ambition to become a doctor bordered on hubris. There were only two black medical schools in the country, and they only admitted about one hundred men per year. But Sweet's chances improved when the United States entered World War I.

The war was an opportunity, said the black leadership, to earn respect through service. Writing in the *Crisis*, W. E. B. Du Bois urged the men of the Talented Tenth to join the war effort. And many of them—class leaders at Howard, Fisk, and Lincoln, who would have competed for slots in America's two black medical schools—heeded the call. Ossian Sweet was not among them. Although he was willing to serve, his eyesight was so poor, he was deemed unfit. And in the fall of 1917, with the world at war, Sweet entered the college of medicine at Howard University in Washington, DC.

Sweet would graduate from Howard and head for Detroit with visions of life as a prosperous member of the Negro elite. But he carried with him an embedded tribal knowledge, the awareness of a race, and specific memories of his childhood in East Bartow, where in the summer of 1901, he saw sixteen-year-old Fred Rochelle burned alive by a mob. Sweet also worried about the more recent violence and risks of his times.

Like Ida B. Wells before him, Sweet was jolted to the reality that social standing was no protection against mobbing. For Wells, the lesson was in the lynching of Tom Moss. For Sweet, it came in reports about the four Johnson brothers who were found shot up in the backseat of a police car in an Arkansas woodlot in 1919. The bodies were still handcuffed. One of the brothers was a doctor and the other was a dentist. Ossian Sweet was a proud striver, but he had no illusions about the hazards of his time.

When Sweet's mother-in-law learned that Ossian and her overproud daughter Gladys had bought a house on Garland Avenue in an all-white section of Detroit, about midway between the inner-city enclave of "Black Bottom" and tony Grosse Pointe, she pulled Ossian close and tucked a pistol into his coat pocket. Sweet already owned a .38 caliber Smith & Wesson revolver, taken earlier as payment from a patient. These were two of the twelve guns that he carried into the Garland Avenue bungalow on moving day.

In the modern gun debate, it is common to talk about what guns and how many guns people need. In that light, Ossian Sweet's twelve guns may seem excessive. But Sweet took a different view. Thinking hard about his exposure, Sweet asked his brothers, a cousin, and several other solid men to stay through the night and carried in two canvas sacks weighted down with a shotgun, rifles, six pistols, and four hundred rounds of ammunition.

Sweet was familiar enough with firearms that the mechanics of self-defense were comfortable, and for his brother Henry, so were the tactics. Henry Sweet had followed Ossian to Wilberforce, where he enrolled in the Cadet Corps. The marching, drilling, and uniforms appealed to him. And in one case, there was an opportunity to put the discussions of strategy and tactics to work when a local black farmer, William Martin, became a target of midnight terrorists.

First, Martin's hayrick was torched. Then shots were fired into his house. This prompted the Wilberforce Cadet commander to put theory into practice, with an ostentatious display of armed drills, a march to Martin's farm and deployment in a defensive perimeter. With this display of force, the attacks on William Martin stopped. Ossian Sweet might have hoped that a similar show of force would earn him a grudging peace in his new neighborhood. But it would not be that easy.[29]

Detroit was a hot destination in the black migration of the early twentieth century. In 1910, there were fewer than six thousand Negroes in Detroit. By 1925, the city's black population had grown to eighty-one thousand. Along with the influx of Negroes came a rising Klan presence. By 1924, the Klan had thirty-five thousand members in Detroit, and Klansmen vied openly for municipal office. In 1925, the Klan put forward a candidate for mayor and that summer demonstrated its growing political power with spectacle. In a huge field on Detroit's west side, a sea of robes and hoods swayed around a fiery cross, and angry men screeched about the scourge of Negroes, Jews, Catholics, Italians, and other "non-Americans."[30]

The Klan surged on anxiety about the building wave of Negro immigration. But for Detroit's Talented Tenth, the increasingly crowded and tumultuous black ghetto of Black Bottom carried things that they too wanted to escape. Some said publicly that the habits and culture that pervaded Black Bottom as southern migrants piled in were part of the reason for increasing racism among whites. The head of the Detroit Urban League, Forrester Washington, with degrees from Tufts and Harvard, criticized that segregation was increasing in the city, "chiefly on account of the loud, noisy, almost nude women in 'Mother Hubbard's' standing around on the public thoroughfares." This assessment was complicated by the reception that Ossian Sweet and other black strivers received when they tried to move onto white blocks.[31]

Ossian Sweet was not the first doctor from Dunbar Memorial Hospital to venture into Detroit's white neighborhoods. And one earlier attempt carried hard lessons that help explain why the first night in his new home, Sweet recruited a squad of men to stay over, and why he carried in two bundles of guns and ammunition. In the summer of 1925, five black families who attempted to move onto white blocks were mobbed and run out by their new neighbors. This tally included Dr. Alexander Turner, a colleague of Sweet's at Dunbar. Turner did not even get to spend the night in his new home on Spokane Avenue. Within hours of moving in, a mob descended, breaking windows and then breaching the door. They trashed the inside and ran off with the few things that the Turners had brought in.

Alexander Turner escaped with his skin, but not his dignity. The story of him cowering on the floor of his flashy, chauffeured Lincoln sedan, and subsequently signing over the deed of his new home to the "neighborhood improvement association" was widely recounted, to the delight of many whites and the horror and shame of blacks.

The image of Turner huddled on the floor of his car haunted Ossian Sweet. Across the community and even among the doctors at Dunbar Memorial Hospital, Turner's retreat was reviled. Perhaps projecting a touch of class envy, one common man criticized, "The dirty coward got down on the floor of his car and made his chauffeur drive through the mob." Another critic complained that Turner "knew when he moved in he was going to have trouble and he should have gone prepared to stay or die."

Removed from the terror of the mob, and mostly behind Turner's back, the doctors at Dunbar uniformly proclaimed that they would have made a stand. And their recommended tools and tactics were quite specific. One armchair defender proclaimed, "I have made up my mind what I would do if a mob comes to drive me out of my home. I have a revolver and a shotgun. I have a rifle. I'm not going to attack anyone that does not attack me, but the first individual that comes over to tear up my home, he'll pay with his life." This was the sentiment in the summer of 1925 when Gladys Sweet pressed her cautious husband to act on the principle that they had a right to live wherever they wanted.

The Sweets bought their new home from Ed and Marie Smith, a nominally white couple who had lived on Garland Avenue for years. Ed Smith was actually a Negro passing for white. But this submerged kinship was no proof against gouging. Like many "first Negroes on my block," the Sweets paid a monstrous premium for the Garland property, roughly $18,500 for a house worth $12,000 to white people.

The Smiths financed the property because Detroit banks would not lend to Negroes. The banks said that blacks drove down property values and no one could predict how far. Here again the Smiths offered no tribal discount. In fact, just the opposite. Ossian and Gladys put 20 percent down and then agreed to pay off the rest over ten years at 18 percent interest.

The economics were familiar. The first few sellers could demand premium prices. Then, as more Negroes bought in the neighborhood, whites would flee, dumping their homes at fire-sale prices. That fear, the worry that their little piece of the American dream would dissolve under a wave of Negroes, combined with the enduring tribalism that fuels racism, pushed the white people of Garland Avenue to organize and take to the streets, to keep the Negroes out.

Ossian Sweet had his own fears, not just of the violence that snagged Al Turner, but also the humiliation that now hounded him. So as they undertook what should have been the happy task of house buying, Ossian proceeded with the resolve of a man headed into combat. After the first hints that he would not be welcome in the neighborhood where he had wildly overpaid for a nice home on a neat corner lot, Sweet told a friend, "Well, we have decided we are not going to run. We're not going to look for any trouble, but we're going to be prepared to protect ourselves if trouble arises." The determination to be a different kind of man from Al Turner would drive Sweet to actions that reverberated nationwide.

By September, the word had spread along Garland Avenue that Negroes had bought the Smith house. Ossian and Gladys actually completed the transaction more than a month earlier. But they decided to delay moving in until after school started, reasoning that fewer kids out on the streets would lessen the chance of a moving-day incident. The strategy seemed to work. The initial move provoked only a clutch of teenage boys running by and yelling "Nigger."

The Sweets resolved to capture the happiness and conviviality of moving into a new home. Two of Gladys's friends, her maid-of-honor and another woman, stopped by to compliment the house and hear Gladys's decorating plans. One of Ossian's hospital colleagues stopped by with a gift. Soon the house warmed with compliments and laughter of guests, now including Ossian's brothers Otis and Henry; the chauffer, Joe Mack; and their handyman, Murray. Things must have seemed almost normal because they lost track of time and failed to appreciate the descending menace of nightfall.

As the sun set, a crowd gathered across the street. Four Detroit policemen walked the block and kept the crowd off the walkway directly in front of the house. Now, fully enveloped in nightfall, the crowd grew to about two hundred.[32]

Sweet called the men upstairs and showed them the guns that he had stowed in the hall closet. They talked about who would stand watch where. They would work in shifts, guns in hand, or close by for those assigned to sleep. But no one really slept. Around midnight, a barrage of stones crashed into the house. Then there was silence. When Gladys looked out the window later that night, the crowd was gone.

The morning was bright and beautiful, oddly cheerful against the previous night's trauma. With two men left to watch the house, Joe Mack drove Ossian and Gladys to shop for furniture and then dropped Ossian off at his office. Sweet worked through a round of patients, then took a call from Hewitt Watson, who had written the insurance policy on the new house. There was some problem with the description of the property and Watson needed to amend the documents. Sweet quickly poured out his tale from the previous night. Watson, unlike some of Sweet's tough-talking hospital friends, immediately volunteered to come over and sit up through the night.

Watson also promised to bring two other agents from the black-owned Liberty Insurance company. Compared to Sweet's colleagues at Dunbar, these three men were relative strangers. It is unclear what motivated their willingness to help. Watson may have empathized with Sweet because he was also the lone Negro on his block. The other two men, Leonard Morse and Charles Washington, Sweet only knew in passing. Whether they would show up as Watson promised remained to be seen.

That evening as they assembled for dinner, Gladys picked up the phone to a hysterical Edna Butler, her guest from the previous day. Butler had overheard a conversation on the streetcar where a Garland resident explained to the conductor, "Some niggers have moved in and we're going to get rid of them. They stayed there last night but they will be put out tonight." Brother Henry chimed in with an unfortunate confirmation of the rumor. While he was keeping watch, a beat cop came to the door and warned vaguely, "you better be on your guard." There had been a meeting last night to plan the details of the coming assault.

Ossian tried to put up a brave front, but he was shaken. Hoping for a display of strength in numbers, he sent his driver to Black Bottom to retrieve their handyman, Norris Murray, on the promise to pay him five dollars to stay at the house again. By the time Mack returned with Murray, the insurance men also had arrived. With his brother Otis and friend William Davis en route, Ossian stepped back from the edge of panic. He tried briefly to act like an ordinary homeowner, inviting the men to sit down at the card table for a couple of hands of bid whist while Gladys put the final touches on dinner.

The veneer of normalcy was obliterated when something heavy crashed into the house. Henry Sweet peeked around the drawn shade and exclaimed, "My God, look at the people!" There were hundreds of them, far more than last night. And tonight, said the rumors, there was a plan of attack, a plan for running them out.

The men dashed upstairs and grabbed rifles, the shotgun, and revolvers. Ossian groped in the closet for one of the revolvers and cartridges. He was unprepared for the effect of adrenaline on his fine motor skills. His hands were shaking so badly that he had difficulty loading the gun.

And then there was calm. The mob did not surge. Whatever had crashed into the house did not explode or catch fire. Sweet thought for a moment that perhaps his colleague Edward Carter was right. These mobs were mainly about intimidation, not action. The idea was a mild comfort and helped Sweet regain his composure. He lay down on the bed, closed his eyes, and relaxed his grip on the revolver.

The brief calm was shattered when a brick crashed through the window. From downstairs someone shouted, "There's someone coming!" Sweet rushed down the stairs, pistol in hand, pushing past Henry, who was headed in the opposite direction, clutching a Winchester rifle. A taxi slowed in front of the house. Before it really stopped, the door flew open. Otis Sweet and William Davies exited at a dead run. Someone in the crowd yelled, "Here's niggers! There they go! Get them!" Otis and William dashed under a hail of stones to the dubious shelter of the bungalow.

They were welcomed in, issued guns, and huddled for cover. They would wish later that they had crouched in the backseat and told the cabbie to drive on.

With rocks and debris crashing down like a hailstorm, Ossian was swept back into fear, pleading to no one really, "What shall I do? What shall I do?" Then, upstairs, another window shattered, followed by two volleys of gunfire. And out in the crowd, two men fell wounded, one of them fatally.

The police on the scene had multiple problems. One of them, who lived in the neighborhood, would initially testify that it was a calm summer night when the Negroes opened fire on their white neighbors, who were just strolling and enjoying the evening. None of that comported with the difficulty of getting the Sweets through the mob, into police cars, and down to the station. It was only a quick-thinking lieutenant, newly on the scene, who leveled his revolver at the mob, freezing them just long enough to push the Negroes into squad cars.

Ossian Sweet had more than ample warning that buying the house on Garland Avenue was a bad idea. Between January and March 1920, the homes of eight Negro strivers recently purchased in or on the boundary of white neighborhoods were firebombed. But in fuller context, Sweet's decision to buy the house on Garland and protect it with a sack full of guns was not irrational. Yes, he knew about Al Turner being mobbed out of his new home. But he also knew about Aladeine and Fleta Mathies. And that made Sweet's Garland Avenue strategy seem plausible.

The Mathieses were part of the latest wave of southern migrants into Detroit. Just arrived from the Georgia countryside, they went in with another couple, the Burtons, to rent an apartment on the border of Black Bottom and an ethnic white neighborhood. As soon as they moved in, the Klan called, first with a threatening letter demanding that they give up the flat. Then menacing men came over to explain why they did not belong. After that, the mob descended.

Two nights in a row, the men of the house stared down the mob, standing under the porch light, armed with rifles. But this strategy raised obvious problems. The men also had to sleep and work. So it was inevitable that at some point the women would be home alone.

Left on their own early in the week, the wives were shocked into action by shattering glass. On raw instinct, Fleta Mathies grabbed her bedside pistol and fired through the broken window. Police were fast on the scene and arrested Fleta on firearms charges.

The Michigan justice system actually worked for Fleta Mathies. Represented by the former head of the Detroit NAACP, she convinced the court that she feared for her life and had fired the gun in self-defense. On the courthouse steps, Fleta was full of defiance, and a touch of hubris, declaring, "The race needs people who are not afraid to die to defend their pride." Whatever the wisdom of that approach, it suggests that Fleta Mathies was playing for higher stakes than her unhappy neighbors. After Fleta's return from jail the threats and midnight attacks ended.

Another incident that Ossian Sweet surely knew about pushed closer to the edge and should have complicated his strategic assessment. Shortly after Al Turner was run out of his home, Vollington Bristol had his own encounter with a mob. Sweet was friends with Bristol. They had arrived in Detroit around the same time. Bristol was a prosperous undertaker who owned several rental properties, including a house on American Avenue that he had rented to a series of troublesome white tenants. Finally, Bristol decided to move into the house himself.[33]

Bristol outstripped his white neighbors on every measure of economics and education. But the neighborhood was only willing to tolerate him as a landlord, not as a resident. After the standard progression from nasty notes to a neighborhood delegation, the mob appeared. Luckily, Vollington Bristol had enough standing to secure a contingent of police guards who resisted the entreaty to "step aside just for five minutes," while the neighborhood men took care of things. Then, as the mob heated up, the police fired warning shots into the air. Someone from the mob fired back. That was enough to precipitate a call for reinforcements that finally sent the crowd running.

Later that night, though, after word of the incident had spread across black Detroit, there was evidence of a now-familiar turn of the black tradition of arms. After midnight, police were still patrolling the area and stopped a group of eight black men on their way to Vollington Bristol's home. They were all armed and were candid about their intent to defend Bristol against further attacks.

Thinking about these incidents, Ossian Sweet might have calculated that a strong show of force would quell hostile neighbors and help him endure the first dangerous days in his new home without any of the more worrisome hazards of gunplay. On the other hand, he also had to consider the July 9 mobbing of John Fletcher on Stoepel Avenue, just a few days after the attacks on Vollington Bristol and only a few blocks away.

This time the mob had a special temptation. The house next to Fletcher's had received a fresh delivery of coal. Just after nightfall, Fletcher's new neighbors appeared and took full advantage of the shiny black missiles. Under a barrage that broke out every window of the house, and amidst venomous cries of "Lynch him," Fletcher laid down rifle fire from an upstairs window, wounding one man in the hip.

In his defense, Fletcher told the simple truth, "I was afraid for my life," and ultimately no indictments were issued. What Sweet did not appreciate is that both Fletcher's case and Fleta Mathies's case were assigned to judges on the local court's progressive wing. These men were far more sympathetic to the plight of Detroit's black population than many of their brethren.[34]

Sweet might actually have been emboldened by the response of the NAACP to this spate of mobbings. From New York, James Weldon Johnson penned an angry missive that was circulated nationwide. "Negroes," he said, "have been driven from their homes by mobs [in Detroit], those who refused to go having defend and themselves in absence of adequate police protection. We now have the spectacle of white . . . newspapers taking sides with the mob and warning Negroes that if they cleave to their citizenship rights they are inviting a 'race riot.'"

These episodes were a high priority for the NAACP. James Weldon Johnson was already focused on the case of Lola Turner, a black woman who was chased out of white neighborhood in Los Angeles by a mob. Were it not for Ossian Sweet, Lola Turner might have been the rallying point for national protest and fundraising.

For James Weldon Johnson, the Sweets presented the possibility of fulfilling his long ambition of a standing legal defense fund that could bankroll important litigation without taking the organization to the brink of insolvency. He imagined a fund of $50,000 raised from the contributions from thousands of black folk. Ossian Sweet would never fully appreciate the politics, egos, and strategic tight ropes that James Weldon Johnson and Walter White navigated between the initial work by the Detroit branch and the decision of the national office to hire the legendary Clarence Darrow, storied defender of Debs and Scopes.

Through reports of their courage and stoicism, the Sweets became national heroes, at least among Negroes. From the jailhouse, Ossian declared, "for a good cause and for the dignity of my people, I'm willing to stay indefinitely in the cell and be punished. . . . I denounce the theory of Ku Kluxism and uphold the theory of manhood with a wife and a tiny baby to protect." Ossian's father, Henry, who traveled from Florida in support of his sons, grew the legend with a colorful and poignant response to Ossian's apology for embarrassing the family by ending up in jail. Henry comforted his sons and commended Ossian's violent stand, telling him, "You got nothing to be embarrassed about. Ain't nothing in the woods that runoff from family but a rabbit. All you were doing was fighting for your family."[35]

The case resonated so strongly among Negroes that it fueled a fundraising juggernaut. When the NAACP took on the case, resources were so thin that it was unclear how the $5,000 fee demanded by the initial team of lawyers would be paid. Funds on hand had been nearly exhausted by another case where the association defended a group of sharecroppers who were convicted of murder under circumstances that seemed like self-defense.

As word of the case spread, so did the community support. After Darrow wrestled the first prosecution to a mistrial, a nationwide tour feting Ossian and Gladys raised more than $75,000—enough to pay for the Sweet's defense, with surplus left to seed the long-discussed and soon-legendary NAACP Legal Defense Fund.

In the black press, the case was compelling copy and was plastered across the front pages nationwide. The *Chicago Defender* repeatedly played the case as its lead story, and publisher Robert Abbott wrote a blistering editorial proclaiming, "If it is true that Dr. Sweet fired into the crowd of whites to keep them from rushing his home, he was certainly within his rights and should be supported by every law-abiding citizen in Detroit. White people in Detroit, as well as other cities, may as well know now as later that our race will no longer run from our homes because they object to us."[36]

The *Washington Daily American* applauded Sweet's violent stand, declaring, "We have learned through the years since slavery passed to fight our enemies with their own weapons. If physical violence is offered we kill in self-defense." A Houston paper exhorted "as goes Dr. Sweet so goes the American Negro." Harlem's *Amsterdam News* called it "possibly the most important court case the Negro has ever figured in the history of the United States. [Sweet represented] the spirit of unity the Negro must more and more evidence if he is to survive. He must face death if he is to live. He must be willing to die fighting when he is right! When police authorities fail to protect him and his family; when courts of law desert him; when his own government fails to take a stand on his behalf, he faces death anyway, and may just as well die fighting!"[37]

The *Arizona Times*, with evidently little worry about advocating political violence, said, "The Sweet case has positively proved to the world at large that the American Negro will fight and stand up for his rights as a citizen until every ounce of blood is spilled from his veins." The editor of the *Cleveland Call*, who witnessed the trial, actually compared Sweet's stoic fearlessness to Christ, reporting that Sweet on the stand was "like one other scene two thousand years ago when One Who Opened Not His Mouth was being baited."

One of the most searing critiques of the case came from W. E. B. Du Bois. Writing for the *Crisis*, Du Bois contrasted the courage of Ossian Sweet to the cowardice Alexander Turner. Sweet, said Du Bois, was a model of manhood for the Talented Tenth. On the decision to fight or flee from the mob, Du Bois prodded the century's New Negroes, "which example would you follow if you were free black and 21." James Weldon Johnson drew the broad lesson from the case, "If in Detroit the Negro was not upheld in the right to defend his home . . . then no decent Negro home anywhere in the United States will be safe." It was a simple and powerful point that spoke to the hopes and fears of countless ordinary folk.[38]

At New York's Abyssinian Baptist Church, the Sweet case consumed the congregation and pushed local concerns off the agenda. Even some of the white press picked up and advanced the Sweets' basic claims. The *New York World* characterized the case as one of clear, legitimate self-defense, declaring that "the Negroes had a right to protect their own lives by firing on those who sought to kill them. The law of America is presumably broad enough to cover the Negro as well as the white man."[39]

Fig. 6.3. Dr. Ossian Sweet. (Courtesy of the Burton Historical Collection, Detroit Public Library.)

The case of *State v. Sweet et al.* ended in the acquittal of eight defendants and a mistrial for Ossian, his brother Henry, and Leonard Morse. The victory was a testament to, well . . . to what? The brilliance of Clarence Darrow? The strong hand of fate? Perhaps to the conscience and humanity of the twelve white men who sat in judgment? Surely it was some of each, although who knows how much. And what to make of the report from snoops at the jury-room door who heard one juror say, "I'll sit here forever before I condemn those niggers"?

Ultimately, it was the simple, earnest testimony of Ossian Sweet that captured the scene. He recounted somberly the mob of hundreds outside his home, stones crashing through windows, and the venomous yelps, "Here's Niggers, Get them, Get them." Asked by Darrow to describe his state of mind at that moment, Sweet conjured the collective consciousness of the race.

> I realized I was facing the same mob that had hounded my people through its entire history. In my mind I was pretty confident of what I was up against, with my back against the wall. I was filled with a peculiar fear, the fear of one who knows the history of my race.[40]

For Darrow, it was left to seal the message, to tug on the pride and shame and guilt of the jurors. His summation, in the marathon style of the day, ran for hours. One observer said that he had never believed the stories that Darrow could make men weep, but now he had seen it. We don't know whether Walter White wept under the power of Darrow's summation. But White clearly had tremendous respect and affection for Darrow. So much so that he gave his firstborn son the middle name Darrow.

The magic of Darrow was that he had something for everyone. It was the same basic message conveyed in multiple cultural dialects. Although it is hard to know precisely what within the six-hour summation especially appealed to pivotal jurors, for black folk there was a crucial moment where Darrow articulated the longing of the race for their own Leonidas. And there he sat, said Darrow, in the person of Dr. Ossian Sweet, who had seen his people

> tied to stakes in free America and a fire built around living human beings until they roasted to death; he knew they had been driven from their homes in the North and in great cities and here in Detroit, and he was there not only to defend himself and his house and his friends but to stand up for the integrity and independence of the abused race . . . a hero who fought a brave fight against fearful odds, the fight for right, for justice, for freedom, and his name will live and he will be honored when most of us are forgotten.[41]

Calculations were made for a subsequent retrial, but the results would be anticlimactic. And until then, at least in the black community, the Sweets were feted as national heroes, and exemplars of the New Negro. While the idea of the New Negro had appeared at least as early as T. Thomas Fortune's 1889 declaration that the old shuffling generation was done, Ossian Sweet showed the New Negro standing and fighting and actually prevailing inside a system that had for so long been rigged against him.

The demands for Sweet to appear around the country were so overwhelming that the NAACP took over the scheduling, declining the countless lesser requests in favor of a high-profile tour starting in New York City at the association's annual meeting. At the Lenox Avenue Baptist Church, 1,500 black folk sprang to their feet when Ossian and Gladys entered the room. They clapped and cheered and cried, and finally stopped only because the old people had to sit down.

From New York, the NAACP sent the Sweets on a tour of the largest branches. More than 2,500 turned out in Philadelphia, 1,200 in Pittsburgh, and 2,000 in Cleveland. Feeding on the adulation of the crowd, Ossian grew beyond himself. The man who thought hard about walking away from the Garland Avenue deal, who trembled loading his revolver, grew positively heroic, intimating that the conflict was preordained.[42]

The final legal maneuver in the Sweet case was prosaic. Prosecutors decided to retry only Henry Sweet, who in initial questioning had admitted firing a rifle. Clarence Darrow teased the truth out of neighborhood witnesses who had conspired to testify that there was no mob outside the Sweet home and that the Negroes started firing without provocation. Deflated by the first trial, some now admitted that the Klan had whipped up anger and urged violent removal of the blacks at a schoolyard rally attended by a crowd of seven hundred. Finally, the evidence was clear that on the night of the shooting, several hundred angry whites were outside the Sweets' house.

Darrow hammered at Michigan's legal definition of *mob* and the presumptions granted to people who fought mob attacks. He shattered the conspiracy of police on the scene to dance around this formula with specious estimates of the crowd that stayed right under the legal definition of *mob*—twelve or more armed people or thirty unarmed people assembled to intimidate or harm. And while it struck different people differently, the fact that twenty-five blacks had died in police custody in 1925 generally dragged down the credibility of police claims that there was nothing out of the ordinary going on until the Negroes opened fire on their incredulous white neighbors.

The white adults of Garland were able to keep their fabricated chronology basically straight, claiming that they heard no glass breaking until after the gunfire, suggesting that the Sweets had not been assaulted before they opened fire. But that crumbled when Darrow asked a simple question and got a truthful answer from one of the children whose parents had brought him out to witness the spectacle.

By the end of it, Darrow put American racism itself on trial. And it is hard to know what precisely caused the all-white, all-male jury to acquit Henry Sweet. Similarly configured juries on far clearer cases of self-defense had happily sent Negroes to prison and the gallows. Was it the beginning of a new age? Was it the residue of co-counsel Arthur Garfield Hays's invocation of the ancient principles and great documents that established the right of self-defense—the Castle doctrine, the federal and state constitutional rights to arms, and even the Emancipation Proclamation, which extolled "necessary self-defense"? Or was it Darrow's exposure of the poisonous tribal prejudice that seeped from witnesses in comments about "Eye Talians," "Pollocks," and Jews? Maybe it was recognition that the Klan tirades against Catholics and the immigrant masses left an awfully small slice of "true Americans" to sustain the republic.[43]

But hopes that the Sweet case alone would stem the tide of residential segregation were disappointed. The same year Henry Sweet was acquitted, the United States Supreme Court upheld the constitutionality of restrictive covenants in residential real estate. It would take another twenty years to reverse that decision. It would be another forty before federal law, drawn out of the cauldron of the 1960s, made housing discrimination illegal.

The ordeal in Detroit took a tremendous toll on the Sweets. During the middle of the trial, Gladys learned she had tuberculosis. The family suspected she contracted it in the long weeks spent in dank Detroit city jails following the shooting. After the trial, she and two-year-old daughter Iva, also afflicted, traveled to Arizona, seeking relief. Gladys found some comfort in the dry desert air, but the disease claimed Iva.

Gladys returned home with a small coffin while Ossian made funeral arrangements. Iva would be buried in Chicago's Roseland Park Cemetery, next to her brother, the boy Ossian and Gladys lost in 1923. Even on the day of the funeral, the petty nastiness of racism intruded. As the procession approached the gates to the cemetery, a white groundsman stepped out and snarled that "Coloreds" had to use the back entrance.

It hurts to think how this petty rebuke must have torn at Ossian and Gladys. And one wonders what was going on in the head and the heart of the man who in the name of white supremacy felt it his duty to dump another shovelful of misery onto parents headed to bury their child.

We can never know what was swirling in the minds of the Negroes standing at the cemetery gates, some crying, the men shooting cold stares. But we do gain some sense of how Ossian Sweet perceived the world that day. He could have turned away from the dirty-fingered groundskeeper and directed the funeral procession to the back entrance. But instead, Dr. Ossian Sweet of Dunbar Hospital, hero of Garland Avenue, drew a gun from his pocket and demanded entry through the front gate.[44]

The next chapter in this saga is frankly so remarkable that it is best just to let one of the witnesses tell it. Black mortician M. Kelley Fritz, the funeral director who stood beside Ossian Sweet when he demanded entry to the front gate of Roseland Park Cemetery to bury his daughter, reported this in a collection of oral histories:

> We had a very prominent man in town. He was a doctor. His child died. We took him out to the cemetery and they said go around to the back gate. He pulled his pistol out and made them open the door. *A few years later his wife died, and the same thing happened. They still wouldn't let him in. He pulled his pistol out. His name was Dr. Ossian Sweet.*[45]

Many of the early stories of Negroes with guns leave us wondering how the lives of those people turned out. This becomes easier to track over time. For Ossian Sweet, we know that after Gladys died of tuberculosis at twenty-seven. Ossian went on to enjoy a period of financial success. He actually moved in to the Garland Avenue bungalow and lived there in relative peace for more than twenty-five years. Two more marriages ended in divorce, and he pursued failed campaigns for state senate, US Congress, and the presidency of the Detroit NAACP.

By the 1950s, friends observed that he was slowing. Some commented that his countenance was darker. He seemed haunted by loss and trauma. And on March 20, 1960, as the modern civil-rights movement was unfolding toward great promise, Ossian Sweet picked up a pistol and shot himself in the head.[46]

Sweet's death by his own hand conjures the modern debate about the multiple hazards of firearms and perhaps even a parable about those who live by the gun. His suicide underscores what we have long known, that the majority of firearms deaths in our exceptionally armed society are suicides, with many of those coming from the population of older men.

The violent final episode of Ossian Sweet's life both complicates and sharpens our sense of the black tradition of arms. It alters our assessment of the hero worship and hyperbole that surrounded Sweet after the shooting at Garland. We wonder now how much the public adulation obscured the anguish and trauma that follows any use of deadly force? How did the event change Ossian Sweet? Without it, would he have been the same man who carried a gun to the funerals of his wife and his child? And what about the thousands of people who flocked into churches to cheer Ossian and Gladys, to cheer an act of violence and bloodshed? Yes, they were celebrating a kind of triumph. But the celebrations elided the full imagery of flesh ripped open by lead and the life-altering trauma it caused for the dusky heroes of Garland Avenue.

Fuller consideration of the black tradition of arms evokes similar themes. It happens whenever we celebrate heroes who fight essential battles. And perhaps celebration is the wrong way to think about what we do here. We celebrate the birth

NEGROES AND THE GUN

of a child. We celebrate the commitment of newlyweds, and the enduring love and patience of a golden anniversary. There is a plain difference between those things and what legions of black folk celebrated in the Sweet case.

We are happy that Sweet survived and we relish the symbolism of his fight. We might even broadly embrace the principle of armed self-defense as a fundamental right and an important private resource. But ultimately we know that shooting someone in self-defense is next to the last thing anyone wants to do. Yes, it is better than dying under a murderous assault. But it is a deeply traumatic thing that scars everyone involved. That bloody reality introduces an element of reserve against glib lessons or platitudes that might attach to unalloyed tales of heroic violence.

Ossian Sweet was not the black Leonidas. Of course, with enough detail, Leonidas himself surely would disappoint the legend. Ossian Sweet in the role of hero is similar. And that actually is better. Sweet was a brave and frightened and flawed man whose story leavens our sense of the black tradition of arms and brings us closer to the perspective that we need in order to consider its implications in the modern era.

CHAPTER SEVEN

FREEDOM FIGHT

"**D**oes *The Crisis* mean to imply that its policy is to defend colored people who kill sheriffs?"

The question was posed by a young Roy Wilkins, future head of the NAACP, writing in 1936 as the new editor of the association's public voice, the *Crisis*. The answer, if one is patient, turns out to be an emphatic yes.

By now the prickly W. E. B. Du Bois had left the NAACP in a huff, his growing economic radicalism and conflicts with Walter White a major source of the split. With roughly five years of service under his belt, Roy Wilkins was already savvy and judicious, prefiguring the man who would shepherd the association through the tumult of the 1960s.

Wilkins faced in 1936 a question at the heart of the black tradition of arms. And consistent with his growing reputation for careful calculation, appeared to answer it both ways. Wilkins, the diplomat, took a law-and-order stance as a matter of broad policy. At the same time, recognizing the practical limits of the law even in the best of circumstances, he championed armed self-defense.

His canvas was the mob killing of William Wales and his sister Cora in Gordonsville, Virginia. The Waleses had resisted local government attempts to take their property for cemetery expansion. Finally, officials tried to pressure William with a specious charge of being forward with a white woman. No one would survive to record the precise details. But two things are clear. The sheriff went to serve a warrant on William Wales. And Wales shot the sheriff dead.

The aftermath is signaled in the title of Roy Wilkins's critique of the episode, "Two against 5,000." It is a blistering commentary that in many ways frames Wilkins's continuing approach to issues of self-defense. Wilkins deploys sharp tools with a sarcastic appraisal of the good citizens who descended on the Wales. "A mob of 5,000 persons including all the sheriffs, constables, deputies and state police for miles around, armed with everything from machine guns on down, was held at bay by a 60-year-old Negro man and his 62-year-old sister for six hours. The pitched battle of two against 5,000 was finally won by the mob only after a gasoline-soaked torch was tossed into the house and the occupants burned to death."[1]

William and Cora turn from victims into heroes as Wilkins celebrates their fight against insurmountable odds. "Even as the flames ate away at their fortress, the man and woman kept up their rifle and shotgun fire until the blazing roof caved in upon their heads." Wilkins mocks the mob, taunting,

> if one has fancy words, this killing was not a lynching. It was sport—sport on a grand scale. Hunting possum compared to this is tiddlywinks. Here were a man and a woman cooped up in a frame house, and all one had to do was shoot. . . . There was a slight flaw in the setup, however. The man and woman had arms and they were not afraid to shoot. . . . The leaders of the 5,000 looked about and took counsel together. They had numbers. They had machine guns. They had sulfur bombs. They had teargas bombs. But the two in the house had rifles, shotguns and perhaps a pistol or two. Not so good. Not half as good as one lone Negro with nothing but his bare hands, easily dangled at the end of a rope. . . . A hanging, manacled Negro cannot shoot back. No, this was a different proposition.

With the coals stoked, Wilkins expands the web of villains to politicians who thwarted the NAACP's long and fruitless pursuit of federal anti-lynching legislation. Again, mocking, he recounts how town authorities, ducking under the Waleses' gunfire, requested reinforcements from the Marine base at nearby Quantico. "You see, gentle reader, the federal government must never interfere with the citizens of a sovereign state who wish to stage lynchings, but it is alright for the sovereign states to call on United States troops when some Negro is crazy enough not to want to be lynched. What the hell is government for, anyway?"

Still innately cautious, Wilkins engages and retreats and engages again the core dilemma of the precipitating bloodshed. "William Wales did kill a Sheriff, did he not? Are the colored people for law and order? Does the *Crisis* mean to imply by this article that its policy is to defend colored people who kill sheriffs?"

Line after line, he dissembles and equivocates. "Colored people have to be for law and order even though the law has given them little protection. They are a relatively helpless minority. They have to place their reliance in the law which the powerful majority has made." But the fact that black folk must favor law and order, said Wilkins, "does not mean that they necessarily approve of the law or the way it is administered or of the people who administer it."

Then, in a more dangerous turn, Wilkins argues that "all too infrequently, [blacks] express their disapproval and resentment in a forthright manner. They have good cause to resort to direct action. It is a marvel of the age that they have been so meek and mild."

But even as he edges toward militancy, Wilkins reflects the long caution against political violence. "The law is stacked against all poor people, and especially against Negroes. Yet they turn to it." Prudence demanded as much because "[Negroes] as a group are not in a position to change the law by democratic means or to defy it with arms."

Wilkins's restraint here sharpens a crucial point. The boundary against political violence is not a bright line. Rather, it is a contestable zone of action and rhetoric that people under disparate influences will navigate differently. It is a zone that prudent men will approach with caution. But some things will push even prudent men into the breach.

One expects a more detailed consideration of whether William Wales's shootout ranged into the forbidden zone of political violence. But Wilkins was now channeling the rage of the community. He was speaking for William and Cora Wales, burned to a cinder, bits of their remains "reposed now on the mantelpieces of many a Virginia home . . . preserved in a jar of alcohol to remind children and grandchildren of the indomitable courage of a brother, father or son of the family who battled to the death to prevent two Negroes from overcoming 5,000 white Virginians."

It was plain desperation, said Wilkins, that explained William Wales's violent stand. Wales "had had his fill of [injustice]. He probably decided that he did not intend to stand anymore from the system set up and maintained to exploit, humiliate and crush him. . . . He probably felt that in this matter he was right and that he was not going to knuckle under to the white folk no matter what happened. Death was preferable to life as he had been forced to live it."

From here, Wilkins engages the range of evils that the NAACP would spend decades fighting in the courts.

> As Wales looked back upon his 60 years what did he see? He saw courts controlled by whites, responsive to whites, giving verdicts pleasing to whites. He saw his race's children cheated out of the schooling for which their parents pay taxes to the state. He saw the separation of the races everywhere, with his having always the little end of the deal. He saw jobs, health, opportunity, prestige, family life and success denied upon the flimsy excuse of skin color. He saw his people hanged, roasted and mutilated by mobs while legislators called points of order and an aspirant to the Presidency fiddled with clauses, phrases, periods and commas in the so-called Bill of Rights.

Confronting the final act of violence, William Wales's gun blast to the chest of a lawman clothed in the authority of the state, Wilkins diverts the blame. William Wales might have pulled the trigger, but American apartheid was the real culprit. "The system killed that Sheriff," Wilkins declared, "Wales was the agent."

Finally, with the worry about respect for badges of authority fully submerged, Wilkins directly answers the starting question: "Yes, *The Crisis* defends William and Cora Wales." But that was not all. Wilkins not only defended William and Cora. He cast them as heroes, boldly celebrating the act of "stubborn, thrilling, crazy bravery by an aging colored man and his sister."[2]

It would be many years before the case of Jerome Wilson earned the kind of attention that Roy Wilkins gave to William and Cora Wales. But the basic scene was the same. Jerome Wilson of Washington Parish, Louisiana, came from a relatively prosperous black family. They owned land, livestock, and guns. Perhaps that made Jerome Wilson proud, a little too willing under the circumstances to claim that he was a man equal to any other. Perhaps if the Wilson clan had been more willing to bow and scrape, Jerome would not have gotten lynched.

Jerome was one of eleven children of John Wilson and Tempe McGee. As the Wilson boys grew older, John bought an adjacent farm for them to make their start. With John's accumulated resources and his boys' energy and ambition, the family thrived. But their relative prosperity rested on a fragile foundation of wavering protection for Negro property and Negro interests that would worry black strivers for years to come.

Like many rural areas, Washington Parish had a cattle-dipping ordinance to combat parasites. Joe Magee was the range rider charged with enforcing the ordinance. Somehow he heard that the Wilsons' old mule had not been dipped. He rode onto their farm, ignoring the Wilson boys sitting on the porch, and headed to the stockyard. One of the boys asked him, "Mister what's your business?" Magee was not accustomed to explaining himself to Negroes and answered vaguely that he was going into the livestock lot. Jerome Wilson told him, "Hell no, you can't go in there if you can't tell us your business." Magee, now on edge, demanded of Jerome, "What is your name, boy?" Jerome said, "You didn't tell me yours—I ain't goin' to tell you mine."

Magee huffed off, but soon returned with two deputies and another man. The Wilson boys were still sitting on the porch and Magee pointed to the ones who sassed him. One of the deputies, Delos Wood, told them to get up and get in the car. Jerome was the first to object. "Go with you for what. . . . We haven't done anything. We're home. Show us your authority."

Deputy Wood responded with the prerogatives of his class and time. "We don't have to have no authority to take you goddamned niggers to jail." Then he drew his gun and advanced. One of the Wilson boys, Moise, grabbed at Wood's gun as he came up the steps. Wood shot Moise in the stomach. The other deputy and a third man fired as well, wounding Jerome and his brother Felton.

Tracking blood through the house, Jerome ran to the gun rack, grabbed a shotgun, and fired out the window, hitting Delos Wood. With Wood down, the range rider, Joe Magee, picked up Wood's pistol and fired at Luther Wilson, wounding him.

The entire Wilson family was eventually carted off to jail. Moise, bleeding from two gunshot wounds to the stomach, died on the cell-room floor. Eventually, the authorities focused on Jerome, and it is some signal of progress that he was not immediately lynched. Indeed, it took nearly six months from the shooting until a mob, unhappy with the pace of the legal proceedings, dragged Jerome Wilson from the Washington Parish jail and killed him.[3]

Roy Wilkins could have used the Wilson saga or any number of other incidents to make all of the points that he pressed in "Two against 5,000." He could have used the shootout in Camp Hill, Arkansas, between a budding black sharecropper's union and a local sheriff that provoked retribution and resulted in the death of at least one black man and the arrest of sixty others. He could have used the gunfight in Fort Dix, New Jersey, spurred by southern MPs who dragged back-of-the-bus protocols north, and a white commander's notice that Negro liaisons with white women would be considered rape per se. There was plenty of fodder for the mill.[4]

Wilkins's primary tools of combat over the years would be intellectual, his battles detached from the violence and blood. But even as he moved pieces across the chess board, lessons about the risks and benefits of defensive firearms were always looming. This was particularly so for an incident in Columbia, Tennessee, that might have changed the trajectory of the entire modern movement.

Aggressive storytellers might say that Negroes with guns nearly cost the life of Thurgood Marshall. Others would say that the armed black community saved Marshall from being lynched. Roy Wilkins was intimately familiar with the situation, so his account seems a fair version.

It started with a dispute between a white counter clerk and two black customers at the Castner Knott Electric Company. Gladys Stephenson and her son came to complain about the quality and price of a radio repair. Negroes carping about slipshod work was outside the boundaries of racial etiquette, and the counterman slapped Gladys Stephenson as a reminder.

But this was 1946, and Stephenson's son James, a Navy veteran with three years' service in World War II, would not abide the old rules. With the brawling instinct of a sailor, James Stephenson set upon the clerk with fists and feet and then pitched him through the plate-glass window of the shop. The police arrested both James and Gladys, punching Gladys in the eye for good measure.

With his prisoners secure, the sheriff recognized the danger of mob violence and moved the Stephensons out of town. He was prescient in this. Because before the day was over, a mob of seventy-five men descended on the jail, unaware that the prisoners had already been moved.

In the black section of town, pejoratively dubbed and then embraced as "Minkslide," word of the frustrated jailhouse mob spread and folk prepared for the worst. In a vivid demonstration of the potential for armed violence to spin out in unintended ways, the next turn was something that most everyone wished they could take back.

Anticipating the mob, the neighbors of Minkslide sat like Du Bois and Walter White before them—lights out, crouching next to doors and windows with rifles, pistols, and shotguns ready. When a group of four white men crossed into the neighborhood, someone shouted, "Here they come." Then there was gunfire. No one knows who fired first. But the result was four white policemen limping away from Minkslide, bleeding from gunshot wounds.[5]

The official response confirmed the long worry about the aftermath of Negroes taking up guns. A force of local and state police along with National Guard troops and armed local men marched in and shot up Minkslide. They destroyed the offices of the black doctor and the insurance company. They shot up the barbershop and pool hall and scrawled *KKK* on the walls of the funeral home. Every Negro home was searched for weapons, and more than one hundred blacks were arrested on charges of insurrection. Two detainees died in custody.

The NAACP denounced the episode in the *Crisis* but championed the residents of Minkslide, who showed, "that Negroes, even in small communities like Columbia where they were outnumbered almost three-to-one do not intend to sit quietly and let a mob form, threaten and raid their neighborhood." Thurgood Marshall, then an NAACP attorney, was assigned to represent the detainees.

Arguing that the defendants could not get a fair trial in Colombia, Marshall got the proceedings moved to Lawrenceburg. But Lawrenceburg posed its own challenges. A professionally appointed sign planted prominently at the city limits warned, "Nigger, read and run. Don't let the sun go down on you here. If you can't read, run anyway." Marshall and his legal team did not chance defying this warning. They stayed in Nashville and drove the two hundred miles back and forth every day.[6]

By some accounts, Marshall escaped lynching only because the black community was already mobilized against mob violence. As the litigation proceeded, Marshall and his co-counsel Alexander Looby and Maurice Weaver were headed back to Nashville when they were stopped by police who claimed to have a warrant to search for whiskey. They searched and found no whiskey. Two minutes down the road, they pulled the car over again. This time they accused Marshall of being drunk. Then they loaded him into the squad car and told Looby and Weaver to get along.

Fearing for Marshall's life, Looby and Weaver refused to abandon him. As a squad car screeched off, Looby and Weaver pursued it along windy back roads to no clear destination. The cruiser finally circled back to Columbia to the magistrate's office. They hauled Marshall inside to an old judge who came in close, sniffed, and declared, "This man isn't drunk, he hasn't even had a drink." The story among black folk was that Thurgood Marshall had been targeted for murder, but "the lynchers failed to carry out their plan because they were cowardly men and they knew ... the entire Columbia Negro community [was] mobilized."[7]

So what should we think about the violence at Minkslide? Wouldn't it have been better if nervous Negroes with guns had not shot policemen? Then again, the violence that sparked the mob, a bigot getting thrown through a window, did not involve guns. And what about the risk to Thurgood Marshall? Black folk claimed that the armed community was a brake on plans to lynch him.

Wondering how our world might be different without Thurgood Marshall's gigantic influence prompts broader questions that shadow analysis of any social movement. How much was the black freedom struggle driven by giants, the great men and women familiar to history? How much can we discern about the freedom movement and the black tradition of arms just by reference to the words and deeds of those famous folk? What do we lose by failing to credit the stories of the countless souls who have faded into obscurity?

Theodore Roosevelt Mason Howard, MD, is of this latter class. Howard evokes comparisons to Ossian Sweet. Both were physicians. Both played significant but underacknowledged roles in the freedom struggle. And both are exemplars of the black tradition of arms. Sweet had notoriety thrust upon him. But Howard made an affirmative, aggressive choice to become a race man. Sweet carried a duffle bag full of guns into his new home in Detroit. Howard built a small empire in the Mississippi Delta and accumulated an arsenal of firearms.

He was born Theodore Roosevelt Howard in March 1908 in Calloway County, Kentucky. His parents scratched out a living picking tobacco. Like many stalwarts of the modern civil-rights movement, Theodore grew up in a rural gun culture where firearms were as common as shovels. People who know that culture will attest that there were countless young boys who ventured out into the fields with guns on assignments like those that ten-year-old Ted got from his mother. On Sundays, she gave him twenty cents to buy four shotgun shells and told him to bring back two rabbits or squirrels for the pot. He wrote later how he was prohibited from wasting shots on quail because "there wasn't enough meat on 'em." This prosaic slice of the black tradition of arms is recorded only incidentally, and some will be dissatisfied with the intermittent written record and the stories of people who were there for the hog killing, chicken-hawk shooting, groundhog sniping, raccoon blasting, and midnight-bump investigation.[8]

Howard's rise was unlikely, much of it owed to the beneficence of his white mentor, Dr. William Herbert Mason. Mason smoothed Howard's road to higher education and actually paid for much of it. When the young Theodore officially adopted the third name Mason and started signing his name T. R. M. Howard, folk whispered, "I told you so," about the long rumors that Dr. Mason actually was Howard's father.

Howard built his professional life in Bolivar County, Mississippi, in the town of Mound Bayou. Mound Bayou, recall, hosted the attempt at enlightened American slavery by Joseph Davis, brother of the Confederate president. By the first half of the twentieth century, Mound Bayou was a haven for black self-determination and an exemplar of black self-help. Booker T. Washington praised it as a model for black economic development. It drew talented folk who had other options, including Benjamin Green, an early black graduate of Harvard Law School who served as mayor from 1919 to 1961.[9]

From his base in Mound Bayou, T. R. M. Howard built a thriving medical practice and a series of lucrative businesses, including a thousand-acre farm, a restaurant, a construction company, and an insurance brokerage. Among Howard's many employees were Medgar and Myrlie Evers, who worked at his insurance agency and would take their lead from Howard into the civil-rights movement.

Later in the movement, Medgar's brother, Charles, said, "People call Martin Luther King Jr. the Negro orator of the century. T. R. M. Howard was as good or better and I heard both of them in their prime." As much as Howard was exalted by blacks, he was reviled by whites. When his civil-rights activism accelerated, Howard responded to mounting threats by preparing to defend himself in the fashion of generations of Negroes before him.

As a young man in the 1930s, Howard treaded gingerly against the backdrop of episodes like the lynching of Tom Robinson that were still a worry in America. Robinson eked out a living working other people's land in the countryside around Emelle, Alabama. His downfall was a contested transaction over a car battery. He had the misfortune of trading with the son of a wealthy white planter. The dispute escalated to a feud and then to a gun battle that left the scion, Clarence Boyd, face-down dead. It was the familiar circumstance where a black combatant won a battle but not the war. A gang of armed men attacked the Robinson clan, killing two of Tom Robinson's sons. Although some in the Robinson family escaped, a mob killed two other blacks in the process of tracking them. Two mutilated bodies were left hanging as a lesson for other defiant Negroes. T. R. M. Howard was traveling through Emelle after this incident and never shook the image of two corpses dangling from tree limbs.[10]

This is the America where Howard came of age and accumulated more guns than he could easily count. When racist administration of Mississippi firearms laws denied Howard a permit to carry a concealed weapon, he had a secret compartment built into his car to hide a pistol. Then he put a gun rack in his car window to exploit the allowance for openly carrying a long gun. A gun rack in a pickup truck is the familiar image. Howard fitted one in his Cadillac.

In 1947, Howard was stopped for speeding. There were five other men in the car. As patrolmen approached, the five passengers drew their pistols and laid them on the floor, hoping to avoid a concealed weapons charge on the argument that the guns were in the open. That tactic failed, and each was fined $100 for carrying a concealed firearm without a permit. Howard was not charged. The story goes that his handgun remained hidden in its secret compartment.[11]

A car full of blacks speeding down the highway illegally carrying concealed handguns conjures modern nightmares. But for men like T. R. M. Howard it was a reasoned, rational calculation. We really can only speculate how widespread the practice was. But we know that Howard and his traveling companions were not unique.

The community attitude about carrying a gun without approval from authorities is suggested in a 1939 report from the *Crisis* that the head of the Greenville, South Carolina, branch of the NAACP was facing charges of illegal concealed carry. The report expressed no surprise that he was carrying a gun and seemed to recognize it as a well-considered tactic and a legitimate act of civil disobedience. According to the *Crisis*, "J. A. Briar, 69, President of Greenville South Carolina branch is the latest victim of the terror the Klan and other groups are using against Negroes in Greenville and vicinity. Mr. Briar was arrested December 1 charged with carrying a concealed weapon."

Briar had been leading a voter-registration fight since early summer. This precipitated a wave of intimidation and threats. According to the *Crisis*, "The first movement to frighten the NAACP was the arrest of William Anderson, president of the Youth Council on the trumped up charge of telephoning a white girl. . . . The arrest of Mr. Briar was the next step. The situation reached a crucial stage early in December when it was reported that all the hardware stores in Greenville were sold out of guns and ammunition and that Negroes were determined to protect themselves in the event any assault was made upon them by the Klan."[12] J. A. Briar faded into obscurity, and who knows how many other such men were never noted at all. T. R. M. Howard is emblematic of such men. We are fortunate that he left a richer record.

In a long career of activism, Howard is most celebrated for his efforts surrounding the Emmett Till murder trial. Howard helped search for witnesses, developed evidence, and opened his home as a safe haven for journalists, witnesses, and visitors. A variety of observers confirm that guns were everywhere. One reporter records "a long gun, a shotgun or rifle, in every corner of every room." Howard typically carried a pistol openly in a belt holster. Every day of the trial, Howard and a caravan of armed men escorted Maime Bradley (Till's mother) and others, including Congressman Charles Diggs of Michigan, to the courthouse.

Journalist Cloyte Murdock, writing for the black monthly magazine *Ebony*, described arriving at Howard's home and having trouble getting her luggage through the front door. She finally wedged in and found the problem. A cache of guns stacked behind the door had fallen over and blocked her entry. Another visitor identified a .357 Magnum revolver and a .45 automatic in holsters looped over the headboard in Howard's bedroom. A Thompson submachine gun rested at the foot of the bed.

If accurate, the report of the submachine gun raises the question of whether Howard had fully complied with the 1934 National Firearms Act, which requires owners of fully automatic firearms to jump through a series of regulatory hoops that would have invited interference by the same local authorities who denied him a permit to carry a concealed handgun. We are left to wonder whether the machine-gun report is just a familiar case of someone ignorant about the technology, misreporting what they saw or another example of Howard defying gun laws.

Some contend that the acquittal of the men charged with Emmett Till's murder marked the beginning of the civil-rights movement in Mississippi. It certainly propelled Howard onto a bigger stage. From that platform, in speeches and in commentary, Howard presented armed self-defense as an essential private resource for blacks. On several occasions, Howard recounted the story of his friend George L. Jefferson, head of the Vicksburg, Mississippi, NAACP. The Klan had burned a cross in front of Jefferson's funeral home. According to Howard, Jefferson called to alert the sheriff that the logistics of Jim Crow required tending:

> They have burned a cross in front of my funeral home. I'm sure that you and everybody in Vicksburg knows where my wife and my family lives. I understand that they are going out there to burn a cross. And, Mr. Sheriff, I just want to tell you that Mississippi law requires separate ambulances for transportation of colored and white persons and inasmuch as the white hearse can't carry a colored man or a colored hearse can't carry a white man, I'm telling you that when that group comes out to my home to burn a cross, I have already got my colored ambulance standing by. I want you to send a white hearse along because somebody's going to be hauled away.

The punch line, rendered to thunderous applause by black audiences, was that no cross was burned at Jefferson's home. The white establishment was less enthused. The *Jackson Daily News* reprinted the full text of Howard's speech and in three separate editorials condemned his "incendiary" language and his "poison tongue."[13]

Throughout his activism, Howard confronted the reality of state failure and overt malice. It fueled his natural stance and political philosophy of self-sufficiency and self-help. The folly of relying on the state for protection was especially evident in an episode where FBI agents were sitting in his office just as a fresh threat came in. The agents were there investigating whether Howard had been the target of extortion. The interview was interrupted by a telephone caller who threatened to kill Howard if he continued to press for integration. Although they had just observed a threat to his life, the agents rebuffed Howard's request for protection and suggested that he contact local authorities. The governor of Mississippi already had refused the NAACP's plea to investigate the roadside shotgun murder of Reverend Henry Lee, with the retort that he did not answer letters from the NAACP. That alone might explain why Howard kept "a small arsenal" in his home.[14]

T. R. M. Howard's practice of arms was not unusual. Witness for example the response when news spread that Howard had received a particularly credible death threat. Howard's nearby neighbor was quickly on the scene with the assurance, "Don't worry about a thing, Doc. Me and a gang of fellows will surround your house tonight and we all have guns." Later, just on the rumor that Howard's wife had been accosted by bigots, fifteen cars full of armed black men sped to Howard's home.[15]

Following the Emmett Till trial, Gus Courts, a black grocer and president of the Belzoni branch of the NAACP, was wounded in a drive-by shooting. Courts had been warned to remove his name from the voting rolls on the pain of economic reprisals and then threats of violence. Howard prodded investigation of the case with the threat of a mass march on Washington. He traveled to Baltimore, New York, Pittsburgh, Los Angeles, and Washington, DC, agitating for a "freedom March to Washington."[16]

Howard's first stop on this tour was the Dexter Avenue Baptist Church in Montgomery, Alabama. The event was hosted by the newly installed pastor, twenty-six-year-old Martin Luther King Jr. Also in the room were two other freedom fighters, Rosa Parks, still just an obscure member of the Montgomery NAACP, and Autherine Lucy, who walked the gauntlet to integrate the University of Alabama.

Each of the three storied figures in the room with Howard that night offers a layer to the evolving black tradition of arms. We already know something about King and will see much more. But Rosa Parks and Autherine Lucy open the chapter of the women whose words and deeds illuminate the tradition of arms in the modern freedom movement.

Fig. 7.1. Representative Charles Diggs *(second from right)*, T. R. M. Howard *(third from right)*, and Mamie Bradley *(fourth from right, and held by Howard)* at the 1955 Emmett Till murder trial. (© Bettmann/CORBIS.)

Justly famous for the act of defiance that sparked the Montgomery bus boycott, Rosa Parks confirms the black tradition of arms in the context of her earliest memories:

> By the time I was six, I was old enough to realize that we were actually not free. The Ku Klux Klan was riding through the black community, burning churches, beating up people, killing people. At the time I didn't realize why there was so much activity, but later I learned that it was because African-American soldiers were returning from World War I and acting as if they deserved equal rights because they served our country. . . .
>
> At one point the violence was so bad that my grandfather kept his gun—a double barreled shotgun—close by at all times. And I remember we talked about how just in case the Klansmen broke into our house, we should go to bed with our clothes on so we would be ready to run if we had to. I can remember my grandfather saying, "I don't know how long I would last if they came breaking in here, but I'm getting the first one who comes through the door." . . . My grandfather wasn't going outside looking for any trouble, but he was going to defend his home. I remember thinking that whatever happened, I wanted to see it. I wanted to see him shoot that gun. I wasn't going to be caught asleep. I remember that at night he would sit by the fire in his rocking chair and I would sit on the floor right by his chair, and he would have his gun right by just in case.[17]

The tradition of arms is further evident in Parks's recollection of the first stages of her activism. When Parks's husband, Ray, started attending late-night meetings of budding activists, the men came with guns and there was always an armed lookout. Initially Ray sheltered Rosa from these meetings. But eventually the couple started hosting groups in their home on Huffman Street. The culture of arms was plainly in evidence. Parks describes it this way. "It was the first meeting we ever had at our house, and it was in the front room. There was a little table about the size of the card table that they were sitting around. . . . The table was covered with guns. I didn't even think to offer them anything—refreshments or something to drink. But with the table so covered with guns, I don't know where I would've put any refreshments. No one was thinking of food anyway."[18]

After her storied defiance helped spring the movement in Alabama, threats and harassment drove Parks out of the state. But before she headed north, the gun was a crucial interim tool. "We did suffer some harassment," Parks recalls, "The threatening telephone calls continued even after the Supreme Court decision. My husband slept with a gun nearby for a time."[19]

Autherine Lucy also sat listening to T. R. M. Howard and Martin King that night at Dexter Avenue Baptist. Lucy had already been snagged by fate. Her desire to go to college required the deployment of big guns, both figuratively and literally. For the legal fight, the already-legendary Thurgood Marshall and his young assistant, future federal court judge Constance Baker Motley, would demand compliance with America's constitutional promises. But before they could appear to wage rhetorical warfare, Motley and Marshall had to survive the night. And here again the gun was an important tool. Judge Motley recalled it this way:

> When Autherine Lucy registered in February 1956 and was finally on campus, a riot broke out. . . . We then went to court with a motion to hold the dean of admissions and members of the board of trustees in contempt for failing to secure Miss Lucy's peaceful attendance. While in Birmingham for this hearing, we stayed in Arthur Shores' spacious new home on the city's outskirts. This house had been bombed on several occasions, but because we could not stay in a hotel or motel in Birmingham, we had to take up Shores' offer of his bomb-prone abode. . . .
>
> When Thurgood and I arrived, the garage door was wide open. Inside were six or eight Black men with shotguns and machine guns who had been guarding the house since the last bombing. . . . When we went to court the next day, the driver of our car and one other man in the front passenger seat carried guns in their pockets.[20]

It is likely that some of the same men came to the rescue after Autherine Lucy was pelted with eggs and gravel as she tried to attend her first class at the University of Alabama. Friends wrapped her up and retreated to a salon in the black section of Tuscaloosa where beauticians washed her hair and cleaned her clothes. As a mob gathered outside, the shop owner called for help and a group of black men armed with rifles and shotguns quickly arrived. This show of force dispersed the crowd. The black men then gave Lucy an armed escort to Birmingham.[21]

In Birmingham, legendary movement leader Reverend Fred Shuttlesworth was protected by a group of armed "Civil Rights Guards" after being threatened and attacked by terrorists.[22] But Shuttlesworth was not simply a passive beneficiary of armed protection. When Freedom Riders from his congregation were attacked in Anniston, Alabama, word spread that many of the injured had been taken to a local hospital. Freedom Rider Hank Thomas recalls, "the people at the hospital would not do anything for us." Then, says Thomas, "a crowd started forming outside . . . and the hospital told us to leave." Reverend Shuttlesworth had already heard this news and was riding to the rescue with a fifteen-car caravan of armed men spurred by Shuttlesworth's promise, "I'm going to get my people. I'm a nonviolent man, but I'm going to get my people."

Transportation was the secondary issue. The primary concern was getting folk out of the hospital and safely through the angry crowd. Here the threat value of the gun was important. As Shuttlesworth's caravan rolled to a stop, the show of force parted the crowd. Thomas recalled how, "each one of them got out with their guns and everything. . . . They had rifles and shotguns and that's how we got back to Birmingham."[23]

Although Fred Shuttlesworth enjoys a higher historical profile, Reverend Ed Gardner was right by his side. In 1956, after multiple pressures forced the Birmingham NAACP office to close, Gardner and Shuttlesworth formed the Alabama Christian Movement to fill the gap. While national attention was focused on the Montgomery bus boycott, Gardner and Shuttlesworth protested bus segregation in Birmingham. More than five hundred protesters went to jail, and Gardner and Shuttlesworth became open targets.

Looking back, Gardner recalled, "they came by my place shooting and all like that, so I had two guards to guard my house. Reverend Shuttlesworth had guards guarding his house. We had a lot of laughs about that. I had a Winchester and I told 'em, *this is a nonviolent Winchester*."[24]

Reverend Gardner's quip about the nonviolent Winchester reflects the long-standing dichotomy between self-defense and political violence. Grassroots activist Austry Kirklin elaborates the two themes in an oral-history account, describing how "We was nonviolent. Nobody never did fight back." Then, without missing a beat and with no worry about inconsistency, she reveals that "Mr. Sims, he used to always carry his gun—him and Joe Smith." Her claim was verified by at least one occasion after a protest march when "they jailed Mr. Sands down there. Kept him three weeks when they found he had a gun." Noting the danger and describing his own preparations, activist T. C. Johnson recalled, "Yes we had little Saturday Night Specials that we'd hide; you couldn't let 'em be caught on you."[25]

After the 1963 bombing of the Sixteenth Street Baptist Church in Birmingham killed four little black girls, novelist John Killens, future Pulitzer Prize nominee, erupted, "Negroes must be prepared to protect themselves with guns." The neighborhood of black strivers that would come to be known as "Dynamite Hill" needed no advice on this point. They set up a community guard system of armed patrols.[26]

Birmingham native and former secretary of state Condoleezza Rice writes vividly about the night in 1963 when a firebomb crashed through the window of a house down the block. Her father gathered the family with the intent of heading to the police station but was reminded by his wife exactly who and where he was. "Are you crazy?" she asked. "They probably set off the thing in the first place."[27]

One is tempted to dismiss Angelena Rice's warning as exaggerated fear, perhaps embellished on recollection. On the other hand, the white man sent to investigate the Birmingham bombings said later, "I had an interview in the state of Georgia since my retirement with the former number one Klansman in Alabama, who stated that former Commissioner 'Bull' Connor paid $500 to get Reverend Shuttlesworth's church dynamited in Birmingham."[28]

The neighborhood bombing chased Condoleezza Rice and her parents temporarily to the home of friends in nearby Hooper City. When they returned late that night, Secretary Rice recalls that her father "didn't say anything more about the bomb. He just went outside and sat on the porch in the springtime heat with his gun on his lap. He sat there all night looking for white night riders." And one wonders here whether Reverend Rice suddenly had a keener appreciation for the long practice of the family matriarch, Condoleezza's great-grandmother, Julia Head, who "to the day she died, would sit on our porch with a shotgun in her lap."

Eventually, Condoleezza Rice recalls, her father and the neighborhood men formed an organized watch. "They would take shifts at the head of the two entrances to our streets. There was a formal schedule, and Daddy would move among them to pray with them and keep their spirits up. Occasionally they would fire a gun into the air to scare off intruders, but they never actually shot anyone." Those tense nights in Birmingham still resonate in Rice's assessment of firearms policy. "Because of this experience, I'm a fierce defender of the Second Amendment and the right to bear arms. Had my father and his neighbors registered their weapons, Bull Connor surely would have confiscated them or even worse."[29]

There is abundant evidence that merely having a gun is only one component of a successful act of armed self-defense and is a guarantee of nothing. That list grows with the recollection of Arthur Shores, who had hosted Thurgood Marshall and Connie Motley in his home on Dynamite Hill not far from the Rice family. In September 1963, his house had been dynamited once already. Shores was on edge. "I was sitting in my living room and said . . . I'm goin' sit out on the porch a little with my double barrel shotgun and kinda watch out. And the moment I got up out of my seat, my front door was blown in and if I'd been a second or two earlier, it would've caught me full in the face."

Shore's story captures multiple facets of the self-defense dynamic. People keep guns because in the critical seconds when violence sparks, outside help, even from well-meaning governments, is at least minutes away. But violence is a whirlwind and launching into it armed, even justly armed, courts unpredictable hazards. The "what if" and "but for" calculations are varied enough to leave us vacillating on questions of policy.

The "what if" calculation looms large in the brutal official response to the 1965 march at the Edmund Pettus Bridge in Selma, Alabama, remembered now in infamy as "Bloody Sunday." The baton charge and tear-gas assaults on black folk dressed in church clothes form some of the most poignant images of the modern freedom movement. But eyewitnesses report how those images might easily have been a record of carnage wrought by political violence.

Wilson Baker, Selma's director of Public Safety, and John Nixon, of the Justice Department, were both on the ground that day in Selma. Baker blames the familiar images of violence on hot-tempered state troopers and a "posse" of private citizens including "a lot of Ku Klux Klan types."[30] According to Baker, the police were instructed not to follow the marchers into Selma city limits. "We were not going to have any part of that thing," Baker recalls, "because I thought at the time that it was time to let them go to Montgomery, if they wanted to go to Montgomery. One reason was I wanted to get them out of Selma. It was selfish, let's be honest about it. . . . I had a thorough understanding . . . that whatever happened across that bridge, once the blacks got back into city limits no one was to follow them back in here. But the posse did follow them back . . . to the church and down in that area and that's where it really got scary."

Once the conflict spilled into the neighborhood around Brown's Chapel, what Baker calls the "civil-rights area," the potential for dramatic shift over from nonviolence into chaos and gunfire was plain. "People were coming out of those houses with shotguns and rifles and pistols," says Baker, "and the horses were running in there and they were trying to ride horses up on the steps of the church and every place else. And Congressman Andrew Young [future UN ambassador and mayor of Atlanta], he played such an important part of saving a bloodbath. He was just running wild up-and-down these apartment units: 'Get back into the house with this weapon. . . . We're not having any weapons out.'" Baker worked the other side of the conflict. "I was there with him helping him. . . . I went to Jim Clark, the Sheriff and told him you get your cowboys, and you get them out of here."[31]

Imagining an alternate scenario in Selma puts a sharp point on an enduring dilemma within the black tradition of arms. How exactly does one mark the line between legitimate self-defense and foolish political violence? Even if coherent in theory, can the distinction be sustained in the heat of conflict? Were those Negroes in Selma who emerged from their homes with guns bent on political violence? Or were they simply reacting in legitimate defense of friends and neighbors? And what if it was really some mixture of both? Does that render the distinction at the heart of the black tradition of arms incoherent?

Certainly claims of self-defense always involve close and complicated factual questions. But for individual self-defenders the stakes are simply exoneration or punishment. In a case like Selma, on the other hand, the stakes were far higher. What if Selma had devolved into a gunfight? The possibilities illustrate a worry that sharpens our definitions of self-defense and political violence, as well as our understanding of the concept of "nonviolence" in the modern freedom movement.

Martin King's response to Robert Williams captured the point. Essential self-defense by individuals pressed to the wall by violent aggressors is the model case. Beyond that model case, where people gather in groups, marching and protesting in ways likely to provoke violent opposition, carrying arms for protection poses a clear hazard. Although we might technically classify this violence as defensive, in the sense that folk in Selma were responding to aggression rather than initiating it, the risk of dramatic political effect is plain. King's formulation respected the model case of individual self-defense but steered well clear of the boundary-land bordering political violence.

Despite Martin Luther King's cautions, the movement's various organized defense groups stepped more aggressively toward the boundary against political violence. As we will see, the Deacons for Defense became the most prominent, but in many other places, organized groups took up arms in defense of their families, communities, and the movement.[32]

In Meridian, Mississippi, a defense group drawn from Porter and Union Baptist Church members guarded the home of NAACP leader Claude Bryant. In April 1964, after an explosion rocked his house, Bryant himself ran into the street with his rifle and shot at the car full of fleeing bombers. It is not clear precisely what type of gun he used. But soon after that incident, Bryant purchased a "high-powered" rifle better suited to the surrounding threats. He would need it.[33]

Three months later, bombers attacked the home of Claude Bryant's brother Charlie. Charlie and his wife Ora were staunch activists in the Macomb County movement. With the front windows blown from her house, Ora Bryant emerged out of the smoke with a shotgun and fired on the fleeing terrorists. Ora Bryant was not the only one on guard that night.

One neighbor described the scene this way: "That car was fired on so many times coming out of there . . . by people straight up the street all through there. . . . And he was shot at when he turned the curve, coming back towards town. . . . And you could hear people hollering 'here he come.'" When the car passed his house, Claude Bryant ran out with his new rifle and fired a full magazine at the fleeing bombers. Afterward, the rumor spread that wounded terrorists were taken out of state for treatment in order to suppress the story of Negro triumph.

The Bryants and their neighbors understood that the fight was not over and followed up by organizing regular armed watches. Annie Reeves, whose husband also helped guard Claude Bryant, recounted sitting in her living room with the lights out, a rifle clutched in her lap. Mr. and Mrs. Matthew Nobles, active members in Claude Bryant's NAACP branch, made their own preparations and stood ready to protect their neighbors. During the worst of it, Matthew Nobles camped on the roof of his house with a rifle while his wife slept fitfully, listening for trouble through an open window, her own rifle at the ready.[34]

In Cambridge, Maryland, several seasons of black protest fueled a backlash in 1963 when white mobs roved through black neighborhoods. Negroes responded with gunfire, and a defense group formed to guard the home of local leader Gloria Richardson.[35] SNCC[36] activist Cleveland Sellers arrived to assist in the Cambridge movement and found that "guns were carried as a matter of course." When one of the local folk offered Sellers a pistol to carry, he was torn between philosophy and practicality. "I decided when I accepted a gun that it was just as necessary to the work we were doing as stirring speeches, picket signs and marches against blatantly racist presidential candidates." (George Wallace was scheduled to appear at the Fairgrounds.)[37]

The same year in St. Augustine, Florida, Korean War veteran and NAACP activist Robert Hayling organized a defense squad after voter registration efforts and protests of continuing segregation prompted shotgun attacks on his home. Hayling bought a cache of rifles and shotguns and made them available to the group of local men who guarded his home and the surrounding neighborhood.[38]

In Natchez, Mississippi, armed Negroes guarded NAACP leader George Metcalf.[39] In Hattiesburg, community men led by army veteran James Nix guarded the homes of Dr. C. E. Smith and J. C. Fairly.[40] A similar defense squad was formed by war veterans in Tuscaloosa, Alabama. The Tuscaloosa defense squad protected the homes of movement activists, rescued teenage demonstrators from a mob, and repelled a Klan attack.[41] And in October 1963, when a carload of Klansmen assaulted activist Goldie Eubanks, Negroes with guns repelled the attack and killed one white man.[42]

∽

The defense groups are only slice of the story of the modern movement. From the leadership to the grassroots, individual preparations for armed self-defense were pervasive. In Arkansas, Daisy and L. C. Bates fought at the forefront of the Little Rock integration struggle. Daisy Bates served as president of the Arkansas Conference of NAACP Branches. She was mentor and advisor to the "Little Rock Nine," who put their skins on the line to integrate Central High School, calling them "her children." Daisy and L. C. Bates were also clear-eyed on the utility of armed self-defense.

Daisy Bates pleaded for federal protection after a firebombing and cross burnings at her home. Federal officials declined to intervene on the argument that they had no jurisdiction. Local law enforcement was overtly hostile and put their primary effort into harassing the armed black men who gathered to guard the Bates home. Against the backdrop of state failure and malevolence, Daisy Bates stood on ancient prerogatives. During the worst of the conflict in Little Rock, the NAACP leader herself repelled a midnight assault with a "volley of gunshots."

Firearms were a familiar tool for the Bateses. In 1934, Daisy and L. C. were stopped by the police in Monroe, Louisiana, on a "Negro Law" charge of "investigation." It came to nothing, except for the record of L. C.'s pistol in the glove compartment. In this, L. C. Bates channeled both community and family tradition. At the end of his life, L. C. listed among his heroes his grandfather who, a generation earlier, in Mississippi, intervened to stop an assault on two of his workers and ended up shooting a white man.[43]

Daisy Bates confirmed the surrounding culture of arms in a 1959 letter to Thurgood Marshall. She confided that that she and L. C. were under continuing threat and "keep 'Old Betsy' well oiled and the guards are always on alert."[44] This would not have surprised Marshall, who found the Bateses' home "an armed camp" when he stayed there in September 1957 while litigating the Little Rock School Board's delay of court-ordered integration.[45]

Today we talk casually about the sacrifices of the civil-rights era. But except for going through it, there is no way to really appreciate what the Bateses endured. Even if we rolled back the clock and could see Daisy on television, perfectly turned out in the latest fashion, we would fail to appreciate that she was sleepless after a new cycle of death threats and that L. C. had sat all night by the window with a shotgun in his lap.

Fig. 7.2. Daisy Bates, "the First Lady of Little Rock." (Courtesy of the University of Arkansas, Special Collections.)

Putting up a strong front was a calculated strategy that masked the wilting effects of economic reprisals and continuing physical threats. People would hear about the fire-bombs and bricks through the window of the neat ranch home that Daisy and L. C. had saved so long for. But only when Daisy disclosed it in her memoir would the public appreciate that she regularly carried a pistol and came perilously close to firing with effect in the fall of 1958 when a carload of toughs rammed into the rear of her station wagon.

When she stopped to survey the damage, they jumped out and threatened to drag her into the street. Daisy Bates's next action demonstrates the tenuous line between legitimate self-defense and something else. An angry young man banged the hood of her car and spit, "You and those damn coons are responsible for the closing of our school. I ought to pull you out of that car and beat you to a pulp." From a casual look at her (she was stunningly beautiful), the young man might have failed to appreciate that Daisy Bates was boiling over with rage, fully sick and tired of threats and plots and the indignities of a lifetime.

Recounting it later, she admitted, "I was so infuriated that I released the lock on the door and simultaneously released the safety catch of my pistol." Like Du Bois and Walter White before her, Daisy Bates stepped right to the edge. It would be worth money to know what caused the young bigot's companion to grab his jacket sleeve and pull him back with a wary, "Leave her alone. C'mon, we'll get her later."

Calculating avoided hazards in a precise way is difficult. We have seen many instances where black folk were armed, but not very effectively. Reading Daisy Bates's account, the intuition is that she was carrying a "woman's gun," a low-powered pistol of the type one army colonel derided as inferior to a hatchet. And, looking at her, one would certainly expect Daisy Bates to carry a lady's gun. But her account of a subsequent early-morning change of guard at her home belies that intuition.

Armed black men were now guarding the Bates home around the clock. But they had jobs and families, so it was not easy. Daisy Bates understood the sacrifice. One morning around daybreak, she went out to her car, where the man on the midnight shift had camped and told him, "You can go now. It will be daylight soon. I can't sleep, so I'll sit in the car for a while." In the thin light of dawn she found a moment of peace, and later described how she, "rested the .45 automatic pistol in my lap while Skippy our cocker spaniel went to sleep on the seat beside me."[46]

Although it is unclear what gun she was carrying the day the car full of toughs crashed into her station wagon, the .45 automatic pistol in her lap that subsequent calm morning was no dainty lady's gun. From 1911 through 1985, this was the gun that left legions of scrawny GIs flinching and complaining about the stout recoil from launching 230-grain slugs at almost a thousand feet per second.

We don't know whether it was her .45 automatic or something else that Daisy Bates fired in October 1957, after she was jerked awake by something crashing through a side window. She rose, gun in hand, to spy a seething little man in her driveway, poised with a vaguely lit missile. She loosed five quick shots that sent him running to a waiting car that sped off.[47]

Following the victory in Little Rock, Daisy Bates traveled around the country, speaking to various audiences, and sometimes recounted episodes of armed resistance by the Negroes of Little Rock. She told about the mother of Elizabeth

Eckford, one of the Little Rock Nine, who sent her husband to town to "buy me a gun with plenty of bullets." And depending on her audience, Bates also revealed that she carried her own pistol and knew how to use it.[48]

One biographer says that Daisy Bates shaped her stories to the circumstances. For some groups, she became more judicious and claimed she and L. C. never actually aimed at anyone.[49] Her appreciation of the need to craft her gun stories to the audience was evidence of the savvy that made her a potent political foe and a valued ally.

When Robert Williams asked the NAACP board to reverse Roy Wilkins's decision to discharge him from leadership of the Monroe NAACP, Wilkins anticipated the political fight and knew that Daisy Bates's support would be vital. On one telling, Wilkins bought the Bateses' allegiance with a promise of $600 per month into the coffers of their ailing newspaper.[50]

Even with such blandishments, Daisy and L. C. Bates were initially equivocal about criticizing Robert Williams. They also remained firm on the importance of private self-defense. Their newspaper, the *Arkansas State Press*, editorialized in May 1959 that "nonviolence never saved George Lee in Belzoni, Miss., or Emmett Till, nor Mack Parker at Poplarville, Miss."[51] But by July, when the NAACP gathered in New York for its annual meeting, Daisy Bates supported Roy Wilkins and provided what some gauged as the decisive condemnation of Robert Williams.[52]

The importance of Bates's support of Wilkins in the Robert Williams affair is underscored by the turnout for the opposition. As we saw in the first chapter, Williams drew considerable support from the grassroots and from the leaders of the branches. He also recruited a formidable ally from the old guard. Now, toward the end of his life, the old lion, W. E. B. Du Bois, entered the fray in support of Williams. As always, Du Bois's sharpest tool was his pen. He deployed it deftly in what was nominally a review of an early biography of Martin Luther King. The review was a platform for Du Bois's criticism of King and endorsement of Williams. "I was sorry," said Du Bois, "to see King lauded for his opposition to the young colored man in North Carolina who declared that in order to stop lynching and mob violence, Negroes must fight back."[53]

Daisy Bates's stance at the NAACP convention was ironic considering what awaited her at home in Little Rock. A few days after returning from New York, the Bateses were again victims of harassment and a bomb attack. Daisy sent the obligatory telegram to the Justice Department in Washington, describing burning crosses, smashed windows, and an explosion. Then, at a more practical level, she supplemented the private guards by taking her own turn in the armed watch, again wielding the .45 caliber Colt automatic pistol.

She would have known by then that this was the same model gun that Robert Williams had strapped to his hip during the conflicts in Monroe, North Carolina.

The irony was not lost on Williams, who wrote her a sympathetic letter with a touch of sarcasm. "I'm sorry to hear that the white racists have decided to step up their campaign of violence against you. I deeply regret that you took the position you did on my suspension. It is obvious that if you are to remain in Little Rock you will have to resort to the method I was suspended for advocating."[54] Strong community support for Williams was still in evidence two years later, at a rally in Harlem, celebrating the anniversary of *Brown v. Board of Education*. People still angry about Williams's dismissal hooted down Daisy Bates and pelted Roy Wilkins with an egg.[55]

Fannie Lou Hamer is exactly the right name for the iron-willed sharecropper's daughter who, after getting death threats for daring to register to vote, quipped, "Well, killing or no killing, I'm going to stick with civil rights." Hamer shared little with Daisy Bates in appearance, deportment, diction, or other markers of class stratification that have long been part of the black American experience. But she surrendered nothing to Bates in her commitment to the freedom struggle.[56]

Fannie Lou Hamer personified the grassroots of the movement. She grew up chopping cotton in the Mississippi Delta and told wrenching stories of how tenuous and desperate that existence could be. The despair is palpable in her account of the whole family scouring picked fields, hoping to find enough cotton scraps to buy dinner. Worse was the episode where a jealous neighbor poisoned the family's three precious mules. "We were doing pretty well. . . . That poisoning knocked us right back down flat. We never did get back up again. That white man did it just because we were getting somewhere."[57] Fannie Lou Hamer would indeed get somewhere. She would stick with civil rights through the storms of the 1960s, registering folk to vote, pressing the struggle as a leader in the Mississippi Freedom Democratic Party, capturing the hearts of callous politicians at two national political conventions, and founding the National Women's Political Caucus.

In some ways, Hamer epitomized the nonviolent theme of the movement. After discrimination, abuse, and beatings, she still urged a scriptural response, "*Baby you gotta love 'em*. Hating just makes you sick and weak." But Fannie Lou Hamer also exhibited an earnest practicality that epitomizes the black tradition of arms.[58] Asked how she survived so many years of racist aggression, Hamer responded, "I'll tell you why. *I keep a shotgun in every corner of my bedroom* and the first cracker even look like he wants to throw some dynamite on my porch won't write his mama again." In this approach, Hamer followed the example of her mother, Lou Ella Townsend, who as a fieldworker at the turn of the century had been threatened, assaulted, and raped. Unbowed, Townsend soldiered on, comforted by a pistol concealed in a bucket.[59] There is some chance that this is the same pistol that Fannie Lou handed to her overnight guest, Stokely Carmichael, when he stayed at her home during a SNCC voter-registration campaign.[60]

Fig. 7.3. Fannie Lou Hamer, circa 1964. (Photograph by Warren K. Leffler, August 22, 1964. Library of Congress Prints and Photographs Division.)

After-the-fact claims like Hamer's "I had a gun and was ready" are easily second-guessed. Who knows what would have happened on the alternate timeline. But on the basic preparations, Hamer's assertions are confirmed by other observers in at least one case where the community responded to a death threat against her. Neighbor Len Edwards recalled how, shortly after the Williams Chapel adjacent to Hamer's home was firebombed, the threat came that Hamer would be killed. Friends hustled Fannie Lou to a neighbor's house and "got shotguns and waited for the cars to drive by."[61]

The image of a shotgun in every corner of Fannie Lou Hamer's bedroom may seem implausible until we consider that she was probably talking about a typical gun of poor folk—that is, the single-shot shotgun, which was generally cheap, durable, and, with the appropriate loads, versatile enough for self-defense, hog killing, and hunting everything from rabbits to deer.

We don't know whether Hamer's guns were passed down, bartered, or bought with scarce cash. But for people familiar with the culture, the image of a couple of single shots leaning in the corner or behind a door is quite common. And many folk, even poor folk, would save and sacrifice to buy or trade for superior tools.

Annie Colton Reeves of Pike County, Mississippi, describes this kind of saving and sacrifice. The Reeveses were as poor as anyone but had invested in a heavy-caliber Winchester rifle, a light-caliber .22 rifle, a shotgun, and two handguns. Annie recalled her father's advice that "it's better to have ammunition than to have food." This was perhaps a calculation that with ammunition one could get food. And that calculation was evident in the training of the six Colton kids to be as familiar with guns as they were with the tools of the field. On the other hand, everyone understood the additional possibilities. This was apparent when Annie brandished a gun and chased off a party of menacing young men with the warning "whenever you get ready to go to hell, you come back."[62]

Women like Annie Colton Reeves and Fannie Lou Hamer offered no high theories about armed self-defense versus political violence. They projected the black tradition of arms in simple words and deeds and in stories passed down of armed black heroes and defiant last stands. Prominently in the first biography of her life, Fannie Lou Hamer proudly recounted a tale from her childhood that had been repeated many times before.

The year was 1924. Fannie Lou was only eight, but the episode kept a hold on her for decades. The venue was a delta plantation where many black men were still working in essential peonage. Joe Pullum was one of them. Pullum was good enough with numbers to know that he had been underpaid. When the plantation owner handed him a wad of cash to recruit more workers from the countryside, Pullum took the money as his due and fixed up his house. The planter tracked down Pullum at his cabin, confronted him, and then shot him. Bleeding from his wounds, Pullum ducked into his house, got his Winchester, and killed the planter where he stood. As Hamer tells it, "a white man that was sitting out in the buggy saw this and he lit out for town. . . . The Negro knew what this meant. As soon as that man got to town, he be coming back with a lynch mob and they would hang him. So he got all the ammunition he had and went on out to Powers Bayou and hid in the hollow of a tree."

The mob did indeed pursue Joe Pullum. "But he was waiting for them," said Hamer. "Every time a white man would peek out, he busted him. Before they finally got him, he'd killed 13 and wounded 26. . . . The way they finally got him was to pour gasoline on the water of the Bayou and set it afire. . . . When they found him, he was . . . lying with his hand on his gun."[63]

On Fannie Lou Hamer's telling, the story of Joe Pullum sounds fantastic, perhaps apocryphal. But outside reports confirm the basics and show that Hamer was not alone in her admiration of Joe Pullum. From Harlem, the widely circulated *Negro World*, voice of Marcus Garvey's Universal Negro Improvement Association, reported the incident under the headline, "Negro Tenant Farmer Shot to Kill and Should Have a Monument." The editors apparently assumed the headline would resonate for the half million readers of the *Negro World*.[64]

For grassroots folk like Fannie Lou Hamer, the story of Joe Pullum was part of the community fabric. The details, perhaps embellished over time, run in stark contrast to the familiar narrative of black victimization. The theme continues in the 1954 account of Holmes County, Mississippi, legend Eddie Noel, preserved in the oral history of Noel's neighbor, T. C. Johnson.

It started in a little country store that was popular with black folk but owned by white men. Eddie Noel's wife worked there as a cook. Someone objected to Noel hanging around, and then there was a fistfight. Soon it was two against one. Noel finally broke loose but was pursued by one of the men brandishing a gun. Noel ran to his car, grabbed his rifle, and killed his pursuer.

Having just shot a white man in rural Mississippi, Eddie Noel knew the drill and fled. The word spread quickly, and Noel's next altercation was against three carloads of pursuing "Klansmen" and a deputy sheriff that Noel fought to a standoff in a roadside shootout.

Noel then retreated home, where reports of his prowess with the gun seem embellished. Noel was an army veteran, transformed by legend into a sharpshooter. One account describes how, "That Sunday . . . they had scattered around the house. This guy was making his move up on the porch and . . . Ed shot him. . . . He got out in the yard, he whirled, flipped the gun over his shoulder, and hit one on top of the house by the chimney. There was another by the car, and he shot that one."

Black oral histories lionize Noel's running fight against hundreds of pursuers, purportedly inflicting multiple casualties, before surrendering in order to spare his family and neighbors the wrath of the mob. White newspaper reports, on the other hand, say that a handful of men went to apprehend Noel and he killed two of them and wounded two others.

Even in exaggerated form, the carnage was secondary to the change in attitude that followed. According to T. C. Johnson, Noel's fight "did give some of the black peoples the idea that they didn't have to take the beatin' and runnin' and the abusement like they had been. I've heard a lot of 'em say it was good that somebody had the courage and the nerve to stand tall like a man."[65]

While many of the fighters in the freedom movement have faded into obscurity, Medgar Evers, one hopes, is still a familiar name. Medgar, his wife, Myrlie, and his brother, Charles, were drawn into the movement by the prodigiously armed T. R. M. Howard. After Medgar sacrificed his life to the struggle, Howard preached his eulogy.[66]

When Medgar was killed, Charles Evers moved from Chicago back to Mississippi and assumed the leadership of the Mississippi NAACP. Indeed, on his telling, Evers took the position by force of will, over the objection of cautious souls like Gloster Current, director of branches at the national office. Based simply on their pedigree, it was fair to worry about the temperament of both of the Evers brothers.

Charles and Medgar grew up in the home of Jim Evers. In Decatur, Mississippi, in the 1930s, that meant something. Within the space of just a few years, at ages when they were trying to figure out how to be men, the Evers brothers witnessed their father's fighting spirit swirl into incidents that ended with the three of them sitting up nights, clutching guns and waiting for lynch mobs.

Jim Evers could not read or write much but was a natural at basic arithmetic. When a local grocer tried to cheat him in settling the week's accounts, Jim Evers called him on it. It was an affront that sent the shopkeeper boiling over. Aiming to avenge the insult of being called a "liar" by a "nigger," the shopkeeper bolted for his pistol, raging at Jim Evers, "I'll kill you, you black sonofabitch."

As his boys looked on, Jim Evers picked up a Coke bottle and warned the man, "Move another step, and I'll bust your damn brains in." The commotion drew a crowd, and Charles and Medgar grabbed bottles and stepped in behind their father. Charles wondered, decades later, why his father wasn't lynched then and there. He speculated that those men knew that Jim Evers was ready to die on the spot and they were not. Not yet ten-years-old, Charles certainly was not ready to die and admitted his instinct to run as the three of them backed out of the store. Later he would repeat his father's calming mantra that "mobbers are cowards."

The walk home was an odd scene. "No one followed us," Charles recalled. "We walked home along the railroad tracks, Medgar on one side of daddy and me on the other. We put our arms around daddy's waist, he put his hands on our heads. We were so happy." He might easily have been describing the night after a Little League game.

Still, no one in the Evers household was naive about the trajectory of these sorts of incidents. The possibility that the humiliated shopkeeper and a gang of sympathizers would descend on the Everses' homestead under the cover of darkness left Jim Evers sitting up nights, resting, without really sleeping, cradling a rifle in his lap.

For the Evers boys, it was a profound lesson. "Some thought daddy was crazy risking his neck, but that's the stock we came from," Charles recalled. "That was part of what it meant to be an Evers." And that grit was rooted deeper than Jim Evers. Family lore had it that Medgar's great-grandfather had fought two white men to the death and then ran off from his childhood home ahead of a lynch mob.[67]

The Everses' fighting lineage struck Charles somewhat differently than Medgar. According to Charles, his younger brother was the "saint" of the Evers kids. Charles tilted the other way. But in the winter of 1935, none of that made a difference, as both the boys sat shivering with their father and two other men, all of them cradling rifles. Jim Evers had broken the Jim Crow rules again.

It was late December and the custom was "No niggers allowed in Decatur around Christmas." But Jim Evers heard his boys talking about the excitement in town and determined to take them to see it. Preparing for the risk, he "put a metal tip on the end of a broom handle and hefted it like a baseball bat."

As they walked down Main Street, a mischievous white boy ran up to throw a firecracker at them. Jim Evers told him drop it or get walloped. The kid ran and told his father, who stormed up, spitting epithets. Jim Evers threatened to give the father the same medicine. He escaped intact only after a sympathetic merchant intervened, admonishing a gathering crowd, "You leave Jim alone. Get on away from here and let Jim alone."[68]

By now, Charles and Medgar knew the drill, and said out loud what their father was thinking, "We better sit up tonight." In a more involved replay of the incident in 1931, Jim Evers recruited two neighbors from across the road. Anticipating retaliation for Jim's affront, the three armed adults, and Charles and Medgar with their .22 rifles, "set up a crisscross" and waited. No one can say how real the mob threat was, only that it did not appear. But for Charles Evers it was another affirmation of his father's grit and the viability of standing up defiant, gun in hand.

By 1946, the Evers brothers had gone to war, spilled blood, and fallen in love with women they could never take back to Decatur, Mississippi. While other men would sit around kitchen tables, telling romantic stories about journeys home with their war brides, Charles and Medgar came home from fighting in Europe and the Philippines still barred from voting. They actually talked about "finding our girls and living in peace in some Central American country where no one cared about race." But fate had a different future in store for the Evers brothers, and for one of them a fight more deadly than the war just endured.[69]

The first battle was over the ballot. In the fall of 1946, Medgar and Charles determined that after their sacrifices in uniform, the United States of America, the state of Mississippi, and the town of Decatur owed them at least the opportunity to go through the motions of democracy. It turns out this was asking too much. And some of the strongest opposition came from the halls of Congress.

It was closing in on a century since the federal government abandoned the brief experiment in Southern Reconstruction and nodded in acquiescence as the Confederate states stripped the franchise from freedmen. One could travel the South through a sea of black souls and find only a handful of them allowed to vote. In Mississippi, the man nominally assigned to represent the interests of Charles and Medgar Evers in the United States Senate, the little homunculus, Theodore Bilbo, advised, "The best way to stop niggers from voting is to visit them the night before the election."

When Charles and Medgar announced that they planned to register and to vote in the next election, word spread fast and the warnings came quickly. Jim Evers was told to talk some sense into his boys. The registration clerk, who had been a friend to the Evers family, pulled them into his office and begged them to wait. Charles Evers appreciated the caution from this essentially decent man, whose meager outreach was enough to earn him the dangerous brand "nigger lover." Charles and Medgar thanked him for the warning but insisted on registering, and the worried clerk did the paperwork.[70]

But registering was different from voting. And on Election Day, Charles and Medgar stepped right to the edge of the precipice before conceding that Negroes did not vote in Decatur. They planned to arrive early, sneak in and out, and be back home before anyone knew the difference. But before the polls were even open, two hundred armed white men were already gathered at the courthouse.

Medgar and Charles had planned for trouble and brought four other men with them. Charles carried a .38 caliber revolver in his pocket. Following a tactical plan that puts modern complaints about voting inconvenience in perspective, the six of them split up, aiming to exploit the three separate entrances to the courthouse.

Through speed and guile, they actually managed to enter the building and get their hands on two ballots. But the ballot box itself had been locked away in a back office that was guarded by armed men stacked three deep. With one hand on his ballot and the other on his revolver, Charles Evers faced down the armed phalanx. Some of the men he had known for years and a few of them he called friends, within the racial constraints of the day.

Charles Evers was launched into some other place when one of those men, "a nice man from the drugstore" whom he had known for years, hissed, "Listen, nigger, ain't nothing happened to you yet." Charles tightened the grip on his gun and spit back, "Ain't nothing going to happen to me!" Writing about it later, Evers said that he was ready to die that day and was pulled back from the edge by his cooler-headed brother. Medgar talked him down with a soft, "Come on, Charlie, let's go. We'll get them next time."

As they backed out of the courthouse, hecklers closed in, hurling epithets and threats. The black men held their guns low and navigated a tense retreat. More anxious nights followed, with the Evers brothers sitting up armed through the night,

Medgar perched in the barn, Charles spotting from the garage. Again they survived the specter of the mob, and by the next year, weathering a campaign of threats and intimidation, they actually voted in the 1947 county elections.[71]

As Medgar and Charles began working on civil rights under the tutelage of T. R. M. Howard, Medgar traveled around the region as a salesman for Howard's insurance business. He started to layer civil-rights talk into his insurance pitch. In 1948, the brothers began canvassing for the NAACP. By 1952, they were labeled race agitators, and the resulting threats against them started Charles Evers sleeping with a gun under his pillow.[72]

As the Evers brothers digested the threats and calculated the toll of the sporadic episodes where Negroes turned up dead on the side of the road, they flirted with the radical idea that had tempted Roy Wilkins a generation earlier. As a young man still working as a journalist in Kansas City, Wilkins seethed over a series of local lynchings and imagined retaliating with raiding parties that would skulk into lynch venues and rain random violence on those who hosted the mob.[73] Charles and Medgar indulged a similar notion that "each time whites killed a Negro" they would "drive to another town, find a bad Sheriff or cop, and kill him in a secret hit and run raid." For both Wilkins and the Evers, this militant fantasy subsided, and they channeled rage into work. Between Medgar and Charles, their different dispositions were evident as the idea ran its course. "Medgar never had his heart in it," Charles recalled, "and over time we dropped it. Medgar was a sweeter man than me."[74]

Change was in the wind. And one continuing influence on the Evers brothers as their activism escalated during the 1950s was the percolating goodwill of "a lot of white folk [who] wanted to do right but the atmosphere was so sick," according to Charles, "that they were scared to speak up." What counts as goodwill here must be considered in the context of the times. Evers was speaking of people who "disliked lynchings but lacked the guts to stop them. So instead they'd warn us. . . . At the first sign of race trouble, white folks warned the niggers they liked. . . . Even the Klan had a few who said leave that poor nigger alone."

In Philadelphia, Mississippi, the infamous venue of the Goodman, Chaney, and Schwerner murders, Charles Evers records that Mayor Clayton Lewis tipped him off to multiple threats and "saved my ass a few times, maybe saved my life." Other men like Howard Cole, owner of WHOC Radio, exhibited goodwill in more ordinary ways. Responding to complaints that the Evers family funeral home was getting shortchanged in its advertising buys because white announcers brought insufficient style to the copy, Cole told Evers to do the ads himself, and then gave him a radio show to boot.

But in many ways these acts of goodwill were reminders of the dangerous current the Evers brothers were bucking. In 1956, Medgar was the NAACP's

Mississippi field director and Charles headed voter-registration efforts. A white friend called to warn Charles, "There is a Negro coming to your house. He'll ask you to drive your cab down to the county line. Don't go. Some Klansmen are waiting there to kill you."

Later that night, just as the caller warned, the fellow showed up following the script that Evers already knew. With his .38 revolver in his pocket, Evers invited the man in and offered him an alternative driver. When the fellow insisted on Evers, Charles sprung the trap. He might have killed the assassins' helper but for the intervention of his wife, Nan.

Things accelerated from there. Howard Cole at the radio station was pressured to cancel Charles Evers's show and a landlord refused to renew the lease on his restaurant. Then a local woman was sent by the Citizens' Council to stage an accident with one of Evers's taxicabs. Economic pressure was a better tool against Charles Evers than physical threats. He set off for Chicago in 1956.[75]

Some said it was better that he was gone because it was not clear Charles had the temperament for the challenges to come. Even in the short space of a visit back to Mississippi, he boiled over into violence after a white cabdriver assaulted Medgar. Charles drove to the taxi stand, brandished a shotgun, and threatened to kill the man who had sucker punched his little brother.

Charles Evers was in Chicago when the news came that Medgar had been shot by a sniper in his driveway and bled to death as his wife and children poured out their grief. Two neighbors, Thomas Young and Houston Wells, heard the shot and ran out to investigate. Wells fired his gun into the air, hoping to scare off anyone who remained lurking. But it was soon clear that this armed response was useless against the damage already done to their friend and neighbor.

Charles Evers returned to Mississippi, buffeted by anger, guilt, and fear. He slept with a pistol within reach, and after the September 15, 1963, bombing of the Sixteenth Street Baptist Church in Birmingham killed four little black girls, Charles Evers indulged his old suicidal fantasies of Mau Mau–style retribution. Then, as his rage subsided, he picked up the mantle of his dead brother.

Now walking the path that had gotten Medgar killed, Charles Evers was guarded by an informal team of armed men who were active in the Jackson NAACP. During particularly tense periods, and on occasions when NAACP leaders and prominent figures like Gloster Current, Roy Wilkins, Thurgood Marshall, and Lena Horne were visiting, the defense group deployed in teams, some sitting with guns in cars outside, others on the porch of Evers's Jackson home.

The Jackson defense group extended its protective reach to local NAACP activist Reverend R. L. T. Smith after his business was targeted by terrorists. Smith surely appreciated the protection but also took his own measures. Charles

Evers recounts, that Reverend Smith "carried a gun and wouldn't have minded using it."[76]

In June 1964, student activists Andrew Goodman, James Chaney, and Michael Schwerner went missing in Neshoba County. Over the coming months, four bombings targeted local black activists. It was a time, Evers recalled, where "I kept a gun in every corner of every room of my house. . . . I felt whites would probably get me, but not like they had Medgar—not in the back, with no return fire."[77]

Charles Evers was not dissuaded by the fact that being armed was no guarantee of safety. The gun plainly had not saved Medgar, who followed T. R. M. Howard's practice of arms. Ruby Hurley, NAACP Youth Program director, recalls, "many times when Medgar and I would be driving together, Medgar would tell us about carrying his gun. . . . He used to sit on it under his [driver's seat] pillow."[78] Medgar's wife, Myrlie, acknowledged that the family "had guns in every room of our house. I slept with a rifle next to . . . the nightstand. He slept with a rifle next to him. We had one in the hall, . . . one in the front room."[79] Just a week before he was murdered, Medgar was startled awake by a crash in the night, jumped from his bed, and grabbed a rifle to investigate.[80] Charles Evers depicts Medgar's concurrent commitment to political nonviolence and private self-defense with no sense of contradiction. "*Medgar was nonviolent, but he had six guns in the kitchen and living room.*"[81]

Medgar Evers's practice of arms is confirmed by John Salter, an American Indian activist who taught sociology at the predominately black Tougaloo College, in Jackson. Salter stopped by Medgar's house one night in 1962 and was greeted by the muzzle of a gun. Inside the house, Salter recalls, "at least half a dozen firearms were in the living room and kitchen." While traveling with Evers to work on voter registration, Salter said that Evers kept a .45 caliber automatic pistol under the pillow he used on the driver's seat and a rifle in the trunk.[82] Salter would subsequently acknowledge his own preparations, explaining:

> Like a martyred friend of mine, NAACP staffer Medgar W. Evers, I, too, was on many Klan death lists and I, too, traveled armed: a .38 Special Smith & Wesson revolver and a 44/40 Winchester carbine. The knowledge that I had these weapons and was willing to use them kept enemies at bay. Years later, in a changed Mississippi, [this deterrent value] was confirmed by a former prominent leader of the White Knights of the KKK when we had an interesting dinner together at Jackson.[83]

Medgar Evers's murder casts critical light on John Salter's assessment. Claims of averted violence are far less evocative than bloody incidents where violence runs unchecked. We are left wondering how to value the statements of John Salter and Charles Evers that guns saved their lives, against the bloody fact that a man with a gun extinguished the life of their beloved brother and friend. One clear lesson is that having a gun is no guarantee of safety. And some will argue further that the gun only introduces new dangers, especially where black self-defenders are left to deal with biased local authorities.[84] But none of this diminished either Charles or Medgar Evers's resolve to arm themselves for self-defense.[85]

For Charles, even the worrisome boundary against political violence did not counsel against the gun. In 1959, he pressed hard against that boundary after a car-bomb attack on Natchez, Mississippi, NAACP leader George Metcalf. Like Robert Williams before him, Evers claimed to reject political violence as fruitless, acknowledging, "the only way we have is through nonviolence. There's no other way."[86] But following the attack on Metcalf, Evers channeled the rage of the community, venting, "We're not going to take it any longer. . . . We're not going to start any riots, but we've got guns and we're going to fight back." A day later, after Governor Paul Johnson ordered guardsmen to Natchez, Evers was again urging the community that group violence was counterproductive.[87]

From the national office, Roy Wilkins scolded Evers, "We have never authorized you, as our representative, to state either privately or publicly, 'we are armed, we have taken all we will take, we will fight' . . . or any sentiments approximating that language. [We cannot] afford these damaging statements in a nationally syndicated newspaper column."[88] Wilkins demanded that Evers issue a statement making this clear. After a follow-up by Evers in the *New York Post* that Wilkins considered unsatisfactory, he drafted a letter demanding that Evers resign. For reasons that remain unclear, Wilkins never sent this letter.[89]

Wilkins already had navigated a similar conflict with St. Augustine, Florida, activist, Robert Hayling, a black dentist who led local voter registration and desegregation efforts. After a shotgun attack on his home, Hayling organized an armed defense squad. He warned the Klan publicly that his guards would "shoot first and ask questions later."[90] Here, Roy Wilkins responded harshly, as he had to Robert Williams. Hayling broke ties with the NAACP. But in a familiar turn, when Martin Luther King came to St. Augustine in 1964, he consented to Hayling's deployment of armed guards for protection.[91]

The movement spills over with lesser-known folk like Robert Hayling whose preparations to defend themselves with guns survive as remnants within a larger story. In South Carolina, a solitary reverend, J. A. Delaine, fired back with effect when terrorists shot into his house.[92] The home of local activist Amzie Moore, of Cleveland, Mississippi, who mentored young activists who would rise to form SNCC, was well stocked with arms and ammunition. A young white activist spending the night at Moore's was "startled when Moore placed a pistol on the night table and suggested that he and his friends use it to repel [intruders]." Not only was his home well fortified, "like most politically active Blacks in the Delta," Moore carried a gun when he traveled.[93]

Shortly after Medgar Evers's murder, Aaron Henry, a Clarksdale, Mississippi, pharmacist and intermittent president of the state NAACP, led a series of protests in Clarksdale, where segregation still reigned and the voting rolls remained tightly restricted. Local folk worried about Aaron Henry's safety after threats on his life circulated. Later, an affidavit to the Justice Department claimed that Clarksdale police chief Ben Collins had offered to pay a Negro named Charlie Black to kill Henry. Henry himself recounts how Collins chided, "Let me take out some life insurance on you. Somebody's gonna kill your ass."

Fearing for Henry's safety, the local NAACP hired professional guards. When the bills came due, folk realized that paying a professional force was unsustainable. So they established a volunteer force of a dozen rotating guards drawn from community men like Reverend Willie Goodlow, whom Henry describes sitting up nights in the living room with a shotgun in his lap. On one occasion as Henry's guards were changing shifts, police chief Ben Collins pulled up, poked around, and then confiscated the pistol that one of the men had laid on his car seat. By Aaron Henry's account, that was the end of the incident. But it is illuminating to consider the additional detail from Charles Evers.[94]

We know from multiple accounts that Aaron Henry and Charles Evers had very different temperaments. And that may explain why Henry fails to mention what Evers describes as a deluge of guns flooding in from black Clarksdale to the Aaron Henry defense effort. According to Evers, when police arrested Henry's guard and confiscated his gun, "that made Negroes of Clarksdale so mad they gave Aaron guns enough for ten lifetimes."[95] Evers's version suggests that Henry was no passive beneficiary of risks taken by other men and actively prepared to defend himself with guns. Anthony Lewis of the *New York Times* confirms Evers's intimation, writing that "after the bombing of his home, Mr. Henry obtained a permit for a revolver." (This evidently refers to a permit to carry a concealed firearm because no permit was needed simply to own the gun).

Charles Evers's richer account of the Aaron Henry episode leaves us wondering what other details have been excluded over the years from judicious recollections of Negroes with guns. Given the abundant surviving evidence of so many of the sober stalwarts of the freedom movement owning and using guns and advocating armed self-defense, it is a fair surmise that the available record shows only a slice of a broader phenomenon populated by a legion of unknown and lesser-known folk.

Among the lesser known and briefly recorded are men like Dr. Emmett Stringer, who served as president of the Mississippi State Conference of NAACP Branches in 1954. For the sin of taking seriously the Supreme Court's decision in *Brown v. Board of Education*, Stringer suffered economic reprisals and then physical threats. His wife's master's degree from Columbia University was no shield against retaliatory firing from her teaching job. Stringer was unapologetic about his response to the growing pressure. "I had weapons in my house. And not only in my house, I had weapons on me when I went to my office. . . . I would take my revolver with me and put it in the drawer, right where I worked."[96]

Daisy Bates and Fannie Lou Hamer are the famous names, but many other black women picked up guns to defend themselves and their friends during the freedom struggle. In one dramatic example in 1962, Rebecca Wilson, of Dallas, Georgia, defied terrorists with pistol fire. It was well past visiting time when she rose to the commotion of seven hooded men on her porch. One of them teased that they wanted to "sell a little politics and leave a card." Then they fired a shotgun through the door. Wilson fired back, five rapid shots, killing one man and wounding a second. Apparently surprised by the return fire, the other men fled.

Wilson later explained, "It was the idea of the masks, I guess. I was scared. I didn't know what I was shooting at. I just had my hand out the door." Even though the dead and wounded men were politically prominent, Wilson's shooting was acknowledged as an act of self-defense, and several of the hooded men were charged with violation of Georgia's KKK-targeted anti-masking law. Fearing retaliation, Wilson accepted an offer of protective custody and then left Georgia for Indiana.[97]

Not every episode ended in gunfire and dead terrorists. But the evidence of armed black women in the modern movement abounds. During the Freedom Summer Project, one student volunteer was shocked to find that her host, "Mrs. Fairly, was armed to the teeth." In a letter home, the student wrote, "I met Mrs. Fairly coming down the hall from the front porch carrying a rifle in one hand and a pistol in the other." In 1965 in Bogalusa, Louisiana, the wife of local activist Robert Hicks used her pistol to fend off Klansmen who had chased a CORE[98] worker to her home. In nearby Ferriday, a rural farmer's wife returned fire when a group of Klansmen shot into her home. And after the brutal beating of her nephew by police in Tuscaloosa, activist Ruth Bolden recounts, "I called my friends . . . to come over here and stay with me that night 'cause I was really scared to death. . . . We had to talk in codes. I said 'come and bring a lot of sandwiches' and he knew what that meant: it was guns and a lot of bullets." Afterward, Bolden began carrying a pistol . . . hidden in her Bible.[99]

In Carroll County, Mississippi, Leola Blackmon invoked faith, fearlessness, and firearms against midnight terrorists who tried to crush local voter-registration efforts. Activists were caught in a bureaucratic game that demanded multiple trips to the registration office. This exposed them to harassment on the roadway by cars full of armed men. Their response was pragmatic. "So some blacks just went home and got their trucks and came back with their guns. . . . We had mens who guarded us, and they was standing out with high power guns. They began to shoot back at this car, and they hit it. . . . That car left there on a flat 'cause they shot the tires out. The laws didn't try to find out who did it."

Later, when someone lit a cross in her yard, Leola Blackmon's reaction was rooted in two different worlds. "I don't feel like I oughta have feared mens," she said, "The one I feared's Jesus Christ. That night when they set that cross afire at my house . . . I thought to cut 'em down, but I didn't. I just let some bullets through behind 'em. I had a rifle. It would shoot sixteen times, and I just lit out up there and started shooting." Leola Blackmon saw her actions as fully consistent with the non-violent movement, explaining, "Well, we said nonviolent when we was protesting the school buses; nobody not s'posed to fight. But that fight was brought on because we were looking for them to hit *us*."[100]

Women like Leola Blackmon defy the intuition that the black tradition of arms was an exclusively male phenomenon. But there is no doubting the dominant role of black men. Just one county over, grassroots activist Hartman Turnbow, was a full-blown exemplar of black male defiance. Turnbow distilled the importance of private self-defense and the basic impulse fueling the black tradition of arms in phrasing unmatched before or since.

Startled awake one spring night in 1963 by crashing glass, flames from a firebomb, and the sound of gunshots, Turnbow proceeded on instinct. He jumped out of bed, grabbed his sixteen-shot semiautomatic rifle, and ran toward the threat. He repelled two armed men from his porch and continued firing as they fled to a waiting vehicle. Turnbow and his family managed to extinguish the flames and save their home. The next day he was arrested on the charge that he had attempted to burn down his own house.[101] The talk among black folk was that that Turnbow actually killed one of the attackers, but the death was called a heart attack in order to cover the identities of the terrorists. Suspicions mounted when SNCC workers surveyed the scene and found a dropped license plate that matched to the sheriff's car.[102]

Turnbow explained his gunfire as perfectly consistent with the nonviolent philosophy of the movement declaring, "*I wasn't being non-nonviolent*, I was protecting my wife and family."[103] While Turnbow answered the worries of northern pacifists with the double negative of non-nonviolence, local folk required no such apologies, and in the Delta, Turnbow was considered a hero.[104]

By the time of the next attack, Turnbow had augmented his arsenal. He described it this way: "The next year when they shot over here, I got a automatic shotgun,

Remington, 12 gauge, and them high-velocity buckshot. So I jumped up and run out and turn it loose a time or two. . . . I reported to the FBI in Jackson. . . . First words they said to me was, 'Don't kill nobody. Don't kill nobody.' . . . I said now here y'all two Mississippi FBI's, talkin bout don't kill nobody. How to you think I feel and they just shootin' all through my house and I got a wife and a 14-year-old daughter?"[105]

Fig. 7.4. Hartman Turnbow speaking at a Holmes County Mississippi church meeting. (The image of Hartman Turnbow, photographed by Sue [Lorenzi] Sojourner, was previously published in *Thunder of Freedom: Black Leadership and the Transformation of 1960s Mississippi* by Sue [Lorenzi] Sojourner with Cheryl Reitan [2013, University Press of Kentucky].)

Hartman Turnbow was not unique in either word or deed. When armed Klansmen attacked the all-black community of Milestone, Mississippi, in 1965, World War II veteran Robert Cooper and other movement activists responded with gunfire of their own. Cooper explained slightly less poetically than Hartman Turnbow, "I don't figure that I was violent. All I was doin' was protectin' myself."

After a cross burning in front of his house, Cooper told the sheriff, "The very next one come up and do something in front of my house, I will be calling the undertaker." The next episode was not a cross burning but a firebomb and then gunshots. When the bomb was tossed, Cooper reports, "I just happened to be out there, and I fired right back on 'em. That's the way I caught 'em 'cause I got the word they was coming by that night to get me. . . . I had my automatic shotgun settin' right at the front door, and I fired up through that oak tree there to let 'em know I was at home."

The terrorists were not easily dissuaded. "Bout an hour after that," Cooper recalled, "I had gone out, got myself stationary. . . . They fired into the house. Then they came right on by me, and just as they got to me, I started firin' on them. Some of them shots hit 'em. One boy, I know, got a load."

Cooper recounts a conversation the next day when the sheriff showed up to arrest him, charging, "'You done shot them fellows, and we gonna put you in jail.' I say, 'Yeah, but I was at home tended to my business when they come shootin into my house. I wasn't out there meddlin; they come there meddlin me. I think I had a right to shoot back at them done shot into my house.' So finally they up and let me out."

Later Cooper explained his decision this way. "I felt that you're in your house, ain't botherin nobody, the only thang you hunting is equal justice. An they gonna sneak by night, burn your house, or shoot in there. And you gonna sit there and take all of it? You got to be a very li'l man with no guts at all."[106]

One wonders from these sorts of accounts whether and how often Hartman Turnbow, Robert Cooper, and folk of similar dispositions carried guns in public. Did they take them to town, to the fields, to church? Certainly the dangers they armed against did not disappear when they ventured from home out into the world.

Although we can never know exactly how widespread it was, there are hints within the culture that creative concealed carry was a minor art form. Recall T. R. M. Howard's rumored secret compartment in his Cadillac. Fannie Lou Hamer's mother, Lou Ella Townsend, carried a gun concealed in a bucket. Medgar Evers hid his pistol in a driver's seat pillow. Fred Kirkpatrick in Louisiana and Ruth Bolden in Alabama capitalized on the practice of church folk to carry around their bibles in big leather covers with room for extras that would fill a decent purse. In with that jumble, Kirkpatrick and Bolden both kept pistols.[107]

But the prize for minimalist creativity goes to the lyrically named Sweets

Turnbow, Hartman Turnbow's life mate. In 1964, Hartman and Sweets traveled to Atlantic City, where the Mississippi Freedom Democratic Party would challenge the whites-only State Democratic Party for representation at the national convention. Fannie Lou Hamer stole the show with wrenching stories of suffering and the uplift of song. But in the wings, Sweets Turnbow schmoozed and cajoled national Democrats to confront the fact that their Mississippi brethren were running a party that would have been a comfortable home to a nineteenth-century Confederate veteran.[108]

People must have thought the rube from Mississippi had brought her lunch or was stuffing buffet leftovers into the brown paper bag she carried up and down the boardwalk. Years later, those who knew the truth would tell that inside the bag was a loaded pistol and how "Sweets never went anyplace without her brown paper bag and gun."[109]

Sweets and Hartman Turnbow no doubt consulted on strategies for concealing and carrying firearms. Although it is unclear whether Hartman was carrying a gun at the Atlantic City convention, Julian Bond records that in Mississippi, Turnbow "used to carry an army automatic in a briefcase, and it's funny to see a man who looks like a farmer and is dressed like a farmer in coveralls and boots and let's say an old hat, with a briefcase. And he opens the briefcase and nothing's in it but an automatic."[110]

SNCC activist James Forman confirmed that keeping and carrying guns was consistent with community norms. Commenting on Hartman Turnbow, Forman observed that "self-defense—at least of one's home—was not a concept new to Southern blacks in 1963 and there was hardly a black home in the South without its shotgun or rifle."[111] Julian Bond echoed the observation: "Almost everybody with whom we stayed in Mississippi had guns, as a matter of course, hunting guns. But you know, they were there for other purposes too."[112]

Margaret Rose was a northern SNCC activist whose particular experience confirms Julian Bond's generalization. After a series of midnight attacks in neighboring counties, Holmes County, Mississippi, Negroes set up armed nightly patrols. Rose reports that the family she stayed with "were up all night.... Mr. on the road patrolling with his new rifle and Mrs. walking from room to room in the house with a shotgun." In the room where one of the children was sleeping, Rose recalled, "was a large shotgun, waiting." Rose was a pacifist, but under the circumstances she acknowledged, "I cannot help feeling more secure knowing that they are armed." In her first letter home, another young CORE volunteer reported, "the first thing that her host family taught her was how to shoot the shotgun which the family kept for protection."[113]

Holmes County grassroots activists Vanderbilt Roby and Bee Jenkins report firsthand their preparations in anticipation of night riders. "I was layin' for 'em," said Roby, "layin' in the bushes for 'em many a night. If they made a shot, I was intending to let 'em have it."[114] Bee Jenkins recalled first the preparation, and then the follow-through: "Oh yeah, they had fire. Ready to shoot lead! They . . . started to burning crosses out there and shooting while we would be on the inside meetin'. . . . So the black men would go and buy them some high-powered rifles and started shooting at those cars. They took off and didn't come back out there."[115]

In Leake County, Mississippi, just over the line from the turmoil in Neshoba, the tradition of arms thrived in the all-black town of Harmony. One of the best firsthand accounts comes from a sturdy, copper-colored woman with the incomparable name of Anger Winson Gates Hudson, to her friends, simply Winson.[116] People who knew the story called her one of the most extraordinary of the many underacknowledged fighters in the civil-rights movement. She played a crucial role in voter registration and served as president of the Leake County NAACP from 1962 through 2001.[117]

As the predictable backlash began, Harmony closed ranks and turned decades of government neglect into a tactical advantage. The roads into Harmony were limited and in abysmal condition. Comparing the Harmony experience to other places plagued by terrorist drive-bys, Winson Hudson described Harmony's ironic advantage. "We had such bad roads so they couldn't just fly in and out like it was a highway."

Harmony was a community of poor folk. With everyone living close to the edge, people were more willing to help their neighbors because they might need it next time. Most folk did not have telephones. But the alternative was in some ways better. "We didn't have no phone," Hudson explained, "but my husband had an old pickup truck, and others did, and plenty of shotguns. When whites came through here, from Frog Bottom, where we lived, to any border, the Harmony men gave a sign. They'd blow that whistle twice, riding through the community, or else they'd shoot in the air and let 'em know to get on board someone was coming in. The Klan never did come in here or get out without being marked or being known."

When Winson Hudson and fifty stout neighbors huddled with Medgar Evers in 1961 to establish the Leake County NAACP, Medgar warned them of the risks and that the government would be no help. When someone asked, "Well, who can we look to for help?" Medgar advised what had long been true, "Nobody—you all will have to stick together."[118]

This advice proved prescient as local terrorists sparked to the arrival of NAACP lawyers Derek Bell and Constance Baker Motley, who came to help on school desegregation. After a newspaper article publicizing the Negroes' grand educational ambitions, a motorcade of angry white men sped through Harmony, firing shots at houses along the road. They made one pass unscathed, Hudson recalled. But "they came through again and that time, some of Dovie's boys—and some more here— were ready for 'em. . . . They ran the whites out of here. They followed 'em back to their homes and shot into them. This stirred things up so bad that even Governor Ross Barnett came out to Harmony and offered to build a junior college up here."[119]

As branch leader, Hudson was specifically targeted for a firebomb, but her diligent preparations thwarted the attack. "I was night watching until 12:00 that night, and the Klan was backing into our driveway. My daughter was living with us while her husband was in Vietnam. . . . I told her to get up and rush into the back room. My husband Cleo and I got ready to start shooting, but by this time, the German Shepherd dog had forced the Klan to move on."

Stymied at Winson's, the bomb throwers drove down the street and launched a flaming missile at her sister Dovie's house. Winson's husband, Cleo, heard the blast and ran up the street to the fight. Winson recalled, "Cleo was shooting, emptying every gun." Dovie survived the attack, which confirmed for the citizens of Harmony the importance of arming and fighting back. It would pay off again when the men of Harmony responded to an attack on the Harmony community center and "shot the Klan truck all up."[120]

Another terrorist tactic was to place bombs in rural mailboxes. If a house was far enough from the road, this could be done without alerting the residents, at least until they opened the box the next morning. When a group of bombers was detected, the word spread quickly and Dovie Hudson put her sons on the lookout.

Fig. 7.5. Winson and Cleo Hudson, 1946, around their tenth wedding anniversary. (From the personal collection of Ms. Hudson.)

"One got one gun and one got the other. And just as they drove up and put the bomb in the mailbox, my boys started shooting. They just lined that car with bullets up and down."[121] Although bravado is generally the province of men, Winson Hudson staked her share in an assessment of the community reaction to continued terrorist attacks. "The more they did to us, the meaner we got."

We have to be cautious about inferring too much from the recorded evidence about the full practice and sentiments of the community. But reports and correspondence of outsiders confirms that the armed stance of Winson Hudson was far from unique. Jane Addams, a white student volunteer from Illinois, lived and worked in Harmony during the summer of 1964. She recorded this in her journal, "Went to Winson and Cleo Hudson's house, helped (sort of) milk the cows, rode the horse.... The whole community was tense the weekend of July 4. Everyone here is armed, but it is a tension of caution, not of fear.... Navy teams are scouring the area [for the missing Goodman, Chaney, and Schwerner]."[122]

There is a similar report from the mother of a white summer volunteer who came south to see firsthand the risks her daughter was taking. She was initially worried by a letter that the host family's house was an "armory with rifles in every room." But ultimately she was comforted by the widely armed black folk, writing, "Cars stopped here last night; prowlers had been seen. Luckily, no trouble has ensued, because at least one of the homes has four rifles ready, and its owner, a Negro farmer, was quite determined to use them in defense of his home."[123] White law student William Holdes expressed similar sentiments in a letter to concerned relatives back north. Holdes was among a group of summer volunteers staying with a black farmer who "hurries us into the house as soon as we get home... [and] has four pistols in the house and certainly has enough fight to use them on an intruder."[124]

By the end of her eighty-six years, Winson Hudson would be feted for her civil-rights heroism. She could joke then about coming up rough and how as a young tomboy she could "ride a bucking horse, and ... kill a hog or anything just like a man." She was an exemplar of the black tradition of arms. And we can fairly wonder whether, absent the gun, she would have survived to enjoy the accolades.[125]

Like any cultural phenomenon, the black tradition of arms filtered through the diverse views and experiences of countless individuals. Many people no doubt eschewed firearms and some were quite literally committed to turning the other cheek regardless of the circumstances. Movement stalwart John Lewis is emblematic. His uncompromising pacifism was grounded in deep religious faith, innate sensitivity, and early trauma.

Lewis was certainly familiar with black gun culture, writing, "My brothers all grew up hunting, just like my father. They still love to hunt, every one of them."

Lewis was the exception within the family, admitting, "I've never been hunting in my life, never fired a gun, never even held one in my hands. . . . I'd always had a visceral aversion to violence of any sort." Lewis speculates that his ardent pacifism may have been rooted in an episode that he describes this way:

> One of my earliest memories—I couldn't have been older than four—was of my mother pleading with my father one afternoon not to leave the house. He had a shotgun in his hand, his face was full of anger, and he was trying to push past my mother toward the door. I don't know to this day what it was about, what had happened out there, beyond that door. But I knew what I saw in my mother's face. It had anguish and terror written all over it. "Don't do it!" I remember watching her plead with my father as she pushed her body full-up against his. "Buddy, *please* don't do it!" . . . I've never heard my mother beg for anything from anyone my entire life, but she was begging my father that day.[126]

Although he disdained the gun, Lewis exhibited a special kind of courage, even as a very young man. This was evident in his resolve to reject armed guards for the SNCC Freedom House in Greenwood, Mississippi, after a series of terrorist attacks. Lewis seems exceptional here, in that his position about protecting the house ultimately was overruled.[127]

The public shift within SNCC toward greater tolerance of violence was evident as early as June 1964, when an activist who had been chased by three carloads of men with bad intentions explained in a *Jet* magazine interview, "I had a shotgun and I'll tell you if they had come in to get me, I would've used it." The young man emphasized that he was still committed to nonviolence during group demonstrations. But even on this point, views were changing.[128]

Informants paid to spy on SNCC reported an increasing tolerance for armed self-defense. Soon journalists were reporting that some SNCC and CORE members had retreated from nonviolence and actually were "urging the contrary." Although many argued that fighting back would only escalate the dangers, some claimed that the capacity for armed self-defense actually reduced the nature and extent of the violence they faced.[129]

Through all of this, John Lewis remained a fierce advocate of unalloyed nonviolence.[130] But it seems he was part of a dwindling minority. One movement historian argues that by the end of the summer of 1964, almost every SNCC worker in the field was armed.[131] Based on his own observations, famous pacifist Bayard Rustin wrote about the period that "young people who formerly were preaching nonviolence in the Student Nonviolent Coordinating Committee, are now advocating quite openly limited forms of violence." Julian Bond disputed Rustin's report, insisting that SNCC did not advocate violence on any scale.[132]

In April 1965, a SNCC worker was arrested in Georgia for carrying three pistols in his car. The discussion of how to respond prompted talk within the group about the philosophy of nonviolence. Some considered any violence counterproductive. Others argued that SNCC faced different and more direct challenges than Martin King and the SCLC,[133] arguing, "They don't do the kind of work we do nor do they live in the areas we live in. They don't ride the highways at night."

Ultimately, the group resolved to hire a lawyer to aid their jailed colleague in Georgia. The broader policy remained officially unchanged, although some accounts say this was just a capitulation to the fact that their nonviolent image was essential to fundraising. Perhaps the true sentiment of the group is measured by a report that most of the members at the meeting were already carrying guns and by the fact that in May 1966, pacifist John Lewis was replaced as SNCC chairman by the more militant Stokely Carmichael.[134]

In Neshoba County, Mississippi, SNCC search teams accompanied by local black men carrying rifles and shotguns searched the woods for evidence of Goodman, Chaney, and Schwerner. At night, the students stayed with local farmers who, with a keen appreciation of the risk that came with sheltering the northern activists, guarded their homes with guns. The coming militancy of SNCC is indicated by the decision of Cleveland Sellers and Stokely Carmichael to take their turns on armed watch.

In an account published in 1973, Sellers was still reluctant to identify the farmer who had sheltered them. He described their "hideout" as a remote country place owned by "an old farmer whom I'll call Jones [since] his life would be in danger if I revealed his name." Jones told Carmichael and Sellers, "I believe that the peckerwoods burned the church and then killed them boys because us church folks was working with the COFO voter registration people. . . . Y'all welcome to stay here and search as long as you want though." Then, with somber practicality, he told them, "I'll be sitting on the front porch with my shotgun every night and there'll be a man in the barn behind the house with a rifle." As the conflict swirled in Neshoba County, bands of angry white men drove through the black section, shooting randomly. In at least two recorded instances, blacks returned fire and wounded one man.[135]

One Mississippi activist whose parents also hosted SNCC workers argued that being protected by Negroes with guns transformed Stokely Carmichael's views on nonviolence. John Jackson was just a young man when Carmichael stayed in Lowndes County with his family. According to Jackson, Carmichael was struck by the idea that "my father had guns and that's why white people didn't mess with [Carmichael] when he was here."[136]

Just like John Lewis, SNCC field secretary Bob Moses was a committed pacifist, his views informed partly by his graduate degree in philosophy from Harvard. Setting policy for student volunteers, Moses adamantly opposed anyone carrying weapons. But Moses was pragmatic about the prospects of drawing grassroots folk to his rigorous pacifism.[137]

In a strategy session discussing how to react to self-defense preparations of local folk, Moses advised that they simply had to accept the fact that "self-defense is so deeply ingrained in rural southern America that we as a small group can't affect it. It's not contradictory for a farmer to say he's nonviolent and also pledge to shoot a marauder's head off."[138] This was essentially Hartman Turnbow's philosophy wrapped in better grammar.

Later, Moses acknowledged, "I don't know if anyone in Mississippi preached to local Negroes that they shouldn't defend themselves. Probably the closest is when I asked Mr. E. W. Steptoe not to carry guns when we go out together at night. So instead he just hides his gun and then I find out later."[139] E. W. Steptoe was from an earlier generation than the young activists. He might have privately scoffed at their naïveté but was too kind to openly deride their pacifist idealism. He simply ignored it.

One student reported that Steptoe "never went out of the door unarmed," carrying a variety of concealed weapons and at a minimum a derringer in his boot. Inside the house, the abundance of guns evoked a kind of wonder on the part of one activist who recounted, "It was just marvelous. . . . Steptoe was always so wonderfully well-armed. . . . You'd go to Steptoe's and as you went to bed he would open up the night table and there would be a large .45 automatic sitting next to you. Just guns all over the house, under pillows, under chairs."

Fig. 7.6. Amite County NAACP President E. W. Steptoe, 1963.
(Used with permission from the Harvey Richards Media Archive.)

This was an extension of the family practice where Steptoe's brothers, five sons, and men of the extended family stood armed watch around the farm during tense periods.[140] And as the details accumulate, it is easier to sympathize with Steptoe's practice of arms. *New York Times* reporter Claude Sitton noted that Steptoe, like many folk, lived out on a rural road where neighbors were farther away than hollering distance. And sometimes neighbors themselves were a worry.

Steptoe's closest neighbor was a white man named E. H. Hurst. He and Steptoe had been childhood friends. But when Steptoe became president of the Amite County NAACP, Hurst, now a state legislator, turned on a dime. At one point, he threatened Steptoe's life. Then in the fall of 1961, Hurst shot and killed NAACP voter-registration activist Herbert Lee. Lee was unarmed, but the sheriff pressured black witnesses to say the shooting was self-defense. Hurst was exonerated without spending a day in jail.[141]

Although he never articulated any grand statements about state failure or malevolent bureaucracies, E. W. Steptoe's actions spoke his assessment of the situation. While there were surely people of goodwill out there, they were irrelevant to his immediate safety. For that, he was on his own. His personal arsenal and practice of arms reflected that simple truth.

In Forrest County, Mississippi, NAACP leader Vernon Dahmer adhered to the E. W. Steptoe school of armed preparedness. Dahmer had pushed the NAACP agenda since the early 1950s when he sued the county sheriff for interfering with black voting efforts. Just like Steptoe, Dahmer was relatively safe against economic reprisals. He owned 200 acres free and clear and drew income from cattle, a sawmill, and a little grocery store.

When northern students came to help with voter registration, some of them stayed with Dahmer and reported back about the "guns, pistols and rifles . . . placed throughout his house." As a demonstration of his preparedness and as a hopeful deterrent against night riders, Dahmer would periodically "just take one of his guns and shoot in the air, just to let folks know he was alive, well and intended to protect his property." When tensions escalated through the early 1960s, Dahmer and his bride, Ellie, sometimes supplemented by local NAACP members, would switch off during the night, between sleeping and sitting up with guns. They continued this practice for several years, up through 1965.[142]

The scene repeats in Leflore County, Mississippi, with NAACP president Dewey Green. After terrorists shot into his home in March 1963, he went to the sheriff and explained that he had made preparations to shoot back next time and that any further attacks would mean a gunfight.[143]Dewey Green was clearly not alone in his philosophy or his preparations.

Within the Leflore branch membership, Mrs. Laura McGhee was also the target of threats after allowing activists to use her farm as a meeting site. Aided by her three sons, Laura McGhee sat watch from the front porch of her rural farmstead, cradling a Winchester repeating rifle of the same style that Ida Wells had recommended to black folk generations earlier. When midnight terrorists stuck an explosive in her mailbox, her boys opened fire on the car. The FBI and local police came out the next day and gave the boys a warning. Laura McGhee answered "fine," that next time *she* would do the shooting.[144]

Laura McGhee's quip might be dismissed as just bluster until one considers other manifestations of her ferocious commitment to basic justice for herself and her family. After one of her boys was arrested during a SNCC protest, Laura McGhee went to the police station with lawyer Bob Zellner. When the desk officer directed Zellner behind closed doors, Laura McGhee wanted to go too. The deputy pushed her back and told her to wait outside. Bob Zellner's account of what happened next cannot be improved upon.

> She says, "The hell I can't [go in]. I come down here to get my son. . . ." He says "You can't go in there" and she says Boppp! hit him right in the eye, right in the eye as hard as I've ever seen anybody hit in my life. . . . I remember his eye swelling up and I remember thinking to myself "God, I didn't know you could *see* something swell up. . . ." And he's losing consciousness, sliding down the door. Meanwhile, Mrs. McGhee is following him on the way down. She's not missing a lick—boom, boom, boom!—and every time she hits him, his head hits the door. Meantime . . . he's going for his gun reflexively, but the man is practically knocked out. . . . They're trying to get from inside the office. The chief is going, "What the hell's going on? Let us out." By this time the cop is slumped down on the floor. When he started going for his gun I . . . pounced on him, simply holding his gun hand. . . . In the meantime I'm saying to Mrs. McGhee, . . . "I think you've got him enough now," cause she was trying to get around me to give him another pop. Meantime . . . every time the chief would try to open the door it would hit the man—whomp—in the head again. I said, "Chief, Ralph is trying to shoot Mrs. McGhee."

Laura McGhee was promptly arrested. But she escaped prosecution after Bob Zellner convinced the police chief that it would be bad for everyone if the story got out. It was a signal of an important turn, said Zellner, evidence that "a new day is coming when a black woman can just whip the yard-dog shit out of a white cop and not have to account for it."[145]

It is not clear whether Bob Zellner ever learned about Mae Catherine Falls, who worked the cotton fields for a northern textile concern for two dollars a day and in 1967 finally had her fill of an abusive field boss who goaded and threatened workers with his walking stick. After Mae Catherine sassed him, a witness reports,

"Mr. Waites got out like he gonna hit at her . . . she got that stick and beat him nearly to death. He left there runnin'. Run off and left his truck. She was the only black woman ever whooped a white man back in the 60s."[146]

Laura McGhee and Mae Catherine Falls were probably more volatile than most. Many folk recoiled from confrontation and gunplay not on philosophical grounds but simply because it was dangerous. And if we need a reminder about the hazards of jumping into that cauldron, even fully armed and committed to self-defense, the death of Forrest County NAACP head Vernon Dahmer is a stark reminder.

In 1966, Dahmer was spearheading the NAACP's voter-registration drive. He collected and delivered the poll taxes for people who were afraid to go down to the courthouse. Then he got on the radio and announced that he would pay the tax out of his own pocket for any Negro who could not afford it. The next night, his home was bombed. Dahmer stormed from the flames, gun in hand, and laid down a hail of lead at the fleeing bombers. But Dahmer's gun did not save him. He died from burn wounds shortly after the attack, his last words, an admonition to black folk about the duties of citizenship. "People who don't vote," he chided, "are deadbeats on the state."[147]

People would draw different lessons from episodes like the murder of Vernon Dahmer. For committed pacifists it was evidence of the futility of violence. But for many black folk on the ground, it was either a neutral signal or actually cut the other way. These contrasting views were evident when Amzie Moore of Cleveland, Mississippi, set down a pistol on the night table in the room where a young white activist was staying overnight. The young man recoiled, stood on principle, and rejected the gun on the argument that violence would imperil the movement. Moore said that he might need it to deal with more immediate dangers during the night.[148]

The multiple unpredictable hazards of armed confrontation are illustrated richly in the circumstances that finally sent Monroe, North Carolina's Robert Williams fleeing the country, charged with kidnapping. The charges eventually were dropped. But the circumstances that provoked them show how guns are a volatile catalyst and how Williams's brand of self-defense edged dangerously close to and perhaps over the boundary against political violence.

After the national leadership ousted him as president of the Monroe branch of the NAACP, fueling his storied debate with Martin Luther King, Williams actually stepped up his activism and formed connections with a variety of more radical groups. With the following he garnered in his fight with the NAACP, Williams expanded his newsletter, the *Crusader*, to national circulation, garnering new friendships and financial support. When Williams wrote in the *Crusader* that the spring of 1961 would witness the payoff of four years of protests to integrate the publicly funded Monroe Country Club swimming pool, supporters in Harlem raised money to buy guns for the "TOTAL STRUGGLE AT THE POOL."

While Williams would say that he never intended to initiate violence and therefore remained under the umbrella of legitimate self-defense, he surely was pursuing group political goals and planning to shield that effort with guns. This was not the easy case of self-defense that most people in the movement would find sympathetic. It was a step in to the treacherous territory of angry, tribal confrontation where just a spark might lead to conflagration.

In June, Williams began leading protests outside the Monroe pool. First they were ignored. But by the fourth day, patience had worn thin and threatening crowds gathered. They hurled the standard litany of epithets, and then several white men fired guns into the air. Williams and the protesters retreated but promised that the next day they would stage a "wade in."[149]

The threat of Negroes in swimsuits, pushing their way into white people's water was explosive. On the afternoon following announcement of the wade-in, a car tried to run Williams off the road. The next day, Williams and three other protesters headed to the pool. At an intersection known as Hilltop, they encountered a crowd of several hundred whites. From across the road, a man driving an old demolition derby car with all the window glass removed floored the accelerator and crashed into Williams's car. The crowd surged.

Williams had a rifle, a 9 millimeter pistol, and his .45 caliber Colt automatic pistol in the car. As he worked a round into the chamber of the rifle, a police car pulled up and one of the officers jumped out and demanded that Williams surrender the gun. For standard episodes of self-defense, the arrival of police ends the claim of legitimate self-help. So it complicates things that Williams pushed the cop back with the butt of the gun and then aimed the muzzle straight in his face. Williams's nightmares were filled with scenes of state agents abetting and even leading lynch mobs. He told the officer basically that.

From the other side of the car, another officer approached and started to draw his gun. But Jay Vann Covington picked up the .45 and beat him to the draw. Both cops backed off. The police report records the episode as "displayed a 45 automatic pistol. No arrest was made." Williams and his passengers escaped the Hilltop intact. But the hysterical cry of an old man in the crowd would resonate over the coming days. "God damn," he cried, "God damn, what is this Goddamn country coming to that the niggers have got guns."[150]

Williams reported the Hilltop incident to the FBI and asked for protection. But given his recent associations, including an acquaintance with the Friends of

Cuba, the agents were more interested in his politics than in protecting him. But the FBI was at least paying attention. Internal reports record an upsurge in racial violence following the Hilltop episode, including a black man named Strand being pulled out of his car and beaten and two carloads of men chasing an unnamed black man who emptied his revolver at them.

Monroe officials attempted to diffuse things by draining the swimming pool and passing an ordinance limiting public protests to ten pickets. Municipal bureaucrats also met to discuss a restraining order prohibiting Williams from carrying firearms.

In the meantime, Williams busied himself delivering the latest edition of the *Crusader* newsletter. Police followed him all over the county as he made deliveries. As he finally turned back to Monroe, they pulled him over and said he was under arrest for a broken taillight. Since they had been following him all day, Williams feared that the stop was just a ruse to carry him off someplace and beat him or worse. Pinched in between two cruisers, Williams followed them as instructed until he saw the chance to break away. Then he raced home, with two cruisers in pursuit.

When the police pulled into Williams's driveway, they faced Mabel at the kitchen door with a 12-gauge shotgun and Robert emerging from around her with a rifle. With their nine-year-old son, John, looking on, Mabel warned the cops that they would not take her husband without a warrant. The officers withdrew and nothing more was mentioned about taillights.[151]

By now, Williams was getting daily death threats. And when a car full of men drove by and fired two shots at the house, the *Crusader* reports that they were surprised by "a quick, almost spontaneous retaliatory firing." Shortly after that, a series of fires broke out at local businesses. All of these were white-owned, except for one owned by a black schoolteacher who had written to the *Baltimore Afro-American*, pleading with northern Negroes to stop sending guns to Robert Williams.

The events in Monroe also drew attention from the Southern Christian Leadership Conference (SCLC) and unaffiliated activists who were expanding the Freedom Rides and other desegregation work to North Carolina. The new activists in town provoked menacing drive-bys of armed white men and two cases where black men fired warning shots into the air.

With tensions high, Williams's home was constantly surrounded by members of his rifle club. There was a typical crowd of close to forty black men congregated outside one evening in late August, when up strode future United States senator Jesse Helms, son of "Big Jesse" Helms Sr., whose brutal arrest tactics Robert Williams witnessed up close as a boy.

In a notable show of courage, or perhaps the hubris of a superior cast, Helms walked up alone, under the hard stares of the crowd of black men. Helms was working as a commentator for a Raleigh television station and had staked his territory with on-air criticisms of newspaper editors who were "so hostile to the Klan but so apologetic for racial extremists [like Martin Luther King] on the other side." Helms had requested an interview with Williams. But most of his questions focused on whether Williams was a Communist and Williams cut it short. Before he left, Helms channeled the bewilderment of so many of his class, asking why Williams was such an agitator when his "father was a good man [who] never gave us any trouble."[152]

The next day, Sunday, the Monroe Nonviolent Action Committee sent several racially mixed groups to white church services. Then they planned a march to the courthouse for speechmaking. Word about Negroes and sympathizers barging into white chapels spread quickly. At the courthouse, an angry crowd of several thousand, including Klansmen from South Carolina and Georgia, was waiting. Any spark to set off the violence would do. The intolerable affront turned out to be Constance Lever, a white girl from the North, marching shoulder to shoulder with young black men. The crowd turned to a mob and surged. Armed black rescuers drove to the perimeter and ferried some of the protesters away. There were multiple exchanges of gunfire throughout the city.

As night fell and rumors spread about a coming wave of Klan violence, people gravitated to Robert Williams's house. Williams had long prepared for this sort of conflict. He assigned clusters of armed men at predetermined spots in the blocks surrounding his home. With preparations made, Williams gathered the crowd and preached his version of self-defense. They should fight gamely, he said, but respect the limits of their task. "They'll come in here burning your homes, raping your women, and killing your children," Williams warned. But then he cautioned, "The weapons that you have are not to kill people with—killing is wrong. Your guns are to protect your families—to stop them from being killed. Let the Klan ride, but if they try to do wrong against you, stop them. If we're ever going to win this fight we got to have a clean record. Stay here, my friends, you are needed most here, stay and protect your homes."[153]

Williams's instructions illustrate the long difficulty of navigating the boundary that defined the black tradition of arms. As conflicts moved from the extremes into the middle of the spectrum, the distinction between self-defense and political violence became muddied. The conservative counsel said to give the political violence boundary wide berth and avoid this perilous middle ground. But in every age, there had been aggressive men who pressed hard on the boundary and some who launched full over into it.

Robert Williams was fully into the danger zone. He would continue to characterize his preparations as defensive. And defensive they were, in the sense of fixed emplacements set in anticipation of aggression. But as the organized work of a group engaged in political struggle, his preparations were manifestly plans for political violence. And but for the navigation error of a hapless white couple, the story of

Monroe might have figured far more dramatically in our collective memory of the civil-rights movement.

As dusk settled on Monroe, Bruce and Mabel Stegall, a white couple from nearby Marshville, drove unwittingly into the midst of Robert Williams's defensive gauntlet. Mabel said later, "we were just surrounded by these niggers, and we couldn't move. There were hundreds of niggers there, and they were armed. They were ready for war. I think they must've been expecting a bunch of white folks to come over through there and they was going to wipe them out." According to one of the black eyewitnesses, Bruce Stegall was drunk and did not help his predicament by questioning, "What's the matter with you niggers? Whatcha pointing those guns at me for? I likes niggers."

With the crowd closing in, Robert Williams fought through and pulled the Stegalls into his house. Mabel said later, "He acted like he wanted to be nice to us . . . Like he wanted to let us go." And that was Williams's claim as well. But the Stegalls wanted Williams to escort them out to safety. Williams had his own problems and responded frankly, "Look lady I didn't bring you in here and I'm not going to take you out. You're free to leave any time you get ready." This statement, along with the decision to move the Stegalls' car out of the street to Williams's driveway, would fuel charges of a "hostage situation" and send Robert Williams fleeing into exile. Mabel Stegall said later, "I was not even thinking about being kidnapped, the papers of publicity and all that stuff is what brought in that kidnapping mess." But at the time, with rumors swirling that the police chief had promised to hang him in the courthouse square, Williams weighed the risk of fighting and decided to flee.

With his family in tow and four guns and five hundred rounds of ammunition between them, Robert Williams skulked out of Monroe through the closing circle of police, a fugitive on the run. They traveled to New York, then into Canada. From there they settled in Cuba, as personal guests of Fidel Castro, who quickly exploited the opportunity. Within a few weeks of his arrival on the Crocodile Island, Williams taunted his Yankee pursuers over the airwaves as host of a show called "Radio Free Dixie," beamed from Cuba across the southern United States. It was not the result he planned, but given the risks he courted, things could have turned out far worse.[154]

Considering that he is the embodiment of the nonviolent civil-rights movement, Martin Luther King is a surprisingly strong affiant of the black tradition of arms. One might be tempted to explain his seeming support of armed self-defense in the storied exchange with Robert Williams as just a reluctant accommodation of the practical and political fact that others in the movement did not have a pristine commitment to nonviolence. More telling are King's personal decisions about armed self-defense. And on that score, at least in the early stages, King embraced defensive arms with the earnest practicality of generations of black folk before him.

King rose to prominence out of the Montgomery, Alabama, bus boycott, which was sparked by Rosa Parks's December 1955 defiance of segregated seating rules. The boycott was the brainchild of E. D. Nixon, who served intermittently as president of the Montgomery NAACP and as an organizer for the Brotherhood of Sleeping Car Porters. Rosa Parks worked for Nixon. It was Nixon who retained white lawyer Clifford Durr to get her out of jail. On the evening of her release, Nixon sat at her kitchen table and prevailed on her to fight.

With Parks on board, Nixon then estimated the revenue generated by Negroes using the bus lines and imagined wielding it as a sword. His wife thought it was a silly plan. It was December. Black folk would not walk to work and shopping in the cold. But E. D. Nixon persisted. His first impulse was to organize a boycott through the NAACP. But he was at that stage a past president of the organization, and the acting head of the Montgomery branch was reticent to undertake the protest without going through channels at the national office.

Roy Wilkins offers a reliable account of what happened next. "Nixon decided on an alternative course of action: he turned to the city's black churches for help. He got on the phone and started calling every minister in town. Reverend King was the third name on his list." King listened politely to Nixon's plan and said, "Brother Nixon, let me think about it for a while."

Nixon called a dozen more ministers before ringing King back. This time the twenty-six-year-old King, newly installed at Dexter Avenue and still preoccupied with finishing his doctoral dissertation, told Nixon that he was interested in the boycott. "I'm glad to hear you say so," Nixon said, "because I've talked to eighteen other people and told them to meet in *your* church tonight. It would've been kind of bad to be getting together there without you."[155]

Nixon later explained that the choice of Dexter Avenue had less to do with King than the location of the church. "If we'da met in the suburbs, insurance mens and doctors and things who were working downtown wouldn't leave the office to go way out. But with it right downtown in the heart there wasn't no question they would walk right around the corner to it, and that's why the meeting was set up there."[156]

As plans for the boycott coalesced, the ministers of Montgomery met at the Holt Street Baptist Church to arrange logistics and elect officers. Black churchmen had long been a relatively conservative force in the community, and this was evident in the Holt Street meeting. As the pastors dithered and schemed how to initiate a boycott so "nobody will know how it happened," E. D. Nixon leapt to his feet so mad, he forgot he was in church. "What the hell you people talkin' bout? . . . How the hell you gonna have a mass meeting, gonna boycott a city bus line without the white folks knowing it? You guys have went around here and lived off these poor washer women all your lives and ain't never done nothing for 'em. And now you got a chance to do something for 'em you talkin' bout you don't want the white folks to know it." Nixon then made it a question of manhood, chiding, "either admit you are a grown man or concede to the fact that you are a bunch of scared boys." This was too much for King, who jumped up and shouted that he wasn't a coward. "That was the moment," said Nixon, "that he got nominated."[157]

Soon after King assumed leadership of the Montgomery Improvement Association, the formal organization that would press the boycott, black folk in Montgomery started to worry about his safety and organized a staff of drivers and bodyguards for him. They brought the guns they had, and fortunately never had to rely on Reverend Richman Smiley's diminutive .25 caliber Beretta, which modern trainers would dismiss as inferior to a bludgeon.[158]

On January 30, 1956, nearly a year into the boycott, King's house was bombed. King had been speaking at a protest meeting and rushed home to Coretta and their two-month-old daughter. He found them unharmed and the parsonage guarded by a loose assembly of armed black men that soon grew into the hundreds. As police pushed through the crowd, one black man brimming with anger was set off by their rough entry to the scene. He challenged the cops, "now you got your .38 and I got mine. So let's shoot it out." King diffused things, telling the crowd, "My wife and baby are all right. I want you to go home and put down your weapons." The armed black men dispersed. But the situation edged toward chaos, and one of the cops later told a reporter, "I'll be honest with you, I was terrified. I owe my life to that nigger preacher."[159]

King dispersed the men with the message, "I want you to love our enemies." But he was at this stage still quite practical about the surrounding threats. Reverend Ralph Abernathy of Montgomery First Baptist Church recalls asking King "if he had any means of protection for himself and his family." King said that all he had was a butcher knife and they decided that "we should go downtown together and buy some weapons for our protection."[160]

King even sought a permit to carry a concealed gun in his car. But local authorities determined that he had not shown "good cause" for needing a permit to carry a firearm. A generation later, protests against the caprice and cronyism that pervaded these types of discretionary permit systems would spark a movement toward nondiscretionary, "shall issue" concealed-carry permits that would become the American norm.[161]

Inflamed by the bombing of the parsonage and another bombing at E. D. Nixon's house, members of King's Dexter Avenue Baptist Church redoubled efforts to protect him. The churchmen came with guns and sat up in shifts guarding his house.[162] Arriving at King's home to assist in the struggle, pacifist Bayard Rustin recalled that the parsonage was "a virtual garrison" with pistols, rifles, and shotguns in every corner of the living room. When Rustin's friend, journalist William Worthy, sat down on a pistol wedged into a chair, King assured them that the weapons were only defensive precautions.[163] Reverend Glenn Smiley, of the Fellowship of Reconciliation, visited Dr. King's home in 1956 and reported back to his employer:

> [King] had Gandhi in mind when this thing started, was aware of the dangers to him inwardly, wants to do it right, but is too young and some of his close help is violent. King accepts as an example, a body guard and asked for permits for them to carry guns. This was denied by the police, *but nevertheless, the place is an arsenal.* King sees the inconsistency, but not enough. He believes and yet he doesn't believe. *The whole movement is armed in a sense,* and this is what I must convince him to see as the greatest evil.[164]

According to Bayard Rustin, a potentially tragic close call shocked King into a more cautious mind-set about the armed guards. The story goes that a delivery boy had ducked behind the hedges near King's home to pee, and was mistaken by one of King's guards as a threat. The armed man almost killed the boy. According to Rustin, the incident pushed King to ban guns from the house.[165]

King is such an iconic figure that we lose the sense of his daily struggle, of how much day-to-day courage his work demanded, and how much pressure he labored under moment to moment. We talk now about King falling to an assassin's bullet, numb to the trauma and outrage of the time. But it sharpens our sense of the angst surrounding King's daily decision making to consider a lesser-known attack that he survived in 1958 in Harlem. He was signing copies of his book *Stride toward Freedom*, when a deranged black woman rushed from the crowd and stabbed him. The attack left a thin, razor-sharp blade lodged in his chest. At Harlem Hospital, a team of doctors removed the blade from flush against King's aorta. They mended the wound, which healed into the shape of a cross over his heart.

We will never know exactly the toll that such things took on King's psyche and resilience. With dangers all around, he leaned heavily on his faith, though we can never really know the extent of his doubts. But ten years later, close to the day he was murdered, the wear and tear was evident in his brief exchange with Roy Wilkins in the Cleveland airport. Wilkins was alone. But King "had three very large men at his side." He called to Wilkins and asked him if he was traveling alone. Wilkins said yes, and King's response reflected his own calculations, "I don't think you should do that. It's too dangerous. You should always have someone with you."[166]

The various influences buffeting King on questions of personal security and self-defense are illuminated by the decision making following the shooting of James

Meredith at the inception of his Mississippi March against Fear. The swirling debate demonstrates the powerful self-defense impulse that King would navigate as he attempted to steer the freedom movement through multiple hazards with just the loose controls of rhetoric.

A veteran of the freedom struggle, James Meredith broke boundaries at the University of Mississippi in 1962, on a platform of nonviolence.[167] On the first day of his 1966 Mississippi March against Fear, Meredith was ambushed by a white gunman. Interviewed from his hospital bed, after doctors had picked a mound of shotgun pellets from his flesh, Meredith made national headlines, railing, "He shot me like I was a goddam rabbit. If I had a gun I could have got that guy. I'm not going to get caught in that situation again." Asked how this statement squared with the philosophy of nonviolence, Meredith snapped, "Who the hell ever said I was non-violent? I spent eight years in the military and the rest of my life in Mississippi."[168]

In some sense, Meredith's rant conveyed a simple intent to defend himself. But in context, the danger that it would incite political violence is plain. Out of the hospital, Meredith maintained his militant stance, confirming that he intended to return to the March against Fear, but this time carrying a gun. Martin Luther King considered Meredith's statement a dangerous flirt with political violence and urged Meredith publicly not to come back armed to the march. This worry about political violence would take center stage in the debate and decisions to come.[169]

Fig. 7.7. James Meredith wounded by a shotgun blast at the beginning of his 1966 March against Fear. (AP Photo/Jack Thornell.)

Meredith's "march" had started as essentially a solo affair to urge black voter registration. By 1966, the protest march was a well-worn tool. Some saw Meredith's march as an empty gesture, and his allies from the days of integrating Ole Miss basically ignored it. There were only four people with him when they crossed into Mississippi and Abrery James Norvell stepped from the brush and laid Meredith flat with a shotgun blast.

Movement leaders raced to the scene and vowed to continue the protest. There was obvious concern about safety. And there was a corresponding worry that security measures would be considered provocative. It was a pointed example of the long-standing worry that security precautions could be construed as battle preparations and self-defense might spill over uncontrollably into political violence.

Those involved were acutely aware that they were walking a tightrope. And the debate about security eventually fractured the coalition that had rallied in support of Meredith. All of the familiar organizations were there: Floyd McKissick, CORE's new director; Martin Luther King, for SCLC; Stokely Carmichael of SNCC; Roy Wilkins for the NAACP; and Whitney Young of the National Urban League.

A primary bone of contention was whether the Deacons for Defense and Justice, a black self-defense organization that had established chapters throughout the South, would be used to protect the marchers. The Deacons, as we will see, were aggressive advocates of armed self-defense and had deployed firearms effectively against terrorists.

The alignment here of King, McKissick, and Carmichael against Roy Wilkins and Whitney Young in the security strategy for the march offers a snapshot of King's thinking about the issues that frame the black tradition of arms. Although there are different accounts of the episode, King, it seems, was the decisive vote in favor of including the Deacons. But the decision was contentious.[170]

As people were arriving for a strategy session at the Lorraine Motel in Memphis, a van full of Deacons pulled up and unloaded, some of them carrying ammunition bandoliers and semiautomatic .30-06 caliber M-1 Garand rifles—the World War II infantry rifle that George Patton called the greatest battle implement ever devised. The leader of the group, Earnest Thomas, was on relatively cordial terms with King, who referred to Thomas as "Deac." Hosea Williams, one of King's aides, objected immediately to the Deacons, scolding Thomas, "Well I'm going to tell you right now, there ain't going to be no Deacons on the March." Thomas countered that the national organizations risked losing the allegiance of grassroots folk "because you getting people hurt, and you get back on them god-damn planes and you fly off and forget about them."[171]

Roy Wilkins and Whitney Young agreed with Hosea Williams. The NAACP had long supported compelling cases of private self-defense. But using the Deacons as security for the march posed real risks of political violence. And that was something that cautious leaders like Wilkins and Young had always worked hard to avoid.

While everyone argued, King sat on the bed, eating his dinner and listening. Finally he interjected with a question to Thomas, "Deac, you mean you're going to march?" It was a judicious move. Thomas responded, "I don't have no intention of marching one block in Mississippi. But we're going to be up and down the highways and byways. If somebody gets shot again, they're going to have somebody to give account to for that."

King's handling of the matter shows a deft political touch. With one question he fashioned a subtle compromise. The March against Fear would remain officially nonviolent. There would be no photographs of Deacons marching with guns. The theme of nonviolence would be projected across the airwaves. But in the background, Negroes with guns would be ready.

King was walking a fine line. It was too close to the edge for Roy Wilkins and Whitney Young, who stormed out of the meeting and withdrew from the march. Two decades later, Andrew Young characterized King's approach this way:

> SCLC was aggressively nonviolent. But Martin made distinctions between defensive violence and retaliatory violence. He was far more understanding of defensive violence. Martin's attitude was you can never fault a man for protecting his home and his wife. He saw the Deacons as defending their homes and their wives and children. Martin said he would never himself resort to violence even in self-defense, but he would not demand that of others. That was a religious commitment into which one had to grow.[172]

There was a powerful element of pragmatism in King's approach. This was evident in the days before the meeting when King stayed at Charles Evers's Queens Road home in Jackson. The place was brimming with pistols and rifles. Evers reports that King never "preached down" to him about the guns and teasingly complimented him, "Charles, I'm nonviolent, but I never feel safer anywhere, with anybody, than in your home."[173]

When the march recommenced, armed Deacons were in the wings. At night, they guarded the campsites. In the mornings while the marchers were assembling, the Deacons were in the vanguard, checking along the road and in adjacent woodlots for threats and questioning whites who lingered too long at the edges of the route. Deacon Charles Sims recalls, "I was carrin' two snub-nosed .38s and two boxes of shells and had three men ridin' down the highway with semiautomatic carbines with 30 rounds apiece."[174]

But the Deacons were not invisible. And some of the reporting of their participation confirmed the worries of Roy Wilkins and Whitney Young. For the marchers on the ground, though, the Deacons were a comfort. Cleveland Sellers recorded that the marchers dismissed the media criticism of the Deacons and made their own practical assessment. "Everyone realized that without them, our lives would have been much less secure." His view was not unanimous.

Fig. 7.8. Deacon Earnest Thomas with a two-way radio, on guard at a church meeting in Jonesboro, Louisiana, in 1965. (© Ed Hollander.)

Among the whites in the march was a minister from Woodbridge, New Jersey. He recoiled at the sight of a big pistol laying on Earnest Thomas's car seat. The New Jersey vicar was "astounded" and advised the misguided black folk that "the movement is no place for guns."[175] Earnest Thomas responded by explaining the basics of the black tradition of arms. No one could demand that blacks surrender their basic right of self-defense. In the same breath, Thomas assured the cleric and skittish journalists that the marchers in the movement were in fact, and would remain, nonviolent. Thomas was a simple man, not an intellectual. But he forcefully articulated for the divinity PhD and the glib journalists the distinction between self-defense and political violence that black folk from the leadership class to the grassroots had been pressing for generations.[176]

Still, the Deacons presented a mixed bag for Martin Luther King. In tense moments he might have appreciated the defensive force they brought to a dangerous scene. But the Deacons also operated much closer to the boundary of political violence than King, and that was a pulsing danger. Even rhetorically they played a more dangerous game. Witness Earnest Thomas's speech at a rally in Yazoo City following the March against Fear: "We plan to practice nonviolence," said Thomas. So far so good.

Then Thomas pushed hard on the contradiction that many others had soft-pedaled. "But we do not intend for any redneck to abuse any black people anymore. . . . If they do, there'll be a blood red Mississippi." People would do their own calculations, but a "blood red Mississippi" conjures images of more than isolated acts of private self-defense.[177] As things escalated, following a blistering speech by Stokely Carmichael that thrust the phrase "black power" into the national lexicon, King warned against use of the "unfortunate" term. He declared wearily, "I'm sick and tired of violence," and pleaded with SNCC and CORE to abandon the black power slogan and to send the Deacons home.[178]

CORE chairman James Farmer had his own difficulties incorporating and explaining the work of the Deacons who were openly protecting CORE workers in the South. His efforts ranged well beyond the ideology of the predominantly white pacifists who founded CORE in 1942. Offering his own version of the boundary central to the black tradition of arms, Farmer distinguished between armed self-defense "outside" the movement and CORE's nonviolent demonstrations. "*You must understand*," said Farmer, "*when a man's home is attacked that's not the movement, that's his home.*"[179]

Pressed on the point that CORE demonstrations involving the Deacons happened in the streets, not in homes, Farmer was unprepared to explain that the boundary against political violence was not a bright line but grey zone sliding toward mounting risks. He deflected the question bluntly, stubbornly repeating that armed self-defense and political violence were fundamentally different.[180] He would eventually retreat to a sharper rendition of the political-violence boundary, arguing in the *Amsterdam News*, "If violence is on the horizon, I would certainly prefer to see it channeled into a defensive discipline than the random homicide and suicide of rioting."[181]

Much like King, Farmer wrestled with the self-defense impulse at a deadly practical level. For Farmer the challenge came in the summer of 1963 in Plaquemine, Louisiana. He was there to support local activists who were fighting against segregated public facilities. When the third of a series of protest marches spun into chaos and then a threat to lynch Farmer, armed black men snatched him from the tumult, guarded him from mobbers, and smuggled him out of town in the back of a hearse.[182]

James Farmer's experience is one confirmation that even before its radical turn, CORE operated against the backstop of local folk with guns. And legendary among that group was Canton, Mississippi's C. O. Chinn, who was sometimes affectionately and sometimes guardedly called, "Bad-ass C. O. Chinn."

Chinn was personally committed to providing security for CORE workers who came to press the movement in Canton. He carried a revolver openly, and, when folk gathered for strategy sessions and rallies, Chinn sat outside the venues in his truck with a gun, scanning the terrain.[183] When Canton police stalked an organizing meeting and menaced one of the female activists, C. O. Chinn's wife walked out to the squad car and scolded them, "You cops don't have anything better to do than sit in front of this office all the time? If you don't, I wish you would find something. I get tired of looking at you." People who witnessed it and knew the culture explained how remarkable this was. The cops "looked at Mrs. Chinn and didn't say a word. Had any other Negro woman in Canton said that, they would've beaten her down to the ground. But they knew she was C. O. Chinn's wife, and no one, black or white, insulted C. O. Chinn's people and got away with it."[184]

Committed pacifists within CORE considered members who flirted with violence to be traitors to the cause. But nonviolence in the face of imminent threats was easier in theory than in practice. Pacifist CORE staffer Meldon Achenson found that he was in a decided minority, writing to his parents, "Nearly everyone in the community is armed to the teeth." He concluded that most folk were "committed to nonviolence only as a tactic."

In West Feliciana Parish, CORE worker Mike Lesser was less conflicted. CORE was holding voter-registration clinics at the Masonic Hall in the evenings. Lesser wrote to his family back north, "We are preaching non-violence, but can only preach non-violence and practice it. We cannot tell someone not to defend his property and the lives of his family and let me tell you, these 15 to 20 shotguns guarding our meetings are very reassuring."

In response to reports that blacks were arming against private threats, the national leadership of CORE pressed its field staff, "Urge the people not to carry guns." These instructions prompted tensions and defiance. In a staff meeting at the end of 1963, two activists angrily responded, "to hell with CORE, we're with the people." Some CORE field staff began carrying guns.[185]

CORE's national office worried that increased militancy would damage alliances with white progressives. Much of CORE's financial support came from northern, white liberals. For many of them, even legitimate acts of self-defense provoked the specter of "black violence," from which they recoiled. The growing radicalization of CORE and the evaporation of white support confirms long-standing fears that black violence would cost white allies.

CORE continued to espouse nonviolence and tried to distance itself from the publicity the Deacons were attracting. But hazards in the field eroded the commitment to nonviolence. The work of the Deacons underscored the importance of self-defense and drew CORE fieldworkers to open advocacy of resistance against violent attacks.[186]

For the white, middle-class pacifists who were the backbone of CORE, armed violence was anathema. CORE leadership attempted to keep the Deacons "in the background."[187] But for the growing black membership of CORE, the practical necessity of armed self-defense was obvious. And in 1965, delegates openly contested the viability of nonviolence during CORE's annual convention.

By 1966, Floyd McKissick had succeeded James Farmer as national director of CORE. Though McKissick maintained a commitment to tactical nonviolence, his ascension marked a shift in policy and his rhetoric was more aggressive. McKissick insisted that "the right of self-defense is a constitutional right and you can't expect Black people to surrender this right while whites maintain it." For CORE's pacifist, white members, this broke the bargain. By the end of 1966, CORE had lost most of its white support and became an almost entirely black organization.[188]

The increasingly darker complexion of CORE chapters in the North corresponded to more sympathy for the Deacons. After the Deacons protected the March against Fear, the Harlem CORE branch endorsed that model, declaring, "In any future action wherein we want to behave in a nonviolent manner we will seek the protection of our brothers to guarantee this right."[189] At the 1966 CORE convention, the northern branches were in agreement, resolving that "CORE accepts the concept of self-defense by the Deacons and believes that the use of guns by CORE workers on a southern project is a personal decision, with the approval of that project's regional directors."[190]

Marking and maintaining the boundary between self-defense and political violence has been the central challenge of the black tradition of arms. Compelling as an idea, it poses an array of practical difficulties, particularly where political violence has some popular appeal. Fuller treatment of the rise and fall of the Deacons for Defense demonstrates this spectrum of challenges.

It was not the first time that black folk had gathered in defense of themselves and their neighbors. But the formation of the Deacons for Defense and Justice in

Jonesboro, Louisiana, in 1964 is important because, unlike community defense groups dating to the nineteenth century, the Deacons operated within living memory and generated a relatively rich documentary record.

From their start in Jonesboro, the Deacons expanded across the South, making contested and probably exaggerated claims of tens of thousands of members across the country. The organization evolved in stages. It grew in part from a failed attempt by the Jonesboro Police Department to co-opt rising black activists by deputizing them and then assigning them to interdict and arrest civil-rights protesters. It was a harbinger of things to come when the black deputies confronted a group of white toughs who were taunting CORE workers at the Jonesboro Freedom House. Offended by commands from Negro police, the whites huffed off and vowed to return with reinforcements. When the news spread across black Jonesboro, dozens of men with guns showed up at the Freedom House, anticipating the fight. The word spread to white Jonesboro as well and the threatened conflict fizzled.[191]

Soon after that, armed Negroes showed up again, this time to guard the courthouse where CORE "testers" of illegal municipal segregation laws were being held after arrest. Although the words of new civil-rights laws guaranteed blacks access to public accommodations, the reality in many places was far different. Across the South, activists "tested" local authorities to see if they would enforce illegal segregation laws. In Jonesboro, the answer was emphatically yes. The protests that followed landed CORE activists in jail and provoked a wave of Klan activity.

A Klan caravan led by the assistant police chief menaced black Jonesboro. Crosses flamed across the countryside. Then a mob of more than one hundred armed white men gathered outside the jail where the CORE activists were held. CORE deployed a phone chain, and before the evening was over, the FBI was stirred to intervene. In the meantime, indeed, for the rest of the night, black men with rifles spied the crowd from adjacent rooftops.

The show of Klan power at the courthouse and police support for a Klan parade through black Jonesboro convinced many folk of the need for something more systematic than the ad hoc decisions of black men to camp on rooftops with rifles. That worry was the seed of the Deacons for Defense and Justice.

Oddly prominent at the beginning was CORE fieldworker Charles Fenton. Fenton was white. He was also a committed pacifist who would maintain allegiance to CORE's nonviolent principles. Fenton had a flair for organizing. And when the fledgling Deacons decided they needed a funding structure and operational protocols, Fenton was their man.

Fenton was never entirely comfortable with the Deacons' self-defense strategy. But nothing would shock him like the night he first arrived at the Jonesboro Freedom House. "I got out of the car," he recalled, "and realized that I was surrounded, absolutely surrounded in an armed camp. They were on top of roofs. They were under the building. . . . They were all around the buildings." Inside the Freedom House, Fenton found more guns stacked in the corners. The men were welcoming, but Fenton reprimanded them. "I told them that I didn't like the guns in the house." Noting that some of the men he sent away that night never returned, Fenton reflected later on his youthful arrogance, "Here was this snotty nosed white boy, coming to the middle of their war and telling them that I didn't like their weapon of choice."[192]

Fenton ultimately struck an accommodation between his ardent pacifism and the practical fact that his host community was widely and justifiably armed. He would help the Deacons organize and expand. He hoped to gain their trust and eventually perhaps win them over to pacifism. As a practical compromise, he asked the men not to carry their weapons inside the Freedom House and concluded that "insofar as the long guns that would have been obvious to everyone, they seem to have complied."

Fenton's ambition to turn the armed black men of Jonesboro toward a robust pacifism seems fanciful. But considering the tension inherent in the name they chose—the Deacons for Defense and Justice—we might forgive his optimism. Although some would say that the name was a ruse to mask their militancy, the initial efforts to restrict membership to mature, working-class men and to exclude hotheads and those with "criminal tendencies" suggests that perhaps Charlie Fenton's ambition was not entirely fanciful.

Some contended that the very existence of the Deacons actually changed the expectations and behavior of people in the community—that it shifted the norm, and actually made folk bolder. There is evidence of this in the aborted cross burning at the home of Reverend Y. D. Jackson. As flames snaked up the kerosene-soaked cross, the Klansmen stood in the open, admiring their work. It was a reasonable thing to do after lighting a cross in the yard of a man who was supposed to turn the other cheek. But the cross burners had miscalculated about both the man and the cheek. Soon they were ducking and running under gunfire from Reverend Jackson's wife, who emptied her rifle at them and was diligently reloading. For black folk in Jonesboro, the incident was emblematic of the resolve that had fueled and was now emboldened by the Deacons for Defense.[193]

The Deacons' growing reputation also raised new hazards. By the beginning of 1965, they were on J. Edgar Hoover's radar. An early FBI assessment gauged them as "more militant than CORE and . . . more inclined to use violence in dealing with any violent episode encountered in civil rights matters." Local law enforcement was also beginning to pay more attention to the Deacons. In January 1965, a member who had spent the day guarding student activists was arrested for public display of firearms as he stood outside a black café with a shotgun balanced over his shoulder.[194]

Although plenty of folk in the movement were armed and committed to self-defense, the Deacons were a strong draw for the national press. Receptive newsmen could have found plenty of stories about Negroes grabbing guns from behind the kitchen door. But the Deacons, courtesy of Charlie Fenton, had put a name on the thing.

The first major coverage of the Deacons appeared in the *New York Times* in February 1965, under the headline "Armed Negroes Make Jonesboro Unusual Town." Although misleading in its implications about the scope of armed self-defense in the movement, it was a sympathetic account. It reported uncritically the Deacons' own assessment of their success; that they had actually prevented Jonesboro from becoming a "battleground" and had averted a threatened lynching of a black boy accused of kissing a white girl. The *New York Times* also interviewed Charlie Fenton, who made a good attempt to explain that the Deacons were a separate, indigenous organization that CORE hoped to win over to the strategy of pure nonviolence.

By formalizing their mission through a corporate charter, the Deacons lured in busy newsmen with an easily verifiable account of their agenda. The decision to incorporate also had a remarkable, almost-comical effect within the membership. Although the source of their misunderstanding is not entirely clear, some the Deacons concluded that the state-granted corporate charter roughly articulating their purpose gave them a broad right to carry firearms for community defense.

Decades later, Deacon member James Stokes remained adamant in this view, explaining, "in the charter, we had to protect people's property and churches and so forth. And therefore couldn't no one take our weapons from us. So we would carry our weapons just like the local law enforcement officers carry theirs." Stokes considered the charter proof against anyone, including police who objected to his gun. He actually carried around a copy of the document, insisting that it entitled him to carry a concealed firearm. Some Deacons were more insistent than others about the power of the charter. And some police capitulated, perhaps uncertain themselves whether the black men's claims about the impressive-looking state document were accurate.[195]

The organization and formality signified by the Deacons' corporate charter also carried with it something more worrisome. In their planning for self-defense, the Deacons also were flirting with the very political violence that they claimed to disdain. The problem is perhaps in the vagaries of the definition. If political violence is something undertaken in pursuit of group goals, almost any sort of organized group violence might qualify. The problem would plague the Deacons, as their activities ranged far beyond the scenario of individuals fighting off imminent threats. Even acknowledging the legitimacy of using violence in defense of another, as the organization grew, the questions became harder.

The March 1965 showdown at Jonesboro High School demonstrates the problem. It fits within the boundary of legitimate self-defense only if one attributes substantial destructive capabilities to the fire hoses that the city was rolling out to blast student protesters. It was a cold day. All the marchers were technically still children. Although lawyers have staked claims of self-defense on less, the fire-hose assault probably would not have killed anyone.

As police directed the fire truck into position, a car full of armed Deacons pulled up. They piled out with guns. One of them warned, "If you turn that water hose on those kids, there's gonna be some blood out here today." After some tense moments and bluster, the firemen rolled up their hoses and drove away.

The question lingers even now, was this a justifiable threat of defensive violence? What difference does it make that the aggressors were agents of the state, operating under nominally legitimate authority? Self-defense against private aggression within the window of imminence, where the state is structurally incompetent, is the model case. Whether the Deacons' threat against the firemen fits within those boundaries depends on the judge.

The point is underscored by comparison to the plain case of self-defense by Deacon Elmo Jacobs. In April 1965, Jacobs came to the rescue of a group of University of Kansas students whose car had broken down. Driving down the highway with a car full of white kids, Jacobs was asking for trouble. He soon found it.

It is unclear whether the attack was premeditated or whether it was just a racist reflex against the interracial group traveling unapologetically on a public highway. Jacobs sensed the danger as a brown station wagon came up fast behind him. The car pulled alongside. Jacobs recalled seeing the barrel of a gun, and then feeling the concussion of the shot. He responded reflexively in a classic case of self-defense, explaining, "Well, that made me went to shooting." The assailants seemed unprepared for Jacobs's gunfire, perhaps anticipating just some nonviolent civil-rights folk. Under a hail of pistol fire, they screeched off, leaving Elmo Jacobs to contemplate the cost of repairing the shotgun blast to his car door.[196]

The Deacons eventually expanded to scores of loosely affiliated chapters. The first significant expansion was the chapter in Bogalusa that would in some ways eclipse the original group in Jonesboro. The Bogalusa chapter started with a larger appetite for risk. They welcomed a class of men that the Jonesboro chapter would reject— men like Charles Sims, who soon would lead the Bogalusa chapter and rise as a force in the brief national movement. Sims served in World War II and earned sergeant's stripes as a shooting instructor. But he was also a brawler who carried a gun long before he joined the Deacons.[197]

Sims reminds us of the common hazards of the gun, stepping more than once into the milieu of intra-racial violence that feeds current worries about black gun crime. Sims's December 1959 conflict with Beatrice Harry is emblematic. Harry and Sims were essentially man and wife, though they had ignored the formalities. After a day of quarreling over nonsense, Harry shot Sims with his own gun. From his hospital bed, Sims told his family not to cooperate in the prosecution of Harry. He admitted that she was just defending herself from a beating at his hands. Sims survived his wounds, reconciled with Harry, and went on to live with her for many years.[198]

Beatrice Harry's shooting of Charles Sims is both familiar and provocative. This brand of violence fuels contemporary policy critiques urging stringent supply-side gun controls. On the other hand, it pays to ask, as we soon will, how much difference there is between Harry's self-defense claim and the claims of countless blacks who fought back against racist violence? The two categories resonate differently on several counts. But from the perspective of the victim, what difference does it really make that her attacker is black or white, a virulent racist or a mercurial lover?

The episode that solidified the Deacons in Bogalusa is an object lesson in the power and hazards of threat and bluff. The threat centered around Bob and Jackie Hicks, whose hosting of white CORE activists raised the hackles of local bigots. As the interracial group was sitting, talking in the living room, the Bogalusa police chief appeared on the porch with a grim warning. A mob was forming to attack the CORE activists. The police could not protect them. They had better leave town, and their black hosts too.

Neither the Hickses nor the CORE activists were inclined to run, although they surely were given pause when the police chief responded to their request for protection, declaring that "he wasn't going to play no nursemaid to some niggers." Shocking as it might have been to the CORE staffers, the police response really was no surprise to Bob and Jackie Hicks. It was, though, a signal that they needed to get busy.

They already had guns in the house. But it was clear that the two white pacifists would be of little use. As word of the threat spread, help arrived in abundance. First, neighborhood women came and carried off the children to safety. Then the men started arriving, a troop of them, carrying rifles and shotguns, and milling about in a mass that defied accurate counting.[199]

Ultimately, the story of impending mob attack was a lie, concocted by the police chief to scare the CORE activists out of town. But it turned out to be more than just a failed ruse. It was, in fact, the spark for the formation of one of the Deacons' most storied chapters.

The episode at Bob and Jackie Hicks's home would also herald a transformation within groups like CORE. The shift was small at first. But the practical lessons were enduring. CORE staffers Bill Yates and Steve Miller were not scared off by the threats or the armed preparations of their hosts. A few days later, they held a meeting at a Negro union hall. They finished up and were driving out of town when they were attacked by a carload of Klansmen who disabled their car with gunfire and then dragged Yates from the vehicle and beat him in the street. Yates and Miller managed to escape the assault and fled to a little black café as several more carloads of Klansmen joined the hunt.

In standard fashion, the CORE workers called for distant saviors and prayed that the call chain would pierce the necessary layers of bureaucracy in time for someone to do something. They were lucky that their black hosts were more practical. While Yates and Miller were feeding coins into the pay phone to plead for help from Washington, San Francisco, and New Orleans, a stream of armed black men slipped into the back of Audrey's Café. Several of them were among the group that had responded to the call of Bob and Jackie Hicks several days earlier. For Steve Miller, the juxtaposition offered a clear lesson. "Up to that point, I embraced the concept of nonviolence. At that point I guess I said, 'Oh, I guess I'm not nonviolent anymore.'"

Eventually, the call chain produced an FBI response and the promise of a protective escort to extract the two CORE workers. When that failed to materialize, the black men formed an armed convoy and took Yates and Miller back to the home of Bob and Jackie Hicks, where they continued to stand guard.

As the Bogalusa organization grew, the provisioning became more sophisticated. Charles Sims recounted how virtually everyone already had some sort of gun. "The average dude own a couple of shotguns. Most of us own pistols and all this type of business." But the army veterans who rose to leadership urged standardization and purchases of ballistically superior firearms. Deacons were discouraged from buying low-powered .22 caliber pistols in favor of more powerful .38 caliber handguns. The organization bought .38 caliber ammunition in bulk to save money. For rifles, the Deacons encouraged high-powered .30-06 caliber rifles like the M1 Garand available from the federal government through the Civilian Marksmanship Program.

Philosophically, the Deacons grounded their strategy on the foundation that freedmen invoked a century earlier. In language reminiscent of black invocations of the Second Amendment in the 1860s, Deacon Bob Hicks declared in the winter of 1965, "Let's back up on the Constitution of the United States and say that we can bear arms. We have a right to defend ourselves since the legally designated authorities won't do it. So this is all we done. That's all."[200]

It wasn't long before the Bogalusa Deacons put their heightened preparations into action. And again the violence swirled around Bob and Jackie Hicks. The target was the resilient Bill Yates, who had been beaten in the street several months earlier. It was now April, and Yates was shepherding a new group of student activists recently arrived from the University of Kansas. On the eve of a planned march on City Hall, Yates was attacked and then chased as he was driving to meet up with student volunteers. A pickup truck pinned his car against the curb. Then a man jumped out of the truck and attempted to break through his windshield. Yates threw the car into reverse and raced backward down the street to the Hickses' house. The attackers broke off the chase when Jackie Hicks stepped out onto the porch with a pistol in her hand.

Fig. 7.9. Robert "Bob" Hicks standing outside his home with his Winchester repeating rifle, assessing the damage after a late-night attack. (AP Photo.)

But the peace did not last long. Later that night, Klansmen returned to the Hickses' home, incensed by the news that white college students were staying there. They probably expected the Hickses to be armed. But they did not appreciate that seven other Deacons were stationed at various points outside, guarding the house.

At around one o'clock in the morning, a car rolled up slowly and a man jumped out with something in in his hand. He tossed it through the windshield of a vehicle owned by one of the white students. Bob Hicks ran outside with his gun to investigate. The terrorists fired a shot from their car, and Hicks fired back. From cover around the house, the Deacons opened fire with reports of at least fifteen shots fired before the midnight terrorists sped out of sight. While everyone in and around the Hickses' home came through the shootout unscathed, black hospital workers said that two Klansmen were shot, and the story was suppressed in order to conceal police complicity in the attack.[201]

This time, the shoot-out made national news. The story ran on the front page of the *New York Post* under the sensational but misleading headline, "Klansmen and CORE in Louisiana Gun Battle." The *New York Post* article failed to appreciate that the Deacons were an entity distinct from CORE. Indeed, it failed even to mention the Deacons by name, referring vaguely to some "Negroes guarding the house."

Still, the Deacons were on the ascent in Bogalusa. In the coming weeks, CORE chairman James Farmer would arrive in town to bolster protests and boycotts against merchants who refused to integrate. When the city fathers agreed to repeal segregation ordinances, a jubilant Farmer celebrated the victory with a speech declaring that the Klan had become "a laughing matter." He was quickly proved wrong.[202]

Almost immediately, the Bogalusa Klan countered with a series of confrontations that culminated in the shooting of two black deputies who had been hired as part of the effort to open up the city bureaucracy to Negroes. The shooting provoked the Deacons to ramp up their organizing and recruitment, and drew more national coverage of their activity. In June 1965, the Deacons made the front page of the *Sunday New York Times*, under the headline, "Armed Negro Unit Spreads in South." The article reported surely exaggerated claims of fifty-five local chapters of the Deacons across the South, totaling more than fifteen thousand members.

The *Sunday New York Times* report also highlighted the same difficult question that Martin Luther King navigated in assessing the role of the Deacons in the Mississippi March against Fear—"Should a civil rights organization committed to nonviolence align itself with the Deacons, and accept their services?" CORE operative Richard Haley answered with a rendition of the long distinction between legitimate self-defense and disdained political violence. Using slightly different terms, Haley argued that affiliation with the Deacons was consistent with the nonviolent movement because the Deacons were practicing "protective nonviolence." Deacons leader Charles Sims embodied the distinction, sitting with a .38 revolver tucked into his waistband while explaining, "I believe nonviolence is the only way."[203]

Any superficial contradiction here was easily resolved by folk who responded with gunfire to midnight attacks on isolated farmhouses. There, the trouble had come to them, their backs were against the wall, and there was no chance of help. But the Deacons, some argued, went seeking trouble and sometimes by their presence provoked it. Charles Sims countered that "the showing of a weapon stops many things," and his assessment is consistent with modern measures of nonshooting defensive gun uses.[204]

On the other hand, there is no denying that guns have both risks and utilities. And brandishing one, particularly in the environments where the Deacons were operating, could be a catalyst for unpredictable results. The *Wall Street Journal* expressed this worry, quoting a Louisiana Klansman who seemingly relished the emergence of the Deacons, declaring, "If violence has to settle this, then the sooner the better." The next piece of national news coverage pressed the point even harder.[205]

Following the story in the *New York Times*, the Sunday *Los Angeles Times* ran its own front-page story on the Deacons, titled "Negro 'Deacons' Claim They Had Machine Guns, Grenades for War." The *L. A. Times* indulged none of the fine distinctions that Richard Haley had sold weeks before to a New York reporter. Drawing from FBI documents leaked to various media outlets, it reported statements from an informant that the Deacons claimed to have a cache of "machine guns and grenades for use in racial warfare." Although these claims were empty boasts, Deacons leaders refused to deny the charge.

The Los Angeles reporting depicted the Deacons as part of an emerging militant trend. It punched the hot buttons of race-driven political violence. And while the Deacons would still avow a commitment to working within boundaries of genuine self-defense, their agenda was plainly sullied. Moreover, it turned out that organizing, fundraising, and speechmaking around a theme of violence made it harder to keep the rhetoric within the boundaries of traditional self-defense. Martin Luther King identified the problem with the criticism that "programmatic action surrounding self-defense" is folly, just a short step from political violence.[206]

Looking back, it is fair to mark the *Los Angeles Times*'s coverage as the beginning of the Deacons' slide into the dangerous boundary-land that separated common self-defense from political violence. And that slide reflected a broader militant trend that dramatically diminished the black tradition of arms in the modern era.

As the Deacons' profile rose, individual members moved into the spotlight. They were not media savvy, and it is unclear exactly how much authority they had to speak for the organization. The group was loose knit. Individual chapters were largely autonomous. So whether Deacons spokesmen were aggressively prescribing a more radical shift, just describing an organic turn already made, or simply exaggerating the sentiment within the ranks is hard to determine. These subtleties were lost on the national press, which now cast the Deacons as part of worrisome militant trend.

Shana Alexander wondered in *Life* magazine "whether it was best to think of the Deacons as armed Negro vigilantes, protection racketeers, Mao-inspired terrorist conspirators, or freedom fighters." Ultimately, Alexander was a good liberal. After interviewing Charles Sims, she wrote, "If I ever have to go to Bogalusa, I should be very glad to have his protection."[207]

The perennial worry about self-defeating political violence is evident in the reported comments of California civil-rights leaders who criticized statements that Charles Sims made during his fundraising tour there. Sims raised hackles with his appearance on the weekly television show of black journalist Louis Lomax. With the conflict over civil rights at a boil, Sims said that the Deacons were prepared to use a level force that would leave "blood . . . flowing down the streets like water." In the national black weekly *Jet* magazine, three prominent Los Angeles civil-rights leaders condemned Sims. Reverend Thomas Kilgore captured the sentiment of the group, declaring, "I disapprove of keeping civil rights workers alive with guns. The nonviolent approach has brought pressure to bear on those elements which discriminate. The Bogalusa movement under the Deacons—a misnomer—represents a danger to 20 million Negroes."[208]

Back in Bogalusa, folk facing more immediate risks had less compunction about being kept alive with guns. Unlike the LA clerics, they were putting their skin on the line to fight for actual enforcement of laws already passed by the United States Congress. After an uneventful march to City Hall in July, protesters planned to follow up the next day. CORE activists were doing much of the planning. Their decisions reflected a discernible trend within the movement.[209]

Just that week, CORE had debated the boundaries and demands of nonviolence. The pacifists prevailed on the point that CORE activists should remain nonviolent. But it was a signal of changes to come that the group affirmatively resolved to accept protection from the Deacons when it was available. The decision was not unanimous. And in the days to come proponents and the dissenters alike would gain lessons about the hazards and unpredictability of violence.

The makeup of the Deacons varied from chapter to chapter. The flagship chapter in Jonesboro tried to screen out hotheads and anyone with a criminal record. The Bogalusa chapter did not. In brash new member Henry Austin, they got both a hothead and someone who had spent two years in military prison for stabbing a man who called him "Nigger."

In early July 1965, activists staged a series of protest marches in Bogalusa. On July 8, the Deacons were on watch during a planned march through town to City Hall. There were hecklers all along the route. Henry Austin and Milton Johnson guarded the rear, driving slowly behind in a car owned by A. Z. Young, one of the older Deacons. As the marchers turned toward City Hall, some white hecklers defied police and moved in close. Then they started throwing rocks and bricks at the marchers, and some young toughs jumped onto the hood of A. Z. Young's car.

Then one of the missiles connected—a brick to the side of the head of a teenage girl named Hattie May Hill. Milton Johnson jumped from the car and dragged Hill into the back seat. But now the mob was on him. Henry Austin came to help, gun in hand. He fired a shot into the air. But the mob was fearless and pressed in. Austin then leveled his revolver and fired three shots. The crowd recoiled as an angry young man named Alton Crowe dropped to the pavement, bleeding from .38 caliber holes in his chest.[210]

So now it had happened. A protest march, undeniably political, had ended in gunfire by a black man, and a white man lay bleeding in the road. This was the danger that had dogged the modern movement—the kind of hazard that had always shadowed the black tradition of arms. Henry Austin's violent reflex showed that the boundary against political violence was not really a line so much as it was a mine-field, a zone of dangerous decision making where individual exigencies crashed into the long-term strategies and aspirations of the group.

Who knows what Alton Crowe thought as he walked over to Main Street that day. Perhaps he hated Negroes with a passion that he could not explain. Perhaps he feared what Negroes, unrestrained, would do to his town, his school, and his way of life. Perhaps he just thought it would be fun to yell, toss a few stones, and shove the wretches back into their place. He probably did not think that one of them would have the audacity to shoot him.

Many men had been lynched across the South for lesser offenses than Henry Austin had just committed. Austin knew this, and so did the police who were quickly on him. The crowd pulsed back at the gunshots. But now, with Austin hand-cuffed over the hood of the car, the impulse to string him up right there started as a murmur and rose to a roar. Austin would not even spend the night in Bogalusa. He was moved to the jail in Slidell on the governor's order.

Alton Crowe survived his wounds and Henry Austin was released on bail. Reactions from across the spectrum were predictable. Initially Deacons leaders denied that Austin and Johnson were part of the group. But then it became clear that local folk considered Austin a hero, and the Deacons embraced him. Governor John McKeithen condemned the Deacons as cowards and trash. Klan leaders were defiant, one of them telling a northern reporter, "I don't care how many guns that bunch of black Mau Mau's has, they don't have the prerequisite guts."[211]

For Martin Luther King, the Alton Crowe shooting was the danger he had long warned against. It was a full plunge into political violence. King quickly condemned the shooting and emphasized the peril of treading into the boundary-land against political violence. It was an interesting comment in contrast to his rhetoric following the Robert Williams incident. There, King recognized and respected the sphere of legitimate, individual self-defense. But here, in the aftermath of an episode that triggered the long worry about political violence, King was supremely cautious, warning that "the line of demarcation between aggressive and defensive violence is very slim. The Negro must have allies to win his struggle for equality. And our allies will not surround a violent movement. What protects us from the Klan is to expose its brutality. We can't outshoot the Klan. We would only alienate our allies and lose sympathy for our cause."[212]

Within a year, though, King would again yield to the practical draw of the self-defense impulse. If FBI reports are to be believed, King was guarded by as many as forty Deacons on July 29, 1966, during a speech in Chicago. Although some of King's aides objected, and Jesse Jackson adamantly so, King reportedly assented to having Deacons from the Chicago chapter act as bodyguards with the proviso that they not be identified as members of the group.[213]

The shooting of Alton Crowe posed a dilemma for CORE as well. The organization had strayed from its pacifist foundation through growing association with the Deacons. If CORE did not disavow the Deacons now, it surely would cost the support of northern white pacifists who would vote by closing their checkbooks. On the other hand, repudiating the Deacons might jeopardize relationships with black folk at the grassroots. As its financial decline would testify, CORE sacrificed the money.

CORE chairman James Farmer, soon to be replaced by the more openly militant Floyd McKissick, reflected the dilemma in a *Wall Street Journal* interview where he attempted to have things both ways. CORE was still committed to nonviolence, said Farmer. But his next statement was, depending on the observer, either an unacceptable equivocation or confirmation of the central theme of the black tradition of arms. CORE's nonviolent stance, said Farmer, did not mean "I have any right to tell a Negro community they don't have the right to defend the sanctity of their homes."

The danger that the Deacons would lose control of their image is evident in *Newsweek* magazine's depiction of them as dangerous, separatist militants on par with Elijah Mohammed's black Muslims. The black press, not surprisingly, took a more sympathetic view. *Jet* magazine ran a front-cover story praising the Deacons as "a determined band of heavily armed Negroes who have vowed to defend themselves with guns from marauding whites who have terrorized black communities in the South."[214]

The response to the *Jet* article suggests that many folk were intrigued by the Deacons. Following the story, the Bogalusa chapter was flooded with calls, offers of support, and queries about starting satellite chapters. In towns across the South, Deacons chapters and other sympathetic but unaffiliated groups sprang up. The actual numbers are hard to pin down because various public statements about membership were deliberately inflated. Still, there is abundant hard evidence of Negroes with guns, under the banner of the Deacons, doing dangerous work.[215]

In Ferriday, Louisiana, a Deacons chapter guarded CORE activists and on January 29, 1966, repelled a bomb attack with gunfire. Across the river in Natchez, the Deacons wrestled with the same questions that had burdened their Mississippi counterparts. Reprising Martin Luther King's March against Fear strategy, Otis Firmin of the Natchez chapter explained his vision, "We don't participate in any demonstrations, any marches, anything like that." But if needed, said Firmin, the Deacons were ready. "We be around, we watch, and we observe and we protect them if they need protecting." And with a candid appreciation of the special and some-times-unspoken legal barriers that applied to Negroes with guns, Firmin answered a recruit's question about getting permits to "tote a weapon." With the same practical approach that had governed generations before him, Firmin explained that they would not dignify the legal charade of the permitting process. Instead, he advised, "We just going to tote weapons."[216]

In Centreville, Mississippi, a fledgling Wilkinson County chapter accompanied a protest march of about two hundred folk who were actually agitating against black teachers who refused to support the voting-rights agenda. Along the route, they passed by a rural gas station whose owner figured that whatever the Negroes were marching for, he was against, and he was willing to press the point with gunfire. As the man stepped from his doorway with a rifle, he faced the muzzles of more than twenty guns pointed by Deacons who accompanied the marchers. The man retreated back into his store and perhaps never learned how little he actually cared about the thing the Negroes were protesting.

There are at least two reports of the familiar dangers of firearms striking fledgling Deacons chapters. In one incident, a young recruit got into an argument with the Woodville chapter leader, drew his gun, and wounded the older man. In another incident, a Deacon from the Woodville chapter shot a black deputy sheriff, confessed his crime, and went to prison.

With the increased publicity and hyperbolic media characterizations of their militancy, the Deacons' star rose among the radical set. A month after Charles Sims raised hackles in Los Angeles, Deacon Earnest Thomas traveled to San Francisco to solicit funds through the Friends of the Deacons Network. He actually met with future Black Panther leader Bobby Seale, who talked about starting a Deacons chapter in California. Thomas was polite but concluded that Seale was too radical for the Deacons. Other groups like the Workers World Party, the Spartacus League, and the Socialist Workers Party proposed alliances with the Deacons and offered financial support.

But leftist politics did not appeal to the Deacons who encountered them. Earnest Thomas's reaction was typical: "I'm not a left-winger. I'm just a capitalist that don't have a damn thing." Charles Sims was of the same mind, declaring that the radical pursuit of "black power didn't do a damn thing but hurt the movement."[217]

If the Deacons had been the most radical force on the scene, the next turn of the black tradition of arms might not have been so dramatic.

CHAPTER EIGHT

❦

PIVOT

In the spring of 1976, Maynard Holbrook Jackson, the first black mayor of Atlanta, urged the United States to "immediately ban the import, manufacture, sale and possession of all handguns." It was a stark departure from the policy and practice of previous generations. The handgun is the quintessential self-defense tool and the black tradition of arms championed self-defense.[1]

Something plainly had changed, because Maynard Jackson was no lone voice in the wind. He was channeling the emerging orthodoxy of the bourgeoning black political class. Beyond his duties as mayor, Jackson chaired the National Coalition to Ban Handguns. He also was president of the Association of Local Black Elected Officials, which was populated by men like Gary, Indiana's Richard Hatcher, one of the new crop of black mayors who rose on the tide of the civil-rights movement. When drug-trade fighting between old-line gangsters and rising black street gangs left twenty-two bodies on the streets of Gary in the span of a few weeks, Hatcher answered with a program of gun controls. Although it mattered little to the gangsters, Hatcher loudly declared that he would deny all future concealed-carry applications and invited objectors to take him to court. Appreciating the weakness of such local measures, black congressmen in Washington proposed national gun confiscation and a constitutional amendment repealing the right to keep and bear arms.[2]

This trend continues strongly into the current conversation. The National Urban League is a sustaining member of the Coalition to Stop Gun Violence, previously the National Coalition to Ban Handguns. In 2003, the NAACP sued gun manufacturers on the theory of tortiously "oversupplying" guns to black people. In 2007, Jesse Jackson was proudly arrested while protesting legal gun sales in the suburbs of Chicago. In 2008 and 2010, the NAACP filed amicus briefs to the United States Supreme Court, supporting blanket gun bans in Washington, DC, and Chicago. Losing those arguments, one of the association's lawyers wrote in a prominent journal that recrafting the constitutional right to arms to allow targeted gun prohibition in black enclaves should be a core plank of the modern civil-rights agenda.[3]

So what happened? Certainly, many things have changed over the long development of the black tradition of arms. But three broad currents explain the dramatic shift to the modern orthodoxy of stringent gun control. First, as the modern civil-rights movement boiled over, black radicals undercut the core distinction that had sustained the black tradition of arms. By invoking self-defense as a justification for overt political violence, they forced black moderates, already buffeted by urban tumult, either to expend precious political capital to brace up the tradition of arms or to back away from it. Second, concurrent with the radicals' apostasy, a strong black political class rose on the wave of a progressive coalition. The newly minted national gun-control movement rested firmly within that coalition and captured the allegiance of the rising black political class, who now faced the challenge of actually governing their recently won domains. Third, as black-on-black gun violence commanded increasing attention, gun bans promised a solution with the compelling logic of no guns equals no gun crime. These three currents explain how, in less than a decade, the robust black tradition of arms was supplanted by the modern orthodoxy of stringent supply controls.

The modern orthodoxy grows from a particular strand of civil-rights advocacy and political strategy that prevailed over competing approaches within the modern freedom movement. By the 1960s, the NAACP, the National Urban League, the SCLC, SNCC, and CORE (the "big five") vied for influence and funding. Out of that mix, the moderate, integrationist NAACP and National Urban League model, capitalizing on coalitions with white progressives, emerged as the dominant form. This triumph was substantially a consequence of the radicalization of the competing organizations.[4]

There was evidence of the divide fairly early on. SNCC and CORE took a more militant path and were viewed as troublemakers by the Kennedy administration. According to one source, John F. Kennedy was pleased that the SCLC rather than SNCC was leading the 1963 desegregation campaign in Birmingham. Kennedy woefully concluded that the "SNCC has got an investment in violence." Contrasting philosophies also were evident in the responses to Lyndon Johnson's request for suspension of demonstrations during the 1964 presidential elections. The NAACP, the SCLC and the National Urban League all granted President Johnson's request in support of his reelection efforts. SNCC and CORE refused.[5]

By 1966, both CORE and SNCC had flirted with violence as a political tactic in the struggle to achieve civil and human rights.[6] CORE, a formally interracial organization founded on Gandhian principles of nonviolence, whose members and leadership were predominately white well into the 1960s, transformed into an almost entirely black organization that threw off its pacifist constraints. SNCC became racially exclusive during the 1966 Atlanta Project. SNCC leaders Stokely Carmichael and H. Rap Brown became more widely known as part of the Black Power movement.[7]

Ultra-radicals like the Black Panthers obliterated traditional boundaries, invoking self-defense as a justification for political violence and confirming the generations-old worry that the approach would trigger overwhelming backlash. This was a tipping point in the development of the modern orthodoxy.[8] The risk of spillover from self-defense into political violence had always shadowed the black tradition of arms. But now radicals upended the distinction.[9] Although some argue that the radicals unwittingly strengthened the hand of moderates, the sharp downward trajectory of the radical organizations shows that political violence as a direct strategy was a failure. The Black Panther Party is emblematic.[10]

Initially designated the Black Panther Party for Self-Defense, the Panthers pushed political violence under the umbrella of self-defense to justify the kinds of tactics that Panther leader Eldridge Cleaver described in the wake of Martin Luther King's assassination. "We put together a little series of events to take place that next night, where we basically went out to ambush the cops. But it was an aborted ambush because the cops showed up too soon." The interruption did not prevent Cleaver and his accomplices from firing nine shots at Officer Richard Jensen, who pulled up as they were loading into vehicles on the way to the ambush site.

The Panthers' blazing downward arc confirmed long-standing fears. The group was decimated by federal, state, and local responses to its open campaign of political violence. Confrontations with the state led to incarceration and deaths of party members. Huey Newton later acknowledged that political violence was counterproductive and launched the Panthers into an unwinnable war with the state that destroyed their outside support.[11] But in 1967, Newton was insistent, "If I'm talking about self-defense, I'm talking about politics; if I'm talking about politics, I'm talking about self-defense. You can't separate them."[12] Writing in the Panthers' weekly newspaper, one member was even more graphic, claiming that "sniping, stabbing, bombing, etc. . . . can only be defined correctly as self-defense."[13]

Splinter groups like the Black Liberation Army were equally extreme advocates and practitioners of political violence under the banner of self-defense. The BLA urged political warfare through the killing of police, both black and white. They claimed credit for the murder of at least two policemen at a Harlem housing project and for the attempted murder of two others who were guarding the home of a lawyer who was prosecuting black revolutionary organizations.[14]

The Revolutionary Action Movement (RAM), which rose to infamy after a bungled attempt to blow up the Statue of Liberty, seemed to recognize no boundaries at all in its plot to kill NAACP head Roy Wilkins. They planned to blame the killing on white assassins with the hope of provoking a race war. The conspiracy fizzled. But testimony in the subsequent prosecution exposed a shocking ruthlessness. Discussing how to respond if Wilkins was with his wife, the triggermen resolved, "We will just have to burn him in her presence."[15]

Official response to the radicals confirmed long assessments of the folly of political violence. From 1966 through 1967, shootouts with police left a line of Black Panthers dead, wounded, and imprisoned. The BLA and RAM withered under similar pressures.[16]

This period is crucial in the development of the modern orthodoxy. Radical organizations were in decline. Urban riots marked a failure of the traditional civil-rights leadership to harness the energy that fueled the violence. Roy Wilkins recounts how "Dr. King was practically run out of Watts when he went to California to see what was going on. . . . Dr. King and the rest of us suddenly found ourselves in the middle of a two-front war. In one direction we had to keep the South from making a Jim Crow comeback in Congress; in the other we had to do something about the ghettos in the cities. No one was really prepared with a strategy or a workable program. We seemed more and more often to fall out among ourselves."[17]

Burning cities drained black political capital, fueled white backlash, and pressed moderate blacks more firmly into the camp of progressive allies. In this environment, it was politically treacherous for moderates to defend the black tradition of arms. When radicals defied the boundary against political violence, more conservative organizations had little to gain by stepping in to repair the damage. Even the attempt would risk the perception of agreement with the radicals, and that would threaten crucial alliances with white progressives. So the voices of moderation— the rising political class and the NAACP, which had cut its organizational teeth defending Negroes who protected themselves with guns—backed away from the generations-old tradition of arms.

There is an early marker of this in 1966. On August 16, representatives from along the spectrum of black politics appeared on the nationally syndicated political talk show *Meet the Press* to address the newly minted slogan "Black Power." It was a high-profile airing of the radical attack on the boundary against political violence.

Opposing the militant implications of Black Power were Martin Luther King of the SCLC, Roy Wilkins of the NAACP, and Whitney Young of the National Urban League. Defending it were James Meredith and Stokely Carmichael of SNCC and Floyd McKissick of CORE. Carmichael is generally credited with launching the phrase in June 1966 in a Greenwood, Mississippi, speech, marking resumption of the March against Fear.[18]

Host Lawrence Spivak's opening to Floyd McKissick was an opportunity for the new director of CORE to affirm his commitment to the boundary against political violence. "There is a difference," said Spivak, "between self-defense and non-violence.... Everybody believes in self-defense.... Am I to understand then that you and Dr. Martin Luther King really are not in disagreement on [this]?" McKissick responded that self-defense and nonviolence are "not incompatible," but he equivocated on whether he agreed with King.

Unable to draw a direct answer from McKissick, the panel put the question to King, whose cautious response reflected the circumstances. Recall King's solid embrace of self-defense in the Robert Williams controversy as "moral," "legal," and a signal of black "courage and self-respect." Now, in the shadow of radical invocations of Black Power, King offered a barely recognizable rendition of the structure he had articulated in the Williams debate and steered hard away from the boundary against political violence. Here is King:

> I believe firmly in nonviolence. . . . I think a turn to violence on the part of the Negro at this time would be both impractical and immoral. . . . If Mr. McKissick believes in that, I certainly agree with him. On the question of defensive violence, I have made it clear that *I don't think we need programmatic action around defensive violence. People are going to defend themselves anyway. I think the minute you have programmatic action around defensive violence and pronouncements about it, the line of demarcation between defensive violence and aggressive violence becomes very thin. The minute the nomenclature of violence gets into the atmosphere, people begin to respond violently and in their unsophisticated minds they cannot quite make the distinction between defensive and aggressive violence.* [Emphasis added.]

Spivak pressed the political violence boundary again in an exchange with James Meredith. The result was a raw, open endorsement of political violence that obliterated the traditional boundary. Referencing Meredith's criticisms of King, Spivak asked,

> Mr. Meredith, don't you think we ought to get straight on the difference between non-violence and self-defense? . . . I think that when Dr. King and others speak about nonviolence they say that groups of Negroes shouldn't take to arms. . . . I don't think that there are many of us who don't believe in the right of self-defense of any Negro against anyone who attacks him. . . . When we talk about non-violence, we are saying that the Negro ought not in groups or alone take up a gun . . . in order to take what he believes belongs to him.

Meredith, perhaps still nursing his gunshot wounds, plunged headlong into forbidden territory.

MEREDITH: The Negro has never entertained the idea of taking up arms against the whites. . . . But now I think the Negro must become part of this mainstream, and if the whites— now in you take Mississippi, for instance—I know the people who shot in my home years ago. They know the people that killed all of the Negroes that have been killed. . . . The Negro has no choice but to remove these men, and they have to be removed.

SPIVAK: Are you suggesting then that if several Negroes are killed or any white men are killed and the law does not punish them, as happens very often in the case of white men too, that people ought to organize as vigilantes and go out and take the law into their own hands and commit violence? You are not saying that, are you Mr. Meredith?

MEREDITH: *That is exactly what I am saying. Exactly.* [Emphasis added.]

CARMICHAEL: If you don't want us to do it, who is going to going to do it?

. . .

SPIVAK: Mr. Meredith, do you mean to tell me that you believe Negroes in this country ought to organize, take up guns?

MEREDITH: This is precisely, I will tell you why, because the white supremacy is a system.

SPIVAK: Mr. Meredith, this doesn't even make sense against 180 million people. If you do it, they are going to do it.

. . .

CARL ROWAN: Mr. Carmichael, do I detect that you agree with Mr. Meredith that the Negro may have to take up arms.

CARMICHAEL: . . . I agree 150 percent that black people have to move to the position where they organize themselves and they are in fact a protection for each other. . . . If in fact 180 million people just think they are going to turn on us and we are going to sit there, like the Nazis did to the Jews, they are wrong. We are going to go down together, all of us.

ROWLAND EVANS: Mr. Wilkins, I want to ask you [about Carmichael's] last statement, do you think it serves the Negro or the white man, his purpose in any way to threaten that the ten percent of the Negro population can, if it has to, drag down this whole country?

. . .

WILKINS: I think Mr. Carmichael—if he weren't where he is, he ought to be on Madison Avenue. He is a public relations man par excellence. He abounds in the provocative phrase. Of course, no one believes that the Negro minority in this country is going to take up arms and try to rectify every wrong that has been done [to] the Negro race if somebody doesn't rectify it through the regular channels.[19]

It is easy to understand how in this environment, the conservative leadership became more circumspect about explaining or excusing black violence, even in self-defense. The distinction between self-defense and political violence was always slippery, and cautious players gave the boundary-land berth. Now, amidst the radicals' chants of Black Power, prudence demanded extreme caution in the treatment of any sort of violence.

For Roy Wilkins, some have argued, the approach had broader strategic implications. Critics point to Wilkins's widely circulated fundraising letter denouncing the Black Power movement while underscoring the NAACP's continued support of integration and nonviolence. Donations to the NAACP quadrupled during 1966 to 1968 when he was vigorously opposing radical cries for Black Power.[20]

Wilkins always denied the accusation that he exploited the fears of Black Power and defended his record in a fashion that rested soundly on the long black tradition of arms. "For 60 years," Wilkins reminded, "the NAACP has asserted the right of Negroes to self-defense against the violence of white oppression. During the Parker affair in the thirties, in the elections of 1948 and 1960s, Negroes have amply shown how aware they were of their own political power. None of these things was new. The younger people were either ignorant of the long record or they chose to ignore it."[21]

Years later, looking back on that time, Wilkins framed the question as,

> whether [the new radicals] were after a revolution. I always believed that for American Negroes revolutionary fantasies were suicidal. To oppose revolution did not mean to fear whites; I knew that anyone who was not cautious in leading a one-tenth minority into a conflict with an overwhelming majority was a fool. You can force a lion one way when you have real artillery, but when you have a powder puff you have to handle yourself differently—if you want to keep your people alive. For all [the radicals'] reckless talk of guns and power back then, I still don't think [they] could tell the difference between a pistol and a powder puff.[22]

Whatever his motivation, Roy Wilkins plainly opposed the radical formulation of political violence as self-defense. Still, in other venues, he continued rhetorical support of a careful, conservative version of the black tradition of arms. In his keynote address at the 1966 NAACP convention, Wilkins both endorsed traditional self-defense and repudiated the radical agenda:

> One organization [CORE] which has been meeting in Baltimore has passed a resolution declaring for *defense of themselves by Negro citizens if they are attacked. This is not new as far as the NAACP is concerned. Historically our association has defended in court those persons who have defended themselves and their homes with firearms.* . . . But the more serious division in the civil rights movement is the one posed by a word formulation that implies clearly a difference in goals. No matter how endlessly they try to explain it, the term "black power" means anti-white

power.... It has to mean separatism.... It is a reverse Mississippi, a reverse Hitler, a reverse Ku Klux Klan....

We of the NAACP will have none of this.[23]

Fig. 8.1. Roy Wilkins in the 1960s. (Photograph by Warren K. Leffler, April 5, 1963, Library of Congress Prints and Photographs Division.)

Martin Luther King displayed his own objection to CORE's radical turn and the Black Power rhetoric by refusing to attend CORE's 1966 convention. King also criticized SNCC radicals, arguing that talk of retaliatory violence failed to appreciate that "the black man needs the white man and the white man needs the black man."[24]

This was an important moment of converging trends. While the radical strategy of political violence as self-defense would soon flame out, coalition politics and the conservative strategy of institutional change within the system were paying off. CORE, SNCC, and even the SCLC (laboring under King's antiwar stance) experienced a decline in external support. The NAACP, on the other hand, enjoyed a substantial increase in outside funding. For many who wanted to support the movement, the NAACP was, increasingly, the only acceptable option.

Important institutional changes were also unfolding. President Lyndon Johnson advanced the War on Poverty with spoils to the black underclass. He pressed for and signed landmark civil-rights legislation and appointed the first black, Thurgood Marshall, to the post of solicitor general and then to the United States Supreme Court. In preparation for Marshall's confirmation hearings, Johnson put him on a national commission to study crime and violence in American cities. "The idea was to keep Marshall's name in the news as a sober, rational voice able to respond to black militants."[25] Adding to the list of firsts, Johnson appointed the first-ever black cabinet officer, Robert Weaver, as secretary of Housing and Urban Development and sent black ambassadors to Finland and Luxembourg.

Within this whirlwind of black advancement, Johnson also signed the 1968 Gun Control Act, six months after the gusher of violence that followed Martin Luther King's April 4 death by gunshot. The timing and meager substance of the law left one prominent liberal skeptic to charge that the Gun Control Act was more a reflex against black violence than a well-considered policy. Among the act's most significant restrictions were import limits on small, cheap handguns derided as "Saturday Night Specials"—a label that combined references to cheap little guns dubbed "Suicide Specials" and the tumult of "Niggertown Saturday Night."[26]

One of the first evident moves in the tip over to the modern orthodoxy occurred in Roy Wilkins's allusion in 1967 to the ongoing work driving the 1968 Gun Control Act. In questioning reflecting the critique that the act was substantially a reflex against black violence, Wilkins, on another *Meet the Press* appearance, was asked by Robert Novak, "Would you be in favor of a massive effort to disarm the Negroes in the ghettoes, just to try to prevent these open-shooting wars such as occurred in Newark last night?" Wilkins's principle response tracked the long tradition of arms. "I wouldn't disarm the Negroes and leave them helpless prey to the people who wanted to go in and shoot them up. . . . Every American wants to own a rifle. Why shouldn't the Negroes own rifles?"

This is a staunchly pro-gun statement, but this was not all that Wilkins said. In a fashion that recalls his 1936 criticism of the killing of William and Cora Wales, Wilkins's first parry actually cut the other way and shows a nascent support for the program of supply-side gun controls that was gaining traction among progressives. Before standing up for the interests of Negroes to own rifles, Wilkins said, "I would be in favor of disarming everybody, not just the Negroes."[27] It is unclear whether Wilkins was referring to nationwide disarmament or disarming everyone in riot-torn cities. Either way, the statement is in tension with the NAACP's long support of armed self-defense and is an early signal of movement toward a stringent gun-control agenda.

Moving into the 1970s, as blacks registered to vote in greater numbers, more black representatives were elected to legislatures. Blacks gained increasingly influential positions in the executive branch, and black administrations came to power in various cities. Even in little Fayette, Mississippi, where a restaurant still thrived on Main Street exhibiting a sign warning, "Every cent spent by a nigger to be donated to the Ku Klux Klan," Charles Evers defeated "Turnip Green" Allen to become the town's first black mayor. Once installed, Mayor Evers adopted a common approach of newly minted black bureaucrats and implemented a ban on the concealed carry of firearms.[28]

This emerging black political class faced a new reality. Products of successful coalition politics and beneficiaries of legislation forged by progressive alliances, they disconnected from the tradition of armed self-defense that was now sullied by the radicals' blurring of the boundary against political violence. With access to new fields of power, the growing political class now could plausibly view the historic reasons for blacks' distrusting the state to protect them as having faded with their own ascendency to power.

This is precisely the time that the national gun-control movement emerged and was quickly ensconced in the progressive coalition. With cities burning and black radicals bent on revolution, politicians and editorialists called for stricter gun legislation. Black mayors and local, state, and national representatives and appointees—having gained power, and now facing the burden of exercising it—embraced the progressive program of supply-side gun control as an answer to the crime and unrest afflicting their new domains.

From here, the modern orthodoxy took hold and flourished as supply-side gun control became an article of faith for progressives. Today, the worry that this demands a level of trust and dependency on government that is incompatible with the black experience is answered with the assertion that "things have changed." And considering the toll that gun crime takes on the black community, we are tempted to conclude that the "things have changed" assessment fully explains and justifies the modern orthodoxy.

But on closer analysis, even stipulating that racist violence and the malevolent state are now nominal concerns (what to do though, with sporadic modern episodes that jolt us back to a darker time?[29]), the "things have changed" assessment raises a series of unexamined questions. Consider, for example, the tacit assumptions about black-on-black crime. This scourge, perpetrated largely by desperate, young, urban men and boys, prompts many to embrace the promise of supply-side gun control. But is this really a new variable that easily explains the shift to the modern orthodoxy? What if it turns out that the black tradition of arms always has required the balancing of violence among the criminal microculture against the self-defense interests of good people? If so, how should we strike that balance today, where some might dismiss the counterweight of self-defense against racist terrorism as a faded concern of an earlier age. And is that even the right balance? Does the tradition of arms just dissolve with the sense that the complexion and character of criminal threats has changed? What about good people in distressed communities who want guns to defend themselves against the predators in their midst?

Wading into these concerns sends us to the root of the black tradition of arms and the realization that the tradition is only incidentally an outgrowth of America's racist past. Fundamentally, the tradition rests on universal principles of self-defense. Those principles are a basic response to structural state failure within the hard boundaries of physics—episodes of imminent violence where it is impossible for the government to act.[30] It is true that the black tradition of arms evolved in a context where state failure was often pernicious. But from the perspective of people at risk, the reason for state failure matters little.[31]

More than a century ago, T. Thomas Fortune urged, "in the absence of law . . . we maintain that every individual has every right . . . to protect himself."[32] Ida B. Wells advocated armed self-defense as a response to government failure, noting the folly of trusting the government "that gave Blacks the ballot, to be strong enough to protect the exercise of that ballot."[33] Wells championed the Winchester repeating rifle on the view that even if the federal government was not overtly hostile, it was not equipped to protect blacks from imminent threats. W. E. B. Du Bois operated on the same impulse, wielding a shotgun to protect his home and family, with a clear appreciation that, for some undetermined period, he was on his own.

A century later, Shelly Parker in Washington, DC, and Otis McDonald in Chicago were similarly besieged. The difference was that their tormentors were not racist terrorists but young black thugs and drug criminals. Within a specific window of risk, they also were on their own against looming threats. We do not begrudge earlier generations of black folk their guns, and their grit might even raise a patch of prideful gooseflesh. But Shelly Parker and Otis McDonald, under the full weight of the modern orthodoxy and over the objection of America's leading civil-rights organization, required intervention by the United States Supreme Court to validate their right to armed self-defense.

Some found it perplexing that when the Court affirmed the individual right to arms, the litigation was fueled by these black plaintiffs. Were they serious? Were they dupes? The answer is that Shelly Parker and Otis McDonald, laboring under the two most restrictive gun-control regimes in the country, were just seeking what generations of black folk before them had sought in response to an array of threats. They wanted access to tools that might give them some additional chance of escaping or defeating violent attackers who were on them before help could arrive.

Standing solidly on the black tradition of arms, Otis McDonald and Shelly Parker agitated through the courts in separate civil-rights challenges, seeking access to handguns to combat threats primarily from a slim criminal microculture of young black men. And that, in a nutshell, fuels the hard questions about the current implications of the black tradition of arms.

How then should the complexion of the threats to the lives and safety of innocents like Shelley Parker and Otis McDonald affect our assessment of supply-side gun-control policies that ground the modern orthodoxy? People must do their own thinking about this. But we all are constrained by the basic inputs. The next chapter details those variables.

CHAPTER NINE

THE BLACK TRADITION OF ARMS AND THE MODERN ORTHODOXY

The black tradition of arms evokes heroic images like Hartman Turnbow repelling Klansmen with rifle fire. The modern orthodoxy responds to the tragic scene of swaggering neighborhood tyrants warring over turf, their gunfire piercing the kitchens and bedrooms of innocent people. These images evoke vastly different reflexes. And that largely explains the appeal of modern orthodoxy.

Supply-control policies at the heart of modern orthodoxy rest on the straightforward logic that no guns equals no gun crime. But fuller consideration raises a litany of questions that reveal the modern orthodoxy as more reflex than considered policy. For example, is the no-guns-equals-no-gun-crime formula realistic in a country that is already saturated with more than 300 million firearms? And what about people who want guns for self-defense? Does the traditional self-defense calculation change when the focus shifts to black-on-black crime? And even granting that modern intraracial violence may resonate differently from the story of Hartman Turnbow, is that enough to turn the tradition of arms on its head? Is it enough to justify, in the name of civil rights, policies like zip code–targeted gun bans that some earnest friends have proposed? These questions trigger wide-ranging intuitions that undergird both the modern orthodoxy and the black tradition of arms. Critical evaluation of these competing approaches requires careful unpacking of the undergirding intuitions and assumptions.

To start, consider the self-defense foundation on which the black tradition of arms rests. Self-defense is a universal exception to the state's monopoly on legitimate violence. State failure drives the self-defense doctrine through the imminence requirement. Private violence is justified where one faces an imminent threat of death or serious bodily harm to which the government cannot respond. *The imminence requirement defines that space where the state, regardless of its motives and ambitions, simply cannot help.*

State failure within the window of imminence is a reality for everyone. But one might expect blacks to be particularly sensitive to it. The window of imminence is often larger in black neighborhoods where various challenges stretch public resources. Certainly state failure is less galling today. Under slavery, Black Codes, and Jim Crow, the state was often just another layer of threat, and reliance on the state for personal security was more obviously an absurd proposition.

Today, the malevolent state is thankfully an anachronism. That makes it easier for those ensconced in government bureaucracies to urge reliance on the state and to ignore the continuing failure of government within the window of imminence. But it is sheer hubris for public officials to ignore the inherent limits on state power and claim that they can protect people within a space where that is impossible as a matter of simple physics.

The odd reticence of modern orthodoxy to acknowledge structural state failure within the window of imminence is highlighted by contrast to the thinking about state failure in the context of other issues on the progressive agenda. For example, progressives have keyed on state failure to support reproductive rights and to expand the range of legitimate violence by abused women. In advocacy for expansion of the battered-woman defense, one school of thought would actually eliminate the imminence requirement in favor of a "no genuine alternatives standard," wherein state failure would justify self-defense absent an immediate threat of death or injury.[1] Here, state failure is urged as the justification for a woman, who endures years of torment, to kill her partner in his sleep. Notice how this feminist advocacy does not depend on any assertion that the state is overtly hostile to the interests of women. It is simply the *fact* of state failure that would justify a broader range of legitimate self-defense by battered women. Compare now the "things have changed" justification for the modern orthodoxy. It would constrict armed self-defense for black folk on the view that government failure is no longer malicious.

Other progressive arguments invoke state failure to justify the right to abortion. One says that "to whatever degree we fail to create the minimal conditions for a just society, we also have a right, individually and fundamentally, to be shielded from the most dire or simply the most damaging consequences of that failure. . . . We must have the right to opt out of an unjust patriarchal world that visits unequal but unparalleled harms upon women . . . with unwanted pregnancies."[2] The modern orthodoxy defies this reasoning even though the principle resonates at least as strongly in the context of armed self-defense. In a society where physical attack is a real danger (especially in communities where the risk is generally higher) and government is a demonstrably incomplete response, the feminist abortion justification is a solid foundation for a robust right of self-defense using standard civilian technology.

Compared to other progressive critiques, the modern orthodoxy seems not fully thought out on the issue of individual exposure within the window of imminent threats. Of course, the discussion of imminence does not settle things. There are other possible ways to justify the modern orthodoxy.

Some argue that in urban communities *where black voters have elected black administrations, gun prohibition should be respected as an exercise of community autonomy*. But the critical question is, how much does black electoral success diminish the worries that make self-defense a crucial private resource? Even the best-intentioned administrations must wrestle with practical, fiscal, and political limitations.

What do we say to the young black woman in Detroit who arrived home after midnight to find her front door broken open and waited three hours for police to respond to her 911 call? At some earlier time, in some other place, such a delay might signal overt racist neglect. But here the problem was simply overtaxed resources. We might discount this worry by saying that slow police response is rare. But how to dismiss the black policy chief's triage approach, focusing only on the worst crimes, letting the others go, and betting that the security bureaucracy can tell the difference?[3]

From the perspective of the victim, how different is the three-hour police response in Detroit from the situation of Mississippi activist Robert Cooper in 1965? Cooper called the sheriff when a cross burst into flames in front of his home and waited until the next day for someone to show up. One difference is that Cooper had an "automatic shotgun" by the door and used it to let the cross burners "know he was home."[4] So was it a good thing that Cooper was armed? Was it a good thing that the young woman from Detroit was not?

It oversimplifies things to assess policy through particular examples. But the reality is that many in our age think in pictures rather than in words, and examples give us a foothold for conversation. Our young woman from Detroit is an unknown and might therefore resonate lightly. Other, more familiar images threaten as much noise as clarity. That is the worry with Otis McDonald, the seventy-six-year-old black man who challenged Chicago's gun ban and was celebrated on the cover of the National Rifle Association's *First Freedom* magazine. It is also the worry with Shelly Parker, the black community activist who challenged the District of Columbia gun ban and whose white lawyers defended her constitutional right to arms as part of a broader libertarian vision.

But other images give us a cleaner focus on the sober, mature members of the community who want tools to defend themselves against violent threats. Consider Mary Thomas, mother of basketball legend Isaiah Thomas. Most descriptions of Mary Thomas manage to work in her front-door stand, sighting down the barrel of a shotgun. Her battleground was the housing projects of Chicago's west side. Her nemesis was the gang culture that has captured and destroyed so many black boys. Mary Thomas had her own boys to worry about and she refused to cede the problem or the solution to some local bureaucrat or some far-off federal program. When the thugs came after her boys, they were answered by the dangerous end of Mary's shotgun and her warning, "There's only one gang here and that's the Thomas gang."[5]

This image leaves many questions hanging. Why did this tactic work for Mary Thomas? She could not follow her boys everywhere. So there must have been something else going on. And what about the danger of escalating violence?

These sorts of questions demonstrate that decisions about firearms use amidst personal crises are fraught with complexity. And that sharpens the question to this: *Does the complexity of interpersonal violence dictate a generic bureaucratic response or does it demand individual choice by people facing perhaps the greatest personal crisis of their lives?*

We know, of course, that having, brandishing, or using a gun is no guarantee of a happy outcome. That has never been the case. Nonetheless, the black tradition of arms has consistently exalted *individual choice* in preparations for dealing with imminent violent threats. The modern orthodoxy, granted its full range, tells people facing violent threats to rely on the generic protections of the state security bureaucracy.

The traditional elevation of private choice on matters of self-defense prompts us to think more critically about the implications of the decision to keep, carry, and use a gun. Consider again the young Detroit woman who waited three hours for the police to come. What if she did have a gun? She might have pulled it, then had it taken and used against her. She might have pulled it and scared off an attacker. She might have fired in self-defense, killing or wounding her assailant. She might have fired and hit or killed an innocent, either with a stray bullet or because she mistook an innocent for an attacker. Even if she lawfully shot a criminal assailant, there is still the trauma of the aftermath and the possibility of being targeted for revenge.

These sorts of concerns drive much of our thinking about whether preparing for armed self-defense is foolish or sound. They reflect our intuitions about the possibilities within a series of future conflicts. Of course we can't proceed just on intuition. And this launches us into *an assessment of the empirical work and social science on which our policy assessments must rest.*

But first a caution. Even in the middle of sterile empirical analysis, some part of our thinking is inexorably visceral. The reason is we are not just discussing what has happened and projecting from that what *will* happen. We are using what *has* happened to project what will happen *to us*. And that introduces a dose of irrationality. Because deep down most of us believe that we are special, particularly blessed, insightful, or resilient in some peculiar way. It is why so many of us hand over currency and special numbers to the lottery man. This sense of individual exceptionalism shades our expectations about the future. It also threatens to shade our sense of the risks and utilities of firearms. We must keep that bias in mind as we view and reason from the data about self-defense and crime with guns.

Let's start with *the details of black gun violence*, which are fairly captured by this summary.

The disproportionate rates of violent crime found among African Americans have been described in numerous studies and reports. For example, the FBI reports that in 1998, African Americans, who constitute 13 percent of the general population, were overrepresented among persons arrested for murder (53 percent), robbery (55 percent), aggravated assault (30 percent), and assault (34 percent). A significant characteristic of violent crime in the United States is that most violent incidents tend to involve an intraracial victim-offender relationship pattern. That is, individuals who commit acts of violence generally commit these acts against members of their own racial group. For example, in 1998, 94 percent of black murder victims were slain by black offenders. Similarly in 1998, 87 percent of white murder victims were slain by white offenders. . . .

The most revealing data regarding the disproportionate impact that violent crime is having on African Americans, particularly black males, is the data on homicide victimization. According to the FBI, in 1998, black males represented 38 percent of known homicide victims, followed in descending order by white males (35 percent), white females (14 percent) and black females (9 percent). High rates of homicide among African Americans also have been reported in compilations of health statistics. According to data compiled by the National Center for Health Statistics, *black males had a homicide death rate of 52.6 per* 100,000 in 1996, whereas white males had a homicide death rate of 4.7 per 100,000.

As a group, violence researchers generally regard individuals in the age range between fifteen and twenty-four as the most murder prone. However, there are significant differences between black and white males of this age in terms of their homicide risk. For example, white males fifteen to twenty-four years of age had a homicide death rate of 6.4 per 100,000 in 1996, whereas *black males of this age range had a homicide death rate of 123 per 100,000*, nearly twenty times greater than similarly aged white males. Moreover, for every age range, black males have higher rates of homicide death than their white male counterparts of the same ages.

A significant trend in homicide patterns involves the increasing youthfulness of homicide offenders and victims. Young black males experienced dramatic increases in both homicide victimization and offending rates in the late 1980s and early 1990s. For example, the number of homicide victims in the fifteen to twenty-four age group increased nearly 50 percent between 1975 and 1992. Moreover, in 1987, homicide accounted for 42 percent of all deaths among young black males. Persons between the ages of fifteen and nineteen experienced the greatest increases in the rate of death due to homicide in this period. Since 1991, homicide rates have been declining among all race-sex subgroups in the United States. However it is important to note that in spite of the declining homicide rates among black males, homicide remains the leading cause of death among black males between fifteen and twenty four years of age.[6]

In the face of this sobering account, the reflex to blame gun proliferation and to wish guns away is natural. The modern orthodoxy translates that reflex into policy with the promise that the right statutory language can solve the problem by dramatically shrinking the gun inventory. Wide endorsement of that approach by the political class implies that it is or should be embraced by anyone who cares about the community. But closer critique reveals both the structural weakness of the supply-control approach and wide diversity within the community about what policy is best.

The no-guns-equals-no-gun-crime logic of supply controls would be compelling if it could be implemented. But that approach was an unworkable policy long before the Supreme Court judged blanket gun bans unconstitutional. It is not as if we are starting from zero and are making a real choice to have guns or not. Americans already own more than 300 million guns and have a deep cultural attachment to them. That simple fact renders supply-side gun controls of the type recently ruled unconstitutional in Washington, DC, and Chicago essentially empty political gestures.

Here is why. International data richly demonstrate how, on average, people defy gun bans at a rate of about 3 to 1. Countries that have registered or banned guns estimate having roughly three illegal guns for every legal one. This is simply the average. In many countries, the defiance ratio is far higher.[7] And none of those places had anything approaching the civilian gun inventory or the robust gun culture of the United States. In the few American jurisdictions that have attempted limited gun bans, estimates of noncompliance are dramatically higher than the international average.[8]

The upshot is that neither the Second Amendment nor weak gun laws are the principle obstacles to successful gun prohibition. The obstacle is that Americans already own nearly half the private firearms on the planet and have an exceptional cultural attachment to them. *So the no-guns-equals-no-gun-crime intuition, even if translated into tough statutory language, does not mean guns will disappear. It just means that much, perhaps most, of the existing 300 million–gun inventory would flood into the black market, tilting firearms possession toward the worst people among us.* I demonstrated this point in detail in a 2008 analysis titled "Imagining Gun Control in America: Understanding the Remainder Problem." That work runs many pages. But my assessment is neatly summarized by former New York City police commissioner William Bratton in a *Wall Street Journal* interview discussing President Obama's gun-control agenda following the massacre in Newtown, Connecticut.

> Mr. Bratton likes what he calls the "symbolism" of this agenda, but he's unsure if its enactment would make a substantive difference. . . . The problem with the gun and ammo bans, he offers, "is that that's going forward." They do nothing about the 350 million firearms, including assault weapons, and hundreds of thousands of extended clips already in circulation. "You can't deal with that retroactively." As for the practical effect of gun control, he notes that "all the studies that were done about assault weapons after the ban ended after 10 years were pretty much inconclusive."[9]

Gun prohibition failed in the District of Columbia and Chicago because anyone who was willing to break the law could get a gun from the leakage out of the hundreds of millions already out there. In practical terms, this core policy of the modern orthodoxy amounted to de jure prohibition but wide *de facto* gun possession by the criminal microculture. The few places like Washington, DC, and Chicago that followed this policy led the nation in gun crime. These were also places where the Parker/McDonald class was essentially under siege. Shelly Parker and Otis McDonald sought stringent rules against gun possession by the criminal microclass and legal access to guns for noncriminals. That approach channels the long the black tradition of arms.[10]

Supply-control policies at the heart of the modern orthodoxy actually command a thinner following in the community than one would presume from the overwhelming black political allegiance to Democrats, who, like it or not, are the party of gun control. Recent national polling asked, "What do you think is more important, to protect the right of Americans to own guns, OR to control gun ownership?" Sixty-six percent of blacks said it was more important to control gun ownership.[11] On the question whether "States and Localities should be able to pass laws banning handguns," 64 percent of blacks said yes.[12] Mid-sixty-percent majorities are consistent with an intuition that blacks would favor gun control. But this is substantially lower than black allegiance to the Democratic Party and presents an interesting contrast with the black leadership, where Democrats rule.

Pressing into the social science, the picture becomes even more complex. *High rates of black victimization from gun crime actually cut two ways.* In a population statistically more at risk from violence, one expects to find both a desire to keep guns from criminals and a parallel desire to possess guns for self-defense. This shows up in what researchers call the "fear and loathing" hypothesis, where firearms purchases accelerate on fears of crime, violence, and civil disorder.

Researchers caution against the simplistic findings from limited questions in popular national surveys. We get a richer sense of patterns of black gun ownership and attitudes toward gun regulation in detailed studies focused at the neighborhood level. *Targeted research contradicts the national surveys at several levels.* In the national surveys, blacks are less likely than whites to report having a gun in the home. But research at the neighborhood level has found the rate of gun ownership between whites and blacks basically the same.

> With regard to differential Black and white attitudes about gun regulation, the number of questions and specificity of the questions made important differences. The policy option with the least support among the groups was the confiscation of all weapons except for those of the police. *The support for confiscation ranged from high of 26% among blacks in high-risk areas to a low of 10.16 among blacks in low-risk areas....*
>
> Support for having the government sell firearms through government owned stores, . . . also varied but Blacks in high-risk neighborhoods were the least supportive—19.4%.
>
> With few exceptions, the survey respondents appeared to be almost evenly divided in their support for and opposition to the regulation of handguns. In most neighborhoods at least 40% of the people questioned supported handgun regulation and at least the same percentage opposed it....
>
> *The results of the computed gun regulation index show that urban residents are less overwhelmingly supportive of gun regulation than is suggested by studies that use the one-item indicator.*[13][Emphasis added.]

Studies focusing specifically on black attitudes show that a significant cohort of blacks favor gun prohibition or other strong limits on the criminal microculture but disfavor blanket prohibition that would impede self-defense by trustworthy people. One study found that blacks actually disfavored gun bans at higher levels than whites, even though more blacks favored measures like permits and registration. This comports with the intuition that people who fear violence will want guns to protect themselves and also favor laws promising to keep guns from criminals (a policy preference arguably underrepresented by the black political class).[14]

A tacit assumption undergirding the modern orthodoxy is that the modern rate of black gun crime is an unprecedented variable that basically ends any debate about the contours of contemporary firearms policy. But it turns out that the black tradition of arms has long demanded balancing the self-defense interest of good people against the costs of criminal violence.

A report sponsored by the National Institute of Mental Health shows that very high rates of homicide victimization and violent crime among blacks is not new. Data from 1925 drawn from selected cities shows that "victimization rates were higher during that era than they are at present. It was not uncommon to find victimization rates in excess of 100 per 100,000." Local government responses to these data reflected the times. Memphis, for example, was described in 1930 as the homicide capital of the nation. The city fathers discounted the news, arguing that "most of the murders were of Negroes by Negroes, so the police and government could not be held responsible."[15]

The 1925 victimization rate in several other cities exceeded modern rates by substantial measures. The black victimization rate per 100,000 of population in Chicago was 101. In Detroit, it was 102 per 100,000. In Cleveland, it was 113. The rate in Memphis peaked at 129 per 100,000. This was surpassed by peak rates of 189 and 207 per 100,000 in Cincinnati and Miami respectively.[16]

Similar trends were reported by preeminent criminologist Marvin Wolfgang in his classic work, *Patterns in Criminal Homicide*. Wolfgang focused primarily on Philadelphia from 1948 through 1952 and surveyed the findings of a variety of earlier studies from around the country. Over the study period, blacks were 18 percent of the population but 73 percent of homicide victims and 75 percent of homicide offenders in Philadelphia.

Then, as now, black males dominated the ranks of victims (77 percent of black victims) and perpetrators (80 percent of black perpetrators). Wolfgang surmised that economic desperation drove the high rates of violence, calculating that 90 to 95 percent of all offenders in the study (black and white) were "in the lower end of the occupational scale."

The availability of guns did not explain Wolfgang's findings. The instrument most used by black murderers was the blade, which accounted for the highest percentage (47 percent) of the homicides. It is unclear precisely how much this reflected the national trend, and Wolfgang noted studies from other cities where shooting was the leading cause of black homicide.

Wolfgang lamented the absence of solid, race-specific data prior to 1921 but summarized a variety of studies conducted as data became available. A 1940 assessment of seven sections of the southern United States concluded that the murder and manslaughter rate for blacks was twelve times that of whites. A study of Birmingham, Alabama, from 1937 through 1944 showed that blacks were 85 percent of homicide convictions and 40 percent of the population. In St. Louis from 1949 to 1951, blacks committed 73 percent of homicides and were 18 percent of the population. Wolfgang cautioned that these data are biased by consistently higher conviction rates for blacks than for whites in the southern states surveyed.

Outside the South, Wolfgang's survey of victimization studies showed a similar trend. Homicide victimization rates per 100,000 during 1920 and 1925 for Pennsylvania were considerably higher for blacks than for whites both in urban and rural areas. In urban areas, whites had a rate of 5.3 per 100,000, compared to 47.1 for blacks. In rural areas, the white rate was 3.4 and the black rate was 45.2. A similar disparity appeared between 1921 and 1930 in a study of 37 upstate New York counties where the homicide victimization rate for whites was 2.8 per 100,000 and 30.4 for blacks.[17]

While we can embrace the modern orthodoxy on the worry about exceptional rates of black victimization and criminality, we cannot say that this is a *new* variable that automatically explains abandonment of the black tradition of arms. Historically, high intra-racial homicide rates show that the black tradition of arms long required balancing between the legitimate self-defense interests of good people against the costs imposed by a microculture of black criminals abusing guns.

More than a century ago, W. E. B. Du Bois dubbed this microculture the "submerged tenth."[18] In his incomparable exposition of Negro life, *The Souls of Black Folk*, Du Bois lamented the rise of "a distinct criminal class" in the urban slums.[19] In his sociological study *The Philadelphia Negro*, Du Bois tracked the activity of a black criminal class that in many ways mirrors the modern criminal microculture.[20] He reported that life in Philadelphia's Seventh Ward in the late 1890s was "hard, noisy and deadly for too many of the Black people there. On Saturday nights [the neighborhoods] disgorged [the] maimed and murdered. . . . Pushed out of economic opportunities . . . it was not surprising that many Seventh Ward Blacks sought release in drugs and crime or savagely turned on each other out of rage or a sense of hopelessness."[21]

Ida B. Wells, the great patron of the Winchester rifle, wrestled with a similarly dispiriting reality. In 1910, she debated a nominally sympathetic white member of the Negro Fellowship League who highlighted the disproportionate level of black crime in Chicago. Facing the difficult reality, Wells said that she could not refute the empirical claims about disproportionate black criminality, "for that is what the figures seem to indicate." She shifted instead to explain the phenomena. "The statistics," she said, "do not mean, as it appears to mean, that the Negro race is the most criminal of the various race groups in Chicago. It does mean that ours is the most neglected group. All the other races in the city are welcomed into the settlements, YMCAs, YWCAs, gymnasiums and every other movement for uplift if only their skins are white.... Only one social center welcomes the Negro and that is the saloon. Ought we to wonder at the harvest which we have heard enumerated tonight?"[22]

This is a familiar brand of response to discouraging news. And though it might blunt some of the harsher policy prescriptions by unsympathetic critics, making excuses for black criminality does not answer the immediate security concerns of black victims.

Black victims of intraracial violence were the dominant concern of leaders from the Mississippi Delta Committee for Better Citizenship. They agitated for "greater punishment for Black criminals who committed offenses against Blacks." The reasoning was summed up by the famously well-armed T. R. M. Howard, who complained that failure to punish black-on-black crime was another manifestation of state malevolence. During a period where racist violence fueled black nightmares, Howard said that the "greatest danger to Negro life in Mississippi is not what white people do to Negroes but what the courts of Mississippi let Negroes of Mississippi do to each other."[23]

Roy Wilkins's 1925 critique of intraracial violence in Kansas City rings similar. Wilkins complained that "getting Kansas City police to enforce the law in black neighborhoods was almost impossible. For a time we ran a murder-a-week campaign . . . to draw attention to the bloodshed that took place at approximately that rate all through the twenties." Wilkins viewed the failure to pursue black criminals as overt state malevolence and evidence of an attitude that "there's one more Negro killed—the more of 'em dead, the less to bother us. Don't spend too much money running down the killer—he may kill another."[24]

This phenomenon was actually systematized by Mississippi circuit judge Sidney Fant Davis, under the heading of "Negro Law." The untutored reader, said Davis, might look at the state civil and criminal codes and conclude that they applied equally to blacks and whites, but "nothing could be farther from the truth." Negro law, said Davis, "determined that certain crimes might be punished or not depending on the racial context." Intraracial violence (which dominated black victimization), bigamy, and theft purely between blacks were routinely ignored or treated as minor matters.[25]

Even black-on-black murder, which as early as 1890 was reportedly the most common form of homicide in Mississippi, passed through a Negro Law filter. Much black-on-black violence was ignored. But where the black victim had some value to or was a favorite of local whites, the prosecution reflected that interest. This was vividly illustrated in the 1911 Sharkey County prosecution of a black man named Judge Collins for the murder of Rube Boyd. The prosecutor argued for the death penalty because "this bad nigger killed a good nigger. The dead nigger was a white man's nigger, and these bad niggers like to kill that kind." The black defense attorney for Collins, thoroughly familiar with the nuances of Negro Law, couched his assessment accordingly. "The average white jury," he explained, "would take it for granted that the killing of a white man's nigger is a more serious offense than the killing of a plain, everyday black man."[26]

Historic rates and treatment of intraracial violence are illuminating. But it is incomplete and ultimately unconvincing to say that exceptional rates of intraracial violence are nothing new. Full assessment of competing policies requires examination of relative costs and benefits of firearms and value judgments that drive firearms policy.

∽◉

We have already seen how very *high rates of gun violence among blacks are disproportionately attributable to young black men.* The tough question is, who are these men? General research shows that most murderers are extreme aberrants with long histories of criminal activity, psychopathology, and violence.[27] The aberrance of murderers is so solidly demonstrated that researchers consider it a general "criminological axiom."[28] If the general trend holds true, the exceptional rate of black homicide is mainly attributable to a slim microculture of aberrants who fall at the extremes of various measures of risk.

The modern orthodoxy does not expressly reject the thesis that exceptional black victimization and criminality are attributable to a slim microculture. But blanket gun bans, like those urged as bedrock policy under the modern orthodoxy do carry the implication that the black community at large cannot be trusted with guns. This is an unavoidable implication of proposals for targeted de jure gun bans in black enclaves, which would be deemed unconstitutional everywhere else. Proponents of this approach probably would prefer that no one have guns. But short of that, some seem willing to settle for targeted gun bans just in places with concentrations of black folk. On the long view, this is quite odd.

Under the banner of civil rights, this strand of the modern orthodoxy brands the entire community with a badge of inferiority through a race-coded deprivation of an established prerogative of American citizenship. It rings similar to nineteenth-century claims "that colored men were unfit for citizenship" and rationalizations of Black Code gun restrictions targeting freedmen.[29] The results of recently overturned gun prohibition laws in Washington, DC, and Chicago confirmed that this prescription only bars legal guns and does little about the flow of illegal guns to the violent microculture. So for a negligible impact on the real targets, these policies stigmatized entire urban enclaves as untrustworthy and left good people unilaterally disarmed against the criminals in their midst.

The focus on *gun control* as a response to the exceptional rate of violence among blacks, and especially among young black men, *is nonetheless politically appealing because it offers a seemingly straightforward solution to a far deeper problem that really has no easy answer*. Consider this summary of the various attempts to explain the exceptional rate of black male violence.

> There exists little consensus among criminologists and other crime scholars regarding "the causes" of black male violence. Numerous explanations have been offered, including biological causes (e.g., head injuries); social disorganization and inadequate socialization; poverty and economic inequality; racial oppression and displaced aggression; adherence to the norms of a subculture of violence; joblessness and family disruption; the cheapening of black life as a result of the imposition of lenient sentences against blacks who assault or murder blacks; and involvement in self-destructive lifestyles centered around heavy drinking, drug abuse and drug trafficking and street gangs. . . . Although they represent a minority viewpoint, some criminologists maintain that racial differences in violent crime offending may stem form genetic/non-acquired biological factors.[30]

This scattered assessment leaves the political class with two choices. One is to focus intently on the criminal microclass while at the same time acknowledging that there is no good, ready diagnosis of their behavior and therefore no easy solution. The alternative is to claim there is a ready solution to the problem—stringent supply-side gun control—but that has failed because of malevolent outsiders who block strong gun laws. On this choice, the appeal of the modern orthodoxy is plain.

The modern orthodoxy has two related advantages that lure the political class. First, it allows one to sidestep difficult conversations about violent self-help. Second, it avoids the stigmatizing class distinctions that come with a hard focus on the microcaste of violent young men.

To the first point, the focus on strict supply controls blunts militant prescriptions for self-help that public officials will naturally find discomforting. That worry is illustrated by the public declaration of Carl Lawrence, president of the New York NAACP, who in the early 1970s urged harsh medicine against the criminal microclass. Lawrence exhorted the "good people" of every harassed community to arm themselves and "take the streets away from the hoodlums."[31]

This is uncomfortable territory for everyone, but especially for progressives, whose political coin is the promise of public solutions to a wide array of problems. Even those who privately acknowledge that people are on their own within the window of imminence will be reluctant to say it and loath to build security policy around a theme of violent self-help. The modern orthodoxy, with its simplistic prescription for gun control, allows one to avoid the conversation about state failure and self-help.

The modern orthodoxy also avoids the political risk of stigmatizing the criminal microclass. The nature of this risk becomes apparent when we consider that the young men and boys of this class are also husbands, lovers, fathers, sons, and grandsons of people who may be willing to condemn the criminal down the street, but will go to the mat to defend their own wayward kin. In places with high offender rates, harsh rhetoric and tough policies against the criminal microclass will step on many toes and commit the sin of airing "family" problems in public.[32]

Careful politicians might navigate this problem by distinguishing between the full population of offenders, which might be relatively high, and the microculture of violent predators, which always has been quite small. But that is a more complicated strategy than the familiar appeal to community victimization and blame-casting onto distant villains.

The modern orthodoxy allows policy leaders to avoid openly choosing between Otis McDonald and the thugs who besieged him. It casts them both as victims of the gun or of the "outsiders" who provided it. It promises to make things safer for everyone by attacking that outside threat. At least that is the script.

But the reality, acknowledged by any serious analysis, is that the success of supply controls depends on taking the gun inventory down toward zero. That is simply impossible in a society that already has nearly as many private firearms as the rest of the world combined. So in practice the modern orthodoxy really *does* choose between the interests of Otis McDonald and the thugs who besieged him. And perversely, it subordinates McDonald's self-defense interest and gives the advantage to his tormentors.

On this balance, the modern orthodoxy seems ill advised. More so because it essentially dismisses promising criminological assessments—like this one from one of the most prolific and sensitive researchers in the field, who advises:

> There is substantial evidence that much could be learned about black homicide and other aspects of black life in the United States if more careful attention were paid to differences among blacks as well as between black and whites. The incidence of homicide among blacks as among non-blacks is significantly correlated with social

class. . . . The study of homicide among blacks may benefit from a within-group as well as a between-group analytical framework.[33]

But even if blacks are reticent to have this public conversation about the family's dirty laundry, shouldn't we at least privilege the interests of innocents and refuse to hand the advantage of arms to their tormentors? Conceding just this much sharpens the remaining analysis in an important way.

Whether it protects innocents like Shelly Parker and Otis McDonald is a crucial gauge of firearms policy. But what really does it mean to protect this class of innocents? What sort of regulatory scheme leaves the Parker/McDonald class better or worse off? *Does giving these people the choice of armed self-defense really offer a plausible chance of good results, or is armed self-defense so dangerous that we can justify taking that choice away?*

We might dismiss the self-defense interest of the Parker/McDonald class by saying that their desire for defensive firearms is simply misguided; that *armed self-defense is ineffective, uncommon, or counterproductive.* This conclusion might rest on a variety of assumptions that, if sound, could leave us confident that, black tradition of arms notwithstanding, the modern orthodoxy represents the clearly better contemporary policy. Those assumptions require careful attention.

Although it has long been debunked, one of the early and sometimes still-repeated claims about gun use is that *you are 44 times more likely* to hurt yourself or someone you love than to use the gun for self-defense. This conjures images of June Cleaver mistakenly shooting Ward when he pops home early from a business trip. The image is false. It is rooted in a study counting gun deaths, most of which were suicides, and ignoring the vast majority of defensive gun uses where no one is shot and the gun is not even fired.[34] The point is underscored by the actual data on the June-shoots-Ward incidents. It turns out that "fewer than 2 percent of fatal gun accidents (FGAs) involve a person accidentally shooting someone mistaken for an intruder."[35]

But even if it turns out that people rarely accidently shoot their loved ones, there is still the objection that *armed self-defense really doesn't work.* The data say otherwise. Survey data show that Americans defend themselves with guns at a startling rate. There have been fourteen major surveys of defensive gun use (DGU), with results ranging as high as 2 million DGUs per year. The figure is contested. But even skeptics who conducted their own surveys obtained similar results. This has led to a variety of other speculations by incredulous critics. Accounting for the various criticisms, the

National Opinion Research Center puts DGUs in the range of 256,500 to 1,210,000, per year.[36] These DGUs do not garner headlines because in the vast majority of cases no shots are fired. There is no indication that this phenomenon excludes blacks.[37]

What about the risk that *you will have your gun taken* and used against you? This concern is generally at odds with the DGU data, and textured research shows explicitly that people actually are better off resisting than submitting. Data from the National Crime Victimization Survey (NCVS) show that a victim's weapon is taken in about 1 percent of cases. The NCVS and other sources also conclude that there is no sound empirical evidence that resistance provokes fatal attacks.[38] In a study of all of the NCVS data on robberies from 1979 through 1985, the firearm offered the most effective form of resistance. Resistance with a gun was the method most likely to thwart the crime and most likely to prevent injury to the victim.[39] The NCVS data show that "the use of a gun by the victim significantly reduces her chance of being injured in situations when a robber is armed with a non-gun weapon."[40]

Another worry about armed self-defense is that *you will hurt yourself or have an accident*. The most compelling rendition of this is the image of children who find the family gun and shoot themselves or a playmate. This scenario triggers our most powerful protective instincts. These intuitions about the risk of accidental gun death may be the most exaggerated aspect of the firearms debate. In one telling example, a group of elite New York lawyers was asked to estimate the number of children under the age of fourteen killed in firearms accidents each year. Essentially everyone in the room of several hundred guessed more than 10,000 per year. Roughly half the room said 50,000 per year. The trend continued, with some saying 100,000 and a few guessing even more.[41]

The National Safety Council reports that for children under the age of fourteen, the death rate from firearms accidents has generally been below 100 deaths per year.[42] This does nothing to diminish the tragedy for the families involved. But it puts things in perspective to note that swimming-pool accidents account for more deaths of minors than *all* forms of death by firearm (accident, homicide, and suicide).[43]

All this said, it is still hard to shake the draw of supply controls, even though we know they are mainly symbolic. The appeal of the "no guns" logic presses through in the intuition that any sort of incremental reduction in the firearm supply will push gun crime proportionately downward. The modern orthodoxy advances this logic through the contention that *easier access to guns explains the exceptional rate of homicide in black communities*.

The data say otherwise. This is demonstrated by the fact that urban areas where disproportionate black murder rates now center generally have stricter gun laws, fewer guns, and more gun crime than rural areas where there are far more guns, easier access to guns, and less gun crime. Among young black males, the gun homicide and victimization rate is higher in urban areas (where gun regulation is stricter and gun ownership is lower) than in rural areas (where gun regulation is looser and gun ownership is higher). But despite the fact that rural blacks own more guns and have easier access to guns, the modern murder rate for young urban blacks has been as much as 600 percent higher than that of their rural counterparts.[44] Overall, blacks own guns at no greater rate than whites, and some surveys say that blacks own fewer guns. A study published in the *Harvard Journal of Law and Public Policy* summarizes the data this way:

> Preventing law-abiding, responsible African-Americans from owning guns does nothing at all to reduce murderers, because they are not the ones who are doing the killing. The murderers are a small minority of extreme antisocial aberrants who manage to obtain guns whatever the level of gun ownership in the African-American community.
>
> Indeed, murderers generally fall into a group some criminologists have called "violent predators," sharply differentiating them not only from the overall population but from other criminals as well. Surveys of imprisoned felons indicate that when not imprisoned the ordinary felon averages perhaps 12 crimes per year. In contrast, "violent predators" spend much or most of their time committing crimes, averaging at least 5 assaults, 63 robberies, and 172 burglaries annually. A National Institute of Justice survey of 2,000 felons in 10 state prisons, which focused on gun crime, said of these types of respondents: "[T]he men we have labeled Predators were clearly omnibus felons . . . [committing] more or less any crime they had the opportunity to commit. . . . Thus, when we talk about 'controlling crime' in the United States today, we are talking largely about controlling the behavior of these men."
>
> The point is not just that demographic patterns of homicide and gun ownership in the African-American community do not support the more guns equal more death mantra. More importantly, those patterns refute the logic of fewer guns equal less death. The reason fewer guns among ordinary African-Americans does not lead to fewer murders is because that paucity does not translate to fewer guns for the aberrant minority who do murder. The correlation of very high murder rates with low gun ownership in African-American communities simply does not bear out the notion that disarming the populace as a whole will disarm and prevent murder by potential murderers.[45]

The general data on violent crime and the gun inventory also refute the instinct that incremental decreases in the gun supply will reduce gun crime. The telling point here is that *the overall gun inventory and gun crime have split in dramatically different directions.* Over the last seventy-five years, the number of guns per 100,000 of population has grown from about 34,000 per 100,000 to roughly 100,000 per 100,000. Yes, we have enough guns literally to arm every man, woman, and child in the nation. But an interesting thing has happened as the gun inventory has grown to this record level.

The more-guns-equals-more-gun-crime assumption has not turned out. While the inventory of civilian firearms has grown steadily, the overall gun homicide rate has oscillated from around three per 100,000 to highs of around six per 100,000. In recent years, *the gun crime rate and violent crime rate (even among blacks) have declined even while the number of guns has risen sharply*. Gun homicides have trended down over recent decades from highs of around 14,000 per year to the current rate of around 8,000 per year. Over this same period, the number of guns in the civilian inventory has continued to grow to its now-record level of more than 325 million firearms. (This estimate is in the middle of a range that includes William Bratton's 350-million-guns estimate on the high end and lower estimates toward 300 million.) Not only have more guns not equaled more crime, both violent crime and gun crime have sharply declined while the gun stock has accelerated to record levels.[46]

One might still respond that *at least stringent supply controls can't hurt*. But this assumes that guns produce no benefits that would be lost under restrictive policies. And that is a difficult assumption to sustain. Several measures show various benefits of firearms ownership. A national study of gun use against burglaries conducted by the Centers for Disease Control (CDC) estimated 1,900,000 annual episodes where someone in the home retrieved a firearm in response to a suspected illegal entry. There were roughly half a million instances where the armed householder confronted and chased off the intruder.[47]

A study of active burglars found that one of the greatest risks faced by residential burglars is being injured or killed by occupants of a targeted dwelling. Many reported that this was their greatest fear and a far greater worry than being caught by police.[48] The data bear out the instinct. Home invaders in the United States are more at risk of being shot in the act than of going to prison.[49] Because burglars do not know which homes have a gun, people who do not own guns enjoy free-rider benefits because of the deterrent effect of others owning guns.[50]

In a survey of convicted felons conducted for the National Institute of Justice, 34 percent of them reported being "scared off, shot at, wounded or captured by an armed victim." Nearly 40 percent had refrained from attempting a crime because they worried the target was armed. Fifty-six percent said that they would not attack someone they knew was armed and 74 percent agreed that "one reason burglars avoid houses where people are at home is that they fear being shot."

The National Institute of Justice study concluded, "The highest concern about confronting an armed victim was registered by felons from states with the greatest relative number of privately owned firearms. . . . The major effects of partial or total handgun bans would fall more on the shoulders of the ordinary gun-owning public than on the felonious gun abuser of the sort studied here. . . . It is therefore also possible that one side consequence of such measures would be some loss of the crime-thwarting effects of civilian firearms ownership."[51]

Comparative assessments are instructive. Only around 13 percent of US residential burglaries are "hot" burglaries, meaning the attempt is made on an occupied residence.[52] This relatively low incidence of hot burglaries is generally attributed to criminals' fear of confronting an armed resident.[53] Home invaders in the United Kingdom seem to operate under different incentives. Compared to the United States, the United Kingdom has far more hot burglaries, nearly half of the total in one counting period. The chances of encountering an armed homeowner are far lower in the United Kingdom. This actually seems to fuel a preference for striking when occupants are home and alarms and locks are disengaged. Because hot burglaries pose higher risks of assault, one estimate says that UK-style gun restrictions in the United States would increase assaults by more than half a million per year, raising the overall American violent crime rate by almost 10 percent.[54]

There is intriguing *anecdotal evidence of firearms benefits in the consequences of targeted firearms policies*. In the period before Florida adopted its "shall issue" concealed-carry laws, the Orlando Police Department conducted a widely advertised program of firearms training for women. The program was started in response to reports that women in the city were buying guns at an increased rate after an uptick in sexual assaults.

The program aimed to help women gun owners become safe and proficient. Over the next year, rape declined by 88 percent. Burglary fell by 25 percent. Nationally these rates were increasing and no other city with a population over 100,000 experienced similar decreases during the period.[55] Rape increased by 7 percent nationally and by 5 percent elsewhere in Florida.[56]

There is a related lesson in the policies surrounding the concealed carry of firearms. The shift here has been revolutionary. Over the past thirty years, state after state has adopted nondiscretionary ("shall issue") licensing, which allows people who pass objective filters of trustworthiness to carry concealed firearms in public. This movement started as a reaction against the old discretionary systems that often were afflicted by cronyism, and, historically, by overt racism. Shall issue licensing is now the national norm.

At the start, many claimed that vetting people for trustworthiness and then allowing them to carry guns would lead to blood in the street. The gun, it was argued, was a powerful catalyst that would turn ordinary people into murderers. By any estimate, that fear did not turn out. With millions of concealed-carry permit holders nationally, the objections that concealed-carry laws would lead to carnage as ordinary people transformed into murderers have been tested and refuted.

The dispute now centers on studies concluding that concealed-carry laws cause reductions in crime and yield billions of dollars of benefits in avoided costs. This assessment matches the intuition that making criminal activity more risky also makes it less likely. These claims have drawn criticisms and rebuttals. In 2005, a National Research Council panel evaluated the literature on both sides. The majority of the panel concluded that the data were inadequate to say whether right-to-carry laws increased or decreased crime. One panel member, political scientist James Q. Wilson, filed a dissent. Wilson had supported gun-control measures in the past and gained fame as the originator of the "Broken Windows" theory of crime control. Wilson concluded that "the best evidence we have is that [right-to-carry laws] impose no costs but may confer benefits." While the debate continues, the striking thing is that the more-guns-equals-more-crime/blood-in-the-streets thesis is not seriously on the table.[57]

Much of the social science on the costs and benefits of private firearms proceeds on broad measures that do not specify distinct racial trends. But some studies have focused specifically on blacks. One study started with data sets about black homicides and then tracked the stories of victims and offenders. Researchers interviewed people familiar with the episode, the parties involved, and people who knew them.

In a sample from selected American cities, the study found that "robbery homicide" was the most frequent type of stranger homicide. But the next finding is surprising. "Young adult black men who are robbery-homicide victims are more often persons described as the robber than the robbed. This pattern appears to prevail in each of the primary sample cities."

In thinking about what is best for the Parker/McDonald class, the next assessment is vital. "Given the higher percentage of robber homicide victimizations in the early years of the interval, one might assume that *targets posing a higher homicide risk for the offender were abandoned in favor of safer targets.*" Note that the idea of hardening targets against the aggressive microculture is the core theme of arguments that armed citizens are a disincentive to crime. Researchers concluded that over a six-year period, robbery homicide was nearly as likely to result in the death of the robber as the robbed and that "*the deterrent efficiency of those who are successful in thwarting a robbery attempt probably exceeds that of the criminal justice system.*"

This is difficult territory. It is easy to see why policy makers might not embrace these data or design rules exploiting this trend. But from the perspective of the Parker/McDonald class—people living in the midst of clear threats and state failure—these data are a welcome affirmation of the benefits of private firearms in the hands of good people. One study underscores that message with this summary.

> The previous evidence illustrating the riskiness of becoming a victim if choosing to engage in robbery is a point seldom made. One must exhibit caution not to overstate the case, considering the low clearance rate for this offense. Yet it appears that robbers are indeed sensitive to the risks associated with the choice of robber targets. . . . Young black males who are insensitive to the risks associated with the choice of a robbery target clearly increase the probability that they will become homicide victims.[58]

The idea that firearms policy in the black community should privilege the Parker/McDonald class of innocents is open to at least two additional objections. Besides the Parker/McDonald class, there is another important class of innocents who are put at risk by firearms externalities— that is, crossfire, stray shots, and accidents for which self-defense is no clear answer. This group actually overlaps with the Parker/McDonald class. But treating it separately gives maximum credit to this interest as a counterweight.

Balancing these interests prompts comparisons between defensive gun uses and accidents and a variety of other balances. The DGU numbers range perhaps into the millions. The accidental death numbers are in the hundreds. People will contest exactly how these inputs should be weighted. And some will suggest other types of comparisons. It is also relevant that these data are drawn from the general population. It may turn out that particular black communities are exceptional in ways that are not reflected in the general data.

Also, one of the negative externalities of even a virtuous armed citizenry is that some percentage of guns owned by good people leak into the black market. Some of these guns are stolen. Others are shared-access guns, legally owned but taken and used by some untrustworthy member of the household. These risks are not fully quantified and are open for debate. They raise arguments for a sharper focus on safe storage, theft reporting, and innovations like frangible ammunition. The government interest in those things might be stronger in some places than in others.

Overall, the social science fairly suggests three important things. First, the problem of intraracial gun violence among blacks is attributable mainly to a distinct criminal microculture. Second, that criminal microclass responds to disincentives that make violent crime more risky. Third, guns in the hands of the Parker/McDonald class are among those disincentives.

Caution is certainly warranted here. The social science on these questions is vast, diverse, and incomplete. And a healthy cycle of criticism, rebuttal, and response is ongoing. It would be a mistake to anoint any particular empirical claim as the last word. Indeed, it is best to think about social-science claims as simply working theories. Still, there is a strong case that arms in the hands of the Parker/McDonald class generate results that compete easily with the modern orthodoxy's combination of promising symbolism and practical failure.

This brings us full circle, back to choice. Empirically it is far from obvious that the Parker/McDonald class is better off disarmed. So it seems fair to give them the option. But choice also resonates beyond cold empirical assessment. As a matter of long practice and policy, the black tradition of arms respected, indeed, exalted, the self-defense interest of individual black people. Though the stakes were tremendous, individuals were never asked to surrender their self-defense interest to advance group goals. The danger that self-defense would spill over into political violence was substantial, putting the entire movement, the freedom of an entire people, at risk. On that measure, the historic risks of the black tradition of arms were just as great or greater than the risks of firearms today. Despite that historic risk, black folk from the leadership to the grassroots upheld individual choice on the question of armed self-defense.

As a broader principle of liberty, the coalition from which the modern orthodoxy grows also has exalted choice as a bedrock principle driving policy on some of the most critical issues within the progressive agenda. It is hard to improve on the Supreme Court's articulation of the principle:

> Matters involving the most intimate and personal choices a person may make in a lifetime, choices central to personal dignity and autonomy, are central to the liberty protected by the Fourteenth Amendment. *At the heart of liberty is the right to define one's own concept of existence, of meaning, of the universe and of the mystery of human life.* Beliefs about these matters could not define the attributes of personhood were they formed under the compulsion of the state.[59]

The values and autonomy the court elevates here are easily reduced further. More basic than *defining* one's own concept of existence is the core interest in *preserving* one's existence against deadly threats. Personal security is the bedrock on which other popular autonomy claims rest. If choice on those matters is central to liberty, how do we deny people some fair measure of choice in circumstances where their lives hang in the balance?

NOTES

INTRODUCTION

    1. The quotations from Turnbow and Hamer are sourced and discussed in detail in chapter 7.

    2. These quotations are sourced and discussed in detail in chapter 1, chapter 7, and chapter 9.

CHAPTER 1: BOUNDARY-LAND

    1. Timothy B. Tyson, *Radio Free Dixie: Robert F. Williams & the Roots of Black Power* (1999) at 57.

    2. Ibid., at 49.

    3. Ibid., at 1-2, 18-25, 49-50, 57; Christopher B. Strain, "Civil Rights & Self-Defense: The Fiction of Nonviolence, 1955-1968," PhD dissertation, Univ. California, Berkley (2000) at 40.

    4. Robert Franklin Williams, *Negroes with Guns* (1962) at 46.

    5. Tyson, *Radio Free*, at 86.

    6. Ibid., at 87.

    7. Ibid., at 50-75, 79-88.

    8. Julian Mayfield, in James Forman, *The Making of Black Revolutionaries* (1972) at 167.

    9. Strain, *Civil Rights*, at 56; William Worthy, "Black Muslims NAACP Target: Raise Funds for Arms for Carolinian," *Baltimore Afro-American* (July 22, 1961); Tyson, *Radio Free*, at 89, 137.

    10. Timothy B. Tyson, *Blood Done Sign My Name* (2004) at 57.

    11. Tyson, *Radio Free*, at 138; Tim Hashaw, *Children of Perdition: Melungeons and the Struggle of Mixed Race America* (2006) at 70-71.

    12. For discussion of defensive gun use, see Nicholas J. Johnson, "Firearms and the Black Community: An Assessment of the Modern Orthodoxy," *Connecticut L. Review* (2013); Nicholas J. Johnson et al., *Firearms Law and the Second Amendment: Regulation, Rights, and Policy* (2012) and chapter 9 of this book.

    13. David T. Beito and Linda Royster Beito, *Black Maverick: T. R. M. Howard's Fight*

for Civil Rights and Economic Power (2009) at 67-68; E. Franklin Frazier, "The Negro and Non-Resistance," *Crisis*, March 1924, at 213-214, reprinted in Herbert Apkether, *Documentary History of the Negro People in the United States*, Vol. 3 (1951) at 449-451, 451.

14. Williams, at 62; Herbert Shapiro, *White Violence and Black Response* (1988) at 459; Forman, at 175; Tyson, *Radio Free*, at 86-89, 137-65.

15. "NAACP Leader Urges Violence," *New York Times*, May 7, 1959.

16. *Carolina Times*, January 5, 1960; *News and Courier*, May 7, 1959, clipping in box A333, group 3, NAACP Papers, Library of Congress; Tyson, *Radio Free*, at 150.

17. Telegram from NAACP executive secretary Roy Wilkins to Robert Williams, president of branch in Monroe, North Carolina, May 6, 1959, box A333, group 3, NAACP Papers, Library of Congress. Wilkins's account is quoted in Julian Mayfield, "Challenge to Negro Leadership: The Case of Robert Williams," *Commentary* (April 1961) at 299. See also Tyson, *Radio Free*, at 86-89, 137-65.

18. Williams, *Negroes with Guns*, at 67. For full text of the resolutions, see Glocester B. Current, "Fiftieth Annual Convention," in *Crisis* (August-September 1959) at 400-10.

19. Both essays are printed in *Southern Patriot* 18, no. 2 (January 1960) at 3; edited versions of the essays appear in *Eyes on the Prize Civil Rights Reader*, edited by Clayborne Carson et al. (1991) at 110 -113. See also Williams, *Negroes with Guns*, at 12-15 (quoting Martin Luther King Jr.).

20. *Baltimore Afro-American*, May 30, 1959; *Ark. State Press*, May 23, 1959; *Ark. State Press*, May 23, 1959; *Southern Patriot* 18, no. 2 (January 1960): 3; *Southern Patriot* 21 no. 2 (February 1963): 2; see also Tyson, *Radio Free*, at 163-164.

21. For continuing support in Monroe, see Williams, *Negroes with Guns*, at 111; Strain, *Civil Rights & Self-Defense*, at 49. For support in the branches, see Brooklyn Branch to Roy Wilkins, May 8, 1959, and Flint Michigan Branch Resolution to the National Board NAACP, May 24, 1959, box 2, CCRI Papers; Charles J. Adams to Roy Wilkins, May 8, 1959, box A 333, group 3, NAACP Papers. Adams wrote to Wilkins, "I support Williams one million percent. . . . Why can't we do like the Indians did down in Carolina last year?"; the Flint Michigan Branch demanded Williams's "immediate reinstatement." Tyson, *Radio Free*, at 156-57.

22. John McCray, "There's Nothing New about It," *Baltimore Afro-American*, May 23, 1959.

23. Roy Wilkins, *The Single Issue in the Robert Williams Case*, box A333, group 3, NAACP Papers, Library of Congress; Address of Roy Wilkins, Freedom Fund Dinner of the Chicago Branch, Morrison Hotel, Chicago, Ill., June 12, 1959.

24. Roy Wilkins, *Standing Fast: The Autobiography of Roy Wilkins* (1982) at 265; *Meet the Press* transcript, July 16, 1967, at 9.

CHAPTER 2: FOUNDATION

1. "The True Remedy for the Fugitive Slave," *Frederick Douglass Paper*, June 9, 1854, reprinted in John R. McKivigan and Heather L. Kaufman, *In the Words of Frederick Douglass: Quotations from Liberty's Champion* (2012) at 111.

2. Robin Santos Doak, *Slave Rebellions* (2006) at 16; Enrico Dal Lago, Constantina Katsari, *Slave Systems: Ancient And Modern* (2008) at 249; Ella Forbes, *But We Have No Country: The 1851 Christiana Pennsylvania Resistance* (1998) at 137.

3. Walter C. Rucker, *The River Flows On: Black Resistance, Culture and Identity Formation in Early America* (2007) at 4-5; Christopher Waldrep, *Roots of Disorder: Race and Criminal Justice in the American South 1817–80* (1998) at 11; Douglas Greenberg, *Crime and Law Enforcement in the Colony of New York, 1691–1776* (1974) at 150-151; Peter H. Wood, *Black Majority: Negroes in Colonial South Carolina from 1670 through the Stono Rebellion* (1974); Harriet C. Frazier, *Slavery and Crime in Missouri, 1773–1865* (2001).

4. Greenberg, at 74, 138-139.

5. Ibid., at 129.

6. The account here is detailed in Frederick Douglass, *The Narrative Life of Frederick Douglass*, reprinted in *Frederick Douglass: The Narrative and Selected Writings* (1984) at 26-56, 68-82. See also William S. McFeely, *Frederick Douglass* (1991) at 8, 13, 43.

7. Greenberg, at 74.

8. Harriet C. Fraizer, *Slavery and Crime in Missouri 1773 to 1865* (2001) at 197, 201, 204-205; Walter White, *Rope and Faggot: A Biography of Judge Lynch* (1929) at 90.

9. Dan T. Carter, *When the War Was Over: The Failure of Self Reconstruction in the South 1865–1867* (1985) at 188.

10. *Dred Scott v. Sandford*, 15 L. Ed. 691 (1857).

11. McFeely, at 5, 8.

12. Waldo E. Martin Jr., *The Mind of Frederick Douglass* (1984) at 188; Frederick Douglass, *Not Afraid to Die*, reprinted in Ronald T. Takaki, *Violence in the Black Imagination* (1993) at 17-35.

13. Stanley Harrold, *Border War: Fighting over Slavery Before the Civil War* (2010) at 25-27, 32, 95; Stephen Middleton, *The Black Laws: Race and the Legal Process in Early Ohio* (2005) at 47-51; Robert C. Smedley, *History of the Underground Railroad in Chester and Neighboring Counties of Pennsylvania* (1883) at 26-29.

14. Nicholas J. Johnson, David Kopel, George Mocsary, and Michael O'Shea, *Firearms Law and the Second Amendment: Regulation, Rights, and Policy* (2012) at 114.

15. Waldrep, *Roots of Disorder*, at 9-10, 25, 29-34.

16. Nicholas J. Johnson, Clayton Cramer, and George Mocsary, "'This Right Is Not Allowed by Governments That Are Afraid of the People': The Public Meaning of the Second Amendment When the Fourteenth Amendment Was Ratified," 17 *George Mason Law Review* (2010) at 853.

17. Kevin Boyle, *Arc of Justice* (2004) at 46; Clifton Paisley, *The Red Hills Florida 1528–1865* (1989) at 134; Harrold, at 129-130.

18. Henry Bibb, *Narrative of the Life and Adventures of Henry Bibb, an American Slave* (2005) at 84.

19. Leon Litwack, *Been in the in the Storm So Long: The Aftermath of Slavery* (1979) at 104.

20. Harrold, at 129-130.

21. Ibid., at 131, 177.

22. Elijah P. Marrs, *Life and History of the Rev. Elijah P. Marrs* (1885) at 17-20, 131, 177.

23. These findings are discussed at length in chapter 9.

24. William Loren Katz, *The Black West* (2005) at 85; Keith P Griffler, *Frontline of Freedom: African Americans and the Forging of the Underground Railroad in the Ohio Valley* (2004) at 62; Francis Fredric, *Escaped Slave, Slave Life in Virginia and Kentucky* (2010) at 86; Harrold, at 131, 179.

25. John P. Parker, *His Promised Land: The Autobiography of John P. Parker, Former Slave and Conductor on the Underground Railroad* (Stuart S. Sprague, ed., 1996) at 119, 118-121.

26. Katz, *Black West*, at 277.

27. William Still, *Still's Underground Railroad Records, with a Life of the Author* (1872) at 124-126; George Hendrick, ed., *Fleeing for Freedom: Stories of the Underground Railroad* (2004) at 148-155.

28. Still, at 124-126; Hendrick, at 148-155.

29. Still, at 48-51.

30. Harrold, at 46, 62.

31. Philip S. Foner and Yuval Taylor, *Frederick Douglass: Selected Speeches and Writings* (1999) at 367.

32. Harrold, at 10, 15, 21-22.

33. Ibid., at 135, 139 -143, 155.

34. "Unconstitutional Laws of Ohio," *Liberator*, April 6, 1838, at 53; Johnson et al. *Public Meaning*, at 838.

35. Lysander Spooner, "The Fugitive Slave Bill," *Liberator*, January 3, 1851, at 1.

36. "The New England Antislavery Convention," *Liberator*, June 3, 1853, at 23; Johnson et al., *Public Meaning*, at 840.

37. Forman, at 376.

38. Harrold, at 101-102, 109.

39. Griffler, *Front Line of Freedom: African Americans and the Forging of the Underground Railroad in the Ohio Valley* (2004) at 54.

40. Harrold, at 102.

41. Ibid., at 103, 111.

42. Ibid., at 98.

43. Ibid., at 177-178.

44. Ibid., at 136.

45. Ibid., at 150- 153, 156- 157, 181.

46. Katz, *Black West*, at 48-52, 63-64.

47. Forbes, at 131-133, 137, 139-140.

48. Earl Ofari, *Let Your Motto Be Resistance: The Life and Thought of Henry Highland Garnet* (1972) at 43.

49. Forbes, at 138.

50. Ofari, at 44; Phillip Foner, *Frederick Douglass* (1964) at 138.

51. *Liberator*, September 8, 1843.

52. Ofari, at 38-39; *Liberator*, December 3, 1843.

53. Forbes, at 134; *Liberator*, September 26, 1851.

54. Jermaine W. Loguen, *The Reverend J. W. Loguen as a Slave and as a Free Man* (1968) at 393-394.

55. Forbes, at 109-110.

56. Ibid., at 111, 119, 123; William Parker, "The Freedman's Story," *Atlantic Monthly*, February 17, 1866, at 281.

57. Forbes, at 124, 129; *Liberator*, November 1, 1850.

58. William J. Simmons, Henry McNeal Turner, *Men of Mark: Eminent, Progressive and Rising* (1887) at 1011.

59. Forbes, at 127.

60. McFeely, *Frederick Douglass*, at 196-197.

61. Ofari, at 44, 61; *Frederick Douglass Paper*, August 20, 1852; "Impartial Citizen," *Liberator*, October 11, 1850.

62. Forbes, at 120-121, 126.

63. Parker's account, *The Freedman's Story*, was published in 1866 in the *Atlantic Monthly*. Dispute about whether this is entirely Parker's work stems from doubts about when and how well he learned to read and write. The work also reflects a level of bravado that cautions skepticism.

64. Forbes, at 296.

65. Jonathan Katz, *Resistance at Christiana: The Fugitive Slave Rebellion, Christiana, Pennsylvania, September 11, 1851* (1974) at 232; Forbes, at 296; Harrold, at 153-154.

66. Johathan Katz, at 234-236; Forbes, at 143-144.

67. Forbes, at 144.

68. Ibid., at 145.

69. Ibid.

70. Ofari, at 45; *Liberator*, March 12, 1858.

71. Frederick Douglass, *Life and Times of Frederick Douglass Written by Himself* (1892) at 281-282; Johathan Katz, at 261.

CHAPTER 3: PROMISE AND BREACH

1. Martin B. Pasternak, "Rise Now and Fly to Arms: The Life of Henry Highland Garnet," PhD dissertation Univ. Mass. (1981) at xi.

2. Joel Schor, *Henry Hyland Garnet: A Voice of Black Radicalism in the Nineteenth Century* (1977) at 12.

3. Ibid., at 4-5, 15.

4. Ibid.

5. Barnet Schecter, *The Devil's Own Work: The Civil War Draft Riots and the Fight to Reconstruct America* (2005) at 99, 301.

6. Joseph Glatthaar, *Forged in Battle: The Civil War Alliance of Black Soldiers and White Officers* (1990) at 122, 129-130, 135.

7. Ibid., at 153, 161.

8. David S. Cecelski, *The Fire of Freedom: Abraham Galloway and the Slaves' Civil War* (2012) at 48; Adam Goodheart, *1861: The Civil War Awakening* (2011); Adam Goodheart, "To Have a Revolver," *Opinionator* (blog), Opinionator.blogs.nytimes.com.

9. Cecelski, at 75.

10. Linda O. McMurry, *To Keep the Waters Troubled: The Life of Ida B. Wells* (Oxford 1998) at 5-8.

11. Cecelski, at 64-66, 75, 78, 119.

12. Christopher Waldrep, *Roots of Disorder: Race and Criminal Justice in the American South, 1817–80* (1998) at 85.

13. Cecelski, at 62, 76, 80-82, 92, 96, 118-119.

14. Glatthaar, at 157-158. Spelling, capitalization, and spacing in this letter have been reproduced to reflect the original.

15. Leslie M. Harris, *In the Shadow of Slavery: African Americans in New York City, 1626–1863* (2003); Cecelski, at 71.

16. Schecter, at 107, 205, 289.

17. August Meier and Elliot Rudwick, *From Plantation to Ghetto* (1970) at 132.

18. Garnet apparently decided not to engage the New York rioters, on the rationale that he would best serve the community by surviving to care for the injured survivors. Schecter, at 154; Cecelski, at 140.

19. Waldrep, *Roots of Disorder*, at 93.

20. Richard M. Reid, *Freedom for Themselves* (2008) at 255; Stephen Hahn, *A Nation under Our Feet: Black Political Struggles in the Rural South from Slavery to the Great Migration* (2003) at 133.

21. Reid, at 258, 284; Roberta Alexander, *North Carolina Faces the Freedmen* (1985) at 130-133; *State v. Joiner* (1850).

22. William McKee Evans, *Ballots and Fence Rails: Reconstruction on the Lower Cape Fear* (1995) at 23.

23. Evans, at 64.

24. Reid, at 273-274.

25. Cecelski, at 182-183.

26. Waldrep, *Roots of Disorder*, at 94.

27. Leon F. Litwack, *Been in the Storm So Long: The Aftermath of Slavery* (1979) at 269.

28. Ibid., at 208.

29. Ibid. at 102, 114, 274, 428, 439.

30. Stephen P. Halbrook, *Freedmen, the Fourteenth Amendment, and the Right to Bear Arms, 1866–1876* (1998) at 2, 12.

31. Nicholas Johnson, David Kopel, George Mocsary, and Michael O'Shea, *Firearms Law and the Second Amendment: Regulation, Rights, and Policy* (2012) at 290-292.

32. Clayton Cramer, Nicholas Johnson, and George Mocsary, "This Right Is Not Allowed by Governments That Are Afraid of the People: The Public Meaning of the Second Amendment When the Fourteenth Amendment Was Ratified," 17 *George Mason Law Review* (2010) at 854; Edward McPhearson, *The Political History of the United States of America during the Period of Reconstruction* (1875) at 118.

33. Halbrook, at 2, 5, 27.

34. Hahn, at 267.

35. Johnson et al., "Public Meaning," at 854; "Right To Bear Arms," *Christian Recorder* (Philadelphia, PA), February 24, 1866, at 1-2.

36. Johnson et al., "Public Meaning," at 858; Letter to the Editor, *Loyal Georgian (Augusta)*, February 3, 1866, at 3.

37. Johnson et al., "Public Meaning," at 856; 2 *Proceedings of the Black State Conventions, 1840 through 1865*, at 302 (Foner and Walker edition 1980).

38. Johnson et al., "Public Meaning," at 858; "Report of the Joint Committee on Reconstruction," 39th Cong. 1st Sess. 219 (1866); *Cong. Globe*, 39th Cong., 1st Sess. 371 (1866).

39. Johnson et al., "Public Meaning," at 856-859; "Joint Committee on Reconstruction," 39th Cong., "Report of the Joint Committee on Reconstruction," 39th Cong., 1st Sess. 140, 219 (1866).

40. Halbrook, at 110-111; *Cong. Globe*, 40th Cong., 2nd Sess. 1996 (March 19, 1868); House Executive Document 329, 40th Cong., 2nd Sess. (1868).

41. Johnson et al., "Public Meaning," at 859; *Cong. Globe*, 39th Cong., 1st Sess. 1033-34 (1866).

42. Johnson et al., "Public Meaning," at 860-861; *Cong. Globe*, 39th Cong., 2nd Sess. 1848 (1868).

43. Kenneth W. Howell, *Still the Arena of Civil War: Violence and Turmoil in Reconstruction Texas, 1865–1874* (2012) at 296.

44. Halbrook, at 97; Donald G. Nieman, "African-American Communities, Politics, and Justice: Washington County Texas, 1865–1890," in Christopher Waldrep and Donald Nieman, *Local Matters: Race Crime and Justice in the 19th Century South* (2011) at 204, 205.

45. George C. Wright, *Racial Violence in Kentucky 1865–1940: Lynchings, Mob Rule and "Legal Lynchings"* (1990) at 46.

46. Elijah Marrs, *Life and History of the Rev. Elijah P Marrs* (1885) at 74-75.

47. Ibid. at 78, 87, 89-90.

48. Halbrook, at 16; "Report of the Joint Committee on Reconstruction, HR," Report number 30, 39th Cong., 1st Sess. 110, 112, 658.

49. Halbrook, at 18, 22, 34, 183.

50. Waldrep, *Roots of Disorder*, at 10, 94, 123, 140-141.

51. Hahn, at 80.

52. Waldrep, *Roots of Disorder*, at 123, 137.

53. Johnson et al., "Public Meaning," at 853; Myrta Lockett Avary, *Dixie after the War: An Exposition of Social Conditions Existing in the South, during the 12 Years Succeeding the Fall of Richmond* (1906) at 263-78; Dan Carter, *When the War Was Over* (1985) at 197.

54. Reid, at 310-311.

55. Halbook, at 77, 78; "President Johnson Asks Advice in Colored Militia Case," *Press*, Philadelphia, PA, November 8, 1867, at 1; "Concerning the Disbandment of the Freedman's Military Organizations," *Press*, Philadelphia, PA, November 7, 1867, at 1.

56. Reid, at 310-311; Evans, at 98-102.

57. Hahn, at 223.

58. Ibid., at 174-177, 181, 186, 274-275, 281.

59. Michael W. Fitzgerald, "Extralegal Violence and the Planter Class: The Ku Klux Klan in the Alabama Black Belt during Reconstruction," in Christopher Waldrep and Donald Nieman, *Local Matters: Race Crime and Justice in the 19th Century South* (2011) at 156-169.

60. Hahn, at, 90, 289-292.

61. Otis A. Singletary, *Negro Militias and Reconstruction* (1984) at 8-13; *Cong. Globe*, 39th Cong., 2nd Sess. at 217.

62. Singletary, at 8-13.

63. Evans, at 71, 99; Singletary, at 8-13.

64. Evans, at 80-81, 84-85, 101-102.

65. Cecelski, at 202, 204.

66. Halbrook, at 121; House of Representatives Report Number 22, February 1, 1871, at 219, 222.

67. Halbrook, at 126-128, 146.

68. Donald G. Nieman, "African-American Communities, Politics, and Justice: Washington County Texas, 1865–1890," in Christopher Waldrep and Donald Nieman, *Local Matters: Race Crime and Justice in the 19th Century South* (2011) at 212.

69. Herbert Shapiro, *White Violence and Black Response* (1988) at 6-7, 12-13, 16, 21.

70. Singletary, at 13, 50, 54-55, 60, 65, 82-99.

71. Christopher Waldrep, "Black Political Leadership, Warren County Mississippi," in

Christopher Waldrep and Donald Nieman, *Local Matters: Race Crime and Justice in the 19th Century South* (2011) at 212, 237, 239-45.

72. Hahn, at 299-305.

73. Ibid., at 306; Lou Falkner Williams, "Federal Enforcement of Black Rights in the Post Redemption South: The Ellenton Riot Case," in Waldrep and Nieman, *Local Matters: Race Crime and Justice in the 19th Century South* (2011) at 176.

74. Hahn, at 306-310.

75. Rayford W. Logan, *The Betrayal of the Negro: From Rutherford B. Hayes to Woodrow Wilson* (Da Capo Press 1997) at 91; Cong. Rec., 56th Cong. 2242-2245; 2nd Sess. 557, 647, 657.

76. Halbrook, at 137, 142-143.

77. Ibid., at 143.

78. Charles Lane, *The Day Freedom Died: The Colfax Massacre, the Supreme Court, and the Betrayal of Reconstruction* (2008) at 35-36, 54, 72-75.

79. Ibid., at 75-80.

80. Ibid., at 93, 97.

81. Ibid., at 9-11, 106.

82. Halbrook, at 166; "The Grant Parish Prisoners," *New Orleans Republican*, June 21, 1874, at 1, 4.

83. Shawn Leigh Alexander, *An Army of Lions: The Civil Rights Struggle before the NAACP* (2012) at 3-4.

CHAPTER 4: NADIR

1. Linda O. McMurry, *To Keep the Waters Troubled: The Life of Ida B. Wells* (1998) at 19-20; *Memphis Argus*, August 24, 1865.

2. McMurry, at 26-30, 128-133.

3. David Levering Lewis, *W. E. B. Du Bois: Biography of a Race* (1993) at 67.

4. McMurry, at 137- 139, 143-145; Lewis, at 67.

5. Paula Giddings, *Ida: A Sword among Lions* (2008) at 214; McMurry, at 147-148.

6. Ida B. Wells Barnett, *On Lynchings* (2002) at 110-111; McMurry, at 158-159.

7. Ida B. Wells, *Southern Horrors*, in *Selected Works of Ida B. Wells-Barnett* (1991), at 42; McMurry, at 161, 164.

8. Giddings, at 74; McMurry, at 128-129.

9. McMurry, at 129, 155.

10. R. L. Wilson, *The Winchester: An American Legend* (1991) at 11.

11. Wright, at 169-170.

12. Margaret Vandiver, *Lethal Punishment: Lynchings and Legal Executions in the South* (2006) at 179.

328   NOTES

13. McMillen, at 226.

14. W. F. Brundage, "The Darien Insurrection of 1899: Black Protest during Nadir of Race Relations," 74 *Georgia Historical Quarterly* 234-253 (1990).

15. Wright, at 170-171.

16. Shawn Leigh Alexander, *Army of Lions: The Civil Rights Struggle before the NAACP* (2011) at 2.

17. Gerald H. Gaither, *Blacks and the Populist Movement: Ballots and Bigotry in the New South* (2005) at x-xi.

18. Joseph Gerteis, *Class and the Color Line: Interracial Class Coalition in the Knights of Labor and the Populist Movement* (2007).

19. Hahn, at 418; William Loren Rogers, "Negro Knights of Labor in Arkansas: A Case Study of the Miscellaneous Strike" 10 *Labor History* 498-505 (1969).

20. Hahn, at 422; William F. Holmes, "The Leflore County Massacre and the Demise of the Colored Farmers' Alliance," 34 *Phylon* 267-274 (1973); Gaither, at 27.

21. *Mob Rule*, in *Selected Works of Id B. Wells*; Alexander, at 158.

22. Joel Williamson, *A Rage for Order* (1986) at 134; Blackmon, at 99, 82.

23. Williamson, at 134-136.

24. Ida B. Wells, *Robert Charles and His Fight to the Death: The Story of His Life. Burning Human Beings Alive. Other Lynching Statistics*, in *Selected Works of Ida B. Wells Barnett* (1991) at 277.

25. Williamson, at 136-141.

26. Wells, *Robert Charles*, in *Selected Works*, at 254, 257-258, 277-278.

27. Louis Armstrong, *Satchamo: My Life in New Orleans* (1954) at 33-39.

28. See chapter 9 for Wells's discussion of black crime in Chicago.

29. *The Civil Rights Cases*, 109 U.S. 3 (1883). Alexander, at 6.

30. Emma Lou Thornbrough, *T. Thomas Fortune: Militant Journalist* (1972) at 14; Alexander, at 5.

31. Thornbrough, at 15.

32. Alexander, at 5, 22; *New York Age*, December 21, 1889.

33. *Compilation of Proceedings of the Afro-American League National Convention* (January 1890) at 18.

34. Michael D'Orso, *Rosewood: Like Judgment Day* (1996) at 54-55.

35. Thornbrough, at 119.

36. Ibid., at 48-49.

37. Ibid., at 182.

38. Ibid., at 16, 48-50, 156, 166, 170, 184, 207-210, 257-258, 264, 296-297, 317, 320-321.

39. Lewis R. Harlan, *Booker T. Washington, the Wizard of Tuskegee* (1983) at 444.

40. Thornbrough, at 193, 198-200.

41. Ibid., at 218; *Washington Post*, August 7, 1901.

42. Ibid., at 279; *New York Age*, September 27, October 4, 1906.

43. Alexander, at 16; *New York Age*, January 5, 1889.

44. Thornbrough, at 368; *Amsterdam News*, June 13, 1928.

45. Giddings, at 397-400.

46. Shapiro, at 77; *Washington Post*, November 21, 1898.

47. Shapiro, at 78; *Washington Bee*, November 5, 1898, *Cleveland Gazette*, November 19, 1898.

48. Tyson, *Radio Free*, at 211; "Bad Nigger with a Winchester: Colored Editors Declare for Armed Resistance to Lynch Law," *Washington Post*, August 10, 1901.

49. Alexander, at 78; Alexander Walters, *My Life and Work* (1917) at 98.

50. Alexander, at 111-113.

51. Andre E. Johnson, *The Forgotten Prophet, Bishop Henry McNeal Turner and the African-American Prophetic Tradition* (2012) at 109-110.

52. Manuscript in John E. Bruce Collection, folder 7, Shomburg Collection, New York Public Library. See also http://www.britannica.com/blackhistory/article-9399827, last accessed October 25, 2013.

53. Alexander, at 16, 113-114, 175-176.

54. Earl Ofari, *Let Your Motto Be Resistance: The Life and Thought of Henry Highland Garnet* (1972) at 135, Appendix 2. Martin B. Pasternak, "Rise Now and Fly to Arms: The Life of Henry Highland Garnet," PhD dissertation Univ. Mass. (1981) at 77.

55. Philip Durham and Everett Jones, *The Negro Cowboys* (1965) at 222-223.

56. William Loren Katz, *Black Indians: A Hidden Heritage* (1986) at 133-135; Quintard Taylor, *In Search of the Racial Frontier: African Americans in the American West 1528–1990* (1998) at 104.

57. Katz, *Black West*, at 13, 16-20.

58. Katz, *Black Indians*, at 135-138; Durham and Jones, at 7.

59. Katz, *Black Indians*, at 138-140.

60. Joel Williamson, *A Rage for Order: Black-White Relations in the American South since Emancipation* (1986) at 164; Katz, *Black Indians*, at 140-149.

61. Taylor, at 30; Katz, *Black Indians*, at 149-151; Daniel F. Littlefield and Lonnie E. Underhill, "Black Dreams and Free Homes: The Oklahoma Territory, 1891–1894," 34 *Phylon* 348-49 (1973).

62. McMurry, at 140-141.

63. Taylor, at 147.

64. Katz, *Black West*, at 230; McMurry, at 142.

65. James Beckworth, *The Life and Adventures of James P. Beckworth as Told to Thomas D. Bonner* (1859); Ray Allen Billington, *The Far Western Frontier: 1830–1860* (1962) at 48.

66. Durham and Jones, at 7-9, 15-16.

67. Wendell Addington, "Slave Insurrections in Texas," 35 *Journal of Negro History* (1950) at 414. For the counting of Texas blacks in 1860, see Taylor, at 54, 76, 104; Durham and Jones, at 16.

68. Taylor, at 60; Ronnie C. Tyler, "The Callahan Expedition of 1855: Indians or Negroes" 70 *Southwestern Historical Quarterly* (1967) at 574 -585, 580.

69. William Katz, *Black West*, at 74.

70. Andrew Forest Muir, "The Free Negro in Jefferson and Orange Counties, Texas," 35 *Journal of Negro History* (1950) at 183-204.

71. W. T. Block, "Meanest Town on the Coast," *Old West*, 10 (Winter 1979); A. F. Muir, "The Free Negroes of Jefferson," at 186; Katz, *Black West*, at 94.

72. Block, at 10; Muir, at 183-206; Katz, *Black West*, at 94.

73. Katz, *Black West*, at 56-58.

74. John Marvin Hunter, *The Trail Drivers of Texas* (1925) at 671; Durham and Jones, at 26.

75. Durham and Jones, at 44-47.

76. Sarah R. Massey, *Black Cowboys of Texas* (2005) at 198, 148; Durham and Jones, at 63, 86-88.

77. Durham and Jones, at 55-56, 69, 85, 130.

78. William A. Keleher, *Violence in Lincoln County, 1869– 1881* (1957) at 110; William Lee Hamlin, *The True Story of Billy the Kid: A Tale of the Lincoln County War* (1959) at 81-83; Durham and Jones, at 101.

79. Taylor, at 84,; Durham and Jones, at 115-129.

80. Clifford P. Westermeier, *Trailing the Cowboy: His Life and Lore as Told by Frontier Journalist* (1955) at 110.

81. Durham and Jones, at 168-169, 204.

82. Arthur T. Burton, *Black Red and Deadly: Black and Indian Gunfighters of the Indian Territory, 1870–1907* (1991) at 4, 25.

83. Katz, *Black Indians*, at 158-160; Burton, at 42, 45, 54.

84. Burton, at 85, 89-90; Katz, *Black Indians*, at 163.

85. Burton, at 110-111.

86. Katz, *Black Indians*, at 146, 178. Burton, 162, 179; Katz, *Black West*, at 146.

87. Frank M. King, *Pioneer Western Empire Builders: A True Story of the Men and Women of Pioneer Days* (1946) at 294; Dane Coolidge, *Fighting Men of the West* (1932) at 72-74.

88. Katz, *Black West*, at 198-199; Taylor, at 175; Frank N. Schubert, "The Suggs Affray: The Black Cavalry in the Johnson County War," 4 *Western Historical Quarterly* 60 (1973).

89. Katz, *Black West*, at 222-223, 272.

90. Tricia Martineau Wagner, *African American Women of the Old West* (2007) at 15-17; James A. Franks, *Mary Fields: The Story of Black Mary* (2000) at 78.

91. Franks, at 42-46, 78, 109-111.

92. Ibid., at 42-46, 78, 109-111; Walter Hazen, *Hidden History: Profiles of Black Americans* (2004); Barbara Holland, *They Went Whistling: Women Wayfarers, Warriors, Runaways, and Renegades* (2002); David Wishart, *Encyclopedia of the Great Plains* (2004); Ben Thompson, *Stagecoach Mary Fields*, at 3.

93. Tricia Martineau Wagner, *African American Women of the Old West* (2007) at 15-17, 22-25.

94. Franks, at 42-46, 78, 109-111.; Thompson, at 5.

95. David Zhang, *Fleet Walker's Divided Heart: The Life of Baseball's First Black Major Leaguer* (1995) at 67-93.

96. Rebecca Goodman and Barett J. Brunsman, "Traveling through Time, Shelby County Historical Society: This Day in Ohio History," 2005 at 39, available at http://www.shelbycounty history.org/schs/archives/blackhistoryarchives/bshangbhisyA.htm.

CHAPTER 5: CRISIS

1. Gerald Horne and Mary Young eds., *W. E. B. Du Bois: An Encyclopedia* (2001); Leon Litwack, *Trouble in Mind: Black Southerners in the Age of Jim Crow* (1998) at 317; Christopher B. Strain, *Pure Fire: Self-Defense as Activism in the Civil Rights Era* (2005) at 24; David Levering Lewis, *Du Bois: Biography of a Race: 1868–1919* (1993) at 354.

2. Lewis, *Du Bois*, at 32-33.

3. The crime rate in Atlanta in 1905 was one of the highest in the country, with black men accounting for about 10,000 of 17,000 arrests—a worrisome indicator even after the modern caution that black arrest rates of this era are not an accurate reflection of true crime levels, considering, among other things, the strong incentives to dragoon black men into the convict labor system. Joel Williamson, *A Rage for Order: Black-White Relations in the American South since Emancipation* (1984) at 146-147; Douglas A. Blackmon, *Slavery by Another Name: The Re-Enslavement of Black Americans from the Civil War to World War II* (2009) at 81.

4. John Dittmer, *Black Georgia in the Progressive Era: 1900–1920* (1977) at 130-131.

5. Lewis, *Du Bois*, at 67.

6. *W. E. B. Du Bois: Encyclopedia*, at 19.

7. Walter White, *A Man Called White* (reprint, 1969) at 10-12; Herbert Shapiro, *White Violence and Black Response: From Reconstruction to Montgomery* (1988) at 102.

8. Recall from chapter 4 that Washington also funded the journalism of T. Thomas Fortune, whose reaction to the riot was typically militant.

9. Shawn Leigh Alexander, *An Army of Lions: The Civil Rights Struggle Before the NAACP* (2013) at 278-282; *New York Times*, October 11, 1906.

10. W. E. B. Du Bois, *Souls of Black Folk*, in *Three Negro Classics*, at 297, 347, 373 375-77.

11. W. E. B. Du Bois, *Crisis*, October 1916 at 270-71; Shapiro, at 91.

12. W. E. B. Du Bois, "Let Us Reason Together," *Crisis*, September 1919, at 231.

13. *Crisis*, October 1911, at 233.

14. *Crisis*, June 1912, at 64.

15. *Crisis*, August 1912, at 192.

16. *Crisis*, October 1911, at 233.

17. *Crisis* August 1913, at 179.

18. *Crisis*, July 1914, at 117.

19. Along the Color Line, *Crisis*, November 1913, at 323.

20. Along the Color Line, *Crisis*, March 1912, at 185.

21. Along the Color Line, *Crisis*, March 1912, at 189.

22. Along the Color Line, *Crisis*, March 1912, at 189.

23. Along the Color Line, *Crisis*, November 1913, at 324.

24. *Crisis*, November 1917, at 41.

25. *Crisis*, January 1918, at 115.

26. Mordecai Wyatt Johnson, "The Faith of the American Negro," *Crisis*, May 1921, at 161.

27. Walter F. White, "The Work of a Mob," *Crisis*, September 1918, at 221-223.

28. *Crisis*, May 1921, at 164.

29. W. E. B. Du Bois, Opinion, *Crisis*, May 1921, at 149.

30. Opinion of W. E. B., Du Bois, *Crisis*, January 1920, at 105-06.

31. George C. Wright, *Racial Violence in Kentucky, 1865–1940: Lynchings, Mob Rule, and "Legal Lynchings"* (1990) at 3, 147.

32. Ibid., at 9.

33. Ibid., at 15-17.

34. Ibid., at 185-186.

35. Ibid., at 187-189; *Commonwealth of Kentucky v. Tom Croe and Others* (1908).

36. Wright, at 188.

37. Neil R. McMillen, *Dark Journey, Black Mississippians in the Age of Jim Crow* (1990) at 225-226; *Meridian Star*, November 6, 1906; *Columbus Commercial*, November 13, 1906. Similar cases were reported in Liberty, Mississippi, and Gunnison. *Jackson Weekly Clarion Ledger*, April 18, 1907; *Jackson Daily Clarion Ledger*, February 12, 1911.

38. Kay Mills, *This Little Light of Mine: The Life of Fannie Lou Hamer* (1994) at 29-30; *Greenwood Enterprise*, February 12, 1904.

39. Horace Mann Bond, and Julia W. Bond, *The Star Creek Papers* (Adam Fairclough, ed., 1997) at 10, 141.

40. David T. Beito and Linda Royster Beito, *Black Maverick: T. R. M. Howard's Fight for Civil Rights and Economic Power* (2009) at 7.

41. Wright, at 189.

42. Nicholas J. Johnson, "Firearms and the Black Community: An Assessment of the Modern Orthodoxy," *Connecticut Law Review* (2013) Part III.

43. Wright, at 190.

44. Ibid., at 191.

45. Ibid., at 123, 140-142, 191-192.

46. Ibid., at 124-125.

47. Ibid., at 116, 124, 132, 136-138, 147.

48. Ibid., at 152; Letter from Edward M. Bacon to Walter White in the NAACP papers, May 19, 1932.

49. Douglas A. Blackmon, *Slavery by Another Name: The Re-Enslavement of Black Americans from the Civil War to World War II* (2008) at 1-2, 69, 79, 81-82.

50. Kevin Boyle, *Arc of Justice: A Saga of Race, Civil Rights, and Murder in the Jazz Age* (2004) at 89.

51. Linda O. McMurry, *To Keep the Waters Troubled: The Life of Ida B. Wells* (1998) at 314, 316.

52. McMurry, at 314, 316; Boyle, at 89.

53. Lindsey Cooper, Special Rep. of *Crisis*, "The Congressional Investigation of East St. Louis," *Crisis*, January 1918 at 115; Boyle, at 89; Elliott, "Race Riot at East St. Louis," *Crisis*, July 1917; McMurry, at 314-316.

54. McMurry, at 314-317.

55. *Franklin v. State of South Carolina*, 218 U.S. 161 (1910).

56. Kenneth W. Goings, *The NAACP Comes of Age* (1990) at 12.

57. Goings, at 12; *Crisis*, November 1910, at 14; McMurray, at 287; Paula J. Giddings, *Ida: A Sword among Lions: Ida B. Wells and the Campaign against Lynching* (2008) at 495.

58. Marvin Wolfgang, *Patterns in Criminal Homicide* (1958) at 84-88.

59. Vincent P. Mikkelsen, "Fighting for Sgt. Caldwell: The NAACP Campaign against Legal Lynching after World War I," *Journal of African American History* (2009) at 464-486; Shapiro, at 147-155.

60. Mikkelsen, "Fighting for Sgt. Caldwell," at 466; Vincent P. Mikkelsen, "Coming from Battle to Face a War: The Lynching of Black Soldiers in the World War One Era," PhD dissertation, Florida State University (2007); NAACP, *Thirty Years of Lynching: 1898–1918* (1919).

61. Mikkelsen, dissertation, at 477-78; *Crisis*, March 1920, at 233.

62. Mikkelsen, "Fighting for Sgt. Caldwell," at 41; *Crisis*, October 1920, at 282.

63. Hubert H. Harrison, *Baltimore Afro-American*, June 10, 1921; Shapiro, at 159; introduction to Hubert H. Harrison Papers, 1893-1927 MS# 1411, Columbia University.

64. 261 U.S. 86 (1923).

65. Goings, at 15.

66. *Moore v. Dempsey*, 261 U.S. 86 (1923).

67. Boyle, at 120.

68. Ibid., at 95.

69. Ibid., at 96.

70. John Lovell Junior, "Washington Fights," *Crisis*, September 1939 at 276-77; Herbert Aptheker, *Volume IV: Documentary History of the Negro People in the United States* (1960) 240-244; V. R. Daily, "Washington's Minority Problem," *Crisis*, June 1939, at 170, 171.

71. Edmund Kersten, *A. Philip Randolph: A Life in the Vanguard* (2006) at 21.

72. August Meier and Elliott Rudwick, *From Plantation to Ghetto* (1976) at 225-228.

73. Kersten, at 18.

74. A. Philip Randolph, "Lynching: Capitalism Its Cause, Socialism Its Cure," *Messenger*, March 1919 at 9-12; August Meier, Elliot Rudwick, and Francis L. Broderick, *Black Protest Thought in the Twentieth Century*, 2nd. ed. (1971) at 85-91.

75. Ibid.; Randolph, at 9-12; Meier, Rudwick, and Broderick, at 85-91.

76. Shapiro, at 171; "Lynching a Domestic Question," *Messenger*, July 1919 at 7-8.

77. Boyle, at 18, 118; "How to Stop Lynching," *Messenger*, August 1919, at 2.

78. Boyle, at 118.

79. "The Negro Must Now Organize All over the World, 400,000,000 Strong to Administer to Our Oppressors Their Waterloo," in Robert A. Hill, ed., *The Marcus Garvey and Universal Negro Improvement Association Papers* (1983) 41, 42, 120212-20, Univ. Ca. Press.

80. Hill, *Marcus Garvey Papers*, at 115-116. Garvey's views were still sufficiently immoderate that the movement was continuously the target of surveillance by British and American intelligence services and police. J. Edgar Hoover identified Garvey as an active radical and expressed regret that he had not yet violated any federal law that would allow his deportation. Finally, in 1927, Garvey was convicted of mail fraud. His sentence was commuted by Calvin Coolidge and he was then deported. Shapiro, at 166. See also Edward Peeks, *The Long Struggle for Black Power* (1971) at 192 (describing Garvey's meeting with Klan leaders).

81. Theodore G. Vincent, *Black Power and the Garvey Movement* (1971) at 19, 191-92. Garvey actually met with Edward Young Clark, imperial wizard of the Klan, and commented that it "will not help us to fight it or its program" because the solution was creation of a black government in Africa.

82. Kersten, at 21; Boyle, at 118.

CHAPTER 6: LEONIDAS

1. Kevin Boyle, *Arc of Justice: A Saga of Race, Civil Rights, and Murder in the Jazz Age* (2004) at 208.

2. Walter White, *A Man Called White* (1948) at 5-12.

3. Kenneth Janken, *White: The Biography of Walter White, Mr. NAACP* (2003) at 3-27.

4. Roy Wilkins, *Standing Fast: The Autobiography of Roy Wilkins* (1982) at 165.

5. Boyle, at 211; Walter White, *The Fire in the Flint* (1924) at 140-141.

6. Walter White, *Rope and Faggot* (1929) at 23-24, 29- 32.

7. Herbert Shapiro, *White Violence and Black Response: From Reconstruction to Montgomery* (1988) at 200; *Crisis*, January 1927 at 141-42.

8. Edward Peeks, *The Long Struggle for Black Power* (1971) at 170; Charles Flint Kellogg, *NAACP* Vol. 1 (1967) at 166.

9. White, *Rope and Faggot*, at 78-79.

10. White, *A Man Called White*, at 70.

11. *Williams v. State*, 122 Miss. 151, 165-167, 179.

12. 120 Miss. 604, 613.

13. *Byrd v. State*, 154 Miss. 747, 754.

14. Walter White, "'The Eruption of Tulsa,' an NAACP Official Investigates the Tulsa Race Riot of 1921," *Nation*, June 29, 1921, at 909–910.

15. Walter White, "Eruption in Tulsa; Resolution and Walter White Report on Tulsa" in NAACP board minutes, June 13, 1921, NAACP Papers, Library of Congress.

16. Scott Ellsworth, *Death in a Promised Land: The Tulsa Race Riot of 1921* (1982) at 48.

17. Walter White, *Eruption of Tulsa*; Ellsworth, at 50-51.

18. Ellsworth, at 52.

19. Ibid., at 3-7.

20. John Hope Franklin, foreword to Scott Ellsworth, *Death in a Promised Land: The Tulsa Race Riot of 1921* (1986) at xv-xvii.

21. Michael D'Orso, *Like Judgment Day: The True Story of the Rosewood Massacre and Its Aftermath* (1996) at 2-11.

22. Rosewood Massacre Report, Part Three, at 5-6.

23. Ibid., at 6.

24. Boyle, at 200.

25. Ibid., at 199; Emma Lou Thornbrough, *T. Thomas Fortune: Militant Journalist* (1972), at 69; James Weldon Johnson, *Along This Way: The Autobiography of James Weldon Johnson* (1933) at 48.

26. Paula J. Giddings, *Ida: A Sword among Lions: Ida B. Wells and the Campaign against Lynching* (2009) at 215; August Meier, *Negro Thought in America* (1963) at 79.

27. Phyllis Vine, *One Man's Castle, Clarence Darrow in Defense of the American Dream* (2004) at 123-24.

28. Boyle, at 73; David Levering Lewis, *Du Bois: Biography of a Race: 1868–1919* (1993) at 151-152.

29. Boyle, at 15 23-27, 67-68, 87, 137, 162; "Posse Chases Man Believed to Be One of Four Who Threatened Colored Farmer," *Xenia Gazette*, October 13, 1924; "Martin Gets Rest While Armed Men Guard Premises," *Xenia Gazette*, October 15, 1924.

30. Boyle, at 4, 8, 24.

31. Ibid., at 119; Vine, at 59.

32. Boyle, at 17, 24- 29, 145-146, 153-157.

33. Ibid., at, 29-37, 99, 151-153.

34. Ibid., at 154-155, 181, 187; "Negroes Shoot a White Youth in New Home Row," *Detroit Free Press*, July 11, 1925; Shapiro, at 187.

35. Boyle, at 163, 194, 205-206, 220, 224, 228, 257; Vine, at 144.

36. "What's Wrong In Detroit?" *Chicago Defender*, September 19, 1925; Boyle, at 203, 219, 245, 307.

37. Boyle, at 245-246; "The Retention of Clarence Darrow," *Washington Daily American*, October 19, 1925; "We Must Fight If We Would Survive," *Amsterdam News*, November 18, 1925.

38. Boyle, at 221, 247, 305.

39. Ibid., at 220, 242; "Law for Whites and Negroes," *New York World*, reprinted in *Chicago Defender*, October 31, 1925.

40. Boyle, at 290, 299; Vine, at 235.

41. Ibid., at 294.

42. Ibid., at 305-306.

43. Vine, at 112, 228.

44. "Baby of Dr. Sweet Dies in Arizona," Chicago Defender, August 28, 1926; Elaine Lataman Moon, *Untold Tales, Unsung Heroes: An Oral History of Detroit's African-American Community: 1918–1967* (1994) at 83.

45. Moon, at 83 (italics added).

46. "Bullet Is Fatal to Negro Doctor, Slay Case Figure," *Detroit Free Press*, March 20, 1960; Boyle, at 346.

CHAPTER 7: FREEDOM FIGHT

1. Roy Wilkins, "Two against 5,000," *Crisis*, June 1936 at 169-170 reprinted in Herbert Aptheker, 4 *Documentary History of the Negro People in the United States* (1974) at 240-244.

2. Wilkins, "Two against 5,000," at 169-170.

3. Horace Mann Bond and Julia Bond, *The Star Creek Papers* (1997) at 123-124; Lance Hill, *The Deacons for Defense: Armed Resistance and the Civil Rights Movement* (2004) at 129.

4. Herbert Shapiro, *White Violence and Black Response: From Reconstruction to Montgomery* (1988) at 226-228, 306-307; Roi Ottley, *"New World A-Coming": Inside Black America* (1969) at 312-314.

5. Roy Wilkins, *Standing Fast: The Autobiography of Roy Wilkins* (1982) at 187.

6. "People's Voice," *Crisis*, March 9, 1946; Editorial, *Crisis*, April 1946, at 105. Wilkins, *Standing Fast*, at 188.

7. Harry Raymond, *Daily Worker*, November 20, 1946; Wilkins, *Standing Fast*, at 187-188. The episode also fostered alliances with progressives. The event prompted the formation of a National Committee for Justice in Columbia, Tennessee, organized by Eleanor Roosevelt and a variety of notable supporters.

8. "Dr. Howard's Safari Room," *Ebony*, October 1969, at 133, 138.

9. David T. Beito and Linda Royster Beito, *Black Maverick: T. R. M. Howard's Fight for Civil Rights and Economic Power* (2009) at 13, 45-46. David T. Beito and Linda Royster Beito, "Blacks, Gun Cultures, and Gun Control: T. R. M. Howard, Armed Self-Defense, and

the Struggle for Civil Rights in Mississippi," *Journal of Firearms and Public Policy* (September 2005).

10. Beito, *Black Maverick*, at xii, 19; "Alabamans Kill Two More Negroes," *New York Times*, July 7, 1930; T. R. M. Howard, "The Negro in the Light of History," *California Eagle*, September 8, 1933.

11. Beito, *Black Maverick*, at 103.

12. "Head of Greenville South Carolina NAACP Is Arrested," *Crisis*, January 1940, at 20.

13. Beito, *Black Maverick*, at 67-68, 136; "An Enemy of His Race," *Jackson Daily News*, October 15, 1955, at 6; Sullens, "Low Down on the Higher Ups," *Jackson Daily News*; "Howard's Poison Tongue," *Jackson Daily News*, October 25, 1955, at 8.

14. Beito, *Black Maverick*, at 108-109, xiii.

15. Akinyele Omowale Umoja, *We Will Shoot Back: Armed Resistance in the Mississippi Freedom Movement* (2013) at 36.

16. Beito, *Black Maverick*, at 138.

17. Rosa Parks and Jim Haskins, *Rosa Parks, My Story* (1992) at 30-33, 67.

18. Parks, at 66- 67.

19. Ibid., at 161.

20. Constance Baker Motley, *Equal Justice under Law: An Autobiography* (1998) at 121-23.

21. E. Culpepper Clark, *The Schoolhouse Door: Segregation's Last Stand at the University of Alabama* (1993) at 57, 71-77; Simon Wendt, *The Spirit and the Shotgun: Armed Resistance and the Struggle for Civil Rights* (2007) at 44.

22. Andrew Michael Manis, *A Fire You Can't Put Out: The Civil Rights Life of Birmingham's Reverend Fred Shuttlesworth* (1990) at 110, 117-18, 169-170.

23. Howell Raines, *My Soul Is Rested: The Story of the Civil Rights Movement in the Deep South* (1977) at 115.

24. Rains, *Soul*, at 141 (italics added).

25. Austry Kirklin, in *Youth of the Rural Organizing Cultural Center, Their Minds Stayed on Freedom: The Civil Rights Struggle in the Rural South, an Oral History* (1991) at 57, 71-77; T. C. Johnson, in *Youth of the Rural Organizing Cultural Center*, at 153.

26. Christopher Strain, "Civil Rights and Self-Defense: The Fiction of Nonviolence, 1955-1968," PhD dissertation, University of California, Berkeley (2000); Coretta Scott King, *My Life with Martin Luther King, Jr.* (1969) at 226; Wendt, *Spirit*, at 39; Condoleezza Rice, *Extraordinary, Ordinary People: A Memoir of Family* (2010) at 92; Diane McWhorter, *Carry Me Home: Birmingham, Alabama—The Climatic Battle of the Civil Rights Revolution* (2001) at 118; George Lavan, "Armed Birmingham Negroes Conduct Own Safety Patrols," *Militant*, September 23, 1963 at 1, 5; Glenn T. Eskew, *But for Birmingham: The Local and National Movements in the Civil Rights Struggle* (1997) at 322.

27. Rice, at 92.

28. Ben Allen in, Raines, *Soul*, at 167-168.

29. Rice, at 13, 92-93; interview by Larry King with Condoleezza Rice, CNN, May 11, 2005.

30. Rains, *Soul*, at 200, 202, 348.

31. Wilson Baker in, Raines, *Soul*, at 202-203.

32. The story was made into a film starring Forest Whitaker, *Deacons for Defense* (Showtime 2003).

33. Wendt, *Spirit*, at 119; Akinyele Omowale Umoja, "Eye for and Eye: the Role of Armed Resistance in the Mississippi Freedom Movement," PhD dissertation, Emory (1996) at 156-158; John Dittmer, *Local People: The Struggle for Civil Rights in Mississippi* (1995) at 266-268, 304.

34. Umoja, "Eye," at 159, 160.

35. Wendt, *Spirit*, at 189; Interview with Gloria Richardson, *Newsweek*, August 5, 1963 at 26.

36. SNCC was the common name of the Student Nonviolent Coordinating Committee. The group was generally referred to by the acronym, which was pronounced "Snick." SNCC grew substantially out of the efforts of Ella Baker to establish a youth arm of the Southern Christian Leadership Conference, commonly called SCLC. See Joanne Grant, *Ella Baker: Freedom Bound* (1998) at 128-130.

37. Cleveland Sellers, *The River of No Return: The Autobiography of a Black Militant and the Life and Death of SNCC* (1973) 67-69.

38. Simon Wendt, *Spirit*, at 187-88.

39. Charles Evers, *Have No Fear: The Charles Evers Story* (1997) at 171; Akinyele O. Umoja, "We Will Shoot Back: The Natchez Model and Paramilitary Organization in the Mississippi Freedom Movement," 32 *J. Black Studies* (2002) at 271, 277.

40. Wendt, *Spirit*, at 128.

41. Ibid., at 42-65.

42. David J. Garrow, *Bearing the Cross: Martin Luther King, Jr., and the Southern Christian Leadership Conference* (1988) at 316-34; David R. Colburn, *Racial Change and Community Crisis: St. Augustine Florida, 1877–1980* (1985) at 50-55, 316-34; Edward W. Kallal, "St. Augustine and the Ku Klux Klan," in *St. Augustine, Florida 1963–1964: Mass Protest and Racial Violence* (1989) 93-176.

43. Daisy Bates, *The Long Shadow of Little Rock: A Memoir* (1962) at 94-96, 111, 162; Grif Stockley, *Daisy Bates: Civil Rights Crusader from Arkansas* (2005) at 24, 27, 186-188.

44. Timothy B. Tyson, *Radio Free Dixie: Robert F. Williams and the Roots of Black Power* (1999) at 57.

45. Stockley, at 132.

46. Bates, at 96, 158-159, 174.

47. Stockley, at 186.

48. Tyson, *Radio Free*, at 159.

49. Stockley, at 186-187.

50. Tyson, *Radio Free*, at 159.

51. *Ark. State Press*, May 23, 1959; Tyson, *Radio Free*, at 163-164.

52. Tyson, *Radio Free*, at 164.

53. Strain, "Civil Rights," at 35; W. E. B. Du Bois, "Martin Luther King's Life 'Crusader Without Violence,'" 12 *National Guardian* (November 9, 1959) at 8.

54. Tyson, *Radio Free*, at 165.

55. Stockley, at 195.

56. Kay Mills, *This Little Light of Mine: The Life of Fannie Lou Hamer* (1993) at 39.

57. Mills, at 9.

58. Evers, at 119.

59. Wendt, *Spirit*, at 121; Charles Payne, *I've Got the Light of Freedom: The Organizing Tradition and the Mississippi Freedom Struggle* (1995) at 233; Chana Kai Lee, *For Freedom's Sake: The Life of Fannie Lou Hamer* (1999) at 9, 11. (Italics added).

60. Fannie Lou Hamer, "To Praise Our Bridges," in 2 *Mississippi Writers: Reflections of Childhood and Youth* (1986) at 321-330; Mills, at 101.

61. Mills, at 101; Hamer, "Praise," at 321-30.

62. Umoja, "Eye," at 68-69.

63. Mills, at 11-12; Hamer, "Praise," at 322-323; Umoja, *We Will Shoot Back* (2013) at 19-20 (reporting the story of Joe "Pullen").

64. Umoja, *We Will Shoot Back* (2013) at 19-20; Mary G. Rolinson, *Grassroots Garveyism: The Universal Negro Improvement Association in the Rural South, 1920–1927* (2007) at 135.

65. T. C. Johnson, in *Youth of the Rural Organizing Cultural Center*, at 154-56.

66. Aaron Henry, *The Fire Ever Burning* (2000) at 150.

67. Evers, at 1-2; Payne, *Light of Freedom*, at 48.

68. Evers, at 16-17.

69. Ibid., at, 47, 49-53, 55, 126. In 1962, the two brothers bought forty acres of land north of Brasilia. They dreamed of building two big houses there and living in the easy peace of a place where they imagined the color line was less acute.

70. Ibid., at 59-60.

71. Ibid., at 64.

72. Ibid., at 62-64, 73.

73. Wilkins, *Standing Fast*, at 14-16, 72, 317.

74. Evers, at 76.

75. Ibid., at 90-96, 104.

76. Ibid., at 194.

77. Ibid., at 106, 129-130; Umoja, "Eye," at 78-80, 171, 178-179; Payne, *Light of Freedom*, at 288.

78. Howell Raines, *My Soul Is Rested: Movement Days in the Deep South Remembered* (1977) at 251-52.

79. Interview with Myrlie Evers in *Voices of Freedom: An Oral History of the Civil Rights Movement from the 1950s through the 1980s* (Henry Hampton and Steve Fayer eds., 1990) at 152; interview with Myrlie Evers, at Eyes on the Prize Interviews, http://digital.wustl.edu/e/eop/eopweb/eve0015.0753.036myrlieevers.html, last accessed September 27, 2013.

80. Umoja, "Eye," at 79; Adam Nossiter, *Of Long Memory: Mississippi and the Murder of Medgar Evers* (1994) at 48, 61; Payne, *Light of Freedom* at 287.

81. Evers, at 117 (italics added).

82. Rains, *Soul*, at 271; John R. Salter, *Jackson, Mississippi: An American Chronicle of Struggle and Schism* (1979) at 24.

83. Quote from "United Liberty: The Unseen in the Gun Debate," at http://www.united liberty.org/articles/10758-the-unseen-in-the-gun-debate, last accessed September 27, 2013. Professor Salter subsequently collaborated with Don B. Kates on a scholarly article titled "The Necessity of Access to Firearms by Dissenters and Minorities Who Government Is Unwilling or Unable to Protect." The collaboration was fueled by their common experience. Kates went south in 1963, the summer after his first year at Yale Law School, in the employ of the Law Student Civil Rights Research Council to work under William Kunstler, who was collaborating on cases with black lawyers in Raleigh.

Traveling into what he describes as "KKK country," Kates carried a Smith & Wesson Chiefs Special in a holster, a Colt Trooper .357 Magnum under the seat, and a semiautomatic M1 carbine rifle in the trunk. These were obviously more guns than he could use at one time, but the tactic made sense on at least one occasion when he was part of a group that stood watch at the rural homestead of a black woman who had been threatened for joining as a plaintiff in several of the local cases that Kunstler was pressing. Interview with Don B. Kates, April 23, 2013. Don Kates would go on to produce an unparalleled body of Second Amendment scholarship and contribute centrally to the Supreme Court's affirmation and elaboration of that right in seminal cases in 2008 and 2010.

84. Wendt, *Spirit*, at 191.

85. Evers, *Have No Fear*. Compare the modern response of NRA board member Roy Innis (who lost a son to gun violence) to Pete Shields, founder of Handgun Control Inc. (who also lost a son to gun violence). Innis followed the Charles Evers approach. Shields and many others in the modern era put their energy into gun control.

86. Robert Penn Warren, *Who Speaks for the Negro* (1965) at 105.

87. Wendt, *Spirit*, at 127; *New York Post*, September 2, 1965.

88. Roy Wilkins to Charles Evers, Wilkins Papers, Sep. 3, 1965, box 7, folder "1965."

89. Simon Wendt suggests Wilkins demurred in recognition of his waning power. Wendt, *Spirit*, at 128.

90. Robert W. Hartley, "A Long Hot Summer: The St. Augustine Racial Disorders of 1964 in St. Augustine, Florida, 1963–1964: Mass Protest and Racial Violence" (David J. Garrow ed. 1989) at 21.

91. Garrow, *Bearing the Cross*, at 317-34; David R. Colburn, *Racial Change and Community Crisis: St. Augustine, Florida 1877–1980* (1985) at 84-89, 212.

92. Richard Kluger, *Simple Justice: The History of* Brown v. Board of Ed. *and Black America's Struggle for Equality* (1976) at 3.

93. Tracy Sugarman, *Stranger at the Gates: A Summer in Mississippi* (1966) at 21, 75; Umoja, "Eye," at 94; Charles Payne, *Light of Freedom*, at 44.

94. Henry, at 154-155.

95. Evers, at 137, 147.

96. Dittmer, *Local People*, at 47.

97. Strain, "Civil Rights," at 76-77; *Baltimore Afro-American*, September 15, 1962, at 1.

98. CORE is an acronym for Congress of Racial Equality.

99. Doug McAdam, *Freedom Summer* (1988) at 21, 90; Wendt, *Souls*, at 324; *Tuscaloosa News*, February 20, 2000.

100. Leola Blackmon, in *Youth of the Rural Organizing Cultural Center*, at 166-67, 174-75. The word *mens*, which appears twice, is from the original oral history.

101. Shadrach Davis, in *Youth of the Rural Organizing Cultural Center*, at 21; Umoja, "Eye," at 112; Wendt, *Spirit*, at 100; *Rains*, Soul, at 262-265; Studs Terkel, *American Dreams Lost and Found* (1980) at 192-200.

102. Reverend J. J. Russell, in *Youth of the Rural Organizing and Cultural Center*, at 25; Umoja, "Eye," at 112- 113.

103. Charles E. Cobb Jr., *On the Road to Freedom: A Guided Tour of the Civil Rights Trail* (2008) at 302; Clayborne Carson, *In Struggle: SNCC and the Black Awakening of the 1960s* (1995) at 89; Turnbow's statement to Charles Cobb in Cobb, *Road to Freedom*, at 302. (Italics added.)

104. Wendt, *Spirit*, at 118; Rains, *Soul*, at 266; Studs Terkel, "Hartman Turnbow: The Diploma," in *American Dreams Lost and Found* (1980) at 192.

105. Raines, *Soul*, at 265.

106. Robert Cooper, in *Youth of the Rural Organizing Cultural Center*, at 93-94.

107. Hill, *Deacons*, at 104; *Tuscaloosa News*, February 20, 2000 (Bolden interview).

108. Joanne Grant, *Ella Baker: Freedom Bound* (1998) at 173.

109. Dittmer, *Local People*, at 286.

110. Raines, *Soul*, at 267.

111. James Forman, *The Making of Black Revolutionaries* (1985) at 376.

112. Raines, *Soul*, at 267.

113. Dittmer, *Local People*, at 254.

114. Vanderbilt Roby, in *Youth of the Rural Organizing Cultural Center*, at 55.

115. Bee Jenkins, in *Youth of the Rural Organizing Cultural Center*, at 139.

116. Anger Winson Gates Hudson was commonly known as Winson Hudson. References here are to Winson Hudson or Hudson or Winson.

117. Winson Hudson, *Mississippi Harmony: Memoirs of a Freedom Fighter* (2002) at 8-9.

118. Hudson, at 58-59.

119. Ibid.

120. Hudson, *Harmony*, at 2, 51-52, 58- 59, 88.

121. Dittmer, *Local People*; Barbara Summers, *I Dream A World: Portraits of Black Women Who Changed America* (1989) at 160.

122. Hudson, *Harmony*, at 77.

123. Alice Lake, "Last Summer in Mississippi," *Redbook Magazine*, November 1964, reprinted in *Library of America, Reporting Civil Rights: American Journalism, 1963–1973* (2003) at 112.

124. Wendt, *Spirit*, at 120.

125. Hudson, *Harmony*, at 28.

126. John Lewis, *Walking with the Wind: A Memoir of the Movement* (1998) at 48-49.

127. Wendt, *Spirit*, at 111, 113; Lewis, *Walking*, at 254-55.

128. Wendt, *Spirit*, at 123; "Shocking Notes on Mississippi Brutality," *Jet*, July 2, 1964 at 6.

129. James Forman, *The Making of Black Revolutionaries* (1972) at 375; Doug McAdam, *Freedom Summer* (1988) at 32; Claiborne Carson, *In the Struggle: SNCC and the Black Awakening of the 1960s* (1995) at 123; Nicholas von Hoffman, *Mississippi Notebook* (1964) at 95.

130. Lewis, *Walking*, at 188-201; Wendt, *Spirit*, at 124; William Sales, *From Civil Rights to Black Liberation: Malcolm X and the Organization of Afro-American Unity* (1994) at 107.

131. Godfrey Hodgson, *America in Our Time* (1976) at 212.

132. Wendt, *Spirit*, at 123-124; Rustin, "Nonviolence on Trial," *Fellowship Magazine* (July 1964) at 5.

133. SCLC (pronounced "S Cee L Cee") is the common reference to the Southern Christian Leadership Conference.

134. Emily Stoper, *The Student Nonviolent Coordinating Committee: The Growth of Radicalism in a Civil Rights Organization* (1989) at 29.

135. Wendt, *Spirit*, at 117; Florence Mars, *Witness in Philadelphia* (1977) at 114, 210; Cleveland Sellers, *The River of No Return: The Autobiography of a Black Militant and the Life and Death of SNCC* (1973) at 88, 90, 210.

136. Strain, "Civil Rights, at 155-156.

137. Lake, "Last Summer," at 113.

138. Wendt, *Spirit*, at 112; Mary King, *Freedom Song: A Personal Story of the 1960s Civil Rights Movement* (1987) at 318.

139. King, *Freedom Song*, at 318.

140. Wendt, *Spirit*, at 109; *Baltimore Afro-American*, March 6, 1965; Umoja, "Eye," at 100.

141. Rains, *Soul*, at 380; Payne, *Light of Freedom*, at 121; Umoja, *We Will Shoot Back* (2013) at 59.

142. Umoja, "Eye," at 103-104.

143. Dittmer, *Local People*, at 150-151; Foreman, *Black Revolutionaries*, at 296; Payne, *Light of Freedom*, at 168-169.

144. Payne, *Light of Freedom*, at 208-209.

145. Ibid., at 213-214; Doug McAdam, *Freedom Summer* (1988) at 279.

146. Austry Kirklin, in *Youth of the Rural Organizing Cultural Center*, at 39.

147. Evers, at 216.

148. Sugarman, *Stranger*, at 75.

149. Tyson, *Radio Free*, at 251-252.

150. Ibid., at 193, 240, 250-255.

151. Ibid., at 259.

152. Ibid., at 271-272.

153. Ibid., at 256-270.

154. Ibid., at 278-285; Strain, "Civil Rights," at 64.

155. Wilkins, *Standing Fast*, at 225-227; Andrew Young, in Raines, *Soul*, at 425.

156. Raines, *Soul*, at 38. (The reference to insurance "mens" is in the original.)

157. Ibid., at 38, 48-49; Wilkins, *Standing Fast*, at 227.

158. Stephen B. Oates, *Let The Trumpet Sound: A Life of Martin Luther King*, at 89-90; Strain, "Civil Rights," at 6.

159. Oates, at 90.

160. Martin Luther King Jr., *Stride toward Freedom: The Montgomery Story* (1959) at 131; Garrow, *Bearing the Cross*, at 60-62; Wendt, *Spirit*, at 8.

161. Strain, "Civil Rights," at 7-8; Nicholas J. Johnson, "A Second Amendment Moment: The Constitutional Politics of Gun Control," 71 *Brooklyn L. Rev.* 715-796 (2005).

162. Wendt, *Spirit*, at 9; Garrow, *Bearing the Cross*, at 62; Wilkins, *Standing Fast*, at 229.

163. Wendt, *Spirit*, at 9; Bayard Rustin, "Montgomery Diary," 1 *Liberation* April 1956, at 7-8; Raines, *Soul*, at 53; Adam Fairclough, *To Redeem the Soul of America: The Southern Christian Leadership Conference and Martin Luther King, Jr.* (1995) at 25.

164. Stewart Burns, *Day Break of Freedom: The Montgomery Bus Boycott* (1997) at 22-23 (italics added).

165. Wendt, *Sprit*, at 24; Raines, *Soul*, at 53; Fairclough, *Redeem the Soul of America*, at 25.

166. Wilkins, *Standing Fast*, at 260, 326.

167. Simone Wendt, "Urge People Not to Carry Guns: Armed Self Defense in the Louisiana Civil Rights Movement and the Radicalization of the Congress of Racial Equality," 45 *Journal of the Louisiana Historical Association*, 261-286 (2004) at 281.

168. Roy Reed, "Meredith Regrets He Was Not Armed," *New York Times*, June 8, 1966; James H. Meredith, "Big Changes Are Coming," *Saturday Evening Post*, August 13, 1966, at 23-27; Wendt, *Spirit*, at 13; "He Shot Me Like . . . a God Damn Rabbit," *Newsweek*, June 20, 1966, at 30.

169. Chester Higgins, "Meredith's Threat to Arm Not Answer, Says Dr. King," *Jet* June 23, 1966, at 17.

170.   Cleveland Sellers, in Hampton and Fayer, *Voices of Freedom*, at 284-286.

171.   Hill, *Deacons*, at 246; Garrow, *Bearing the Cross*, at 477; Oates, *Let the Trumpet Sound*, at 397-398; Sellers, *River of No Return*, at 162.

172.   Hampton and Fayer, *Voices of Freedom*, at 287.

173.   Evers, at 214.

174.   Hill, *Deacons*, at 246; Garrow, *Bearing the Cross*, at 477; Oates, *Let the Trumpet Sound*, at 397-398, Sellers, *River of No Return*, at 162, 166; Raines, *Soul*, at 422; Hampton and Fayer, *Voices of Freedom*, at 281-295.

175.   Strain, "Civil Rights," at 137; "Marchers Upset by Apathy," *New York Times*, June 14, 1966, at 19.

176.   Wendt, *Spirit*, at 137; *New York Times*, June 14, 1966; "Earnest Thomas, Deacons," *New York Times*, June 10, 1966; Hill, *Deacons*, at 10.

177.   Wendt, "Urge the People," at 280; Margaret Long, "Black Power in the Black Belt," *Progressive*, October 1966, at 21.

178.   *New York Times*, June 21, 1966; Martin Luther King Jr., *Where Do We Go from Here: Chaos or Community?* (1967) at 30; Joanne Grant says that SNCC staffer Willie Ricks was actually the first to shout the phrase from the crowd and Carmichael took it from there. Joanne Grant, *Ella Baker: Freedom Bound* (1998) at 193; Dittmer, *Local People*, at 396.

179.   Wendt, "Urge the People," at 280; interview with James Farmer, WABC-TV, April 25, 1965 (CORE Papers); Hill, *Deacons*, at 17. (Italics added.)

180.   Wendt, "Urge the People," at 280.

181.   Strain, "Civil Rights," at 125; James Farmer, "Deacons for Defense," *Amsterdam News*, July 1965, at 15.

182.   James J. Farmer, "A Night of Terror in Plaquemine, Louisiana" (1963), reprinted in Henry Steele Commager, *The Struggle for Racial Equality* (1972) at 134-144.

183.   Wendt, *Spirit*, at 109; Anne Moody, *Coming of Age in Mississippi* (1968) at 303, 331.

184.   Moody, at 333-365.

185.   Wendt, "Urge People," at 277-278; Strain, "Civil Rights," at 199; Fred Powerledge, *Free at Last? The Civil Rights Movement and the People Who Made It* (1991) at 573; Wendt, *Spirit*, at 140; Neil A. Maxwell, "Militancy on the March," *Wall Street Journal*, June 24, 1966.

186.   Wendt, "Urge People," at 279-282.

187.   Ibid., at 279; James Farmer, *Freedom When?* (1965) at 65.

188.   Ibid., at 281-85; Tyson, *Radio Free*, at 290-91; Lester A. Sobel, *Civil Rights 1960–66* (1967) at 376.

189.   Wendt, *Spirit*, at 141; *New York Times*, June 10, 1966. Harlem branch president and future CORE chairman Roy Innis would lose a son to gun violence and serve on the board of directors of the National Rifle Association.

190.   Wendt, *Spirit*, at 141.

191.   Hill, *Deacons*, at 2, 134-135.

192. Ibid., at 25, 35-39, 43-45; Wendt, *Spirit*, at 142.

193. Ibid., at 40.

194. Ibid., at 45, 50, 55.

195. Ibid., at 56-57, 62; *New York Times*, February 21, 1965.

196. Hill, *Deacons*, at 76-77.

197. Ibid., at 69, 108- 109.

198. Ibid., at 109.

199. Ibid., at 93-94, 109-110.

200. Raines, *Soul*, at 418; Hill, *Deacons*, at 97- 98, 105, 107.

201. *New York Post*, April 8, 1965; "Bogalusa Riflemen Fight off KKK Attack," *Jet*, April 22, 1965, at 5; Hill, *Deacons*, at 118-119.

202. Hill, *Deacons*, at 119, 128; *Louisiana Weekly*, May 30, 1965; *Bogalusa Daily News*, May 24, 1965.

203. Hill, *Deacons*, at 133; *New York Times*, June 6, 1965; Strain, "Civil Rights," at 121; Grant, *Black Protest*, at 358; "Deacons Organize Chicago Chapter," *New York Times*, April 6, 1966 at 29.

204. Strain, "Civil Rights," at 141; Grant, *Black Protest*, at 361. For nonshooting defensive gun uses, see chapter 9.

205. Strain, "Civil Rights," at 126; Fred L. Zimmerman, "Race and Violence: More Dixie Negroes Buy Arms to Retaliate against White Attacks," *Wall Street Journal*, July 12, 1965, at 1, 15.

206. Hill, *Deacons*, at 134-135; *Los Angeles Times*, June 13, 1965.

207. Shana Alexander, "Visit Bogalusa and You Will Look for Me," *Life*, July 2, 1965 at 28.

208. Hill, *Deacons*, at 138-139.

209. Ibid., at 136-138.

210. "CORE Shifts to Politics: Tackles Media Money Problem," *Jet*, July 1965, at 8-9; Hill, *Deacons*, at 140-142.

211. Zimmerman, "Race and Violence"; Hill, *Deacons*, at 142-143. Lance Hill conducted numerous personal interviews of Deacons members in his definitive work on the group. Hill reports that Henry Austin was not prosecuted for the shooting of Alton Crowe. Local authorities, anxious to avoid further confrontation, apparently determined not to prosecute Austin if he would leave town. Austin shows up in New Orleans shortly after the shooting and remained active in the Deacons chapter there. Hill, *Deacons*, at 213, 220, 240, 253. Communications with Lance Hill, July 2013.

212. Hill, *Deacons*, at 144.

213. "Investigative Report, Deacons for Defense and Justice," November 22, 1966, FBI Files citied in Hill, *Deacons*, at 144, 231-232; *Louisiana Weekly*, July 17, 1965; Hill, *Deacons*, at 144, 231-232.

214. "The Deacons," *Newsweek*, August 2, 1965, at 28-29; Louis Robinson and Charles Brown, "Negro Most Feared by Whites," *Jet*, July 15, 1965, at 14-17.

215. "Guns, Pickets Down: Talks Begin in Bogalusa Racial Crisis," *Jet*, June 24, 1965; "Bogalusa Riflemen Fight off KKK Attack," *Jet*, April 22, 1965, at 5; "Denied Deacons Shot Bogalusa White Youth," *Jet*, July 22, 1965, at 5; *New Orleans Times Picayune*, July 15, 1965; *Bogalusa Daily News*, July 15, 1965; Hill, *Deacons*, at 149, 167.

216. Hill, *Deacons*, at 193.

217. Ibid., at 211, 218-224; *New York Times*, September 5, 1967.

CHAPTER 8: PIVOT

1. Maynard Holbrook Jackson Jr., "Handgun Control: Constitutional and Critically Needed," 8 *N. C. Cent. L. J.* (1976) at 189; *District of Columbia v. Heller*, 554 U.S. 570 (2008).

2. Roy Wilkins, *The Autobiography of Roy Wilkins: Standing Fast* (1963) at 341; Robert Sherrill, *The Saturday Night Special* (1975) at 23; *Kellogg v. City of Gary*, 562 N.E.2d 685, 688 (Ind. 1990). Rep. Major Owens (D–Brooklyn, NY) proposed repeal of the Second Amendment at 102d Cong. 2nd Sess., H.J. Res. 438; 139 Cong. Rec. H9088 at H9094, Nov. 10, 1993; Illinois congressman Bobby Rush proposed gun confiscation at Evan Osnos, "Bobby Rush; Democrat, U.S. House of Representatives," *Chicago Tribune*, December 5, 1999; *Archer v. Arms Technology* 669 N.W.2d 845, 854–55 (Mich. Ct. App. 2003).

3. "Rev. Jesse Jackson Arrested at Gun Shop Protest," Associated Press, Sunday, June 24, 2007; *NAACP v. AccuSport, Inc.*; Michael B. de Leeuw, "Ready, Aim, Fire? *District of Columbia v. Heller* and Communities of Color," *Harv. Blackletter L. J.* (2009) at 133, 137.

4. Doug McAdam, *Freedom Summer* (1988) at 90; Doug McAdam, *Political Process and the Development of Black Insurgency* (1982) at 153-154, 183-185.

5. Akinyele O. Umoja, "The Ballot and the Bullet: A Comparative Analysis of Armed Resistance in the Civil Rights Movement," 29 *Journal of Black Studies* (1999) at 558, 568.

6. Ibid., at 568.

7. Michael Levine, *African Americans and Civil Rights: From 1619 to the Present* (1996) at 198-208. See also Umoja, at 563.

8. Doug McAdam, *Political Process and the Development of Black Insurgency* (1982) at 183. "We Love Everybody Who Loves Us," youtube.com/watch?v=Cz3isgUZe5Y, uploaded April 9, 2007, by "Malcolm X," http://malcolmxfiles.blogspot.com/; "The Complete Malcolm X."

9. This conflation was evident in Malcolm X's declaration that "the biggest criminal against whom Blacks need to defend themselves [was] Uncle Sam." Ultimate assessment of Malcolm X is complicated by the evident shift in his outlook after his pilgrimage to Mecca. After a fiery speech in Selma, Alabama, Malcolm whispered to Coretta King, "will you tell Dr. King that I'm sorry I won't get to see him? I had planned to visit him in jail, but I have to leave. I want him to know that I didn't come to make his job more difficult. I thought that if the white people understood what the alternative was, that they would be willing to listen to Dr. King." Henry Hampton

and Steve Fayer, *Voices of Freedom: An Oral History of the Civil Rights Movement from the 1950s through the 1980s* (1990) at 221-222.

10. Simon Wendt, "The New Black Power History, Protection or Path Toward Revolution? Black Power and Self-Defense," *Souls*, October-December 2007, at 320, 328.

11. Hampton and Fayer, *Voices of Freedom*, at 327-328, 515- 516.

12. Strain, "Civil Rights & Self-Defense: The Fiction of Nonviolence, 1955–1968," PhD dissertation, University of California, Berkley (2000) at 164; Bobby Seale, *Seize the Time: The Story of the Black Panther Party and Huey P. Newton* (1968) at 71, 116-117.

13. Strain, "Civil Rights," at 172; Don Cox, in "The Black Panther Party: Its Origin and Development as Reflected in Its Official Weekly Newspaper *The Black Panther Black Community News Service*," Staff Study by the Committee on Internal Security, U.S. Congress, House of Representatives, 91st Congress, Second Session, October 6, 1971 at page 26.

14. Kenneth O'Reily, *Racial Matters: The FBI's Secret File on Black America, 1960–1972* (1989) at 321.

15. Wilkins, *Standing Fast*, at 325; Strain, "Civil Rights," at 215.

16. Hugh Pearson, *The Shadow of the Panther: Huey Newton and the Price of Black Power in America* (1994).

17. Wilkins, *Standing Fast*, at 314; Hampton and Fayer, *Voices of Freedom*, at 298.

18. Some people who were there say it was SNCC staffer Willie Ricks who said it first, but one account indicates that it was already sufficiently in use that to Ricks's shouted question "What do you want?" the crowd was already primed to demand "Black Power!" Joanne Grant, *Ella Baker: Freedom Bound* (1999) at 193.

19. *Meet the Press* transcript, August 21, 1966, at 10- 26.

20. Wendt, *Spirit*, at 145; Herbert Haines, *Black Radicals and the Civil Rights Mainstream 1954–1970* (1988) at 84; Manfred Berg, "Black Power: The National Association for the Advancement of Colored People and the Resurgence of Black Nationalism during the 1960s," in *The American Nation-National Identity-Nationalism* (Knud Krakau, ed., 1997) at 235-262. ("Almost quadrupling its income between 1966 and 1968, the NAACP undoubtedly benefited from its adamant opposition to the new slogan.") Id. at 239.

21. Wilkins, *Standing Fast*, at 316.

22. Ibid., at 317.

23. Roy Wilkins, "Whither Black Power," *Crisis*, August-September, 1966, at 353- 354; Wendt, *Spirit*, at 141-146.

24. Wendt, *Spirit*, at 144; Martin Luther King Jr., *Where Do We Go From Here: Chaos or Community?* (1967) at 54; David Garrow, *Bearing the Cross: Martin Luther King, Jr., and the Southern Christian Leadership Conference* (2004) at 490.

25. Juan Williams, *Thurgood Marshall: American Revolutionary* (1998) at 334.

26. Sherrill, at 283-295; Nicholas J. Johnson et al., *Firearms Law and the Second Amendment: Regulation, Rights, and Policy* (2012) at 731.

27. *Meet the Press*, Sunday, July 16, 1967, at 9; Sherrill, at 283-295.

28. Michael L. Levine, *African Americans and Civil Rights: From 1619 to the Present* (1996) at 193, 211; "Progress Report 1967: Political Victories Climax Year of Strife and Explosion in Nations Black Ghettos," *Ebony*, January 1968 at 118-122; Charles Evers, *Have no Fear: The Charles Evers Story* (1996) at 241-243, 256, 263-264. Coleman Young of Detroit was an outlier, declaring "I'll be damned if I'm going to let them collect guns in the city of Detroit while we're surrounded by hostile suburbs and the whole rest of the state who have guns, and where you have vigilantes practicing Ku Klux Klan in the wilderness with automatic weapons." Bill McGraw, *The Quotations of Mayor Coleman A. Young* (2005) at 29.

29. See, for example, the incidents recorded by the Southern Poverty Law Center at http://www.splcenter.org/get-involved/stand-strong-against-hate.

30. Nicholas J. Johnson, "Self Defense," *J. L. Econ. & Pol'y* (2006) at 187. Nicholas J. Johnson, "Principles and Passions, the Intersection of Abortion and Gun Rights," 50 *Rutgers L. Rev.* (1997) at 97-197.

31. I address the objection that opposition to gun control is the cause of this government failure in Nicholas J. Johnson, "Imagining Gun Control in America: Understanding the Remainder Problem," 43 *Wake Forest L. Rev.* (2008) at 837.

32. Emma Lou Thornbrough, "T. Thomas Fortune: Militant Editor in the Age of Accommodation," in John Hope Franklin and August Meier, *Black Leaders of the Twentieth Century* (1980) at 22-23.

33. Jacqueline Jones Royster, Ida B. Wells Barnett, *Southern Horrors and Other Writings* (1997) at 70.

CHAPTER 9: THE BLACK TRADITION OF ARMS AND THE MODERN ORTHODOXY

1. Benjamin C. Zirpursky, "Self-Defense, Domination and the Social Contract," 57 *U. Pitt. L. Rev.* (1996) at 579, 605. See also critiques of the utilization of principles of self-defense to expand rights on the progressive agenda, in Nicholas J. Johnson, "Principles and Passions: The Intersection of Abortion and Gun Rights," 50 *Rutgers L. Rev.* (1997) at 97-197; Nicholas J. Johnson, "Self-defense?" 2 *Geo. Mason J. L., Econ. & Pol.* (2006) at 187; Nicholas J. Johnson, "Supply Restrictions at the Margins of Heller and the Abortion Analogue: Stenberg Principles, Assault Weapons and the Attitudinalist Critique," 60 *Hastings L. J.* (2009) at 1285.

2. Robin L. West, "The Nature of the Right to an Abortion," 45 *Hastings L. J.* (1994) at 961, 964-965.

3. Alex P. Kellogg, "Black Flight Hits Detroit," *Wall Street Journal,* June 5, 2010; "Crime-ridden Camden, N.J., Cuts Police Force Nearly in Half," January 18, 2011, by the CNN

Wire Staff, http://www.cnn.com/2011/US/01/18/new.jersey.layoffs/index.html (last accessed October 1, 2013).

4. Robert Cooper, in *Youth of the Rural Organizing Cultural Center. Their Minds Stayed on Freedom: The Civil Rights Struggle in the Rural South, an Oral History* (1991) at 93.

5. Melissa Isaacson, "One Tough (But Sweet) Mother," *ESPN Chicago.com* (January 14, 2010).

6. William Oliver, "The Structural-Cultural Perspective: A Theory of Black Male Violence" in *Violent Crime: Assessing Race and Ethnic Differences* (Darnell F. Hawkins, ed. 2003).

7. Project of the Graduate Institute of International Studies, Geneva, *Small Arms Survey 2007: Guns in the City* (2007) at 47-51. Nicholas J. Johnson, "Imagining Gun Control in America: Understanding the Remainder Problem," 43 *Wake Forrest Law Review* (2008) at 847-860.

8. For a full discussion, see Johnson, "Imagining Gun Control," at 837.

9. David Feith, "William Bratton: The Real Cures for Gun Violence, William Bratton, the Once (and Possibly Future) New York Police Commissioner, on the President's Gun-Control Plans and the Need for 'Certainty of Punishment," *Wall Street Journal*, January 18, 2013; Johnson, "Imagining Gun Control," at 851-856. There is no precise count of firearms in America. Estimates of the gun stock proceed based on surrogate information. In 2012, my coauthors and I calculated approximately 323 million. See Johnson, et al., *Firearms Law*, chapter 12 (online). There is general agreement that the number exceeds 300 million. William Bratton's estimate of 350 million firearms is on the high end of the spectrum. It also accounts for record levels of gun buying over the last several years in response to gun-ban proposals.

10. The affiliated position of spot firearms bans only for beleaguered black communities is also a demonstrably failed experiment. The proffered excuse for that failure, and for the extraordinary levels of gun violence in rare places that banned guns, was that criminals were getting guns from other jurisdictions. The solution, proponents said, was to extend stringent gun restrictions to neighboring jurisdictions. But it was never realistic to expect the extraordinarily restrictive policies of a handful of municipalities to catch hold nationwide. And even if a national gun ban were enacted, the words would not make more than 300 million guns disappear but would instead send a large fraction of them into the black market.

11. *Pew Research Center Publications, Views of Gun Control—A Detailed Demographic Breakdown* (January 2011).

12. *Pew Research Center, Public Divided over State, Local Laws Banning Handguns* (March 2010).

13. Paula D. McClain, "Firearms Ownership, Gun Control Attitudes and Neighborhood Environment," 5 *Law & Policy Quarterly* (1983) at 299-300, 304-308.

14. Pauline Brennan, Alan Lizotte, and David McDowall, "Guns, Southerness and Gun Control," 9 *Journal of Quantitative Criminology* (1993) at 289, 304.

15. Harold M. Rose and Paula McClain, *Black Homicide and the Urban Environment*, Final Report, Grant #5 RO1 MH 29269-02, Submitted to Center for Minority Group Mental Health Programs, National Institute of Mental Health (January 1981) at 174-175.

16. Ibid., at 175.

17. Marvin E. Wolfgang, *Patterns in Criminal Homicide* (1958) at 31-37, 40-45, 84, 90-95.

18. W. E. B. Du Bois, *The Philadelphia Negro: A Social Study* (1889) at 97, 311, 318; David Levering Lewis, *W. E. B. Du Bois: Biography of a Race* (1993) at 206.

19. W. E. B. Du Bois, *The Souls of Black Folk*, in *Three Negro Classics* (1999) (1965) at 241, 249, 259, 284-94, 297.

20. Du Bois, *Philadelphia Negro*, at 235-268.

21. Lewis, *Du Bois*, at 186-187; W. E. B. Du Bois, *The Autobiography of W. E. B. Du Bois: A Soliloquy on Viewing My Life from the Last Decade of its First Century* (1962) at 195, 241, 249, 259, 284-94, 297; W. E. B. Du Bois, "Notes on Negro Crime Particularly in Georgia: A Social Study Made under the Direction of Atlanta University by the Ninth Atlanta Conference. Ed." (1904).

22. Linda O. McMurry, *To Keep the Waters Troubled: The Life of Ida B. Wells* (1998) at 294; Alfreda M. Duster, *Crusade for Justice: The Autobiography of Ida B. Wells* (1970) at 301-302.

23. David T. Beito and Linda Royster Beito, *Black Maverick: T. R. M. Howard's Fight for Civil Rights and Economic Power* (2009) at 67-68, 73.

24. Roy Wilkins, *Standing Fast: The Autobiography of Roy Wilkins* (1982) at 65. Wilkins was fully committed to the idea of black criminals being apprehended and punished in accordance with the law but was militantly opposed to mobbing that scooped up innocent men and punished anyone without a proper finding of guilt. This is an interesting contrast with some modern critiques arguing that punishment of black criminals at current rates is inherently problematic. See, Michelle Alexander, *The New Jim Crow, Mass Incarceration in the Age of Colorblindness* (2012).

25. Neil R. McMillan, *Dark Journey: Black Mississippians in the Age of Jim Crow* (1990) at 202-204.

26. Ibid., at 203; *Collins v. Mississippi*, 100 Miss. 435, 437 (1911); *Butler v. Mississippi*, 146 Miss. 505 (1927).

27. Delbert S. Elliott, "Life Threatening Violence Is Primarily a Crime Problem: A Focus on Prevention," 69 *Colo. L. Rev.* (1998) at 1081, 1093.

28. David Kennedy and Anthony Braga, "Homicide in Minneapolis: Research for Problem Solving," 2 *Homicide Studies* (1998) at 263-290; Robert J. Cottrol, "Submission Is Not the Answer: Lethal Violence, Microcultures of Criminal Violence and the Right to Self-Defense," 69 *U. Colo. L. Rev.* (1998) at 1029.

29. Charles Lane, *The Day Freedom Died: The Colfax Massacre, the Supreme Court and the Betrayal of Reconstruction* (2008) at 5; Robert Cottrol and Raymond Diamond, "Never Intended to apply to the White Population" 70 *Chi.-Kent L. Rev.* (1995) at 1307-1335; Clayton Cramer, "The Racist Roots of Gun Control," *Kan. J. L. & Pub. Pol'y* (1995) at 17.

30. Oliver, *Structural-Cultural Perspective*, at 280.

31. Robert Sherrill, *The Saturday Night Special* (1973) at 125.

32. Darnell Hawkins, ed., *Homicide among Black Americans* (1986).

33. Ibid., at 8. Hawkins followed his 1986 work with two additional books: *Ethnicity, Race and Crime: Perspectives across Time and Place* (1995) and *Violent Crime: Assessing Race and Ethnic Differences* (2003). One of the better concrete prescriptions for addressing the problem is provided in David M. Kennedy, *Don't Shoot: One Man, a Street Fellowship and the End of Violence in Inner-City America* (2011).

34. The result comes from counting 743 gunshot deaths in King County, Washington. For every case where a gun in the home was used in a justifiable killing, there were 4.6 criminal homicides, 37 suicides, and 1.3 unintentional deaths. Arthur L. Kellermann and Donald T. Reay, "Protection or Peril? An Analysis of Firearm-Related Deaths in the Home," 314 *New Eng. J. Med.* (1986) at 1557-1560; Stevens H. Clarke, "Firearms and Violence: Interpreting the Connection," *Popular Gov't.* (Winter 2000) at 3, 9; Gary Kleck, *Point Blank: Guns And Violence in America* (1991) at 114; Gary Kleck and Marc Gertz, "Armed Resistance to Crime: The Prevalence and Nature of Self-Defense with a Gun," 86 *J. Crim. L. & Criminology* (1995) at 150-181.

35. "With about 1400 FGAs in 1987, this implies that there were fewer than 28 incidents of this sort annually." Kleck, *Point Blank*, at 122.

36. Gary Kleck and Mark Gertz conducted an especially thorough survey in 1993, with stringent safeguards to cull respondents who might misdescribe a DGU story, yielding a midpoint estimate of 2.5 million DGUs annually. See Gary Kleck and Marc Gertz, "Armed Resistance to Crime: The Prevalence and Nature of Self-Defense with a Gun," 86 *J. Crim. L. & Criminology* (1995) at 150. Eighty percent of these DGUs involved handguns, and 76 percent did not involve firing the weapon but merely brandishing it to scare away an attacker.

Marvin Wolfgang, one of the most eminent criminologists of the twentieth century and an ardent supporter of gun prohibition, reviewed Kleck's findings and commented, "I am as strong a gun-control advocate as can be found among the criminologists in this country. . . . I would eliminate all guns from the civilian population and maybe even from the police. I hate guns. . . . Nonetheless, the methodological soundness of the current Kleck and Gertz study is clear. . . . I do not like their conclusions that having a gun can be useful, but I cannot fault their methodology. They have tried earnestly to meet all objections in advance and have done exceedingly well." Marvin Wolfgang, "A Tribute to a View I Have Opposed," 86 *J. Crim. L. & Criminology* (1995) at 188, 191-192.

Philip Cook of Duke and Jens Ludwig of Georgetown were skeptical of Kleck's results and conducted their own survey for the Police Foundation. That work yielded an estimate of 1.46 million DGUs per year. Philip Cook and Jens Ludwig, *Guns in America: Results of a Comprehensive National Survey of Firearms Ownership and Use* (1996) at 62-75. Cook and Ludwig argue that their own study produced implausibly high numbers. For a response to Cook and Ludwig, see Gary Kleck, "Has the Gun Deterrence Hypothesis Been Discredited?" 10 *J. Firearms & Pub. Pol'y* (1998) at 65.

The National Opinion Research Center argues that Kleck's figures are probably too high, and the National Crime Victims Survey (a government survey that does not actually ask about DGUs but reports volunteered information) is too low. The NORC estimates annual DGUs in the range of 256,500 to 1,210,000. Tom Smith, "A Call for a Truce in the DGU War," 87 *J. Crim. L. & Criminology* (1997) at 1462. Gary Kleck notes "there are now at least 14 surveys, with an aggregate sample size of over 20,000 cases, and all of the surveys indicate at least 700,000 DGUs [per year]." Gary Kleck, "The Frequency of Defensive Gun Use," in Don B. Kates and Gary Kleck, *The Great American Gun Debate* (1997) at 159.

37. Gary Kleck and Marc Gertz, "Armed Resistance to Crime: The Prevalence and Nature of Self-Defense with a Gun," 86 *J. Crim. L. & Criminology* (1995) at 150, 175. The Kleck/Gertz survey found that at least 80 percent of DGUs involved handguns and that 76 percent did not involve firing the weapon but merely brandishing it to scare away an attacker.

38. Gary Kleck and Jongyeon Tark, "Resisting Crime: The Effects of Victim Action on the Outcomes of Crimes," 42 *Criminology* (2005) at 861, 903.

39. Kleck, 35 *Soc. Probs.*, at 7-9; Gary Kleck and Miriam DeLone, "Victim Resistance and Offender Weapon Effects in Robbery," 9 *J. Quantitative Criminology* (1993) at 55, 73-77; Gary Kleck and Marc Gertz, "Armed Resistance to Crime: The Prevalence and Nature of Self-Defense With a Gun," 86 *J. Crim. L. & Criminology* (1995) at 150, 174-75; William Wells, "The Nature and Circumstances of Defense Gun Use: A Content Analysis of Interpersonal Conflict Situations Involving Criminal Offenders," 19 *Just. Q.* (2002) at 127, 152.

40. Lawrence Southwick, "Self-Defense with Guns: The Consequences," 28 *J. Crim. Just.* (2000) at 351, 362, 367.

41. This visceral concern is sometimes exploited for political advantage. See discussion of Washington State Initiative 676, in Nicholas Johnson, "A Second Amendment Moment: The Constitutional Politics of Gun Control," 71 *Brooklyn Law Review* (Winter 2005) at 786-788.

42. National Safety Council, *Injury Facts* (2011) at 143.

43. Stephen Breyer, *Breaking the Vicious Circle: Toward Effective Risk Regulation* (1995) at 5, 7 (airplane and vaccine data). "The likelihood of death by pool (1 in 11,000) versus death by gun (1 in 1 million-plus) isn't even close." For children in age range 0–19 years, it showed firearms-related deaths of 3,067 from homicide, suicide, and accidents. This broke down into 138 accidents, 683 suicides, and 2,161 homicides, 25 from legal intervention, and 60 undetermined. National Safety Council, *Injury Facts* (2011) at 143.

44. Lois A. Fingerhut et al., "Firearm and Nonfirearm Homicide among Persons 15 through 19 Years of Age," 267 *J. Am. Med. Ass'n* 3048, 3049 tbl. 1.

45. Kates and Mauser, "Would Banning Firearms Reduce Murder and Suicide? A Review of International and Some Domestic Evidence," 30 *Harvard J. Law and Public Policy* (2007) at 649.

46. Alfred Blumstein and Joel Wallman, *The Crime Drop in America* (2006).

47. Robert Ikeda et al., "Estimating Intruder-Related Firearms Retrievals in U.S. Households, 1994," 12 *Violence & Victims* (1997) at 363.

48. Richard Wright and Scott Decker, *Burglars on the Job: Streetlife and Residential Break-Ins* (1994) at 112-113.

49. James Wright, Peter Rossi, and Kathleen Daly, *Under the Gun: Weapons, Crime and Violence in America* (1983) at 139-140; Gary Kleck, "Crime Control through the Private Use of Armed Force," 35 *Soc. Probs.* (1988) at 1, 12, 15-16.

50. David Kopel, *Lawyers, Guns, and Burglars*, 43 *Ariz. L. Rev.* (2001) at 345, 363-366. For more, see Philip Cook and Jens Ludwig, "Guns & Burglary," and David Kopel, "Comment," both in *Evaluating Gun Policy* (Jens Ludwig and Philip Cook eds., 2003).

51. James Wright and Peter Rossi, *Armed and Considered Dangerous: A Survey of Felons and Their Firearms* (expanded ed. 1994) at 146, 151, 155, 237.

52. U.S. Bureau of Justice Statistics, "Household Burglary," *BJS Bull.* at 4 (1985).

53. George Rengert And John Wasilchick, *Suburban Burglary: A Tale of 2 Suburbs* (2nd ed., 2000; study of Delaware County, Penn., and Greenwich, Conn.) at 33; see also John Conklin, *Robbery and the Criminal Justice System* (1972) at 85.

54. Gary Kleck, *Point Blank: Guns and Violence in America* (1991) at 140.

55. Gary Kleck and David Bordua, "The Factual Foundation for Certain Key Assumptions of Gun Control," 5 *L. & Pol'y Q.* (1983) at 271, 284; Gary Kleck, "Policy Lessons from Recent Gun Control Research," 49 *J. L. & Contemp. Probs.* (1986) at 35, 47.

56. Don Kates, "The Value of Civilian Handgun Possession as a Deterrent to Crime or Defense against Crime," 18 *Am. J. Crim. L.* (1991) at 113, 153. One set of commentators argued that the drop in Orlando rapes was statistically insignificant, being within the range of possibly normal fluctuations. David McDowall et al., "General Deterrence through Civilian Gun Ownership," 29 *Criminology* (1991) at 541. But this objection was based on a model that would have found statistical insignificance even if gun-based deterrence had eliminated all rapes in Orlando. Kleck, *Targeting Guns*, at 181.

57. John Lott Jr., *More Guns Less Crime: Understanding Crime and Gun Control Laws* (3d ed. 2010); James Q. Wilson, "Just Take away Their Guns," *New York Times Magazine*, March 20, 1994, at 47; National Research Council, *Firearms and Violence: A Critical Review* (2005) at 270; Nicholas J. Johnson, "A Second Amendment Moment, The Constitutional Politics of Gun Control," 71 *Brooklyn L. Rev.* (2005) at 715, 747-764.

58. Rose and McClain, at 117, 270.

59. The quote is from *Planned Parenthood v. Casey*, 505 U.S. 833 (1992), upholding a woman's right to choose abortion. For more on the intersection between the right to arms and reproductive rights claims see, *Nordyke v. King*, 644 F.3d 776 (9th Cir. 2011); J. Harvie Wilkinson III, "Of Guns, Abortions, and the Unraveling Rule of Law," 95 *Virginia L. Rev.* (2009) at 253; Nicholas J. Johnson, "Supply Restrictions at the Margins of Heller and the Abortion Analogue," 60 *Hastings L. J.* (2009) at 1285; Cass R. Sunstein, "Second Amendment Minimalism: Heller as Griswold," 122 *Harv. L. Rev.* (2008) at 246; Nicholas J. Johnson, "Self Defense?" 2 *Journal of Law Economics and Policy* (2006) at 236; Nicholas J. Johnson, "Principles and Passions: The Intersection of Abortion and Gun Rights," 50 *Rutgers L. Rev.* (1997) at 97.

SELECT BIBLIOGRAPHY

Addington, Wendell. "Slave Insurrections in Texas." *Journal of Negro History* (1950).

Alexander, Michelle. *The New Jim Crow: Mass Incarceration in the Age of Colorblindness* (2012).

Alexander, Shawn Leigh. *An Army of Lions: The Civil Rights Struggle before the NAACP* (2012).

Apkether, Herbert. *Documentary History of the Negro People in the United States* (1974).

Armstrong, Louis. *Satchamo: My Life in New Orleans* (1954).

Avary, Myrta Lockett. *Dixie after the War: An Exposition of Social Conditions Existing in the South during the 12 Years Succeeding the Fall of Richmond* (1906).

Bates, Daisy. *The Long Shadow of Little Rock: A Memoir* (1962).

Beckworth, James P. *The Life and Adventures of James P. Beckworth as Told to Thomas D. Bonner* (1859).

Beito, David T., and Linda Royster Beito. *Black Maverick: T. R. M. Howard's Fight for Civil Rights and Economic Power* (2009).

Bibb, Henry. *Narrative of the Life and Adventures of Henry Bibb, an American Slave* (2005).

Billington, Ray Allen. *The Far Western Frontier: 1830–1860* (1962).

Blackmon, Douglas A. *Slavery by Another Name: The Re-Enslavement of Black Americans from the Civil War to World War II* (2008).

Block, W. T. *Meanest Town on the Coast* (1979).

Blumstein, Alfred, and Joel Wallman. *The Crime Drop in America* (2006).

Boyle, Kevin. *Arc of Justice: A Saga of Race, Civil Rights, and Murder in the Jazz Age* (2004).

Brundage, W. F. "The Darien Insurrection of 1899: Black Protest during the Nadir of Race Relations." *Georgia Historical Quarterly* (1990).

Burns, Stewart. *Day Break of Freedom: The Montgomery Bus Boycott* (1997).

Burton, Arthur T. *Black, Red and Deadly: Black and Indian Gunfighters of the Indian Territory, 1870–1907* (1991).

Carson, Clayborne. *The Eyes on the Prize Civil Rights Reader* (1991).

———. *In Struggle: SNCC and the Black Awakening of the 1960s* (1995).

Carter, Dan T. *When the War Was Over: The Failure of Self-Reconstruction in the South 1865–1867* (1985).

Cecelski, David S. *The Fire of Freedom: Abraham Galloway and the Slaves' Civil War* (2012).

Clark, E. Culpepper. *The Schoolhouse Door: Segregation's Last Stand at the University of Alabama* (1993).

Cobb, Charles E., Jr. *On the Road to Freedom: A Guided Tour of the Civil Rights Trail* (2008).

Colburn, David R. *Racial Change and Community Crisis: St. Augustine Florida, 1877–1980* (1985).

Commager, Henry Steele. *The Struggle for Racial Equality* (1972).

Conklin, John. *Robbery and the Criminal Justice System* (1972).

Cook, Philip, and Jens Ludwig. *Guns in America: Results of a Comprehensive National Survey of Firearms Ownership and Use* (1996).

Coolidge, Dane. *Fighting Men of the West* (1932).

Cottrol, Robert J. "Submission Is Not the Answer: Lethal Violence, Microcultures of Criminal Violence and the Right to Self-Defense." *University of Colorado Law Review* (1998).

Cottrol, Robert J., and Raymond Diamond. "Never Intended to Apply to the White Population." *Chicago-Kent Law Review* (1995).

Crowder, Ralph L. *John Edward Bruce: Politician, Journalist, and Self-Trained Historian of the African Diaspora* (2004).

Dal Lago, Enrico. *Slave Systems: Ancient and Modern* (2008).

Dittmer, John. *Black Georgia in the Progressive Era: 1900–1920* (1977).

——. *Local People: The Struggle for Civil Rights in Mississippi* (1995).

Doak, Robin Santos. *Slave Rebellions* (2006).

D'Orso, Michael. *Like Judgment Day: The True Story of the Rosewood Massacre and Its Aftermath* (1996).

Douglass, Frederick. *The Narrative and Selected Writings* (1984).

Du Bois, W. E. B. *The Autobiography of W. E. B. Du Bois: A Soliloquy on Viewing My Life from the Last Decade of Its First Century* (1962).

——. *Notes on Negro Crime Particularly in Georgia: A Social Study Made under the Direction of Atlanta University by the Ninth Atlanta Conference* (1904).

——. *The Philadelphia Negro: A Social Study* (1899).

——. *The Souls of Black Folk* (1903).

Durham, Philip, and Everett Jones. *The Negro Cowboys* (1965).

Ellsworth, Scott. *Death in a Promised Land: The Tulsa Race Riot of 1921* (1982).

Eskew, Glenn T. *But for Birmingham: The Local and National Movements in the Civil Rights Struggle* (1997).

Evans, William McKee. *Ballots and Fence Rails: Reconstruction on the Lower Cape Fear* (1967).

Fairclough, Adam, Horace Mann Bond, and Julia W. Bond. *The Star Creek Papers* (1997).

——. *To Redeem the Soul of America: The Southern Christian Leadership Conference and Martin Luther King, Jr.* (1995).

Farmer, James. *Freedom When?* (1965).

Foner, Philip S. *Frederick Douglass: Selected Speeches and Writings* (1999).

——. *Frederick Douglass* (1964).

——. *Proceedings of the Black State Conventions, 1840 through 1865* (1980).

Forbes, Ella. *But We Have No Country: The 1851 Christiana Pennsylvania Resistance* (1998).

Forman, James. *The Making of Black Revolutionaries* (1972).

Franklin, John Hope. Foreword to *Death in a Promised Land: The Tulsa Race Riot of 1921*, by Scott Ellsworth (1986).

Franks, James A. *Mary Fields: The Story of Black Mary* (2000).

Frazier, E. Franklin. "The Negro and Non-Resistance." *Crisis* (March 1924).

Frazier, Harriet C. *Slavery and Crime in Missouri, 1773–1865* (2001).

Fredric, Francis. *Escaped Slave: Slave Life in Virginia and Kentucky* (2010).

Gaither, Gerald H. *Blacks and the Populist Movement: Ballots and Bigotry in the New South* (2005).

Garrow, David J. *Bearing the Cross: Martin Luther King, Jr., and the Southern Christian Leadership Conference* (1988).

Gerteis, Joseph. *Class and the Color Line: Interracial Class Coalition in the Knights of Labor and the Populist Movement* (2007).

Giddings, Paula. *Ida: A Sword among Lions* (2008).

Glatthaar, Joseph. *Forged in Battle: The Civil War Alliance of Black Soldiers and White Officers* (1990).

Goings, Kenneth W. *The NAACP Comes of Age* (1990).

Goodheart, Adam. *1861: The Civil War Awakening* (2011).

Graduate Institute of International Studies. *Small Arms Survey* (2007).

Grant, Joanne. *Ella Baker: Freedom Bound* (1998).

Greenberg, Douglas. *Crime and Law Enforcement in the Colony of New York, 1691–1776* (1974).

Griffler, Keith P. *Frontline of Freedom: African Americans and the Forging of the Underground Railroad in the Ohio Valley* (2004).

Hahn, Steven. *A Nation under Our Feet: Black Political Struggles in the Rural South from Slavery to the Great Migration* (2003).

Halbrook, Stephen P. *Freedmen, the Fourteenth Amendment, and the Right to Bear Arms, 1866–1876* (1998).

Hamer, Fannie Lou. *To Praise Our Bridges* (1967).

Hamlin, William Lee. *The True Story of Billy the Kid: A Tale of the Lincoln County War* (1959).

Hampton, Henry. *Voices of Freedom: An Oral History of the Civil Rights Movement from the 1950s through the 1980s* (1990).

Harlan, Lewis R. *Booker T. Washington: The Wizard of Tuskegee* (1983).

Harris, Leslie M. *In the Shadow of Slavery: African Americans in New York City, 1626–1863* (2003).

Harrold, Stanley. *Border War: Fighting over Slavery before the Civil War* (2010).

Hashaw, Tim. *Children of Perdition: Melungeons and the Struggle of Mixed Race America* (2006).

Hawkins, Darnell. *Ethnicity, Race and Crime: Perspectives across Time and Place* (1995).

———. *Homicide among Black Americans* (1986).

———. *Violent Crime: Assessing Race and Ethnic Differences* (2003).

Hendrick, George. *Fleeing for Freedom: Stories of the Underground Railroad* (2004).

Henry, Aaron. *The Fire Ever Burning* (2000).

Hodgson, Godfrey. *America in Our Time* (1976).

Holland, Barbara. *They Went Whistling: Women Wayfarers, Warriors, Runaways, and Renegades* (2002).

Horne, Gerald. *W. E. B. Du Bois: Encyclopedia* (2001).

Howell, Kenneth W. *Still the Arena of Civil War: Violence and Turmoil in Reconstruction Texas, 1865–1874* (2012).

Hudson, Winson. *Mississippi Harmony: Memoirs of a Freedom Fighter* (2002).

Hunter, John Marvin. *The Trail Drivers of Texas* (1925).

Janken, Kenneth. *White: The Biography of Walter White, Mr. NAACP* (2003).

Johnson, Andre E. *The Forgotten Prophet, Bishop Henry McNeal Turner and the African-American Prophetic Tradition* (2012).

Johnson, James Weldon. *Along This Way: The Autobiography of James Weldon Johnson* (1933).

Johnson, Nicholas J. "Firearms and the Black Community: An Assessment of the Modern Orthodoxy." *Connecticut Law Review* (2013).

———. "Imagining Gun Control in America: Understanding the Remainder Problem." *Wake Forest Law Review* (2008).

———. "Principles and Passions: The Intersection of Abortion and Gun Rights." *Rutgers Law Review* (1997).

———. "A Second Amendment Moment: The Constitutional Politics of Gun Control." *Brooklyn Law Review* (2005).

———. "Self Defense." 2 *Journal of Law Economics and Policy* (2006).

———. "Supply Restrictions at the Margins of Heller and the Abortion Analogue: Stenberg Principles, Assault Weapons and the Attitudinalist Critique." *Hastings Law Journal* (2009).

Johnson, Nicholas J., Clayton Cramer, and George Mocsary. "'This Right Is Not Allowed by Governments That Are Afraid of the People': The Public Meaning of the Second Amendment When the Fourteenth Amendment Was Ratified." *George Mason Law Review* (2010).

Johnson, Nicholas J., David B. Kopel, George Mocsary and Michael O'Shea, *Firearms Law and the Second Amendment: Regulation, Rights, and Policy* (2012).

Katz, Jonathan. *Resistance at Christiana: The Fugitive Slave Rebellion, Christiana, Pennsylvania, September 11, 1851* (1974).

Katz, William Loren. *Black Indians: A Hidden Heritage* (1986).

———. *Black West: A Hidden Heritage* (1986).

Keleher, William A. *Violence in Lincoln County, 1869–1881* (1957).

Kennedy, David M. *Don't Shoot: One Man, a Street Fellowship and the End of Violence in Inner-City America* (2011).

Kersten, Edmund. *A. Philip Randolph: A Life in the Vanguard* (2006).

King, Coretta Scott. *My Life with Martin Luther King, Jr.* (1969).

King, Frank M. *Pioneer Western Empire Builders: A True Story of the Men and Women of Pioneer Days* (1946).

King, Martin Luther, Jr. *Stride toward Freedom: The Montgomery Story* (1959).

———. *Where Do We Go from Here: Chaos or Community?* (1967).

King, Mary. *Freedom Song: A Personal Story of the 1960s Civil Rights Movement* (1987).

Kleck, Gary. *Point Blank: Guns and Violence in America* (1991).

——. "The Factual Foundation for Certain Key Assumptions of Gun Control." *Law and Policy Quarterly* (1983).

——. "Policy Lessons from Recent Gun Control Research." *Journal of Law and Contemporary Problems* (1986).

Kluger, Richard. *Simple Justice: The History of* Brown v. Board of Ed. *and Black America's Struggle for Equality* (1976).

Lake, Alice. "Last Summer in Mississippi." *Redbook* (November 1964).

Lane, Charles. *The Day Freedom Died: The Colfax Massacre, the Supreme Court, and the Betrayal of Reconstruction* (2008).

Lee, Chana Kai. *For Freedom's Sake: The Life of Fannie Lou Hamer* (1999).

Levine, Michael. *African Americans and Civil Rights: From 1619 to the Present* (1996).

Lewis, David Levering. *W. E. B. Du Bois: Biography of a Race* (1993).

Lewis, John. *Walking with the Wind: A Memoir of the Movement* (1998).

Litwack, Leon F. *Been in the Storm So Long: The Aftermath of Slavery* (1979).

——. *Trouble in Mind: Black Southerners in the Age of Jim Crow* (1998).

Lizotte, Alan. *Guns Southerness and Gun Control*, Journal of Quantitative Criminology (1993).

Logan, Rayford W. *The Betrayal of the Negro: From Rutherford B. Hayes to Woodrow Wilson* (1997).

Loguen, Jermaine W. *The Reverend J. W. Loguen as a Slave and as a Free Man* (1968).

Manis, Andrew Michael. *A Fire You Can't Put Out: The Civil Rights Life of Birmingham's Reverend Fred Shuttlesworth* (1990).

Marrs, Elijah P. *Life and History of the Reverend Elijah P. Marrs* (1885).

Mars, Florence. *Witness in Philadelphia* (1977).

Martin, Tony. *Race First: The Ideological and Organizational Struggles of Marcus Garvey and the Universal Negro Improvement Association* (1976).

Martin, Waldo E., Jr. *The Mind of Frederick Douglass* (1984).

Massey, Sarah R. *Black Cowboys of Texas* (2005).

Mayfield, Julian. "Challenge to Negro Leadership: The Case of Robert Williams." *Commentary* (1961).

McAdam, Doug. *Freedom Summer* (1988).

——. *Political Process and the Development of Black Insurgency* (1982).

McClain, Paula D. "Firearms Ownership, Gun Control Attitudes and Neighborhood Environment." *Law & Policy Quarterly* (1983).

McFeely, William S. *Frederick Douglass* (1991).

McGraw, Bill. *The Quotations of Mayor Coleman A. Young* (2005).

McKivigan, John R. *In the Words of Frederick Douglass: Quotations from Liberty's Champion* (2012).

McMillen, Neil. *Dark Journey: Black Mississippians in the Age of Jim Crow* (1990).

McMurry, Linda O. *To Keep the Waters Troubled: The Life of Ida B. Wells* (1998).

McPhearson, Edward. *The Political History of the United States of America during the Period of Reconstruction* (1875).

McWhorter, Diane. *Carry Me Home: Birmingham, Alabama—The Climatic Battle of the Civil Rights Revolution* (2001).

Meier, August, and Elliot Rudwick. *Black Protest Thought in the Twentieth Century* (1971).

——. *From Plantation to Ghetto* (1970).

——. *Negro Thought in America* (1963).

Middleton, Stephen. *The Black Laws: Race and the Legal Process in Early Ohio* (2005).

Mikkelsen, Vincent P. "Coming from Battle to Face a War: The Lynching of Black Soldiers in the World War One Era." PhD dissertation, Florida State University (2007).

——. "Fighting for Sgt. Caldwell: The NAACP Campaign against Legal Lynching after World War I." *Journal of African American History* (2009).

Mills, Kay. *This Little Light of Mine: The Life of Fannie Lou Hamer* (1994).

Moody, Anne. *Coming of Age in Mississippi* (1968).

Moon, Elaine Lataman. *Untold Tales, Unsung Heroes: An Oral History of Detroit's African-American Community: 1918–1967* (1994).

Motley, Constance Baker. *Equal Justice under Law: An Autobiography* (1999).

Muir, Andrew Forest. "The Free Negro in Jefferson and Orange Counties, Texas." *Journal of Negro History* (1950).

National Association for the Advancement of Colored People. *Thirty Years of Lynching: 1898–1918* (1919).

Nossiter, Adam. *Of Long Memory: Mississippi and the Murder of Medgar Evers* (1994).

Oates, Stephen B. *Let the Trumpet Sound: A Life of Martin Luther King* (1994).

Ofari, Earl. *Let Your Motto Be Resistance: The Life and Thought of Henry Highland Garnet* (1972).

Oliver, William. *The Structural-Cultural Perspective: A Theory of Black Male Violence and Violent Crime: Assessing Race and Ethnic Differences* (Darnell F. Hawkins, ed. 2003).

O'Reily, Kenneth. *Racial Matters: The FBI's Secret File on Black America, 1960–1972* (1989).

Paisley, Clifton. *The Red Hills Florida 1528–1865* (1989).

Parker, John P. *His Promised Land: The Autobiography of John P. Parker, Former Slave and Conductor on the Underground Railroad* (Stuart S. Sprague, ed. 1996).

Parks, Rosa. *My Story* (1992).

Pasternak, Martin B. *"Rise Now and Fly To Arms": The Life of Henry Highland Garnet* (1994).

Payne, Charles. *I've Got the Light of Freedom: The Organizing Tradition and the Mississippi Freedom Struggle* (1995).

Pearson, Hugh. *The Shadow of the Panther: Huey Newton and the Price of Black Power in America* (1994).

Peeks, Edward. *The Long Struggle for Black Power* (1971).

Powerledge, Fred. *Free At Last? The Civil Rights Movement and the People Who Made It* (1991).

Project of the Graduate Institute of International Studies, Geneva, *Small Arms Survey 2007: Guns in the City* (2007).

Raines, Howell. *My Soul Is Rested: Movement Days in the Deep South Remembered* (1977).

Rengert, George, and John Wasilchick. *Suburban Burglary: A Tale of 2 Suburbs* (2000).

Rice, Condoleezza. *Extraordinary Ordinary People: A Memoir of Family* (2010).

Rogers, William. "Negro Knights of Labor in Arkansas: A Case Study of the Miscellaneous Strike." *Labor History* (1969).

Rose, Harold M., and Paula McClain. *Black Homicide and the Urban Environment, Final Report, National Institute of Mental Health* (January 1981).

Rucker, Walter C. *The River Flows On: Black Resistance, Culture and Identity Formation in Early America* (2007).

Sales, William. *From Civil Rights to Black Liberation: Malcolm X and the Organization of Afro-American Unity* (1994).

Salter, John R. *Jackson, Mississippi: An American Chronicle of Struggle and Schism* (1979).

Schecter, Barnet. *The Devil's Own Work: The Civil War Draft Riots and the Fight to Reconstruct America* (2005).

Schor, Joel. *Henry Hyland Garnet: A Voice of Black Radicalism in the Nineteenth Century* (1977).

Schubert, Frank N. "The Suggs Affray: The Black Cavalry in the Johnson County War." *Western Historical Quarterly January* (1973).

Seale, Bobby. *Seize the Time: The Story of the Black Panther Party and Huey P. Newton* (1968).

Sellers, Cleveland. *The River of No Return: The Autobiography of a Black Militant and the Life and Death of SNCC* (1973).

Shapiro, Herbert. *White Violence and Black Response* (1988).

Sherrill, Robert. *The Saturday Night Special* (1973).

Simmons, William J. *Henry McNeal Turner, Men of Mark: Eminent, Progressive and Rising* (1887).

Singletary, Otis A. *Negro Militia and Reconstruction* (1984).

Smedley, Robert C. *History of the Underground Railroad in Chester and Neighboring Counties of Pennsylvania* (1883).

Sobel, Lester A. *Civil Rights 1960–66* (1967).

Still, William. *William Still's Underground Railroad Records: With a Life of the Author* (1872).

Stockley, Grif. *Daisy Bates: Civil Rights Crusader from Arkansas* (2005).

Stoper, Emily. *The Student Nonviolent Coordinating Committee: The Growth of Radicalism in a Civil Rights Organization* (1989).

Strain, Christopher B. "Civil Rights & Self-Defense: The Fiction of Nonviolence, 1955–1968." PhD dissertation, University of California, Berkley (2000).

Sugarman, Tracy. *Stranger at the Gates: A Summer in Mississippi* (1966).

Summers, Barbara. *I Dream a World: Portraits of Black Women Who Changed America* (1989).

Takaki, Ronald T. *Violence in the Black Imagination* (1993).

Taylor, Quintard. *In Search of the Racial Frontier: African Americans in the American West 1528–1990* (1998).

Terkel, Studs. *American Dreams Lost and Found* (1980).

Thornbrough, Emma Lou. *T. Thomas Fortune: Militant Journalist* (1972).

Tyler, Ronnie C. "The Callahan Expedition of 1855: Indians or Negroes." *Southwestern Historical Quarterly* (1967).

Tyson, Timothy B. *Blood Done Sign My Name* (2004).

———. *Radio Free Dixie: Robert F. Williams and the Roots of Black Power* (1999).

Umoja, Akinyele O. "The Ballot and the Bullet: A Comparative Analysis of Armed Resistance in the Civil Rights Movement." *Journal of Black Studies* (1999).

———. *We Will Shoot Back : Armed Resistance in the Mississippi Freedom Movement* (2013).

———. "We Will Shoot Back: The Natchez Model and Paramilitary Organization in the Mississippi Freedom Movement." *Journal of Black Studies* (2002).

Vandiver, Margaret. *Lethal Punishment: Lynchings and Legal Executions in the South* (2006).

Vincent, Theodore G. *Black Power and the Garvey Movement* (1971).

Vine, Phyllis. *One Man's Castle: Clarence Darrow in Defense of the American Dream* (2004).

Von Hoffman, Nicholas. *Mississippi Notebook* (1964).

Wagner, Tricia Martineau. *African American Women of the Old West* (2007).

Waldrep, Christopher. *Roots of Disorder: Race and Criminal Justice in the American South 1817–80* (1998).

Waldrep, Christopher, and Donald Nieman. *Local Matters: Race Crime and Justice in the Nineteenth-Century South* (2011).

Warren, Robert Penn. *Who Speaks for the Negro* (1965).

Wells Barnett, Ida B. *Crusade for Justice: The Autobiography of Ida B. Wells* (1970).

———. *On Lynchings* (2002).

———. *Selected Works* (1991).

———. *Southern Horrors* (2002).

Wendt, Simon. "The New Black Power History, Protection or Path toward Revolution? Black Power and Self-Defense." *Souls* (2007).

———. *The Spirit and the Shotgun: Armed Resistance and the Struggle for Civil Rights* (2007).

———. "Urge People Not to Carry Guns: Armed Self Defense in the Louisiana Civil Rights Movement and the Radicalization of the Congress of Racial Equality." *Journal of the Louisiana Historical Association* (2004).

West, Robin L. "The Nature of the Right to an Abortion." *Hastings Law Journal* (1994).

Westermeier, Clifford P. *Trailing the Cowboy: His Life and Lore as Told by Frontier Journalists* (1955).

White, Walter. "'The Eruption of Tulsa': An NAACP Official Investigates the Tulsa Race Riot of 1921." *Nation* (1921).

———. *A Man Called White* (1969).

———. *Rope and Faggot: A Biography of Judge Lynch* (1929).

Wilkins, Roy *Standing Fast: The Autobiography of Roy Wilkins* (1982).

Williams, Juan. *Thurgood Marshall: American Revolutionary* (1998).

Williams, Robert F. *Negroes with Guns* (1962).

Williamson, Joel. *A Rage for Order: Black-White Relations in the American South since Emancipation* (1986).

Wilson, R. L. *The Winchester: An American Legend* (1991).

Wishart, David. *Encyclopedia of the Great Plains* (2004).

Wolfgang, Marvin. *Patterns in Criminal Homicide* (1958).

Wood, Peter H. *Black Majority: Negroes in Colonial South Carolina from 1670 through the Stono Rebellion* (1974).

Wright, George C. *Racial Violence in Kentucky 1865–1940: Lynchings, Mob Rule and "Legal Lynchings"* (1990).

Wright, James, Peter Rossi, Kathleen Daley. *Under the Gun: Weapons, Crime and Violence in America* (1983).

Wright, James, and Peter Rossi. *Armed and Considered Dangerous: A Survey of Felons and Their Firearms* (1994).

Wright, Richard, and Scott Decker. *Burglars on the Job: Street Life and Residential Break-Ins* (1994).

Youth of the Rural Organizing Cultural Center. *Their Minds Stayed on Freedom: The Civil Rights Struggle in the Rural South, an Oral History* (1991).

Zhang, David. *Fleet Walker's Divided Heart: The Life of Baseball's First Black Major Leaguer* (1995).

Zirpursky, Benjamin C. "Self-Defense, Domination and the Social Contract." *University of Pittsburgh Law Review* (1996).

INDEX